BRINGING NEW TECHNOLOGY TO MARKET

BRINGING NEW TECHNOLOGY TO MARKET

❖ ❖ ❖

KATHLEEN R. ALLEN

DIRECTOR, TECHNOLOGY COMMERCIALIZATION ALLIANCE
GREIF ENTREPRENEURSHIP CENTER
MARSHALL SCHOOL OF BUSINESS
UNIVERSITY OF SOUTHERN CALIFORNIA

Prentice
Hall

UPPER SADDLE RIVER, NEW JERSEY

Library of Congress Cataloging-in-Publication Data

Allen, Kathleen R.
 Bringing new technology to market / Kathleen R. Allen.
  p. cm.
 Includes bibliographical references and index.
 ISBN 0-13-093373-2
  1. High technology—Marketing. 2. High technology industries. I. Title.
HF5415 .A432 2002
658.5—dc21   2002017056

Senior Managing Editor: Jennifer Glennon
Editor-in-Chief: Jeff Shelstad
Assistant Editor: Jessica Sabloff
Editorial Assistant: Kevin Glynn
Senior Marketing Manager: Shannon Moore
Marketing Assistant: Christine Genneken
Managing Editor (Production): John Roberts
Production Editor: Kelly Warsak
Permissions Coordinator: Suzanne Grappi
Associate Director, Manufacturing: Vincent Scelta
Production Manager: Arnold Vila
Manufacturing Buyer: Michelle Klein
Cover Designer: Bruce Kenselaar
Composition: BookMasters, Inc.
Full-Service Project Management: BookMasters, Inc.
Printer/Binder: The Maple Press Company
Cover Printer: Phoenix Color Corp.

Credits and acknowledgments borrowed from other sources and reproduced, with permission, in this textbook appear on appropriate page within text.

Pearson Education LTD.
Pearson Education Australia PTY, Limited
Pearson Education Singapore, Pte. Ltd
Pearson Education North Asia Ltd
Pearson Education, Canada, Ltd
Pearson Educación de Mexico, S.A. de C.V.
Pearson Education–Japan
Pearson Education Malaysia, Pte. Ltd

10 9 8 7 6 5 4 3 2 1
ISBN 0-13-093373-2

To the students, scientists, and engineers at the University of Southern California who are developing the technologies that will shape our future, and to George Bekey, Lloyd Greif, Tom O'Malia, Isaac Maya, Pablo Valencia, and Phil Weilerstein for their enormous support and encouragement.

BRIEF CONTENTS

PART I: THE FOUNDATIONS OF TECHNOLOGY COMMERCIALIZATION   1

Chapter 1   Innovation and Commercialization   1
Chapter 2   Recognizing and Screening Technology Opportunities   27
Chapter 3   Developing and Testing a Technology Business Concept   50
Chapter 4   High-Technology Product Development Strategies   84

PART II: INTELLECTUAL PROPERTY   109

Chapter 5   The Concept of Intellectual Property   109
Chapter 6   Licensing Intellectual Property   131
Chapter 7   Intellectual Property Strategy   144

PART III: FINANCIAL STRATEGY FOR TECHNOLOGY START-UPS   168

Chapter 8   Building and Valuing the Business Model   168
Chapter 9   Funding the Technology Start-Up   189
Chapter 10   Funding Growth   209

PART IV: THE TRANSITION FROM R&D TO OPERATIONS   235

Chapter 11   Moving from R&D to Operations   235
Chapter 12   Marketing High Technology   256
Chapter 13   Growing the High-Tech Venture   286
Chapter 14   Entrepreneurial Venturing Inside a Corporation   311
Chapter 15   Developing a Business Plan for Sustained Innovation   335

CONTENTS

PREFACE   XIII

PART I: THE FOUNDATIONS OF TECHNOLOGY COMMERCIALIZATION   1

CHAPTER 1   Innovation and Commercialization   1
Technological Change and Basic Economic Principles   2
The Foundations of Technological Innovation   7
Overview of the Innovation and Commercialization Process   16
Organization of the Text   20
Case Study: Innovation in the Palm of His Hand   23

CHAPTER 2   Recognizing and Screening Technology Opportunities   27
Creativity: The Spark That Ignites Innovation   28
Opportunity Recognition   34
Sources of Opportunity   35
Screening Technology Opportunities   37
Case Study: The Art of Invention: Yoshiro Nakamatsu and Claude Elwood Shannon   46

CHAPTER 3   Developing and Testing a Technology Business Concept   50
Developing a Business Concept   51
Conducting a Feasibility Analysis   54
Analyzing the Industry   55
Analyzing Technical Feasibility   62
Market Analysis   64
Analyzing Distribution Channel Alternatives   67
Analyzing the Founding Team   70
Constructing a Feasible Business Model   71
Feasibility Analysis Outline   73
Case Study: Zondigo: Chaos in the Wireless World   77

CHAPTER 4   High-Technology Product Development Strategies   84
The New Product Development Process   87
Metrics for Product Development Success   97

Outsourcing Technology Innovation   100

Case Study: IDEO: Where Innovation Is the Culture   105

PART II: INTELLECTUAL PROPERTY   109

CHAPTER 5   The Concept of Intellectual Property   109

The Theory Behind Intellectual Property Protections   110

Trade Secrets   112

Copyrights   114

Trademarks   116

Patents   118

Case Study: Gordon Gould: The Father of Laser
Technology   128

CHAPTER 6   Licensing Intellectual Property   131

The Licensor's View of the Licensing Process   132

The Licensee's View of the Licensing Process   136

The License Agreement   137

Licensing Strategy   139

Case Study: P&G: Finding Value in the Licensing Network   142

CHAPTER 7   Intellectual Property Strategy   144

Developing a Patent Strategy   146

Developing a Trademark Strategy   152

Issues in Intellectual Property Strategy   155

Case Study: Robotic Surgery to the Rescue   165

PART III: FINANCIAL STRATEGY FOR TECHNOLOGY START-UPS   168

CHAPTER 8   Building and Valuing the Business Model   168

Radical Innovation Business Models   169

Constructing the Most Effective Business Model   172

The Drivers of Value   173

Financial Models for Assessing Value   180

Case Study: Pixstream Inc.: The Value of Intangible
Assets   186

CHAPTER 9   Funding the Technology Start-Up   189

Start-Up Risks and Stages of Financing   190

Seed Capital   192

Early Stage Capital   195

Government Funding Sources   202

The Costs of Raising Capital   203

Case Study: Prepare for the Money Hunt   206

CHAPTER 10   Funding Growth   209

Debt vs. Equity   210

Financing Strategy for Growth   211

Venture Capital Funding   213

The Private Offering   221

The Initial Public Offering   223

Presenting the Company to Investors   228

Case Study: From Riches to Rags and Back?: When Going Public
            May Not Be the Right Path   231

**PART IV: THE TRANSITION FROM R&D
            TO OPERATIONS   235**

CHAPTER 11   Moving from R&D to Operations   235

Challenges in Transitioning from Project to
            Operations   236

Organizational Models   239

Legal Forms of Organization   242

Case Study: Quantum Dots   253

CHAPTER 12   Marketing High Technology   256

The Characteristics of Technology-Intensive Markets   257

Key Decisions for Technology-Intensive Markets   259

Understanding Customer Needs   266

Collecting Market Intelligence   270

Pricing High-Technology Products   271

Developing a Marketing Plan   275

Promoting High-Technology Products   276

Case Study: Will GPS Ever Cross the Chasm?   282

CHAPTER 13   Growing the High-Tech Venture   286

The Nature of Growth   288

Conventional Growth Strategies   292

Growth Through R&D   294

Growth Through Co-operation and Acquisition   297

Strategies for Setting Technology Standards   304

Case Study: Rapid Growth with BlackBerry?   308

**CHAPTER 14 Entrepreneurial Venturing Inside a
                Corporation   311**

The Nature of Corporate Venturing   313

The Role of Change in Facilitating Corporate
        Venturing   314

The Paths to Corporate Venturing   319

Success as a Corporate Entrepreneur   324

Case Study: New Pig Corporation: A Study in Corporate
        Innovation   331

**CHAPTER 15 Developing a Business Plan for Sustained
                Innovation   335**

The Audience for the Business Plan   336

The Components of the Business Plan   337

Time Is of the Essence   348

Case Study: An Illuminating Business Plan   352

INDEX   355

Bringing New Technology to Market is the first text designed to address the entire technology commercialization process, from idea to market. Today, as technology drives innovation and companies seek more effective ways to exploit the intellectual property they create, it is important for students in business, engineering, and the sciences to understand the processes that result in successful new technology products in the market. Consequently, the subject of technology commercialization is becoming an important part of the graduate and undergraduate curricula in schools of business, engineering, and science. *Bringing New Technology to Market* presents a comprehensive look at the issues related to the transfer and commercialization of new technology. High-tech businesses with patentable technology, whether engineering technology, biotechnology, or information systems technology, display different business models, processes, and characteristics from mainstream types of businesses. Therefore, CEOs, CTOs, managers, entrepreneurs, faculty, and students need to understand this phenomenon and learn how to successfully commercialize the intellectual property they develop.

Technology is different from any other type of new product. For one thing, the market responds differently to technology; customers are slow to accept a new technology with which they are not familiar. The entrepreneur who introduces a new technology must, therefore, devise a strategy that captures early adopters in a variety of niches in order to develop sufficient momentum to push the technology into the mainstream market. The development of new technology is generally a longer and more expensive process than that for other products. Securing intellectual property to protect technological products, processes, and know-how is also a critical component of the commercialization process. New technologies are commercialized in a variety of ways, but the underlying commonality is an entrepreneurial approach that seeks to create new value. Whether technology is developed inside the laboratories of a large company or in an entrepreneur's garage, the need for a fast-cycle process with checkpoints and criteria that must be met is essential to success.

This book was written to address all of these issues. Although it was prepared for a graduate-level course, it can be used equally well in undergraduate courses. It was designed with 15 chapters to permit teaching the material comfortably in one semester. The text is compatible with an overview course presenting the broad picture of the technology commercialization process. Because it contains application tools, it is also appropriate for a course where students are moving through the commercialization process with real inventions they have developed or technology they have acquired for the purposes of commercialization.

Bringing New Technology to Market embodies three major themes. The first is new value creation. For companies to be successful in sustainable technology innovation, it is critical that they punctuate their incremental or value-added innovations with radical or value-creating innovations. Creating new value is the most important way that a company can distinguish itself from its competitors. Therefore, the commercialization process as discussed in this book makes it possible for a company to successfully combine the development and exploitation of both incremental and radical innovations. The second theme is speed. As windows of opportunity for new technologies are shrinking, product development timelines are by necessity shortening, creating a real dilemma for product developers—how to produce superior high-technology products faster, yet at prices the market will tolerate. This book presents methods, based on empirical research, that result in faster time to market without sacrificing quality or value creation. The third theme is entrepreneurship. The tools that entrepreneurs employ to recognize and create opportunity, test a business concept in the market, and gather the resources to execute the business concept are the same tools required to successfully navigate the technology commercialization process. In this book, these entrepreneurial tools are applied in the context of a new technology venture, whether that venture is a start-up, a venture inside a large organization, or a spin-off venture from a large corporation.

Bringing New Technology to Market contains many features designed to benefit faculty, students, and others interested in technology commercialization.

- The book covers the entire spectrum of the commercialization process, from idea conception through prototyping and testing, intellectual property acquisition, market analysis, and product launch. *Readers will have a single source for the latest information and research in technology commercialization.*
- It recognizes the broad spectrum of technology industries with examples from information systems, industrial engineering, biotechnology, and other technical industries. *The book is adaptable and compatible with courses in engineering, science, and business.*
- Each chapter has a small real-world case that relates to the topic of the chapter. *Readers will be able to discuss the content of the chapter through the practical environment of the case.*
- Each chapter contains real-world examples of concepts presented in a readable style. *Readers will be able to easily see how theory translates into practice.*
- The book follows a logical progression in its development from idea conception to market launch. *Readers can learn the process through a natural progression where each new concept builds on the previous one.*
- The book treats the topic of feasibility analysis, a critical component of the commercialization process. *Readers will learn how to develop a business concept for a new technology and test that concept in the market.*
- The book contains three chapters on the development, acquisition, and management of intellectual property, which is a critical aspect of the technology commercialization process. *Readers will understand their rights regarding the intellectual property they develop or acquire, and how to manage that IP to create wealth.*

Every chapter contains a short case or profile of a real entrepreneur, inventor, or company grappling with the commercialization process. Other real-life examples are sprinkled throughout the chapters to keep the topics grounded in reality. Current and relevant research is the basis for the chapter content and additional resources, both books and Internet resources, are given at the end of each chapter. In addition, questions at the end of the chapter serve to provoke stimulating discussions in class or may form the basis for a class assignment.

Available with this text is an instructor's manual, as well as a Web site where professors can download PowerPoint slides, the instructor's manual, and sample syllabi for the course (*www.prenhall.com/allen*).

ACKNOWLEDGMENTS

I would like to acknowledge the help and advice of Jon Gordon and his colleagues at Weston Benshoof Rochefort Rubalcava MacCuish LLP for their review of the intellectual property chapters. I would also like to express my appreciation to David Groves for his assistance with the research and to my former students, Lucrezia Bickerton and Casey Horton (MBA 2001), who contributed the Zondigo case study. Special thanks to my husband John Allen, Gentech Corporation; Dr. Ken Jordan, Jordan Neuroscience; and Drs. Eugene DeJuan and Mark Humayan of the Doheny Retina Institute at the University of Southern California for serving as beta sites for many of the concepts presented in the book.

Special thanks to Jennifer Glennon, Kelly Warsak, and Jennifer Welsch for their very helpful comments and for keeping me on track.

CHAPTER

1

INNOVATION AND COMMERCIALIZATION

OVERVIEW

This chapter will examine

❖ the effect of technological change on economic principles

❖ the foundations of technological innovation

❖ key disruptive technologies for the new millennium

❖ the innovation and commercialization process

INTRODUCTION

Today, companies seeking to commercialize their technologies face a dynamic set of challenges, attitudes, and values. The demand for better, faster, cheaper technology products is a dilemma that few companies have successfully overcome. Intellectual property, once a cost center for most corporations, has now become an important revenue center—a critical competitive advantage for the firms that hold it and a significant disadvantage for those that do not. Incremental innovation—improving on what has already been done—has traditionally helped a company survive and compete. Today, however, it is radical innovation that is critical for long-term sustainability.[1] Unfortunately, although many companies have successfully commercialized incremental innovations on existing technologies, they have been far less successful in bringing radical innovations or breakthrough products to market.

Thousands of new products are produced every year by corporations attempting to increase their market share and stay competitive, but the vast majority of these products fail to make a profit for the companies that spent millions creating and marketing them. Very few companies have enjoyed the consistent new product success of Hewlett-Packard, 3M, and Pfizer, and many have disappeared from the corporate map because they failed to innovate and were overtaken by their more agile counterparts.

Fully 40 percent of major corporations in business in 1975 are not in business today.[2] One of the explanations for this dismal record is that companies are still trying to link emerging technologies with existing markets when they should be linking emerging technologies with emerging markets.[3] What customers want today, they will not want tomorrow. Satisfying customers today and anticipating their latent needs for the future is like trying to hit a moving target. Now more than ever, it is important to understand how to effectively commercialize new technology products.

TECHNOLOGICAL CHANGE AND BASIC ECONOMIC PRINCIPLES

On August 9, 1995, when Netscape Communications went public and its stock more than doubled in less than 24 hours, it signaled the start of the Internet IPO market. It was the gold rush of the 1990s. Companies that followed—Priceline.com, eBay, and E*Trade—enjoyed successful IPOs with no major products, no profits, and virtually no customers. Between November 1998 and November 1999, 10 companies showed first-day price increases greater than 300 percent, despite generating little or no profit.[4]

This was certainly not the first time that a technology company had gone public with no sales and no product yet ready for commercialization. In 1980, biotech giant Genentech, in one of the largest stock run-ups ever, went public. Its stock shot from $35 a share to $88 dollars a share in less than an hour.[5] Yet, it was not until 1985 that Genentech finally received approval from the U.S. Food and Drug Administration (FDA) to market its first product, Protropin, a growth hormone for children with growth hormone deficiency. This was the first recombinant pharmaceutical product to be manufactured and marketed by a biotechnology company.

Until the 1980s, technological change was nowhere to be found in economic growth models, which relied solely on inputs of capital and labor. In the 1980s, the work of Paul Romer and others identified technological change as a critical component of a growth model that responds to market incentives.[6] Technological change comes about when a company identifies new customer segments that appear to be emerging, new customer needs, existing customer needs that have not been satisfied, and new ways of manufacturing and distributing products and services. Technological change has been behind the record growth that many companies have achieved. For example, Intel would not have experienced the high rate of growth it saw in the mid-1980s had it not redefined the way it saw the business, starting in 1979 when CEO and founder Andy Grove announced that Intel would discontinue its memory chip business (it controlled 30 percent of the market) and focus on microprocessors. One year later, IBM released the IBM PC with an Intel 8080 microprocessor, and the rest is history. Redefinition of the business resulted in a completely different strategy for doing business.

Key shifts in basic economic principles resulting from the rapid pace of technological change precipitated major changes in business strategy. With the dot-com implosion of April 2000 and the subsequent crash of technology stocks, many believed that business would return to its pre-dot-com ways, but that has not happened. The period from 1998 to 2001 was a period of great experimentation and creativity that shook nearly every industry in one way or another. It also had a profound impact on basic economic principles. We will look at five of these adjustments to long-standing economic principles and how the changes affect competitive strategy.

THE FINANCIAL REVOLUTION

Venture capital (VC) funding is the fuel that powers the engine of innovation. VC funding has soared from about $5 billion annually in 1988, a peak year to that point, to about $100 billion in 2000.[7] This increase in the level of investment has had an important impact on the rate of technological change. Without the enormous infusion of capital to such companies as Genetech, Cisco, and Netscape, the Internet age would have come about much more slowly. The availability of capital accelerates innovation exponentially. In fact, the primary reason that technological innovation has not benefited countries such as Germany and Japan to the same extent that it has the United States is their lack of access to the same levels of venture capital.

Venture capital speeds up the pace of innovation and stimulates new competition, but it does not normally fund basic research that produces radical innovation. Because basic research is a lengthy process with no particular commercialization goals in mind, its funding typically comes from the nonprofit sector and through government grants, university research centers, and corporate research and development (R&D) funds. But when basic research identifies potential applications in the market, venture capital can serve to hasten the development process. One example of the impact of venture capital on the pace of innovation is the Human Genome Project. Originally, the project was funded with government and nonprofit money with the purpose of mapping the human genome. The target completion date to produce the complete mapping of the human genome was 2005. When venture-capital-funded Celera Genomics, a Maryland-based start-up, entered the picture, the Human Genome Project was impelled to complete its task in record time. Both the government and Celera announced the mapping of most of the human genome in June 2000, five years earlier than planned.[8]

Just as the availability of capital can stimulate innovation, the lack of capital can sharply curtail innovation efforts. For example, from 1987 to 1991, available venture capital declined by more than 50 percent and first-round financing for start-up companies fell 75 percent, significantly inhibiting innovation efforts.[9] The decline in the value of technology stocks that began in the spring of 2000 precipitated another shift of venture capital funds away from the technology sector, which, if it lasts for any significant length of time, could seriously inhibit innovation efforts. Innovation depends on easy access to capital. Unfortunately, venture capital is highly sensitive to the economy, and to the stock market in particular.

FIRST MOVER TO SCALE

One interesting idea to come out of the new economy was that to succeed, a business must be first in its market and scale out quickly, that is, the business must position the company's brand in as many places as possible as quickly as possible. However, history teaches that being first mover is more often a liability than a benefit. For example, not many people under the age of 40 remember VisiCalc. VisiCalc was the first major computer spreadsheet. Ultimately, it lost in the marketplace to Lotus 1-2-3; Lotus then lost to Microsoft Excel, the third mover. The ubiquitous PalmPilot, with its Graffiti handwriting recognition software, was not the first personal digital assistant (PDA) in the market. It came years after Apple's Newton MessagePad. The Newton MessagePad is a classic story of a first-mover company that did not listen to its customers. Its developers concentrated on producing a complex technology that customers did not appreciate because it did not solve their basic needs. The Newton MessagePad was designed to read its owner's personal handwriting. In engineering terms, that meant that the computer chip inside the Newton MessagePad had to adapt itself to millions of variations in handwriting—a nearly impossible task. Consequently, the Newton MessagePad often gave incorrect results and frustrated its user.

These examples are just two of the many cases where the second, third, or even fourth company entering the market prevailed over the pioneering company. In fact, most of the major brands that dominate the marketplace today were not pioneers in their industries. According to Jim Collins, author of the best-selling book *Built to Last*,[10] the companies that prevail are simply better at what they do. It is his belief that, except in rare cases, "best beats first, even if it takes a long time." There is an interesting story about a young product manager who, in the early 1980s, walked into the office of Cyril Yansouni, the general manager of the Hewlett-Packard personal computer group. The young man was very concerned that Hewlett-Packard would lose a once-in-a-lifetime opportunity to be the best in portable and personal computers. The wise Yansouni calmly responded that Hewlett-Packard might fail at being first, but it would learn from its mistakes and the mistakes of others. "We don't have to be first so long as in the end we figure out how to be best. It might take 10 or 15 years, but we'll figure it out."[11]

America Online (AOL) is another example of a technology company that achieved success by being better, not first. In 1992, AOL only had 200,000 members compared to Prodigy's 2 million members.[12] AOL ultimately beat its competitors and acquired them because it subscribed to a strategy of continual improvement—listening to its customers and constantly making changes for the better.

SCARCITY

When Adam Smith proposed his market system over 200 years ago, it was based on the concept of scarcity, the idea that people make choices based on limited resources.[13] Knowledge products, which are at the core of the new economy, present a problem for economists because knowledge defies the law of scarcity. For example, if someone sells a car, he no longer owns it; but, if someone sells an idea, he still owns it. In fact, he can sell it many times—it will never be used up. In traditional economic theory, industries experience diminishing returns when unit costs start to rise. In other words, the gain from producing an additional unit goes down. With information-based products, such as software, books, and movies that can be digitized, there are increasing returns, because information is costly to produce but inexpensive to replicate. Consequently, industries that deal in information products have high fixed costs and extremely low variable costs that afford them huge economies of scale.

Economies of scale are perhaps the biggest reason that new entrants have a difficult time breaking into a market. Economists recognize that in the information age, the benefits of economies of scale accrue not only on the supply side, but also on the demand side due to what they call "network effects" or "network externalities." In other words, the real value of an information product is realized as more people use the product. Microsoft Windows is valuable to customers precisely because so many people use it in business, resolving compatibility issues. These network effects create strong barriers to entry for the companies that benefit from them, making it more difficult for competitors to enter the same market. This concept of increasing returns is not exclusive to the information age. In 1890, for example, gas, electricity, and railways enjoyed increasing returns as well, chiefly from the network effects of more people using the system. The more people who use a system, the cheaper the cost to maintain it.

MONOPOLIES

Joseph Schumpeter, a 20th-century economist who is often thought of as the father of entrepreneurship, espoused the theory of "creative destruction," which proposed that monopolies actually stimulate innovation and growth by allowing the firm a quiet period with no rivals. According to the theory, without the ability to operate as a temporary monopoly, a firm will be faced with competitive pricing that does not allow it time to recoup its costs before it must compete on price. The U.S. Patent and Trademark Office was created expressly to ensure inventors a temporary monopoly. Without that quiet period free of competition, inventors would have no incentive to invest heavily in innovation, particularly disruptive or radical innovation. That being said, in the new economy, not only has the time from concept to market declined precipitously, but the quiet time of temporary monopoly for the pioneering firm has declined as well. Today, with technology life cycles shortening, different core technologies competing for the same customers, and global companies increasing their technological innovation investment, it is difficult for any company to survive and prosper with only a monopoly status. Every company needs to build a diversified barrier of competitive advantages, of which a temporary monopoly is one, albeit very significant, advantage.

BETTER, FASTER, CHEAPER

The new economy is driven by the demand for higher quality products, faster production and distribution, and lower prices. Consequently, the dilemma for entrepreneurs is how to crush the competition, produce at Internet speed, and still make sure the customer is happy—a nearly impossible task. Speed is one of the key competitive advantages in the new product arena. The ability to get new products to market in record time so as to take advantage of increasingly smaller windows of opportunity has never been more critical to success. Speed produces:

- **Competitive advantage.** The business can gain a foothold in the market before competitors become aware of what they are doing.
- **More profit potential.** The business has shortened the time to market.
- **Fewer surprises.** The business gets the product to market before customers' tastes and preferences change.[14]

The longer it takes to develop a new product and bring it to market, the less likely it will still meet customers' needs. Every aspect of the product development environment is changing at such a rapid pace that any lag time in commercializing a new technology can make it obsolete by the time it hits the market. Getting to market quickly can also mean higher profits. It is estimated that a 6-month jump on competitors in a market accustomed to 18- to 24-month design lives can translate into as much as three times the profit over the market life of the design.

❖ **Key Technologies to Watch**

In the world of technology, opportunity comes from looking ahead, sometimes very far ahead, so that a business can position itself to pioneer the application of a new technology when it reaches the commercialization stage. MIT has identified 10 technologies to keep an eye on.[15] Here five technologies are profiled and an additional five to watch out for are listed.

1. **Brain–machine interfaces.** At Duke University, neurobiologist Miguel Nicolelis is pioneering the use of neural implants to study the brain. His goal is to better understand how the brain works so that systems can be designed that will allow for brain control of computers and other machines—essentially brain–machine interfaces. The ultimate goal of the project is to permit human brains to control artificial devices that will restore lost sensory and motor functions to the physically challenged. See *www.neuro.duke.edu/Faculty/Nicolelis.htm.*

2. **Flexible transistors.** Everything is becoming or will become digital. This requires cheap and flexible integrated circuits. Recently, a materials scientist at IBM's Watson Research Center, Cherie Kagan, discovered a way to create transistors from materials that combine the speed of inorganic materials with the flexibility and affordability of organic materials. Her findings could result in faster circuits that would deliver sharper flat-panel video displays and bring down the cost of wall-panel displays. See *www.watson.ibm.com/.*

3. **Data mining.** The ability to search through gigabytes of data to find meaningful relationships and patterns goes well beyond the world of Amazon-style e-commerce. With the flow of information increasing at astronomical rates, the corporate world is demanding a way through the morass. Usama Fayyad, referred to by some as the "father of data mining," recognized the need for data mining when he took a summer job with General Motors while a graduate student at the University of Michigan. He wanted to find a way to allow a service technician to query a database based on any aspect of a vehicle, for example, engine capacity, model, etc. He developed a pattern recognition algorithm to solve the problem. That was just the beginning. Today, data-mining technology has begun to move into methods for extracting meaningful relationships from free-form text documents. Fayyad has commercialized his efforts through a data-mining company called digiMine.com. See *www.digimine.com.*

4. **Digital rights management.** One of the biggest challenges facing the Internet today is the conflict between the owners of intellectual property (books, music, video, etc.) and Internet users who believe that any content distributed over the Internet should be free. Spinning out of research at Xerox's Palo Alto Research Center (PARC), Ranjit Singh's company, ContentGuard, wants to solve the pain faced by content providers and allow them to follow their content to see "who is passing your content to whom." ContentGuard is an encryption device that lets content providers control who receives and distributes their proprietary content. See *www.contentguard.com.*

5. **Microphotonics.** The telecommunications industry has seen dramatic technological advances, but more is coming in the form of microphotonics—
   technologies that direct light on a microscopic scale. Microphotonics has the
   potential to unclog the integration of fiber optics and electronic switching in
   the telecommunications backbone. Technologies such as photonic crystals,
   the work of MIT physics professor John Joannopoulos, have the best chance
   of solving the problem through optical circuits that will process data at the
   speed of light. Joannopoulos' dream is an all-optical Internet that will carry
   1,000 times more data than current fiber optics. See *webrle.mit.edu/groups/g-
   SUR.HTM.*

Here are an additional five technologies to watch out for.

1. **Biometrics.** The identification of individuals by specific biological traits.
2. **Natural language processing.** Speech recognition, speech generation, and
   natural language understanding.
3. **Untangling code.** The ability to trace and record every operation that a software application performs to allow a programmer to make global fixes.
4. **Robot design.** Using robotics to perform complex tasks.
5. **Microfluidics.** The ability to control and manipulate fluids at the microscale
   for applications in genomics and pharmaceutical development.

THE FOUNDATIONS OF TECHNOLOGICAL INNOVATION

Innovation happens when old ideas are juxtaposed in new ways. When Alessandro
Volta designed the eudiometer, his purpose was to explode bad smelling gases with
electricity, but his invention ultimately achieved its real value as the spark plug.
Wilhelm Maybach, while working for Daimler in Germany, juxtaposed a newly
invented perfume sprayer with gasoline and invented the carburetor. Whether in the
conception of a new idea or in the development of applications of that idea, creativity
plays a vital role.

   Today, innovation occurs at ever-increasing rates, but for the most part, this innovation has been incremental in nature, improving on something that already exists.[16]
As the speed of innovation continues to increase, incremental innovation will become
continuous in nature and require escalating levels of creativity to sustain it. The next
section looks at the role creativity plays in invention and innovation.

THE ROLES OF CREATIVITY AND INVENTION IN INNOVATION

Innovation and invention both require creativity, but there are distinct differences
between the two activities. Invention relies solely on creativity, whereas innovation
requires a plan.[17] Innovation, the improvement of something that already exists, occurs
at a much faster pace than invention, and is more directly affected by market shifts.

Furthermore, innovation does not just refer to products and processes, but also to innovations in engineering, manufacturing, purchasing, and marketing—essentially every aspect of the business.

The ability of an inventor to view the world not as others see it, but in unique configurations, allows the inventor to create something that others are not able to conceive. The inventor takes the impossible and makes it possible. By examining a sticky cocklebur he had plucked from his clothing under a microscope, Swiss engineer George de Mestral discovered a way to bind cloth without hooks or buttons—Velcro. The black residue that clings to oil rig pumps was not considered to have any value, but chemist Robert Chesebrough decided to try to extract something of value from it and succeeded in reducing the black goop to a white jelly. He named the new product Vaseline. It has become one of the most successful products in history, being used as hair tonic, a salve, and fish bait. Creativity and the invention process will be addressed in more detail in Chapter 2.

THE ROLE OF BASIC RESEARCH IN INVENTION AND INNOVATION

Research driven solely by curiosity, unfettered by existing technology, is quickly becoming rare. Years ago, major corporations funded institutes or entire divisions devoted to basic research. One notable example was Bell Telephone Laboratories, which invented the transistor in 1947 as a result of theoretical and experimental investigations into the properties of semiconductors. The period from the late 1950s to the mid-1980s has been called a golden era for academic research. People came from all over the world to study and conduct research in the United States.[18]

Today, however, most of the major corporate research units no longer exist or do not devote the bulk of their efforts to basic research. Basic research is frequently bypassed in favor of applied research with shorter time frames. This change is largely driven by the availability of massive amounts of capital and media hype that showcases researchers who have scored major successes in the entrepreneurial world. It is no wonder then that the federal government is the dominant financial supporter of basic research as it is not constrained by time. In fact, the time lines on many research grants far exceed the market viability of the technology, particularly in the information technology area. However, even government entities are feeling the pressure to respond more quickly to the market. For example, the National Science Foundation (NSF), a primary supporter of academic research, now demands that research projects not only be of high interest, quality, and importance, but that they demonstrate the solution to a societal need or goal. Chapter 9 explores the resources for R&D and looks more closely at the role of basic research in the technology transfer and commercialization process.

DEFINING INNOVATION

Invention is often a random and unpredictable process, whereas innovation is a manageable process that turns an invention into something useful having commercial value.[19] In the past, innovation typically involved the design of new products. Today, it has taken on a much broader definition. Now, innovation is also about creating new ways of doing things, and may include the development of new processes or distribution strategies. For example, oil companies certainly make money by selling fuel, but they also make money by improving the drilling and distribution process. Oil companies now mine data archives to find ways to modify their systems to conserve on energy costs, and they pass those savings on to customers.

Researchers have constructed many frameworks to assist in the definition of innovation and innovative products: technology push versus market pull, evolutionary versus revolutionary, radical versus incremental, and sustaining versus disruptive. They all essentially refer to the same concept. In this book, disruptive or radical technology will be used to refer to technology that derives from new knowledge and displaces previous technologies and sustaining or incremental technology to refer to technologies based on existing knowledge.

SUSTAINING VERSUS DISRUPTIVE MODEL OF INNOVATION

The sustaining versus disruptive model of innovation was developed by Clayton Christensen of Harvard in his work identifying innovations that are paradigm shifters—those that radically change the way we do things.[20] These paradigm-shifting innovations are disruptive technologies. A sustaining technology is compatible with existing standards and addresses current needs in the market, whereas a disruptive technology makes existing standards obsolete and addresses future needs. Disruptive technologies represent not a simple change from one technology to another, but a radical change at a systemic level with far-reaching implications. These technologies come about when the needs of the customer can no longer be met inside the current technology parameters, and they are successful only when the change they bring about produces significant improvements in features, benefits, and costs.[21]

Historically, disruptive technologies only came along once every couple of decades or so, but today these technologies appear on an almost annual basis. Christensen noted that a critical differentiating factor between disruptive technologies and sustaining technologies is that the latter tend to be more profitable earlier for their inventors because they are more easily absorbed into the market as they are based on technologies that customers already understand. Curiously, disruptive technologies often do not reap their full value until they achieve mass-market acceptance. They are typically characterized as cheaper, smaller, simpler, and more convenient than the existing technologies. However, these pioneering products often display poor performance. When Sony introduced its battery-powered transistor radio in the late 1950s, it produced a very poor quality of sound by any standard, but it served the needs of the early adopters, teenagers who wanted to listen to the new rock-and-roll music out of earshot of their parents. Over time, the transistor radio became cheaper, smaller, and produced a better quality of sound.

Sustaining technologies improve on existing technologies, most often in the area of performance. Each generation of Palm's successful PDA has improved on the previous version in terms of performance. However, the PalmPilot was not the pioneer in the PDA market. The Apple Newton MessagePad, a disruptive technology designed to be an alternative to paper daily organizers, pioneered the PDA market. It performed poorly and consequently never reached the required mass-market acceptance.

Once mass acceptance has been achieved, disruptive technologies ultimately have a positive impact on the economy, producing new categories of products and services, not to mention new companies and many jobs. However, in their early stages, disruptive innovations are not easy to distinguish from poor ideas. Intel's Andy Grove uses what he terms "inflection points" to identify when an idea moves from mere idea to disruptive technology. Grove defines an inflection point as "a time in the life of a business when its fundamentals are about to change. That change can mean an opportunity to rise to new heights. But it may just as likely signal the beginning of the end."[22]

Disruptive technology does not rely on a specifically defined customer need, but instead addresses a latent need, a need the customer has yet to recognize. Leifer et al. classified radical or disruptive innovation into three categories:[23]

- **Innovation within the markets of existing business units.** Here, the goal is to replace existing technologies for the same customers and market. For example, GE's magnetic resonance imaging technology was a disruptive technology designed to serve the same market that its Medical Systems business unit had been serving. The belief is that current customers familiar with a company's technology are more likely to adopt a disruptive technology from a company with which they are familiar.
- **Innovation in the "white spaces" between a company's existing businesses.** In this category, a disruptive technology falls somewhere in the space between existing business units and either results in a new business unit or serves to expand the scope of an existing unit. The technology, although new to the company, is still within the scope of its strategic objectives. Closely related to this concept is fusion innovation, which consists of those innovations that emerge from a combination of distinct disciplines or bodies of knowledge to create new disciplines and applications without necessarily creating an entirely new body of knowledge. For example, nanotechnology is the result of combining molecular biology and engineering.
- **Innovation outside a company's current strategic objectives.** Here, the disruptive technology opens up new markets to a business that are significantly different from its current markets and objectives. This type of innovation results in the highest degree of uncertainty for a business because the company is moving in areas with which it is not familiar.

RADICAL INNOVATION AND THE INCUMBENT'S CURSE

The theory of the "incumbent's curse" has permeated much of the research on radical innovation.[24] The theory is as follows: An independent or corporate-sponsored inventor comes up with a radically new device. In attempting to gain support from large firms in the industry, the inventor encounters resistance and indifference and is forced to raise the funds to launch the device on his own. If the inventor succeeds and the technology becomes the new standard in the industry, the inventor typically responds to the threat of new technology in the same way that firms responded to the inventor's device. Because incumbents have significant investments in their current technology, they often suffer from technology inertia, that is, fear of straying too far from their successes.[25] Consequently, most new radical innovation has come from small firms that have no sunk costs in existing technology or turf to protect. To overcome the obstacles to radical innovation, established companies have to break away from traditional strategic thinking and the arrogance that comes from having achieved success with their core products. As highly successful companies like Hewlett-Packard,

Corning, and Motorola have done, businesses need to "punctuate ongoing incremental innovation with radical innovation."[26]

Entire industries have been destroyed by a pioneering technology (gas lighting, typewriters, and the telegraph, to name a few) yet large companies often fail to invest in radical innovation or scan the environment for emerging disruptive technologies before it's too late. There are many reasons why companies tend to avoid this radical innovation.

- **Smaller perceived incentives.**[27] Radical technologies produce no income for long periods of time, whereas incremental innovations of an existing technology can produce income almost immediately. Therefore, it would actually hurt a company's revenue picture to introduce a radical technology.
- **The tendency to focus on their core competencies.** Incumbent firms tend to filter out information that does not relate to their core technologies. This filtering often prevents them from seeing potential threats from small innovative firms.
- **Inability to change routines.** Because existing routines have helped the company achieve success with its current technology, the firm is reluctant to change what it does well. Chances are that a switch to a new technology might actually make the firm's current routines obsolete, and this is something the incumbent firm does not want to do.

KEY DISRUPTIVE TECHNOLOGIES FOR THE NEW MILLENNIUM

Disruptive technologies change the world; they move us in new directions and affect all areas of our lives. The Internet is merely one in a long series of technological shifts we have experienced and will continue to experience into the future. Past disruptive technologies have included Edison's light bulb, eyeglasses, moveable type, the steam engine, elevators, structural steel, the birth control pill, and lasers, among many others.

Some economists, like Robert Gordon from Northwestern University, argue that the five major periods of innovation in the past 100 years that preceded what we now call the digital or information revolution were more important on an individual basis than the digital revolution is as a whole.[28] Those five periods of dramatic innovation included the discovery and application of electricity, the internal combustion engine, modern chemistry, plumbing, and the mass media, all of which were disruptive technologies that changed the world. Although no one would deny the importance of any one of those technologies, we are now experiencing the development of more disruptive technologies in a shorter span of time than at almost any other time in the past.

The Internet as a disruptive technology has changed the way business is conducted and has had a profound effect on society in general. However, like a child in adolescence, the Internet has not yet found its perfect place in the whole scheme of things. It is currently going through a trial-and-error period just as any disruptive technology does. It does appear, however, that the Internet has survived the first phase. The rush to offer retail services and products online (business-to-consumer market) and to provide similar services and consolidation of distribution channels in the business-to-business marketplace taught users a lot about what the Internet can and cannot do. The dot-com implosion forced the marketplace to debate the real value of e-commerce. Although the Internet and e-commerce changed some of what business does, it did not make everything that came before it obsolete, as some might suggest. Louis Gerstner, Jr., the CEO who turned around a failing IBM, claims that the "Internet is going to be remembered a lot like the way we see the importance of the electric motor today—it was first used in heavy industries, but eventually it was absorbed and adopted by every industry."[29] The Internet will change the way much of business is transacted, but it does not allow business people to forget all the fundamentals of good business practice. According to Gerstner, superior businesses today will result from technology leadership and operational leadership, not an Internet presence.

Three disruptive technologies that will affect innovation and opportunity in every industry for the foreseeable future are the Human Genome Project, nanotechnology, and wireless technology.

THE HUMAN GENOME PROJECT

Arguably the most important scientific finding of the 1990s was the mapping of the human genome, which was announced in June 2000. Two teams of researchers, one private, one government-funded, found that humans have only about 30,000 genes, far fewer than originally thought. Surprisingly, they also discovered that genetic differences between any two people are relatively small. The mapping of the human genome

---

❖ Are We Heading Toward a Nano Economy?

As recently as 5 years ago, nanotechnology, engineering and science at the molecular level, was considered on the edge, not quite equivalent to the paranormal phenomena that form the basis of the television series *The X-Files*, but close. In the not-so-distant past, nanotechnology was seen as possible, but not likely to become a reality for decades. However, in a world where everything seems to be moving faster, nanotechnology has become a commercial reality—at least to the many entrepreneurs who have chosen to start ventures in that area and believe in its commercial viability.

Bob Gower, a former chemical industry executive, and Richard Smalley, the 1996 Nobel Prize-winning chemist who discovered *fullerenes,* a new class of carbon compounds, have founded Carbon Nantechnologies Inc. (CNI) to produce and market carbon nanotubes (pipe-shaped molecules), a type of fullerene that holds extraordinary electrical and heat conducting properties. Nanotubes can be bundled together to form fiber that is 100 times stronger than steel. Gower and Smalley have the potential to create nanowires and transistors in ultradense integrated circuits, which can be used in such things as flat-panel displays and in electromagnetic shielding for cell phones.[30] See *www.cnanotech.com* for more on CNI.

In another area of nanotechnology, BioForce Laboratory, Inc. has become the leading developer of next-generation, ultraminiaturized laboratory tools for labs working at the molecular level in the area of disease identification and diagnostics as well as drug and gene therapy development. See *www.bioforcelab.com* for more on BioForce Laboratory, Inc.

opens the door to genetic therapies targeted at an individual's specific genetic makeup and ultimately to the ability to cure the most devastating of diseases. At the same time, it invites opportunity in ethically challenging areas such as human cloning that will have to be dealt with in the coming decades.

As a result of the Human Genome Project, hundreds of business opportunities have been created. Companies such as PE Biosystems Group and Qiagen make equipment that genomics companies use to sequence and assemble genes. Diagnostic laboratories see opportunities in gene-based diagnostic tests. Drug makers are counting on the ability to make more effective medicines by tailoring them to a patient's genetic profile. However, despite all of these opportunities, it will probably take up to a decade or more for most companies to realize profits from these scientific discoveries.

NANOTECHNOLOGY

Another major scientific advance is nanotechnology. Nanotechnology comprises those technologies that operate in the nanometer area of scale. *Nano* is a term used by scientists to refer to 1 billionth (10^{-9}) of a metric unit. This means that 1 nanometer is 1 billionth of a meter, or 1 millionth of a millimeter.[31] Try to imagine storing the data from five high-density floppy disks on a thousandth of a millimeter. Or, consider that 10 nanometers are 1,000 times smaller than the diameter of a human hair.

As with many great scientific discoveries in the past, the new emphasis on nanotechnology was born out of a need—in this case, to develop a nonsilicon chip. Why is it necessary to develop a nonsilicon chip? The reason stems from the fact that over the past 35 years the number of transistors on a single chip has increased 5,000 times, from 2,300 in 1971 to 10.5 million on the Pentium III processor.[32] Trying to pack that many transistors on a single silicon chip has become a very costly process. Replacing the silicon chip with less expensive molecular computing components may be a way to reduce the financial barriers faced by the microprocessor industry. Some research suggests that future generations of molecular machines will actually build themselves by growing complex lattices of crystals.[33] Scientists at UCLA, in conjunction with Hewlett-Packard Laboratories, have created a crude prototype of what will be a computer based on exotic molecules, rather than silicon, that is expected to lead to microprocessors that are billions of times more powerful and compact than today's most advanced chips. Nanotechnology is clearly opening the door to a wealth of innovation.

WIRELESS TECHNOLOGY

It all started with the cellular telephone. Then came the cellular modem, the digital alphanumeric pager, and the PDA with wireless access to the Internet. Today, anyone can check inventory levels, monitor shipping progress, send and receive e-mail, or buy and sell stock transparently with the help of a Web-enabled cell phone or PDA.

The worldwide market for wireless applications is predicted to grow from $10 billion today to $74 billion by 2005.[34] Nokia, Motorola, and Ericsson dominate the mobile phone market with about 53 percent of worldwide sales. However, Web-enabled handheld devices are just the beginning. One MIT graduate, Alex Lightman, founder of Charmed Technology, believes that people will become walking Internet portals through wearable wireless technology.[35] Charmed Technology produces everything from a digital business card that reads and stores data from other business cards to the more cutting edge wearable wireless computer kit. Lightman believes that wireless technology is an extension of the senses that permits an individual to have an interface with everything wherever they go.

Certainly there are a multitude of devices and applications being developed that will take advantage of the freedom of wireless communication, including the ability to construct a business LAN without having to wire a building. At this point, the real challenge to rapid growth of the wireless industry is the lack of agreement on an industry-wide communications standard.

The three disruptive technologies discussed here, in combination with the Internet, are having an impact on the economy and society in ways that may not be understood for years to come. Both disruptive and sustaining technologies emerge from a process that requires creation, invention, and innovation.

STIMULATING INNOVATION

Whether the subject is sustaining or disruptive technology, successful innovation comes only after intense questioning of existing products and patterns, and going beyond the limits of existing capabilities. Sustaining or incremental innovation will meet customer needs for a time, but it must be supplemented by periods of disruptive or radical innovation.[36] Therefore, creating a company culture that encourages innovation is critical to long-term success in the marketplace. In addition to the availability of capital, innovation is stimulated by four fundamental factors:[37]

- Globalization
- Sophisticated customers in fragmented markets
- Widely diversified and changing technologies
- Shrinking cycle times

These factors will be considered in more detail.

GLOBALIZATION

The number of companies competing in the global marketplace has been increasing dramatically since the 1980s. When global expansion is combined with the fact that most new products come from products already in the market, it is easy to see why the marketplace has become so competitive. Companies from every part of the world are imposing their standards on products and processes and a technology company must be ready to respond rapidly to threats that may come from a competitor in another part of the world. As competition has intensified, so has the potential for innovation.

SOPHISTICATED CUSTOMERS

Customers, whether consumers or businesses, have so many choices today that innovators find they need to differentiate their products on many levels just to compete. Customers demand superior performance and value-based pricing as the starting point for competitive advantage. Innovators must exceed those criteria, surpassing customer expectations to stand out from the crowd. Moreover, customers are savvy about technology and the value or lack of it when it comes to incremental improvements, which is why at some point the benefits to customers of incremental innovations decline and the potential for acceptance of a radically new innovation increases.

RAPIDLY CHANGING TECHNOLOGY

With the marginal cost of added technology capability being very small, many companies seek to compete by adding more and more capability to their products. However, customers are not willing to pay for "bells and whistles" that do not satisfy a specific need just because those enhancements are technologically available. Customers do not purchase the technology per se, but rather the solution to a particular problem—the benefit of the technology. To compete, successful companies must not only produce innovative technologies and their associated products, they must also develop innovative processes that are integrated with their products, making it difficult for a competitor to produce at the same quality level and at the same cost.

SHRINKING PRODUCT DEVELOPMENT TIMELINES

A new product no longer has a long life cycle before it becomes obsolete. Where 50 years ago a new tool would have an 18-year life and a new toy would have a 16-year life, today those life cycles have shrunk to 5 years.[38] These shortened product life cycles are forcing companies to innovate constantly just to stay ahead of the game. They are also effectively shortening the temporary monopoly enjoyed by companies with proprietary technology.

EFFECT OF INNOVATION ON COMPANY SUCCESS

Today, new products account for an average of 33 percent of company sales revenues.[39] Success in technology ventures has been measured by market share, stock value, return on investment, profit, and even survival in the case of new ventures. First-mover advantage is also considered a measure of success in the commercialization process. First movers derive their advantage by securing intellectual property protection, specifically patents, on a particular technology, or by preempting others from gaining access to resources by recognizing and controlling a scarce resource—retail shelf space, key location, limited raw materials, or skilled labor—before others see its value.[40] First-mover advantage will be discussed in Chapter 12 when entry and growth strategies are considered, but suffice it to say here that first-mover has its disadvantages as well. Second movers often benefit from the pioneer's work and are able to develop around the protected technology without incurring the heavy costs of basic research. The second mover also is free from the costs and delays associated with compatibility issues with complementary products.[41] One study found a negative correlation between R&D intensity and success, that is, the greater the investment in R&D, the less chance of success.[42] Therefore, it appears that the uniqueness of a technology in and of itself does not determine success but rather the ability to successfully commercialize that technology in the market.

However, a more recent study has confirmed that even though first-mover advantage does not indicate success in the long term, it does give the firm an advantage in seeking funding and also provides an initial quiet period or temporary monopoly during which to establish a foothold in the market and build brand loyalty before having to deal with direct competitors.[43]

Yet another of the determinants of success with new products is the ability to effectively navigate the innovation and commercialization process. This issue will be taken up in the next section.

OVERVIEW OF THE INNOVATION AND COMMERCIALIZATION PROCESS

The innovation and commercialization process is not linear. In fact, it moves more like a pinball machine—taking off in one direction until it hits a snag, then bouncing off in another direction. This chaotic process continues until the goal is achieved. Innovation is an iterative process where the inventor learns from his mistakes and builds on that learning. Figure 1-1 depicts the innovation and commercialization process as categories of activities. Within each category are many nonlinear, often chaotic activities. The broad categories will be discussed briefly here and in more detail in the chapters to follow. A more elaborate commercialization process will be introduced later in the book.

INVENTING AND INNOVATING

The invention and innovation process generally consists of four broad categories of activities: connection, discovery, invention, and application. Briefly, connection involves recognizing a relationship that might lead to a discovery, which is the "ah ha" or "eureka!"

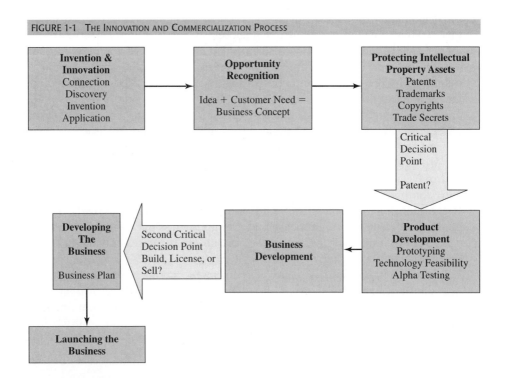

FIGURE 1-1 THE INNOVATION AND COMMERCIALIZATION PROCESS

phenomenon that occurs when something new is discovered. From this discovery comes an invention that has the potential to produce applications in a variety of different contexts. The invention and innovation portion of the process will be discussed in more depth in Chapter 2.

OPPORTUNITY RECOGNITION

Inventing a new device or process or innovating on an existing one is important, but that process alone will not produce an opportunity. An opportunity is the intersection of an idea and a market need or space. It is often reflected in a business concept statement that describes the product/process, the customer/end-user for the technology, the benefits and applications of the technology, and the distribution strategy. This concept statement will provide a basis for testing the feasibility of the opportunity in the market. Chapter 3 discusses opportunity recognition and concept development in more detail.

PROTECTING INTELLECTUAL PROPERTY ASSETS

Early in the invention and innovation process, the inventor will need to find ways to protect the intellectual property (IP) assets that are being created. Many inventors fail to realize how important it is to legally protect their work so that they have the option to apply for a patent or other form of IP at the appropriate time. The protection of innovative ideas and inventions is critical to successful commercialization. However, determining which type of protection to choose and which strategy will best meet commercialization goals is also vital. Part II of this book addresses intellectual property issues.

REACHING THE FIRST CRITICAL DECISION POINT: WHETHER TO PATENT

The first critical decision point is whether to seek patent protection for the invention or innovation, assuming the technology qualifies according to the requirements of the U. S. Patent and Trademark Office (PTO). Three questions must be answered at this juncture.

- Does the technology appear to be a feasible design?
- Is a patent necessary to the successful commercialization of the technology?
- Does the technology meet the PTO requirements?

For some products, getting a patent will take longer than the window of opportunity will allow. For others, a patent will provide a brief quiet period to enter the market without competitors. After deciding whether or not to patent, the inventor will also have to develop a prototype and determine if the product is technically feasible. The patent process will be discussed in Chapter 5.

PRODUCT DEVELOPMENT, PROTOTYPING, AND TECHNOLOGY FEASIBILITY

Every new product goes through a design, development, and prototyping phase during which the feasibility of the technology is tested. Today, designing right the first time, shortening the time to market, prototyping early, and outsourcing noncore capabilities are critical components in an effective product development process in a dynamic environment. Field-testing with potential users at various stages in the process will reduce the chance of error in the final product. Product development is the subject of Chapter 4.

DEVELOPING AND TESTING THE BUSINESS CONCEPT

Determining if the invention or innovation is commercially feasible requires a thorough analysis of the industry and market, the capabilities and shortcomings of the founding team, and the resources required to start the venture. This stage points to the relationship between innovation and the market. Research has found that the chances for commercial success are greater when technology and market factors are considered together.[44] In fact, boundary spanning in the organization, as Kanter refers to it,[45] is necessary to build a competitive advantage, as the information required to judge feasibility will need to come from a variety of sources both internal and external to the founding team. Feasibility analysis is the subject of Chapter 3.

REACHING THE SECOND CRITICAL DECISION POINT: LICENSE, SELL, OR BUILD

Inventors have three basic choices: They can license the right to manufacture and market their inventions to an existing company and collect royalties on sales, they can sell the technology outright to another company, or they can build a company to manufacture and sell their invention. This is a particularly difficult decision for researchers and inventors who work in university environments, research institutes, government laboratories, or for large corporations. Deciding to start a company probably means having to leave their current position and seek resources to support the start-up—a culture shock at best—whereas licensing or selling outright may offer more flexibility. Who owns the technology an inventor develops is a question that also affects this second critical decision point. These issues are discussed in Chapters 9 and 10.

DEVELOPING THE BUSINESS

Once a business concept is judged to be feasible and the decision has been made to create a company, it is necessary to develop the infrastructure for the business. This is typically accomplished by preparing a comprehensive business plan that documents the operations of the business, policies, a marketing and growth plan, and a complete set of financial statements, as well as updated industry, market, and team analyses from the feasibility study. Business development also entails setting up the legal structure of the business and the distribution of equity to the shareholders. If the inventor/entrepreneur is seeking outside capital, negotiations with investors will also take place. The inventor/entrepreneur will need to negotiate with strategic partners to implement certain areas of the business plan. Preparing a business plan is the subject of Chapter 15.

BUSINESS MODELS FOR INNOVATION

The venture capital community, which, in large part, is the economic driver of innovation, has made it clear that it is interested in ideas with relatively fast turnarounds, preferably through an IPO or an acquisition. It generally has no interest in building companies to endure over the long term, as its mandate is to provide a superior return to its investors in 3 to 5 years. Jim Collins, author of *Built to Last*, refers to this phenomenon as "built to flip."[46] In other words, an entrepreneur builds a company for the sole purpose of taking it public or being acquired. Had this same environment existed 50 years ago, would companies like Merck, Hewlett-Packard, or Sony exist in their current forms?

The speed with which venture capitalists want a return on their investment precludes their investing in disruptive or breakthrough innovation, which is generally the result of basic research, a very long-term proposition at best. They focus instead on generating vast amounts of wealth quickly, rather than on the more long-term endeavors of creating value, taking risk, and satisfying customers. The built-to-flip phenomenon is not new. Evidence of this lack of desire to build an enduring company was found in the Silicon Valley of the 1980s. The time frame for flipping the business was longer then— 7 to 10 years—but when measured against enduring companies of 50 or more years, it was relatively fast. Ashton-Tate and Osborne computers were the built-to-flip companies of their age. The build-to-sell model and the inventor platform model are considered here.

The Build-to-Sell Model   Many research and development companies in the biotech, medical technology, and other similar industries where product development lead times are long, set up a company simply for the purpose of designing and developing a device and then selling the technology to a large, established company for manufacturing and distribution. For example, Cardiometrics was a California-based company founded in 1986 to develop a device that would measure the amount of coronary disease in a patient. In 1997, EndoSonics, a heart-catheter company, acquired Cardiometrics in a deal that made economic sense. EndoSonics already had an effective distribution channel in place that would extend Cardiometric's reach far more rapidly than the start-up could achieve on its own.[47] A similar situation occurs on a regular basis in the biotech industry. For example, a research team forms a company for the purpose of developing a gene therapy and positions itself to be acquired by a major pharmaceutical company. That way, the scientists/inventors reap the rewards of their years of laboratory work without having to put together an infrastructure to market and distribute their product. They are also typically free to continue their research positions while enjoying the wealth they have created from their inventions.

The Inventor Platform   Sometimes a company is formed around a creative genius who carries the vision for the company and without whom the company would have no purpose. In reality, the sole purpose of the company is to serve as a creative platform for the ideas and inventions of its founder. One could argue that Microsoft exists for the sole purpose of developing and propagating the technology ideas of its founder, Bill Gates. Certainly, that was true of Polaroid for Edwin Land, its founder. General Electric was founded out of the genius of Thomas Edison, who developed the light bulb and then handed the invention off to people who could build a company infrastructure around it and commercialize it. Business models and how to structure the most effective one for a particular situation will be the subject of Chapter 8.

LAUNCHING THE BUSINESS

The actual start-up of the business includes such activities as finding and negotiating for facilities, hiring personnel, stocking inventories of raw materials and components, and organizing the operations of the business. The transition from research to operations is often jarring for engineers and scientists who would much prefer to remain in their laboratories working on new products. For this reason, it is vitally important that any decision to launch a business include the decision to bring on management expertise to run the operations. These issues are discussed in Chapters 11 and 13.

ORGANIZATION OF THE TEXT

This book is organized to take the reader through the commercialization process by first laying the groundwork in Part I: The Foundations of Technology Commercialization, which has four chapters. The first chapter examined the fundamentals of innovation and the innovation process. Chapter 2 explores how creativity leads to invention and innovation, and Chapter 3 explores the development of a business concept around a technology to see if the technology and product is economically feasible. Part I closes with Chapter 4, which looks at the product development process and the creation of a prototype.

Part II: Intellectual Property covers the protection of technology and establishment of proprietary rights. Chapter 5 examines the fundamentals of intellectual property and how to acquire intellectual property rights. Those intellectual property rights can be licensed to create revenue streams. Strategies for licensing and license agreements are discussed in Chapter 6. Finally, Chapter 7 discusses offensive and defensive strategies for protecting and defending intellectual property rights.

Part III: Financial Strategy for Technology Start-Ups, examines how to develop a business model for a technology product. Chapter 8 addresses how to value intellectual property based on whether it is tangible, intangible, or know-how. Chapter 9 deals with the issue of how to calculate funding needs for a start-up venture and how to find the most appropriate source of funding. Chapter 10 continues the discussion of funding by looking at how to fund growth through IPOs, mergers, and buyouts.

Part IV: The Transition from R&D to Operations examines the many unique issues related to technology ventures. Chapter 11 deals with transitioning a company from a research lab to a real business operation. Chapter 12 explores the unique marketing and distribution issues that high-technology ventures face when they try to move a pioneering technology across the chasm to mass acceptance. Chapter 13 moves beyond start-up to rapidly growing the business, something that can happen very early in the life cycle of a high-technology business. Because many new ventures today are started under the umbrella of a parent company or as a spin-off from a large corporation, Chapter 14 discusses the distinct issues related to these types of ventures. Part IV concludes with Chapter 15, which discusses how to develop a business plan for a technology company.

❖ SUMMARY

The process of taking an invention from idea to business concept to market—technology commercialization—faces a unique set of challenges and opportunities in a fast-paced market. Products must be developed faster, prototyped earlier, and brought to market in record time. Small entrepreneurial companies are in a good position to do that as they tend to be more flexible and fast to respond to environmental changes. In contrast, established companies find that they must break away from traditional strategic thinking and the inertia they tend to experience from having achieved a measure of success with their core products. Creativity and innovation are essential to the development of disruptive technologies, which can result in many new companies and thousands of new jobs. First movers with disruptive technologies can achieve a market advantage but often are overtaken by second and third movers with improved versions of the technology. The key disruptive technologies to watch are the Human Genome Project, wireless technology, and nanotechnology. The technology commercialization process is an iterative one made up of invention and innovation, opportunity recognition and concept development, intellectual property protection, product development and testing, feasibility analysis, and development of the business.

❖ DISCUSSION QUESTIONS

1. Why is continual innovation critical to business success today?
2. In what ways has the product development process changed and why?
3. When it comes time to commercialize an invention, what options are available to an inventor to navigate the business side of commercialization, and what are the advantages and disadvantages of each?
4. Choose one of the principal disruptive technologies for the next decade. What are two possible businesses that could be developed to exploit that technology that were not mentioned in the text?
5. What are the advantages and disadvantages of a first mover or pioneering strategy? Under what conditions would first mover be essential?

❖ RESOURCES

Allen, Kathleen. *Launching New Ventures.* 3d ed. Boston: Houghton Mifflin Company, 2002.

Christensen, Clayton M. *The Innovator's Dilemma.* Boston: Harvard Business School Press, 1997.

Cooper, Robert G. *Winning at New Products.* Cambridge, MA: Perseus, 2001.

Gross, Michael. *Travels to the Nanoworld: Miniature Machinery in Nature and Technology.* New York: Plenum Trade, 1995.

Koehn, Nancy F. *Brand New: How Entrepreneurs Earned Consumers' Trust from*

Wedgwood to Dell. Boston: Harvard Business School Press, 2001.

Leifer, Richard, Christopher M. McDermott, Ginan Colarelli O'Connor, Lois S. Peters, Mark Rice, and Robert W. Veryzer. *Radical Innovation: How Mature Companies Can Outsmart Upstarts.* Boston: Harvard Business School Press, 2000.

Ridley, Matt. *Genome.* New York: HarperPerennial, 2000.

❖ INTERNET RESOURCES

Blueprint of the Body
www.cnn.com/SPECIALS/2000/genome/
CNN special report on the Human Genome Project

E-Business Research Center
www.cio.com
Good source of e-commerce case studies

Genetics Timeline
www.msnbc.com/news/341113.asp
A look into the future at the effects of genetic research

Nanotechnology
www.zyvex.com/nano/
A description of nanotechnology and a variety of links to nanotechnology-related sites

NanoTechnology Magazine
planet-hawaii.com/nanozine/
A comprehensive source of information and resources on the field of nanotechnology

The National Human Genome Research Institute
www.nhgri.nih.gov/
The first analysis of the genome sequence

MIT Technology Review
www.techreview.com/
Excellent source of articles on the latest technologies

Wireless Design & Development
www.wirelessdesignmag.com/
A resource for the wireless industry

INNOVATION IN THE PALM
OF HIS HAND

How many new products can claim a cult-like status with more than 150 Web sites devoted to extolling its virtues? The PalmPilot can. In 1996, Jeff Hawkins and his long-time partner Donna Dubinsky introduced the PalmPilot and blew the other PDAs out of the water. Today, after selling over 2 million units, the pair has left the company they founded to start a similar company with an advanced product that will reach an even wider audience than the PalmPilot has.

Where did the idea for this breakthrough product come from? It was Hawkins' fascination with cognition and neurobiology—the physical basis of human intelligence—that put him on the path to inventing the PalmPilot. So passionate was he about the brain that in 1986, he left his career in business to enroll in a graduate-level biophysics program to begin to understand how the brain works. His research resulted in two insights that influenced his work at Palm Computing. His first insight was that the brain is not like a computer because it has no processor, no software, and no random-access memory. Instead, the brain uses auto-associative memory, which has the ability to generalize, fill in missing information, and work with incomplete or inaccurate data. Hawkins went on to develop a way to apply auto-associative memory to data that varies over time. That insight resulted in the handwriting recognition software, Graffiti, for which the PalmPilot is known.

Hawkins' second insight involved "understanding—that is, how we know something. Intelligent systems don't just act; they anticipate. They make predictions about their environment."[48] Auto-associative memory assists the brain in making predictions. Hawkins' ultimate goal was to develop products that incorporate auto-associative memories and intelligence in a way that lets them understand the world. However, he was a long way from that goal back in the 1980s.

Hawkins graduated from Cornell University in 1979 with a degree in electrical engineering and began work for Intel. He left Intel after 3 years to seek an opportunity that would give him more responsibility, which he found for a time at GRID Systems, a small Silicon Valley company that was doing work in portable computing. After a "sabbatical" from GRID to earn his degree in biophysics at UC Berkeley, he went back to GRID, which had by then been acquired by Tandy Corporation, under an agreement whereby he licensed to the company his patented PalmPrint software and became the vice president of research. His job was to develop pen-based hardware and software. In 1992, he introduced the first real pen-based computer, the GRIDPad. Although it was slow, too large, and lacked aesthetics, it began a revolution and foretold the future of handheld computing. Huge companies like IBM, NEC, and Samsung also announced their forays into the handheld, or PDA market as it was dubbed by John Sculley, then CEO of Apple Computers.

Never happy in large organizations, Hawkins finally left Tandy to form Palm Computing in January 1992. Needing funding, he sought out Bruce Dunlevie, a venture capitalist who happened to sit on the board of directors at Geoworks, a company that writes operating systems for portable computers. Between

Dunlevie's firm, Sutter Hill Ventures, and Tandy, Hawkins was able to raise $1.3 million to fund his new venture.

Hawkins was wise enough to realize that his strength was as the idea person, so to make sure that the business was run properly, he hired Donna Dubinsky, a Yale graduate who ran Apple Computer's distribution network. The success of PalmPilot can be attributed in large part to the success of the partnership between Jeff Hawkins and Donna Dubinsky. They had compatible strengths and usually agreed, but they were not free from mistakes.

In the early days, they took on several big partners: Casio to manufacture the handheld device, Geoworks to provide the operating system, Intuit to provide personal financial software, and America Online as the Internet Service Provider. The problem came when they discovered that a committee of all the partners was making every decision, both major and minor. Consequently, it is no surprise that their first product, Zoomer PDA, bombed. It was big, expensive, and terribly slow. The only fortunate outcome of their first failure was that it was not the first PDA in the market. Apple had released its Newton MessagePad 2 months before, and the hype over it and subsequent ridicule over its ineffectiveness overshadowed Zoomer's faults.

Rather than try to improve on the Zoomer, Hawkins and Dubinsky decided to conduct in-depth interviews with Zoomer users. What they learned changed the entire direction of the company. They learned that people were not purchasing a PDA as a replacement for the computer, but to replace paper, the daily paper record keeper they toted around. They also learned that users appreciated the ability to transfer files from their PC to their PDA. Hawkins decided that it was time for a radical shift in how they viewed the PDA. At the time, PDA developers had been focusing on handwriting-recognition software as the basis for communication, which was an impossible feat because it meant that the software had to recognize millions of different combinations and permutations of handwriting. Hawkins believed that they should reverse their thinking and ask the customer to learn a few easy charac-

ters that would enable the software to better understand their handwriting. As a result, Graffiti was born. Hawkins also believed that the device should be small enough to fit in a shirt pocket.

This time they were not going to make the same mistakes. Hawkins and Dubinsky formed a virtual company and outsourced hardware design and manufacturing. However, funding for marketing was a problem. Dubinsky figured they would need $5 million to properly launch this product, which they were calling "Touch-down." Raising that amount was difficult, and the young company soon found itself in dire straits financially. Dubinsky frantically looked for a potential strategic partner with enough synergy to make the deal worthwhile. She finally found that partner in U.S. Robotics, the fast-growing modem manufacturer. U.S. Robotics was trying to make its way into Silicon Valley, and Palm offered a solution. Hawkins and Dubinsky wanted $5 million in cash, but U.S. Robotics surprised them with an offer to buy Palm. After much debate, the partners agreed to become a division of U.S. Robotics for $44 million in stock, and Touchdown became the Pilot. The first PalmPilots shipped in April 1996 and by mid-summer, it was impossible to keep up with demand.

When 3Com, the network hardware company, acquired U.S. Robotics, Hawkins and Dubinsky found themselves once again in a very large company. These two entrepreneurs, who enjoy the small company environment, decided to leave 3Com to build a brand new company and a new type of PDA geared toward the consumer rather than the businessperson. In 1998, the two left to found Handspring and devote themselves to developing new hand-held products. Their first product, the Visor, has the ability to be a pager, an MP3 player, a global-positioning satellite receiver, as well as an organizer. Their goal is to provide customers with the features they want, not with a lot of unnecessary bells and whistles. They now find themselves in the strange position of licensing their operating system from 3Com and competing to some degree in the same market space. In what is quickly becoming a crowded market,

Hawkins and Dubinsky face the challenge of differentiating themselves in ways that are valuable to customers and that create new value. They wonder how they can do a better job of finding the gaps in the market before their competitors find them. ■

Sources: Adapted from Pat Dillon, "The Next Small Thing," *Fast Company*, 15 (June 1998): 97; Pat Dillon, "This Is Jeff Hawkins on Brains," *Fast Company*, 15, (June 1998): 104; Pat Dillon, "Exit Interview: Jeff Hawkins, Inventor of the PalmPilot," *PalmPower*, August 1998 (*www.palmpower.com*); *www.handspring.com*; Stephanie Miles, "Palm Cofounder Shares Design Philosophy," *Cnet News*, October 20, 1999 (*www.cnet.com/news/*); *www.palm.com*.

❖ NOTES

1. Clayton Christensen, *The Innovator's Dilemma* (Boston: Harvard Business School Press, 1997), 208–211.
2. R. N. Foster, "Managing Technological Innovation for the Next 25 Years," *Research-Technology Management* 43, 1 (January–February 2000): 29.
3. Greg A. Stevens and James Burley, "3,000 Raw Ideas = 1 Commercial Success!" *Research-Technology Management* (May–June 1997).
4. NASDAQ, November 1998 to November 1999.
5. *www.gene.com/gene/about/corporate/history/timeline/1980.jsp*
6. Paul Romer, "Increasing Returns and Long-Run Growth," *Journal of Political Economy* 94 (1986): 1,002–1,037.
7. Michael J. Mandel, "The Next Downturn," *Business Week* (October 9, 2000): *www.businessweek.com/2000/00_41/b3702001.htm*.
8. The Human Genome Project, U.S. Department of Energy, *www.ornl.gov/hgmis/*.
9. Mandel, "The Next Downturn."
10. James C. Collins, "Best Beats First," *Inc.* (August 2000): 48–52.
11. Ibid.
12. Kara Swisher, *AOL.com* (New York: Times Books, 1999).
13. Pam Woodall, "Survey: The New Economy: The Beginning of a Great Adventure," *The Economist* (September 23, 2000) Vol. 356, No. 8189, pp. 55–57.
14. Robert G. Cooper, *Winning at New Products* (Cambridge, MA: Perseus, 2001), 3.
15. "10 Emerging Technologies That Will Change the World," *MIT Technology Review* (January–February 2001). *www.techreview.com*.
16. Andrzej M. Pawlak, "Fostering Creativity in the New Millennium," *Research-Technology Management* 43, no.6 (November/December 2000): 32.
17. Leonard S. Cutler, "Creativity: Essential to Technological Innovation," *Research-Technology Management* 43, no. 6 (November/December 2000). *www.iriinc.org/webiri/index.cfm*.
18. Marinus Los, "Creativity and Technological Innovation in the United States," *Research-Technology Management* 43, no. 6 (November/December 2000). *www.iriinc.org/webiri/index.cfm*.
19. William L. Miller and Langdon Morris, *4th Generation R&D* (New York: John Wiley & Sons, 1999), pp. 1–4.
20. Christensen, *The Innovator's Dilemma.*
21. Miller and Morris, *4th Generation R&D*, 8.
22. Andrew Grove, *Only the Paranoid Survive* (New York: Doubleday, 1996).
23. Richard Leifer et al., *Radical Innovation: How Mature Companies Can Outsmart Upstarts* (Boston: Harvard Business School Press, 2000), 6–7.
24. Rajesh K. Chandy and Gerard J. Tellis, "The Incumbent's Curse? Incumbency, Size, and Radical Product Innovation," *Journal of Marketing* 64, no. 3 (July 2000) pp. 1–17.
25. F. M. Scherer, "Historical Research in Marketing," *Journal of Marketing* 44 (Fall 1980): 52–58.

26. Leifer et al., *Radical Innovation: How Mature Companies Can Outsmart Upstarts*, 4.

27. Kathleen Conner, "Strategies for Product Cannibalism," *Strategic Management Journal* 9 (Summer 1988): 9–27.

28. Robert Gordon, "Does the New Economy Measure Up to the Great Inventions of the Past?" *Journal of Economic Perspectives* 4 no. 14 (Fall 2000) 49–74.

29. Robert Buderi, "What New Economy," *MIT Technology Review* (February 2001): 45–50.

30. David Rotmann, "Nanotechnology Goes to Work," MIT Technology Review, (Jan/Feb 2001). *www.technologyreview.com/articles/rotman0101.asp*.

31. Gross, *Travels to the Nanoworld*, New York: Plenum Trade, 1999.

32. J. R. Heath, P. J. Kuekes, G. S. Snider, and R. S. Williams, "A Defect-Tolerant Computer Architecture: Opportunities for Nanotechnology," *Science* 280 (June 12, 1998): 1,716–1,721.

33. Ibid., pp. 716–721.

34. Doug Harper, "A Wireless Frontier," *www.manufacturing.net/ind/ Industrial Distribution* (December 2000).

35. Hans Ibold, "Wireless Wearables," *Los Angeles Business Journal* (January 15, 2001). *www.labusinessjournal.com/*.

36. Leifer et al., *Radical Innovation*; pp. 1–4.

37. K. Clark and T. Fujimoto, *Product Development Performance* (Boston: Harvard Business School Press, 1991).

38. Christoph von Braun, "The Acceleration Trap," *Sloan Management Review* 32, no. 1 (Fall 1990): 49.

39. A. Griffin, *Drivers of NPD Success: The 1997 PDMA Report* (Chicago: Product Development & Management Association, 1997).

40. M. Lieberman and D. Montgomery, "First-Mover Advantage," *Strategic Management Journal* 9 (1988): 41–58.

41. Russell Slaybaugh, "Investigation into the Effects of an Inventive Idea on the Success of a Firm," unpublished paper prepared for BAEP 551, Marshall School of Business, University of Southern California, 2000.

42. R. Stuart and P. Abetti, "Start-up Ventures: Towards the Prediction of Initial Success," *Journal of Business Venturing* 2, no. 3 (1987): 215–230.

43. M. Lieberman and D. Montgomery, "First-Mover Disadvantages: Retrospective and Link with the Resource-Based View," *Strategic Management Journal* 19 (1998): 1,111–1,125.

44. H. Noori, *Managing the Dynamics of New Technology* (Upper Saddle River, NJ: Prentice Hall, 1990).

45. R. Kanter, "Supporting Innovation and Venture Development in Established Companies," *Journal of Business Venturing* 1 (1985): 47–60.

46. Jim Collins, "Built to Flip," *Fast Company* (March 2000). *www.fastcompany.com*.

47. Ibid.

48. Pat Dillon, "This Is Jeff Hawkins on Brains," *Fast Company* 15, (June 1998): 104.

RECOGNIZING AND SCREENING TECHNOLOGY OPPORTUNITIES

OVERVIEW

This chapter will examine

❖ the role of creativity in innovation

❖ opportunity recognition

❖ sources of opportunity

❖ screening technology opportunities

INTRODUCTION

A good place to begin this chapter is by distinguishing between an idea and an opportunity. Ideas are plentiful; they come to everyone throughout the day, but they're typically dismissed or are not assigned any value or potential. An opportunity, on the other hand, is an idea that can be turned into a business or commercialized in some manner. A raw technology may be a great idea for technology's sake, but unless there is an application for that technology, a need in the marketplace, and a way to make money, it remains merely an idea.

Today, nearly every technology company is in pursuit of the next great breakthrough product. This pursuit is usually a focused quest for potential opportunities that are compatible with the company's goals. Sometimes the search starts from the top down—a request from top management for new ways to serve customers and solve their problems. In this market-driven model, external market forces drive the firm to find an innovative solution to a problem in the market. While logical, this approach carries the risk that a technology solution will not be found or that significant compromises must be made in using it to solve a particular problem. The invention of the catalytic converter for automobiles was the result of a need in the market to find a way to reduce cold-start emissions that polluted the air. It was, in effect, a compromise solution to pollution reduction—the alternative being reducing the number of cars on the road.

Other times, a scientist or engineer working in a laboratory makes a serendipitous connection that, with experimentation, eventually leads to a new product idea. In this model, technology is the driving force for innovation. In effect, this model is based on a solution looking for a problem, as a market need has not yet been demonstrated. The danger here is that the inventor spends time and money on a technology for which there is no need. Haptic technology, the ability to provide kinesthetic sensation in a virtual environment, was driven by the technological challenge of finding a way to simulate touch in a digital environment. Initially, there was no market need for people to touch and feel the shapes of objects on a computer screen. However, as the science of haptics has evolved, real-world applications are becoming apparent, for example, in three-dimensional design where development teams are geographically separated and in applications for the visually impaired. Identifying an application for a core technology is the first step toward opportunity recognition.

Both approaches to opportunity recognition work and should be employed in any company that wants to stay on the leading edge of innovation. Unfortunately, at the same time that the quest for the next radical innovation is taking on new levels of importance, more and more corporations are disbanding their basic research units. Research efforts have shifted to short-term projects with immediate payoff, but regrettably, radical or breakthrough innovation is not normally born out of this type of research. Radical innovation is usually the result of years of basic research with no defined outcome necessarily in mind. As a result, corporations are increasingly turning to university research institutes and departments for the basic research that will lead to a radical innovation.

This chapter explores how opportunity comes about and how businesses and inventors screen initial ideas and opportunities so that they can focus on those that have the greatest potential for success.

CREATIVITY: THE SPARK THAT IGNITES INNOVATION

Creative people do not always have a specific idea in mind when they begin to search for an innovation; what they do have is a method or way of going about that search. Two famous inventors, Claude Elwood Shannon and Yoshiro Nakamatsu (see the end-of-chapter Case Study) solved problems by drawing on their skills and experience to come up with innovations. What creative people have in common is state-of-the-art knowledge in their discipline, curiosity, imagination, persistence, and motivation, as well as the courage to think independently and an ability to recognize and seize opportunities.[1]

The commercialization process itself is a creative process, not a scientific one. From the discovery of the business idea to product development, feasibility analysis, and business planning, the application of creativity to all of these areas is what sets successful entrepreneurial ventures apart from their competitors. Research has examined creativity from both a process and an outcome perspective. The process view, which dominates the literature, proposes that creativity is about the production of unique and useful ideas.[2] In contrast, the outcome view proposes that creativity is about the generation of valuable and useful products, services, procedures, and processes.[3] The earliest creativity research focused on individual personality factors and cognitive skills (language, thinking processes, and intelligence).[4] Later, researchers moved on to look at the context in which people are creative. They found that particular environments seem to be compatible with creative activity, specifically those without constraints, that provide rewards for creativity, and in which teamwork is effective.[5] The most recent studies of creativity have incorporated organizational variables such as policies, structures, culture, and training. Although we do not know much about the specific conditions that promote creativity inside organizations, we do know that creativity occurs both at an individual and a group level, and is a matter of choice on the part of the person involved.[6]

UNDERSTANDING THE CREATIVE PROCESS

Creativity is not a linear process, but an iterative one. Although there are no right and wrong ways to be creative, research suggests that there are definite activities that occur in any creative process. These activities are connection, discovery, invention, and application.[7] Using one of the greatest inventors of all time, Leonardo Da Vinci, the next sections will consider these activities.

CONNECTION

While designing a canal system for the city of Florence, Italy, Leonardo Da Vinci noticed a connection between tree branches and the canal system. He used a metaphor to describe that connection: Canals are tree branches. This association with trees opened up a whole new way of looking at canals. Inventors can achieve a creative connection when they bring together two disparate ideas using devices such as metaphor, analogy, symbolism, or hypothesis.

DISCOVERY

Once a connection is made, the inventor begins to explore it further. Da Vinci began drawing tree branches and examining them closely, conducting experiments and learning everything he could about how trees manage the flow of nutrients and water through their systems. He extrapolated his findings to how water flows through canals. This was an important discovery.

INVENTION

Once a discovery has occurred, it can often result in an invention, which is the application of the discovery in the real world. Da Vinci's understanding of the inner workings of tree branches was the stimulus for a hydraulic device to control water levels in the canals so that a boat could cross under a bridge. Da Vinci found the inspiration for many of his inventions in nature.

APPLICATION

Numerous other inventions also came out of da Vinci's discovery about the nature of tree branches, including a means to create a waterway from Florence to the sea and ideas for mills powered by wind and water. The most creative inventions come about from stepping outside of what is known. Da Vinci was an inventor who was willing to do that. Unfortunately, many inventors never see beyond their initial invention to applications in other industries because they often unknowingly set up challenges and barriers to their own creativity.

CHALLENGES TO CREATIVE THINKING

Once creative thinking becomes a habit, it is relatively easy to turn it on and off at will; however, achieving that skill takes practice and time. Unfortunately, most people unintentionally set up barricades to achieving a creative mindset, in other words, they do not give themselves the opportunity to be creative. Here are some barriers to creativity:

- Lack of time set aside for brainstorming
- Lack of confidence and a fear of being criticized for doing something unusual or going outside mainstream thought
- The belief that they have no creative skills

Recognizing the roadblocks is the first step. The next is to be proactive about acquiring a creative mindset and skills and to prepare an environment that permits creative thinking. Some people find that they are at their most creative when they are jogging or lying in a hammock looking at the sky. Others, like Dr. Yoshiro Nakamatsu (see end-of-chapter case study), use a variety of environments to stimulate creative thought. Thomas Edison's greatest invention was not the light bulb, but the environment for radical innovation that he created in his research and development laboratory.

The environment in which a person works or lives can either stimulate or deaden creative tendencies.[8] If the work environment is rigid, inflexible, and has many layers of management, chances are it is also very standardized, the goal being to have everyone do things the same way. This type of environment is not conducive to creative thinking. To overcome negative environments like this, inventors and entrepreneurs minimize any distractions—they close the door and shut off the phone and e-mail when it's time to do some creative thinking. It's important to take some time every day to let the mind wander and play with ideas. Eventually creative thinking will become a habit that can be turned on at will. It's also helpful to identify places that seem to stimulate the greatest ideas and plan to spend time there to exercise creative skills. Yet another way that inventors and entrepreneurs stimulate their brains and challenge themselves to think out of the box is to put themselves in an unfamiliar environment, even at work. An unfamiliar environment can stimulate the mind to form new associations and connections that could lead to a discovery. Inventors who typically work in the lab with scientists, for example, might spend a week with the marketing and sales people. It gives them a whole new perspective that can be taken back to their research and applied to solving problems.

DEVELOPING CREATIVE PROBLEM-SOLVING SKILLS

No matter how complex or dynamic a problem is, only a few major factors actually affect the ultimate solution. But, surprisingly, most people have difficulty identifying the major factors in a problem. More often than not, they tend to identify those factors that easily come to mind or are most important to them.[9] The problem-solving process involves one of two modes: divergent or convergent thinking. Divergent thinking pulls a person away from a central point to explore different directions and ideas, whereas convergent thinking brings that person back to a focused thought.

In general, there are four basic types of problems:

1. **Simplistic.** When there is only one answer to the problem.
2. **Deterministic.** A formula produces one answer.
3. **Random.** Different answers are possible and can be identified.
4. **Indeterminate.** Many different answers are possible, but getting to the correct one requires all of the information or the right formula.

Developing radical innovations typically involves solving complex problems, usually those that are random or indeterminate. Solving these types of problems consists of scanning for ideas and information, integrating and processing the ideas and information, and then evaluating and selecting solutions.[10] These problems often need to be solved in a group process, so the outcome is not known until action is taken.[11]

The more information there is, the easier the problem is to solve, whereas the less information there is, the more difficult it is to solve. In the latter situation, limited information must be expanded upon. One good technique for doing this is to state a problem and then restate it in different ways. For example:

Initial problem statement: We don't have enough lab space.
Restatement: There are too many people for the space we have.
Restatement: How can we reduce the number of people we have?
Restatement: How can we use the space we have more effectively?

There are many more possible restatements of this problem, but what this exercise points out is that any problem can and should be viewed from a number of different perspectives. Here are some suggestions for restating problems using the original problem statement.[12]

- Write the opposite of the original statement.
  We have too much lab space.
- Broaden or narrow the focus. Put the statement in larger or narrower context.
  What would we do with more lab space?
- Ask "why" at least four or five times to get to the root of the problem.
  Original: We need more lab space.
  Why? Because we don't have room for all our researchers.
  Restatement: How can we accommodate all the researchers we need?
  Why? Because we have had to hire more to complete our work on time.
  Restatement: How can we get more researchers without having to provide lab space?
  Why? Because we don't have the funding to add more lab space right now.
  Restatement: Can we outsource some of the research to another lab?
  Why? Because we need to finish the project on time.
  Restatement: How can we finish the project on time?

It is clear that by the time the question has been asked and restated four times, the problem is not really how to get more lab space, but how to finish the project on time. Without going through this process, a wrong assumption about the source of the problem would have been a likely outcome.

AN ENGINEERING APPROACH TO CREATIVE PROBLEM SOLVING

Engineers and scientists are well trained in structured problem-solving skills, but they sometimes stumble when asked to apply creative, out-of-the-box thinking to those skills. Recognizing that, Clegg and Birch came up with a four-step problem-solving approach that is analogous to an engineering process:[13]

1. **Surveying.** In this first stage, information needed to solve the problem is gathered and a goal is set for the end of the process. Too many people skip over this initial stage and do not spend enough time defining the problem; then they wonder why the solution they arrived at did not work. This stage involves the use of both divergent and convergent thinking. Some of the critical tasks that should be accomplished at this stage include repeatedly asking "why" until the root problem is identified, recognizing roadblocks to achieving the solution (the goal), looking at the problem from new angles, drawing a map of the problem so all the relationships that affect it can be seen, and reconfirming the goal of the problem-solving task.

2. **Building.** Based on the information gathered in the first stage, a method for getting from the destination to the goal is devised that also identifies potential obstacles along the way and uses creativity to overcome them. Clegg and Birch suggest a variety of tools to employ in this stage, including getting past obstacles by making them invisible—challenging long-held assumptions; building "what if" scenarios; and questioning the original destination chosen, since there is no right answer to a problem.

3. **Waymaking.** This stage takes what has been built and turns it into a fully operational "transportation system." Waymaking is an iterative process that may require revising something that was done earlier. Here the views of the stakeholders are considered, the ideas that will continue are chosen, and the advantages and disadvantages of the approach are examined.

4. **Navigating.** Using the path that was built, the solution can be planned and implemented. Resources required for the journey are determined as well as a way to track progress and mark the arrival at the goal.

TRIZ APPROACH TO INNOVATION

TRIZ is a Russian acronym that translates to "the theory of inventive problem solving." It is one of a number of new problem-solving tools that allows engineers to quickly design breakthrough products by applying innovative thinking. The natural creativity of engineers has often been stifled by several factors, including rigid company hierarchies that limit interaction, the fear of failure, and overdependence on computers.[14]

The TRIZ approach focuses on the problem itself in the belief that the problem posed is rarely the actual problem that has to be solved. Most technology problems are a complex mix of useful functions and dysfunctional or harmful functions, so the first task for the engineer is to determine where to begin. Problems suitable for the TRIZ approach include the following:[15]

- **Technical conflict and physical contradiction.** Many technical conflicts occur when an attempt to solve one problem creates another. For example, if an engineer creates a beverage can with very thin walls, it may no longer be able to support the weight of cans stacked on top of it.
- **Inventive problem.** Many engineering problems involve a trade-off in a situation concerning a conflict and a contradiction where the engineer is put in the position of inventing a solution to resolve the conflict. In other words, before the original problem can be solved, the discovered conflict must be resolved. For example, suppose the problem involves the development of a device for applying labels to envelopes that go through the mail system at the post office in a manner that is much faster than what is currently being done. So, speed is the critical factor. A device is created that does an excellent job of applying labels within the required parameters for speed, but the reality is that envelopes going through the system are of varying sizes and thicknesses, which causes the speed at which labels can be applied to vary as well. The engineer must now solve the conflict with varying sizes of envelopes before the goal of speed can be achieved.
- **Ideal machine.** Once a device or invention has been conceptualized, the engineer now tries to find the simplest way to make the invention work; that is, how can the device be simplified, what can be taken out, and what can be replaced with something simpler.

TRIZ consists of five important processes:

1. **Inventive principles.** TRIZ uses 40 inventive principles derived from the analysis of millions of patents in a variety of industries and from an array of creative minds. These principles are used to find solutions to conflicts, contradictions, and inventive problems. They are the basic tools of the TRIZ method.
2. **Known physical, chemical, and geometric effects.** When a problem is identified, the engineer then studies commonly known physical, chemical, and geometric effects associated with it to generate solutions to the problem.
3. **Sufield analysis.** An analytical technique where symbolic equations are used to represent engineering problems. Use of this technique leads the engineer more easily toward the problem's solution.
4. **Functional analysis and trimming.** During the TRIZ process, engineers identify the functions of the product and the functions of all the components in the product. The goal of this step is to maximize functionality and minimize cost.
5. **Technology lifecycles and forecasting.** Using demand life cycles, technology life cycles, TRIZ invention classification, and TRIZ patterns of evolution of engineering systems, the engineer can make next-generation product forecasts.[16]

TRIZ also provides a way to resolve conflicts in technical designs. The traditional way that these conflicts have been resolved is through compromise, but compromise does not produce the optimal solution, as an improvement in one area could result in problems in another. TRIZ is also useful for technology forecasting and concept development[17] and has been very successful in reducing cycle times and generating new ideas. For example, the TRIZ process produced 60 patentable ideas in 1 day for improving an auto component that had been operating poorly for 5 years.

OPPORTUNITY RECOGNITION

Opportunity recognition happens when an entrepreneur sees a need in the marketplace and identifies a way to satisfy that need. Biotech scientists saw a way to apply genetics to the world of agriculture to increase yields and rid farmers of the problems associated with using pesticides. In contrast, opportunity creation occurs when an entrepreneur creates a demand for something that people did not previously know that they needed. How many people knew they needed personal computers in the late 1970s? Recall the discussion in Chapter 1 about incremental innovation and disruptive or radical technologies. Most new products are the result of incremental or evolutionary innovation—recognizing a need in the market that can be served by the incremental improvement of an existing technology. Disruptive or radical innovation creates an opportunity that never existed previously by making the preceding technology obsolete.

HOW OPPORTUNITY RECOGNITION HAPPENS

A growing body of research is providing an understanding of how entrepreneurs recognize opportunities. One thing is certain: The vast majority of people who find business opportunities find them in industries with which they are familiar or in a business for which they have worked.[18] Moreover, entrepreneurs who network in a variety of social circles tend to recognize more opportunities. In fact, the number of weak ties or connections outside immediate family and friends in the entrepreneur's network is positively correlated to the number of opportunities recognized.[19]

The literature is unclear as to whether opportunity recognition is a planned process. Some of the early research claimed that planning is not involved in opportunity recognition.[20] However, more recent research attributes opportunity recognition with active, well-planned searches for opportunities.[21] The reality is that both active searches and serendipity play significant roles in the ability of entrepreneurs to discover new opportunities.[22]

THE OPPORTUNITY RECOGNITION PROCESS

Hill, Schrader, and Lumpkin[23] created a five-step framework of the entrepreneurial opportunity recognition process. Note that their process is not linear. Instead, it is an iterative process with many feedback loops.

1. **Preparation.** Every entrepreneur brings prior knowledge and experience to the process, making the opportunity recognition process idiosyncratic to each entrepreneur.
2. **Incubation.** This is a period of time during which the entrepreneur contemplates the solution to the problem.
3. **Insight.** This is the moment when the entrepreneur sees the solution to the problem—the "eureka!" moment.
4. **Evaluation.** The process of defining a business concept and testing it in the marketplace to see if it is feasible.
5. **Elaboration.** The planning and the creation of a company to execute the business concept.

THE BOTTOM LINE

The real value of research lies in its ability to be applied in the real world. Unfortunately, for every characteristic, behavior, or process used to describe opportunity recognition, the reality is that it is a unique journey for each person. There are no formulas for success, and there are many uncontrollable variables: experience, social networks, knowledge, age, resources, and so forth. One graduate student used the analogy of a lightning strike, saying that although it cannot be predicted exactly where lightning will strike, what is known is that it will happen and there are some guidelines that suggest where it is likely to strike.* Similarly, entrepreneurs have a higher probability of recognizing an opportunity if they:

- Increase their knowledge and experience in an industry in which they are interested.
- Build a diverse network of strong and weak professional ties.
- Develop an opportunistic mindset.
- Exercise patience. The incubation period can sometimes take a long time.

SOURCES OF OPPORTUNITY

Chapter 1 explored the invention process. However, today, technology opportunities can come from many other sources. This section looks at how to find opportunity outside the realm of basic research, including capitalizing on the research of others.

STUDY AN INDUSTRY

Learning an industry is one of the most important first steps in finding opportunity, as most inventor/entrepreneurs discover their best opportunities in industries in which they have had experience. Trends, changes, and emerging needs in an industry present gaps or white spaces that can be turned into opportunities. A good place to start is by mapping the value chain in the industry to learn not only how the industry works, but also who the major players are. Once the industry has been mapped, consider the following questions:

- How are customer needs changing in this industry?
- What opportunities could arise from these changes?
- What are the industry drivers?
- How do businesses become profitable in this industry?
- What are some alternative scenarios to what is currently believed about the industry or seen occurring in the industry?

A good example of what not to do is what AT&T did in the late 1980s. The National Science Foundation (NSF) asked AT&T to take control of the Internet because it no longer wanted to administer it.[24] However, AT&T's view of the future was that its centrally switched telephony technology was going to dominate, and the

---

*Thanks to Ryan Vuletic, MBA 2000, Marshall School of Business, University of Southern California.

Internet had no place in that future. Of course, had AT&T considered any alternative scenarios—both best and worse case, it might have been in a better position to recognize changes occurring in the industry and position itself to respond quickly. For more information on how to analyze an industry, see Chapter 3.

SEARCH THE PATENT LITERATURE

The U.S. Patent and Trademark Office's database contains millions of U. S. and foreign patents. Searching their archives is an excellent way to spark an idea. In fact, searching the archives of patents now in the public domain could lead to an invention that was never commercialized. Most patents were never brought to market because they either had no inherent commercial value or their owners did not understand how to commercialize the invention they had developed.

TALK TO CUSTOMERS

More new product ideas have come from customers than probably any other source. Customers experience the pain of not having something they need, and they readily communicate that pain if someone is listening. The best way to understand customer needs is to use an anthropological approach to market research. What did Jane Goodall do when she wanted to understand the habits of chimpanzees? She moved in with them and lived with them for months on end. No one expects entrepreneurs to move in with their customers and devote months to understanding their needs, but they can spend a day in the life of their customer, shadowing what the customer does and listening carefully to that customer's pain. The cardiac device division of Hewlett-Packard needed to ensure that its measurement devices were thoroughly tested and worked the way their customers, the hospital staff, needed them to work, as it was literally a matter of life and death. The team spent weeks at the hospital observing and listening in order to create the best product.[25] Surveys, focus groups, and interviews are excellent ways to gather information, but nothing beats camping out with the customer.

LOOK INTO UNIVERSITY OPPORTUNITIES

For years the pharmaceutical industry has relied on university research laboratories for basic research leading to new drugs. The Human Genome Project is one example of how government, university, and public/private partners can work together to create new products and knowledge. In combinatory chemistry, companies such as Millennium Pharmaceuticals, Inc. have developed software models to build and analyze virtual chemicals that demonstrate biological effects. They can use these models to search for molecules that display similar effects and, using the capabilities of outside partners, test thousands of potential effects per day. With other partners, they can conduct animal and human testing.[26]

The basic research performed by university professors and researchers may result in the next major breakthrough in science and engineering. However, most researchers conduct their research without any thought of commercializing their discovery. A university's technology transfer office is a good place to look for ways to collaborate with university researchers to commercialize their technology.

INVESTIGATE GOVERNMENT SOURCES

Many government agencies regularly publish requests for proposals (RFPs) for technology that they would like to see researched and turned into inventions that can be commercialized. Agencies like NASA (National Aeronautical and Space Administration) own technology developed under government contracts that they will license to companies. Other federal agencies and laboratories that deal in technology transfer include the Department of Commerce, the Department of Defense, and the Department of Energy. See the end-of-chapter resources for Internet sources on licensing opportunities.

FIND NEW VALUE IN EXISTING TECHNOLOGY

Increasingly, companies are finding that some of their greatest opportunities lie with technologies whose patents have lain dormant because, for whatever reason, the company did not move forward with the transfer or commercialization of the technology. Intellectual property in the form of patents and trademarks is the new opportunity frontier. More and more companies are building growth strategies around finding new value in existing and oftentimes archived technologies. IBM was perhaps one of the earliest companies to reap the financial rewards of new royalty streams by licensing existing intellectual property. Through a judicious effort to mine its patent archives for new applications, it was able to boast its annual royalty stream from $30 million in 1990 to over $1 billion today. This revenue stream represents approximately one-ninth of its annual pretax profits, and it goes directly to its net profit. To achieve that same level of profit, IBM would have to sell about $20 billion in additional products each year, one-fourth of its worldwide sales.[27]

OTHER SOURCES

In addition to the sources already discussed, trade associations are a good source of technology-related information. Also consider trade publications, suppliers, and distributors. The Internet can play a role in finding opportunity. Patent exchange sites have sprung up that allow inventors to post their issued patents for licensing or sale (see the end-of-chapter resources for the URLs of some of these sites). Finally, some entrepreneurs have identified opportunities through direct mail solicitations to universities, corporations, government agencies, or trade associations.

SCREENING TECHNOLOGY OPPORTUNITIES

Idea generation and opportunity recognition are the starting points for technology commercialization. Ideas come easily; it is more difficult to generate opportunities from ideas. Therefore, it makes sense to have a process for screening opportunities. A small company or start-up venture may only have one product that is its raison d'etre—the reason it is in business. This company may not require a screening process. However, a larger company requires a more complex decision-making process because

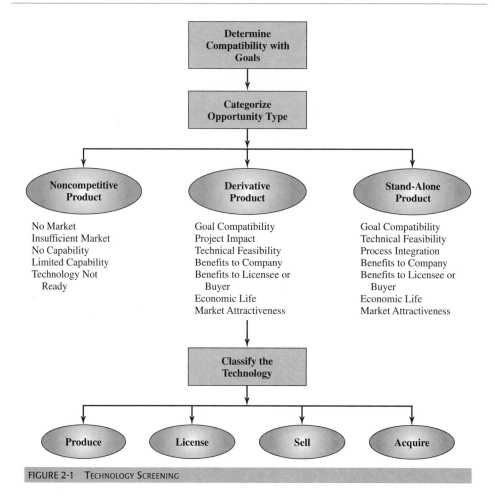

FIGURE 2-1   TECHNOLOGY SCREENING

it may already have a variety of products and processes that it has commercialized, thus the impact of a new opportunity may be more critical.

The phrase *Fuzzy Front End* (FFE) first began appearing in the product development literature in 1985. It refers to the portion of the product development cycle between when a new product project should start and when it actually does start, in other words, all the activities leading to the ultimate decision to proceed with a project into product development.[28] Today, this concept has taken on a more critical meaning as the window of opportunity for new products continues to shrink and anything that slows a company's ability to recognize an opportunity and act on it quickly can mean the difference between profits and no profits. The ability to quickly screen new product ideas becomes a vital organizational skill. Reinertsen has modeled the FFE in economic terms. Simply stated, the amount a person is willing to bet on a new product is a function of the probability of its success, the value of that success, and the cost of failure. Altering any one of these values will change the economics of the bet.[29]

In general, in a company with a technical/invention staff, 20 percent of that staff generates 80 percent of the development projects, and the initial screening of those projects takes place through informal discussions. Typically, the team has a good sense of what is possible and what is most compatible with the company's goals. Therefore, many potential projects can be eliminated fairly quickly as not feasible under the current circumstances. This is the first step of the screening process. The second step is to categorize the nature of the opportunity. Is the opportunity:

- A stand-alone product or platform technology completely unrelated to the company's existing portfolio?
- A derivative opportunity based on the company's core technology?
- A noncompetitive product with no commercial potential?

Derivative products are those that arise from the original stand-alone or platform technology and typically involve incremental innovations. These products normally easily fit within the company's capabilities; in fact, most fit so easily that companies often take on more projects than they can handle. The question then becomes, does this derivative product meet company goals? Does it have a big enough impact to make it worthwhile to put limited resources towards it? If the answer to these questions is "yes," then the screening filters discussed under stand-alone products are appropriate.

Noncompetitive products are those that can be determined rather quickly and that have no market value or the market is not sufficient to make the effort involved in developing them worthwhile. These are also products for which the company has limited or no capability for or for which the technology is years from being ready to use. When inventors and entrepreneurs brainstorm new product ideas, these types of products are the ones that stand out as irrational, but they are included in the brainstorming to prevent inhibiting the flow of ideas.

SCREENING STAND-ALONE PRODUCT OPPORTUNITIES

Stand-alone or platform technologies generally involve starting a new business to commercialize the technology or diversify the current product line. In either case, there are several issues that need to be addressed when deciding whether to go forward with initial product development and feasibility analysis.

QUANTIFY AND QUALIFY THE BENEFITS TO THE COMPANY

First and foremost, will taking on this project meet company goals? In general, development of a new technology opportunity should not be undertaken unless it is compatible with the strategic direction the company is taking. What is this technology opportunity going to do for the company? Will it allow the company to diversify its current offerings? Will it provide an opportunity to be a pioneer and capture a certain segment of the market? Is there a process that can be integrated with the product technology to strengthen the proprietary aspects of the technology? It is important to understand what the tangible and intangible benefits to the company will be. Are they worth the investment in time, money, and effort to develop and commercialize this technology?

QUANTIFY AND QUALIFY THE BENEFITS TO A POTENTIAL LICENSEE OR BUYER

Screening a technology opportunity for potential commercialization means looking at that technology from the customer's point of view. In this case, the customer is the potential licensee or buyer, most likely another company. Why would that customer want this technology, and why would they want to license or purchase it from this company? When the tangible and intangible benefits of the technology to the customer cannot be identified, the customer will not be convinced to go forward with the transaction.

CALCULATE THE ECONOMIC LIFE OF THE TECHNOLOGY

Although a patented technology has a legal life, that is, the length of time for which the patent is valid, it also has an economic life, the length of time during which it can generate revenue for the business. The earning period is affected by a number of factors:

- **The probability that the competition will be able to design around the patent and develop a competing product.** Competition could force the company to spend more marketing dollars to assure brand loyalty and expend more on research and development to continually improve on the product design and functionality.
- **The probability that the patent will be challenged.** Patents and patent infringement are covered in Chapters 5, 6, and 7, but suffice it to say here that one way that companies battle in the marketplace is to tie up their competitors in patent litigation.
- **Higher than estimated technology development costs.** It is difficult to predict with any degree of accuracy the total costs of developing a new technology from concept to production quality prototype; therefore, companies often estimate on the high side to keep from getting in the middle of R&D only to discover that they have run out of money. This means that many projects are not undertaken because the expected costs are too high and it would take too long to recoup them in the marketplace.
- **Potential impact of new laws.** Federal and state governments and their agencies regularly pass laws that affect the development of new technologies. Those laws can range from environmental protection regulations to regulations on stem cell research, all of which affect the kinds of technologies that can reach the marketplace. A new law passed while a technology is in the market can serve to shorten or cut off its economic life or, in some cases, breathe new life into a fading technology.
- **Escalation of supply pricing or actual loss of supply.** The prices of raw materials and components for technology development change over time. If those changes are significant, they can effectively reduce the economic life of the technology as competitors take advantage of alternate supplies with more cost-effective pricing. Likewise, the loss of access to raw materials can also cut off the economic life of a new technology.

DETERMINE THE ABILITY OF THE TECHNOLOGY TO BE TRANSFERRED

A technology needs to carry a strong form of intellectual property protection—usually a patent—to be able to be transferred without losing proprietary rights. It must also be capable of being produced or used in an environment other than the inventor's, that is, it must not be so tied to the company's in-house technology that it cannot be separated from it. Whether the technology is captive—essential to the company's core business—or nonessential, is important to determine so that transferring it is beneficial to the company, not detrimental.

IDENTIFY THE RESOURCE REQUIREMENTS TO TRANSFER THE TECHNOLOGY

Technology is rarely transferred without also providing some level of know-how to assist the licensee in using the technology appropriately. Some technologies depend so much on the know-how of the inventor or the invention team that it is difficult to transfer the technology to another firm to manufacture and distribute it or to develop additional applications. It is important to determine how the company's know-how will be transferred and if it will be necessary to put someone from the licensor's company inside the licensee's company for a time to help them through the process. Moreover, licensees will not learn of the technology without some marketing effort on the part of the inventing company. Both of these scenarios require money and human resources.

IDENTIFY THE RISKS ASSOCIATED WITH THE DEVELOPMENT

Product development is an inherently risky proposition, but it is made even more so by the requirements of today's dynamic environment. With everyone on the team moving as quickly as possible to get the product to market in as short a time as possible, there is no time to respond to things that go wrong. Moreover, routines that worked well previously fall apart under the pressure of fast-track development. With limited resources and short time frames, it is important to identify risks and determine how to deal with them in advance.

Every development project carries with it two basic types of risk: technical and market.[30] Technical risks arise when product developers are unable to build a product that meets the required specifications, whereas market risks occur when the company has misread the market or has failed to meet the needs of the customer. It is natural that engineers tend to focus on technical risks, but the reality is that most product failures are due to market risk. The work of Robert Cooper over 25 years studying 2,000 new products, has made it clear that new product success depends on six factors:[31]

- A superior product that is unique in the market
- A clearly defined product at the earliest stages of development
- Well-researched market and technical feasibility analyses
- A well-executed marketing plan
- A well-executed technology plan
- Cross-functional teams with representation from all the functional areas of the business

Note that the only factor that falls within the product development domain is the technology plan; the rest reside in market research.

Managing risk through the product development process is accomplished by continually looking for ways to reduce the probability that an identified risk will occur. Given that the amount of equity an entrepreneur has to give up to investors is directly related to the level of risk in the venture, this risk reduction strategy is the very one that entrepreneurs use to reduce the risk to potential investors, and thereby also reduce the amount of equity they need to give up to investors. For example, some of the technical risk is reduced at the prototype stage because there is a working model that can be tested. Market risk is reduced when the technology is proven with potential customers. Investors will make the decision to risk their capital on a new technology when the inventor has reduced the technical and market risk to the investors' level of comfort.

Potential risks are identified through creative brainstorming. The most effective risk brainstorming is performed in cross-functional teams, due to the fact that most risk crosses more than one functional area. By bringing together engineers and business people, it is more likely that both technical and market risks will be uncovered. The following are some ways to reduce risk during the product development process.

- **Use off-the-shelf or proven components whenever possible.** Where a particular component has worked well in a previous product, it should be used in the new product if possible.
- **Don't force a solution.** Sometimes two options appear workable, and the risk of choosing one and being wrong is more costly than producing both. For example, Black & Decker was attempting to determine the best handle size and shape for a battery-powered screwdriver. Certainly, this was a critical decision. Should it go with the thinner handle that held two cells and was more comfortable for smaller hands or with the thicker handle that held three cells and provided more power? Ultimately, Black & Decker decided to continue designing both until further market research could prove one more valuable than the other.[32]
- **Talk to the customer.** The best way to reduce risk in any technology screening and product development process is to get continual input from the customer. That means letting customers talk directly to design engineers. Pelco, Inc., a leader in video surveillance equipment, brings its customers to the manufacturing floor and creates rapid prototypes of their ideas on the spot. This saves design time and gives the customers a vested interest in Pelco's success.
- **Tackle the riskiest issues first.** When screening a technology idea, the natural tendency is to focus on the issues that carry the lowest risk and save the tougher issues for last. It is always more prudent to identify the highest risk with any development project first and make sure there is a way to reduce that risk. Otherwise, it could put the project in jeopardy after time and effort have been spent taking care of less critical risks.

The goal of risk management is to avoid failure. However, if a company is too concerned with avoiding failure, it may not take the appropriate risks necessary to achieve great successes. Invaluable information that may never have been learned otherwise is gained from failure. Product screening and development are inherently iterative processes that rely on trying one thing, testing another, and continually moving in a forward direction based on lessons learned.

CLASSIFYING TECHNOLOGIES AFTER THE INITIAL SCREENING

After the initial screening, opportunities should be classified as to how they might be commercialized or transferred. There are four major categories into which these technologies might be classified: produce the technology, acquire a technology, license the technology, or sell the technology. In some cases, a combination of these may be possible.

PRODUCE THE PRODUCT

Although the natural course of action would be to produce a product or technology that the company has invented, this is not always the best course of action. The company may not have the expertise or resources to properly produce the product; therefore, it may make more sense to use the capability of another company that does have those skills and resources. Alternatively, the inventing company may have the appropriate capability for a particular application of the technology, but not for other applications of the technology in other industries. In that case, it will seek companies that have those capabilities and give them the right to manufacture and distribute the product for that application. Companies that have the ability to produce the technology generally do so because they may be the only company with the capabilities to produce the product. In addition, they may produce the product in-house because they want to retain control of their intellectual property or they do not intend to patent the technology, keeping it as a captive application and trade secret for use in their business.

ACQUIRE THE TECHNOLOGY

Not all entrepreneurs are inventors, and not all inventors have the ability to take their inventions to market. Consequently, technology acquisition is a viable solution when an entrepreneur does not own the technology needed or does not have the resources to develop it. In many cases, acquiring the technology will speed the time to market with a new product because the entrepreneur will not have to spend time and resources in the typically lengthy R&D phase. Opportunities abound, not only in highly valued technologies, but also in those that have been undervalued or misapplied. Many of the sources of opportunity mentioned earlier in the chapter can be used to find needed technology. Before acquiring any technology, however, it is important to address some critical questions:

- What specifically is required in the way of technology?
- How much risk can the company incur?
- How much will it cost to acquire the technology versus developing and manufacturing it in-house?
- Is time a critical factor?
- What are the desired commercial features of the technology?
- Will the seller indemnify the company for patent infringement if it uses the technology?

LICENSE THE TECHNOLOGY

By licensing technology, a company has the opportunity to create multiple revenue streams and get the technology into more markets than it could probably achieve on its own. This is critically important when the company is trying to create the standard in a particular technology. It must get that technology adopted in as many markets as possible in order to create the momentum needed to establish it as the standard in the industry. Licensing is the subject of Chapter 6.

SELL THE TECHNOLOGY

Some inventors and entrepreneurs choose to sell outright the technologies they create. In some cases, they see their businesses as product development firms, not manufacturing, marketing, or distribution firms, and they would prefer to leave the commercialization task to someone else. There are other reasons that many new technologies are sold by the companies that create them. If the technology is not captive, that is, not tied to other company technologies or processes, and it has a patent position, it is a good candidate for a sale. This strategy is particularly useful if the product is in a different market than the company's core products and the buyer has a strong position in that market. Another reason to sell a technology is when the buyer has better access to needed raw materials, has underutilized manufacturing capacity in that area, or is already manufacturing the product but with a different, less advanced technology.

Once technology opportunities have been recognized and screened, it is time to turn those technology opportunities into business opportunities. Chapter 3 discusses how to develop and test a business concept.

❖ SUMMARY

Never before has creativity played such a vital role in the development of technology. Traditionally, creativity was applied to generating ideas for new products, but today it must also be applied to finding new ways of doing things—new marketing strategies, new distribution channels, and new organizational strategies. The creative process involves the connection of disparate ideas, discoveries, inventions, and applications. Natural creativity is often stifled by the barriers that people set up for themselves—not giving themselves time to be creative, fear of being criticized for being different, and the belief that they have no creative skills. These barriers can be overcome by developing an environment that inspires creativity and by making time for creative thought. Creative problem-solving skills such as restating the problem, asking why five times to get at the root of the problem, broadening or narrowing the scope of the problem, and working with the opposite of the problem can also be used. Creativity is the source of opportunity recognition, that is, an idea that has business potential. The ability to recognize opportunity can be enhanced by increasing knowledge and experience in an industry, building a diverse network of strong and weak ties, and developing an opportunistic mindset. Sources of opportunity include the patent literature, the industry of interest, customers, universities, government sources, online patent exchanges, and existing technologies in a company's archives. Technology opportunities need to be screened to determine whether they will result in a stand-alone product, a derivative opportunity based on core technology that the company already has, or a noncompetitive product with no commercial potential. With a stand-alone product, it will be important to determine what its economic life is, if it has transfer capability, and what it would take to transfer the technology. It will also be necessary to consider the risks associated with this technology opportunity. Once the technology has been classified, a decision to produce the technology, acquire it from someone else, sell it, or license it must be made.

❖ DISCUSSION QUESTIONS

1. Provide two examples that illustrate the difference between an idea and an opportunity.
2. What two challenges do you face in becoming more creative? How will you deal with those challenges?

3. Why is studying an industry one of the most important things you can do to find an opportunity?
4. What do we mean when we speak of the economic life of a technology product? How does that compare with technology life and product life?

❖ RESOURCES

Clegg, Brian and Paul Birch. *Imagination Engineering.* New York: Pearson Education Limited, 2000.

Crouch, T. D. "Why Wilbur and Orville? Some Thoughts on the Wright Brothers and the Process of Invention." In *Inventive Minds: Creativity in Technology,* edited by R. J. Weber and D. N. Perkins, 80–96. New York: Oxford Press, 1992.

Gelb, Michael J. *How to Think Like Leonardo Da Vinci: Seven Steps to Genius Every Day.* New York: Dell Books, 2000.

Gladwell, M. "Six Degrees of Lois Weisberg." *New Yorker,* January 11, 1999, 52–63.

Habino, S., and G. Nadler. *Breakthrough Thinking.* Rocklin, CA: Prima Publishing, 1990.

Hall, D., and D. Wecker. *Jumpstart Your Brain.* New York: Warner Books, 1995.

Jones, Morgan D. *The Thinker's Toolkit.* New York: Three Rivers Press, 1998.

Pfenninger, Karl. H., Valerie R. Shubik, and Bruce Adolphe. *The Origins of Creativity.* London: Oxford University Press, 2001.

Smith, Rolf. *The 7 Levels of Change.* Chicago: Summit Publishing Group, 1997.

van Oech, R. *A Whack on the Side of the Head.* New York: Warner Books, 1990.

Weick, K. E. "Small Wins in Organizational Life." *Dividend* 24, 1 (1993): 2–6.

❖ INTERNET RESOURCES

Business Opportunities Handbook: Online
www.busop1.com/
This site features articles about running a small business. Also lists business opportunities

Creativity Web
www.ozemail.com.au
An Australian site with many articles on various aspects of creativity. Check out the article called "What Can I Do to Increase My Creativity?" to get started. It's at *www.oze mail.com.au/~caveman/Creative/Techniques/intro.htm*

Federal Technology Transfer Offices on the Internet
www.nalusda.gov/ttic/guide.htm
This site will guide searchers to technology transfer offices at federal laboratories and related sites

Where Really Bad Ideas Come From
www.inc.com/search/1114.html
This great article by Ron McLean discusses how successful entrepreneurs learned from their failures

Where Great Ideas Come From
www.inc.com/search/908.html
A great article by Susan Greco discussing how successful entrepreneurs come by their ideas

Thinking up a Storm
edge.lowe.org/
A brief article on brainstorming

THE ART OF INVENTION: YOSHIRO NAKAMATSU AND CLAUDE ELWOOD SHANNON

Opportunity recognition is a personal journey. Although there are guidelines and suggestions to help bring out latent creativity and teach creative skills, each person creates opportunity in his own unique way. If one were to give an award to a great master of creativity and innovation, it would very likely go to Dr. Yoshiro Nakamatsu, the holder of more than 2,300 patents, more than double the 1,093 of Thomas Edison. Many of Dr. Nakamatsu's inventions are part of our daily lives, such as the compact disc player and the digital watch. Others serve niche markets, such as a golf putter and a water-powered engine. If one were to give an award to one of the people most responsible for the digital age as we know it, that award would go to Dr. Claude Elwood Shannon. Dr. Shannon gave us the modern concept of digital information and paved the way for the computer and information revolution. Although these two men are from different parts of the world, they share many similarities in how they approach the creative process.

Yoshiro Nakamatsu's parents, recognizing his natural curiosity as a child, encouraged his early interest in invention. In Japan, creativity was not part of a child's academic education; on the contrary, children were under extreme pressure to compete and succeed in a standardized educational system. However, Nakamatsu attributes his intellectual ability to the skills that were engrained in him throughout his schooling. For example, Japanese children are taught to memorize until the age of 20 because the Japanese believe that the brain requires this kind of discipline to prepare a person for free-associating at a later age. Some feel that it is the combination of regimentation and freedom that brings about superior levels of creativity.

Nakamatsu subscribes to a three-step process for generating new ideas, and each process requires a different location. He begins the creative process in his "static" room, which contains items only found in nature: a rock garden, running water, plants, and wood. The walls are painted white. He uses this room to free-associate or brainstorm, generating lots of ideas without judging them to be good or bad. Next, he moves to his "dynamic" room, which has black-and-white-striped walls, leather furniture, and audio/video equipment. He begins his session in this room by listening to jazz, then transitions to easy listening, and finally ends with Beethoven's Fifth Symphony, which helps him draw conclusions from his idea generation phase. The third step entails a trip to his swimming pool where he employs a special method for holding his breath and swimming underwater. He calls it "creative swimming." He has even developed a Plexiglas writing pad so that he can remain underwater while recording his thoughts.

Nakamatsu believes that what you feed your body affects your creative abilities. He eats only the best foods and abstains from alcohol. In addition, he has developed his own "brain food," called Yummy Nutri Brain Food, which consists of dried shrimp, seaweed, cheese, yogurt, eel, eggs, beef, and chicken livers!

In the United States, another inventor, equally eccentric, preceded Nakamatsu, but their inventions would eventually overlap in some industries. In 1948, when Claude Shannon was a 32-year-old researcher at Bell Laboratories, he wrote a theoretical treatise, "A Mathematical Theory of Communication," demonstrating how information could be defined and quantified with precision, unifying all the previous technologies in communication. He further proposed that all types of information media could be encoded in binary digits, or *bits* (the first time that term was used in print). Once the information was digitized, he believed that it could be transmitted without error. At the time, this was an enormous conceptual leap that would later lead to the development of today's error correcting codes and data compression algorithms, as well as to compact discs and Nakamatsu's floppy disks. His theorem explains how computer modems are able to transmit compressed data at tens of thousands of bits per second over ordinary telephone lines without error. Shannon's theory gave engineers the math tools they needed to calculate channel capacity—how much information could go from point A to point B without errors.

As amazing as his foresight was in that paper, it was almost overshadowed by the dissertation he wrote years earlier in 1940 that outlined a blueprint for the computer age. Until that time, it was thought that communication required electromagnetic waves to be sent down a wire. In his dissertation, Shannon proposed that the logical values "true" and "false" could be denoted by the numeric symbols 1 and 0, which meant you could transmit pictures, words, and sounds by sending a stream of 1's and 0's down a wire. The most compelling outcome of his proposition was that circuits could make decisions, which was the basis for the work in artificial intelligence that we know today.

After completing his doctoral degree in mathematics in 1940 at MIT, Shannon went to work for Bell Labs, where he would spend the next 31 years, and also became a professor at MIT. In 1948, with co-author Warren Weaver, he published "A Mathematical Theory of Communication," which formed the basis for what is known today as information theory. By the early 1950s, his theory had become a buzzword. Shannon was hounded by the press and received request after request for lectures and new research papers. Shannon, who disliked celebrity, eventually retreated from the research world, stopped teaching, and in 1978 retired to his home in Winchester, Massachusetts.

Shannon was famous for his creative problem solving. He loved attacking problems from angles that no one had ever thought of. Like Nakamatsu, he had his eccentricities, like riding a unicycle in the Bell Labs' hallways at night while juggling. He was constantly inventing, particularly things that had funny motions. A classic was his "Ultimate Machine," a box that contained a very large switch on the side. When you pressed the switch, the top of the box would rise, and a large hand would pop out and shut off the switch, returning the lid to its original position. That was its sole purpose!

The mind of the inventor is unlike any other. It is always in motion, constantly playing with new ideas. Even at play, both Shannon and Nakamatsu continued to invent offbeat items and concepts that reflected their childlike wonder at the world and all of its possibilities. ■

Sources: Adapted from: Charles A. Gimon, "Heroes of Cyberspace: Claude Shannon," *Info Nation* (*www.skypoint.com/~gimonca/shannon.html*); M. Mitchell Waldrop, "Reluctant Father of the Digital Age: Claude Shannon," *MIT Technology Review*, July-August, 2001 64–71.

❖ NOTES

1. Andrzej M. Pawlak, "Fostering Creativity in the New Millennium," *Research-Technology Management* 43, no. 6 (November–December 2000): 32.

2. R. D. Deazin, "Multilevel Theorizing About Creativity in Organizations: A Sensemaking Perspective," *Academy of Management Review* (April 1999); R. Drazin, "Professionals and Innovation: Structural-Functional versus Radical-Structural Perspectives," *Journal of Management Studies* 27 (1990): 245–263; T. M. Amabile, "A Model of Creativity and Innovation in Organizations." In B. M. Staw and L. L. Cummings, eds., *Research in Organizational Behavior*, 10 (Greenwich, CT: JAI Press, 1988): 123–167.

3. Deazin, "Multilevel Theorizing About Creativity in Organizations: A Sensemaking Perspective,"; R. W. Woodman, J. E. Sawyer, and R. W. Griffin, "Toward a Theory of Organizational Creativity," *Academy of Management Review* 18 (1993): 293–321.

4. B. Singh, "Role of Personality versus Biographical Factors in Creativity," *Psychological Studies* 31 (1986): 90–92; F. Barron and D. M. Harrington, "Creativity, Intelligence, and Personality," *Annual Review of Psychology* 32 (1981): 439–476; H. Gardner, Frames of Mind (New York: Basic Books, 1993).

5. Amabile, "A Model of Creativity and Innovation in Organizations," G. R. Oldham and A. Cummings, "Employee Creativity: Personal and Contextual Factors at Work," *Academy of Management Journal* 39 (1996): 607–634; M. D. Mumford and S. B. Gustafson, "Creativity Syndrome: Integration, Application, and Innovation," *Psychological Bulletin* 103 (1988): 27–43; R. Payne, "The Effectiveness of Research Teams: A Review." M. A. West and J. L. Farr, eds., In *Innovation and Creativity at Work* (Chichester: Wiley, 1990), 101–122.

6. K. J. Klein, F. Dansereau, and R. J. Hall, "Levels Issues in Theory Development, Data Collection, and Analysis," *Academy of Management Review* 19 (1994): 195–229.

7. Todd Siler, *Think Like a Genius* (New York: Bantam Books, 1996).

8. T. M. Amabile, "A Model of Creativity and Innovation in Organizations."

9. Morgan D. Jones, *The Thinker's Toolkit* (New York: Three Rivers Press, 1998).

10. H. Mintzberg and D. Raisinghani, "The Structure of Unstructured Decision Processes," *Administrative Science Quarterly* 21 (1976): 246–275.

11. K. B. Clark and T. Fujimoto, "Overlapping Problem Solving in Product Development." In K. Ferdows, eds., *Managing International Manufacturing* (Amsterdam: North–Holland, 1989), 127–152.

12. Jones, 1998, 65.

13. Brian Clegg and Paul Birch, *Imagination Engineering* (New York: Pearson Education Limited, 2000).

14. Dinah Greek, "Beginners' Guide to Genius," *Professional Engineering*, 12, no. 7 (1999): 44.

15. Paul R. Syiem, "An Introduction to TRIZ: A Revolutionary New Product Development Tool," *Visions*, January 1996.

16. Ibid.

17. Ibid.

18. Charlene Zietsma, "Opportunity Knocks— Or Does it Hide? An Examination of the Role of Opportunity Recognition in Entrepreneurship," In *Frontiers of Entrepreneurship Research* (Wellesley, MA: Babson College, 1999), *www.babson.edu/ entrep/fer/papers99/X/X_C/X_C.html*; Gerald E. Hills, Rodney G. Shrader, and G. T. Lumpkin, "Opportunity Recognition as a Creative Process." In *Frontiers of Entrepreneurship Research* (Wellesley, MA: Babson College, 1999), *www.babson.edu/ entrep/fer/papers99/X/X_C/X_C.html*.

19. Robert P. Singh, et al., "Opportunity Recognition Through Social Network Characteristics of Entrepreneurs." *Frontiers of Entrepreneurship Research* (Wellesley, MA: Babson College, 1999), *www.babson. edu/entrep/fer/papers99/X/X_C/X_C.html*.

20. I. Kirzner, *Competition and Entrepreneurship* (Chicago: University of Chicago Press, 1973).

21. C. Herron and H. J. Sapienza, "The Entrepreneur and the Initiation of New Venture Launch Activities," *Entrepreneurship: Theory & Practice* 17, no. 1 (1992): 49.

22. Zietsma, "Opportunity Knocks-Or Does it Hide? An Examination of the Role of Opportunity Recognition in Entrepreneurship," *www.babson.edu/entrep/fer/papers99/ X/X_C/X_C.html*.

23. Gerald E. Hills, Rodney G. Shrader, and G. T. Lumpkin, "Opportunity Recognition as a Creative Process," *www.babson.edu/ entrep/fer/papers99/X/X_C/X_C.html*.

24. P. Schwartz, "The Official Future, Self Delusion, and Value of Scenarios," *Financial Times* (May 2, 2000): 6–7.

25. Robert G. Cooper, *Winning at New Products*, 3d ed. (Cambridge, MA: Perseus Publishing, 2001): 162–63.

26. Kevin G. Rivette and David Kline, "Discovering New Value in Intellectual Property," *Harvard Business Review* 78, No.1 (January-February 2000): 54.

27. Ibid.

28. Donald G. Reinertsen, "Taking the Fuzziness Out of the Fuzzy Front End," *Industrial Research Institute, Inc.* (November/December 1999): 25–31.

29. Ibid., 25.

30. Preston G. Smith, "Managing Risk as Product Development Schedules Shrink," *Industrial Research Institute, Inc.* (September/October 1999): 25–32.

31. Cooper, *Winning at New Products,* pp. 53–57.

32. Smith, "Managing Risk as Product Development Schedules Shrink," 30

DEVELOPING AND TESTING A TECHNOLOGY BUSINESS CONCEPT

OVERVIEW

This chapter will examine

❖ business concept development

❖ feasibility analysis

❖ industry analysis

❖ technological feasibility analysis

❖ market analysis

❖ evaluation of distribution channels

❖ building the founding team

❖ construction of a feasible business model

INTRODUCTION

Before an entrepreneur ever considers formally starting a business, it is vitally important that he develop a concept, test it, and prove it in the marketplace. In 1993, Rob Vito met a Hungarian inventor who had developed a patented transmitter box into which he plugged a computer. The inventor plugged the box into a wall socket and began transferring data over copper electrical wiring to a computer in another room. Vito saw a huge opportunity in this invention, but was not sure how to turn it into a viable business. Partnering with the inventor, he raised $18 million to start Elcom Technologies and converted the technology into a series of consumer products. He knew that ultimately the technology should be embedded in electronic products, but to attract the attention of the major manufacturers, he had to prove consumer demand for the capability. In other words, he had to test his concept in the market.

This chapter will help the reader learn how to take a business opportunity and test it through a process called *feasibility analysis*. Feasibility analysis is an analytical tool and a process by which the entrepreneur can examine a business concept and establish the conditions under which he is willing to go forward with the concept. The results of feasibility analysis determine:

- Whether there are customers for the concept
- Whether there is a market sufficiently large enough to sustain a business
- Whether customers will buy the product from the entrepreneur
- The conditions required for the entrepreneur to feel confident to move into the business planning stage (e.g., an appropriate founding team, a way to deliver the product, required start-up resources, etc.)

Testing the business concept is an essential first step. It makes no sense to develop a complete business plan unless the concept is feasible. In fact, many high-tech companies are able to secure funding just on the strength of a feasibility analysis. This is particularly true in the biotech area where funding is needed in the very early stages of product development. Because of the importance of the business concept to both feasibility analysis and the business plan, the chapter begins with a discussion of how to develop a business concept.

DEVELOPING A BUSINESS CONCEPT

Coming up with the idea for a product or technology is really the easy part. Much more difficult is the progression from idea to opportunity to business concept to feasible business (see Figure 3-1). In Chapter 2, the focus was on creativity and opportunity recognition; that is, identifying great ideas that could become commercial opportunities. Not all inventions that come out of the innovation process have commercial potential. For those that do, a business concept will need to be developed. A business concept is a formal description of an opportunity that incorporates four elements: the

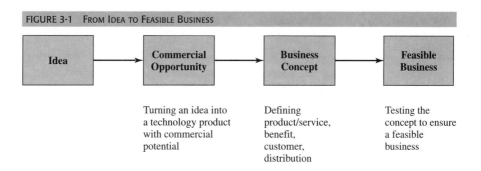

FIGURE 3-1   FROM IDEA TO FEASIBLE BUSINESS

product or service being offered, the customer definition, the value proposition (the benefits to the customer), and the means by which the benefits will be delivered to the customer—the distribution channel.

Todd Greene was sold on his invention, a patented razor fashioned like a miniature yellow jet ski designed to make it easy to shave the head. He tried to sell his product to the Schick division of Warner-Lambert Co., but they rejected it. Determined to bring his invention to market, Green decided to start his business on the Internet.[1] What would a business concept for this product look like?

> **Product:** A 2.25-inch-long razor called the HeadBlade
> **Customers:** Men who like to shave their heads
> **Benefits:** Provides a way for the user's hand to become the handle of the razor, giving the user better control of the blade
> **Distribution:** Direct to the consumer via the Internet (*www.headblade.com*)

A clear and concise concept statement incorporating these four elements might look like this:

> HeadBlade Co. LLC provides a state-of-the-art way for men to shave their heads by making the user's hand the handle, allowing for better control of the blade. HeadBlade is delivered direct to the consumer through the Internet site.

The exercise of forcing the concept into a couple of well-constructed sentences is important. Too many entrepreneurs, particularly inventor-entrepreneurs, when asked about their new businesses, begin a long drawn-out discussion of the technology and never get to the business proposition. That's fine if the audience is another scientist or engineer, but if the listener is a potential investor or other interested party, that person will quickly deduce that the entrepreneur hasn't considered the market and business potential of the invention. By devising a concise, two-sentence concept statement, the entrepreneur is prepared, no matter what the situation, to present the business in a way that shows the listener that the entrepreneur knows what she is talking about. Of course, the concept statement presented here is not yet complete. As it is, it is certainly clear and concise, but it lacks a compelling story, something that grabs people's attention: How is the product going to change the world? How is it going to take away the customer's pain? Without a compelling story, it is unlikely that the listener's attention will be held long enough to get him interested in the business. The next sections explore these components in more detail.

DEFINING THE BUSINESS

Understanding what business the entrepreneur is in is very important., Too many entrepreneurs define their businesses so narrowly that they have nowhere to move if the market or the economy changes. Using the HeadBlade concept statement, it appears that HeadBlade is in the consumer products business. This is preferable to saying that HeadBlade is in the razor business. Narrowing the business to the razor business would limit the potential of the business if shaving technology changed or if Greene wanted to diversify the business. Instead, HeadBlade positions itself in the broader consumer market, allowing itself the opportunity to move in a number of different directions as the company grows. In fact, HeadBlade now offers accessories, apparel, and other branded items.

Part of defining the business is describing the product or service that is being offered. Most businesses today offer both products and services from their inception, thus both products and services will add value to the offering. If the entrepreneur has developed a core technology, depending on who the customer is, the entrepreneur may be selling the core technology to another company to develop applications or he may have developed an initial application to demonstrate the technology. For example, Niagara Broadband developed an ultra-high-bandwidth operating system with the potential for multiple applications in a number of industries. To demonstrate the value of this technology to potential partners and investors and to its first customers—major telecommunications carriers—Niagara developed an initial application, a real-time, high-definition video application called "Virtual Presence" that interested parties could use to experience the benefits of the technology.

BENEFITS

Identifying the features a product offers is easy; identifying the benefits customers are looking for is a more difficult proposition, but it is one of the most important things to do in preparing an invention for market introduction. Entrepreneurs can understand the concept of customer benefit if they put themselves in the customer's shoes and ask, "what's in it for me?" Customers want to know why they should purchase the entrepreneur's product over someone else's and why they should buy it from the entrepreneur as opposed to someone else. If these questions cannot be answered, chances are the customer will not make the purchase.

To discover what customers really consider to be benefits it's important for the entrepreneur to talk to them to confirm the entrepreneur's predictions about customer expectations. The easiest way to begin is to look at the benefits associated with the product's features. To use the HeadBlade example, suppose one of the features of the product is the ergonomics of the handle. The tendency is to say that the benefit the product is providing customers is a better handle for shaving heads. Actually, the ergonomically superior handle is really a feature of the product, not a benefit to the customer. The benefit is what's in it for the customer, and that is normally something intangible like convenience, better health, speed, or reliability. In this case, the benefit is comfort and better control of the razor blade.

Once the benefits have been identified and associated with the features of the product, it is time to consider other intangible benefits that the company can offer customers that will differentiate it from its competitors. Help in finding those benefits will come from market research and also from the industry analysis. Will customers see a benefit in a company that builds long-term relationships with its customers? Is the company customizing its product to meet their specific needs? These are examples of benefits that are not tied to product features.

SOME QUESTIONS PRIOR TO FEASIBILITY

Once the business concept is well defined, it is a good idea to do a quick test to see if a feasibility study is warranted. This quick test will eliminate many weak business concepts with minimal research, as it relies solely on the entrepreneur's own knowledge and the opinions of others that the entrepreneur seeks out in the process. Here are the questions to think about:

1. **How interested am I in this opportunity?** Remember that starting a new business is a labor of love. It takes more time and energy than any job, so the entrepreneur must be passionate about the business concept.
2. **Who else is interested in this business concept?** A business requires customers, and perhaps investors. Therefore, people other than the entrepreneur must be interested in the business concept.
3. **Will people actually buy the product?** It is easy for people to express interest in the product, but how many of them would write a check to actually purchase it? If they are not willing to pay what the product is worth, the entrepreneur will definitely want to rethink the concept.
4. **Why me?** Why is the entrepreneur the right person to execute this concept? Knowing what the entrepreneur brings to the table is a vital part of deciding if the concept is feasible.
5. **Why now?** Why is this the best time to launch the venture? Why has no one already done this? Or, has somebody done this and failed?

When these questions have been answered satisfactorily, the entrepreneur is ready to conduct a feasibility analysis.

CONDUCTING A FEASIBILITY ANALYSIS

It is not an understatement to say that conducting a feasibility analysis is one of the most important things to do prior to starting a business. It forces the entrepreneur to undertake some due diligence on the concept and think critically about whether the most important questions have been answered before starting a business. In general, the feasibility analysis will answer three broad questions about the potential business:

1. **Are there enough customers to make the business work?** The business may have a great technology and a business concept that seems to make sense, but if the market is too small, there may not be enough profit to make the effort worthwhile. Learning that in advance of starting the business will put the entrepreneur in a better position to make adjustments to the concept to broaden its niche. Or, the entrepreneur may decide that this concept is not worth pursuing.
2. **Do the capital requirements to start the business make sense?** The amount of capital and other resources required to start the business must be in line with other businesses in the same industry and must be within the reach of the entrepreneur.
3. **Does the entrepreneur have the right team put together to execute the concept?** Most investors look at the team first and the concept second because they know that it takes an excellent team to make a business work. The entrepreneur must identify people or businesses that can fill any gaps in the founding team.

Conducting a feasibility analysis is like digging at an archeological site. As the layers of sand and rock are pushed away, more and more about the era that is being studied

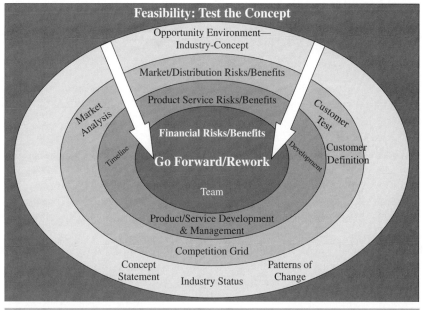

FIGURE 3-2 THE NATURE OF FEASIBILITY ANALYSIS

is learned until the researcher finally discovers that bone or skeleton that answers all his questions. Figure 3-2 depicts the layers of investigation in a feasibility analysis. The next sections discuss these layers in more detail.

ANALYZING THE INDUSTRY

The industry, a group of similar businesses that typically interact in the same environment, is the broadest level of analysis. Whether it is accomplished before the opportunity is recognized or after the development of a business concept, the industry analysis provides enormous insight into how similar businesses work and interact. Moreover, understanding an industry makes it easier to find appropriate strategic partners, customers, money sources, and effective distribution channels.

Industries are not static, they are dynamic, living organisms that move through stages much like a person progresses from birth to death. Figure 3-3 depicts the stages of the industry growth cycle. The stages are as follows:

1. **Birth.** A new industry emerges, the result of a disruptive technology, like the semiconductor, or a radically new kind of service, like fast food.
2. **Growth and adaptation.** In the early stages of the new industry, there is a lot of volatility as companies maneuver for the strongest position and strive to be the one to establish the standards for everyone else. At this point, there is a lot of uncertainty and the risk is high. Intellectual property rights give the firms that hold them an advantage—a temporary monopoly in which to introduce their technologies.
3. **Differentiation and competition.** As more and more firms enter the industry, competition becomes fierce, prices come down, and standards are established.

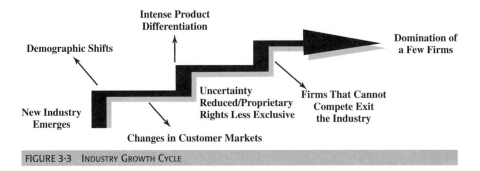

FIGURE 3-3   INDUSTRY GROWTH CYCLE

4. Shakeout. At some point, the competition reaches such a high level of intensity that those firms that can no longer compete exit the industry, leaving only a few major players.

5. Maturity and decline. Every industry eventually reaches a mature state with a few dominant firms. Over time, if these firms do not continue to invest in R&D or if new firms do not find a way to enter the industry and shake it up, the industry will decline.

Every industry's life cycle is a little different. Some industries reach maturity sooner or later than others or go through each stage at different rates. Emerging industries are those just coming into being, such as genetic therapy, nanotechnology, and wireless technology. In an emerging industry, technological uncertainty exists for a relatively long period of time until the major technology developers enter the industry and determine the best technology. Therefore, at the outset, products or processes are not standardized, thus production costs are very high. Companies in an emerging industry may have difficulty obtaining raw materials because supply chains are not well established. Furthermore, buyers in an emerging industry are few in number and are considered early adopters who are willing to pay a premium to experience state-of-the-art technology. Understanding where the industry is in its life cycle is important to the overall business strategy, and, in particular, the new venture's entry strategy. The subject of entry strategy is taken up in more depth in Chapter 15.

USING A FRAMEWORK FOR ANALYSIS

The work of Michael Porter serves as a reliable framework for analyzing an industry, with some modifications to account for the effect of technology, the Internet, and the information age. Porter describes five forces that affect every industry, and by extension the profit potential and competitive strategy of a business in that industry.[2] A sixth force—technology—has been added to this framework to reflect the dynamic nature of industries over time. The six forces are:

1. Barriers to entry in the industry
2. Threat of substitute products
3. Buyer power
4. Supplier power

5. Degree of competitor rivalry

6. Technology

Each of these factors is considered now in more detail.

BARRIERS TO ENTRY

Some industries erect very difficult barriers for new entrants to overcome. Firms in the industry may have achieved economies of scale in marketing, production, and distribution that allow them to lower their prices because their production costs are less. The new venture's costs to produce are typically high, making it very difficult for new companies to compete. In this situation, small companies often band together in strategic alliances to create economies of scale that allow them to compete.

Another difficult barrier to overcome is brand loyalty. Existing products have a loyal customer base for which the switching costs are great. Overcoming brand loyalty means introducing a technology that is obviously superior to existing technology or partnering with one of the major players to gain entry. This latter strategy is also a way to reduce the costs of entering an industry that typically has high costs for R&D, plant and equipment, and marketing, and allows the entering firm to compete on the same level as established companies. It also gives the new venture access to established distribution channels. Other barriers to entry include government regulations and industry hostility. Knowing these barriers in advance can help to the entrepreneur design an entry strategy that is not doomed from the start.

THREAT FROM SUBSTITUTE PRODUCTS

In any industry, companies compete not only with products that are very much like theirs, but also with substitute products in other industries that perform the same basic function, though in a different way or at a different price. For example, HeadBlade certainly competes with razors manufactured by the major players in the industry, Schick, Gillette, and others, as well as producers of clippers and scissors.

BUYERS' POWER

In many industries, established companies have gained a level of buying power that makes it very difficult for a new business to compete. These established companies can force down prices from their suppliers so that they can purchase supplies and raw materials at prices the new venture cannot. They also pose the threat of backward integration, which means that the buyers purchase their suppliers in order to control the supply chain, effectively locking out smaller companies. Companies like Microsoft, General Motors, and Boeing carry a lot of clout as buyers in their respective industries, and they can command the best prices from their suppliers.

SUPPLIERS' POWER

Suppliers can also exert power in an industry where the number of suppliers of a particular raw material or component is few relative to the size of the industry or where the industry is not a primary customer of the supplier. Suppliers can raise prices or change quality. Suppliers also pose a threat of forward integration, which means that they purchase the outlets for their raw materials, effectively controlling the price at which they are sold.

DEGREE OF COMPETITOR RIVALRY

A highly competitive industry will drive down prices and also the return on investment. In this type of industry, price wars and advertising battles are common. This is a very challenging environment for a new venture. The new venture must identify a niche from which it can enter the industry without attracting the attention of the major players. Another effective strategy is for the new venture to position itself to be acquired by a larger firm.

TECHNOLOGY

Technology not only enables business goals, it also drives change. Industries based on digital technology are well aware of this. These industries move quickly, often without a lot of elaborate planning, because the windows of opportunity are small and close very quickly. Many researchers now claim that any industry whose principal product includes information cannot take the time to undertake conventional planning processes; moreover, the frequency of technological shifts since 1996 has made forecasting a very challenging task.[3] Technology has made every industry more dynamic, more virtual than physical, and more intuitive than analytical. Rather than enjoying 3-to-5-year planning cycles, many companies are finding that they can only forecast out 12 to 18 months with any degree of accuracy. In addition, technology has precipitated the destruction or shortening of many value chains and disrupted the economic models of many industries and the businesses in them.

ANALYZING THE COMPETITION

One of the most important aspects of an industry analysis is to study the competition. Learning their strategies and goals, how they have positioned themselves in the industry, and what motivates them will put the entrepreneur in a better position to find gaps that can be leveraged. Using a competitive grid is an excellent way to organize the information gathered about competitors. The grid consists of a simple matrix where the competitors are listed in the first column and subsequent columns compare these competitors on a variety of variables such as product features, benefits, distribution strategy, and marketing strategy. Putting the entrepreneur's business concept into the matrix as well helps visualize how it stacks up against the competition. For an example matrix, see Table 3-1.

Finding competitive intelligence on a company is no easy task. An Internet search of the competitors' Web sites, examples of their advertising, and a look at their facilities is a good place to start because it will reveal something about who their customers are and what their stated goals are. If any competitors are public companies, financial information such as revenues, operating expenses, and the like can be found in the companies' annual reports and quarterly Securities and Exchange Commission (SEC) filings. In addition, data on competitors' current market strategies, management style and culture, pricing strategy, customer mix, and promotional mix is important information. Here are some suggestions for gathering competitive information:

- If possible, visit competitors' physical sites to talk to employees and customers and to observe what goes on.
- Purchase competitors' products to understand their features and benefits. The purchase transactions will also provide valuable information about how they treat their customers.

TABLE 3-1 Competitive Grid for Nutritional Concepts

	Product	Unique Features/Benefits	Price	Promotion	Weaknesses
Enutrition.com	• Online supplements and beauty products	• Boasts great customer service • Wide selection • Detailed descriptions of their products	• Depends on amount of products purchased	• Free shipping on orders $20 or more • Free newsletter • Ads in magazines, on radio, and Internet	• No personalized health evaluation available • No article and resource information available • Advertisements confusing in correlation with business mission
Ediets.com	• Online health evaluation with meal plans and support staff	• Largest support group community including message boards • Large staff with good personalization	• Free brief evaluation • $10 start-up fee for detailed evaluation and plan • $10 a month (min. 3 months)	• Free brief evaluation • Ads on the Internet, radio, and magazines • Free newsletter	• Very small selection of supplements • No groceries or online database • Confusing to know if they sell anything besides their evaluations
Mothernature.com	• Natural products and information distributor	• Product supplement planner • Widest selection of product categories from supplements to groceries to fashion • Message boards	• Depends on products purchased • $3.95 for shipping	• Free shipping for purchases over $50 • Ads on TV, magazines, and radio • Free newsletter	• Does not focus on personalization • Evaluation very weak • No focus on core team

(Continued)

TABLE 3-1 (*Continued*)

	Product	Unique Features/Benefits	Price	Promotion	Weaknesses
Wholepeople.com	• Online shopping from natural foods to supplements along with nutritional advice	• Will offer wide selection of food and supplements with retail store backing them	• Advice is free	• None	• Failure of first e-commerce site • Personalization and products not integrated
Vitaminshoppe.com	• The largest selection of vitamins and supplements	• Wide variety • Easy search categories • Have 78 retail locations to go with Web site • Resource center	• Depends on products purchased • Shipping dependent on purchase (minimal)	• Free color catalog • Ads in newspapers, magazines, billboards, and radio	• No online community • Does not focus on personalization • No focus on core team • No grocery or book purchases
NutritionalConcepts.com	• Personalized health evaluations complete with all implementation tools (supplements, groceries, books, and beauty products)	• The only Web site offering a complete personalized health evaluation with home delivery of the products necessary to implement the plan • Live support staff • A personalized Web page for members	• Personal health evaluation—$50 • Membership after evaluation—$15 per month • Product sales per customer and delivery costs dependent on amount purchased	• Free delivery for purchases over $75 • 1 month free membership for new members and existing clients • Ads in local Chicago newspapers, local cable, and billboards • Free newsletter	• Size and awareness on a national scale

Source: Created by Mike Minsky while a student in the Greif Entrepreneurship Center at the University of Southern California, *Nutritional Concepts Business Plan,* p. 18.

- Study public companies that serve as benchmarks of excellence in the industry. Three valuable sources are Hoover's Online (*www.hoovers.com*), the U.S. Securities and Exchange Commission (*www.sec.gov*), and OneSource (*www.onesource.com*).
- Check government Web sites, which are good sources of industry information. Some of them are listed in the Internet Resources for this chapter.
- Find trade associations dedicated to the industry. They are the industry watchers and can provide a wealth of valuable information, as can trade shows.

A PLAN FOR INDUSTRY ANALYSIS

An effective industry analysis will rely on data from both secondary and primary sources. Secondary sources are those studies and statistics compiled by others, whereas primary sources are the many ways that the entrepreneur collects data, such as interviews, surveys, observation, and so forth. A good way to begin is by identifying an industry's NAICS code. NAICS is the North American Industry Classification System, which permits common standards and statistics across North America. It replaced the Standard Industrial Classification System (SIC). Information about NAICS can be found at the NTIS (U.S. Department of Commerce National Technical Information Service) Web site at *www.fedworld.gov*. The big improvement with this system is that it now covers 350 new industries, including high-tech areas such as fiber optic cable manufacturing, satellite communications, and computer software reproduction. Also, instead of the familiar four-digit SIC code, it uses a six-digit code that accommodates a larger number of industry sectors. Like the SIC code, the NAICS code can be used to find statistics about size of the industry, sales, number of employees, and so forth.

The following are some of the questions about the industry that should be answered:

- **Is the industry experiencing growth?** Growth can be measured in a number of ways: sales volume, number of employees, units produced, number of new industry entrants. An industry that is growing provides more opportunities for new entrants.
- **Where are the opportunities in this industry?** Is this an industry ripe for consolidation? Are there opportunities to innovate in marketing, distribution, or manufacturing?
- **How does the industry respond to new technology?** How quickly does the industry adopt new technology? Does technology play an important role in the competitive strategies of companies in this industry?
- **How much is spent on R&D?** The amount of R&D investment in the industry will have an impact on the start-up capital requirements for a new venture and will also provide an idea of how fast the product development cycle is.
- **Who are the major competitors?** Which firms dominate in the industry? What are their strategies?
- **Are young firms surviving in the industry?** If there are no young firms in the industry, it is usually an indication that entry barriers are high and an industry shakeout has already occurred. Many young firms suggest that the industry is still in the early stages of development and growth.
- **Where is the industry going?** What will the industry look like in 5 years? What about 10 years? What are the long-term trends?

- **What are the threats to the industry?** Is there a chance that an emerging technology will cause the industry to become obsolete?
- **What are the gross margins in the industry?** The gross margin is a financial measure that determines how much room there is to make mistakes and how much of every dollar the company takes in is available to pay overhead and make a profit. An industry that has gross margins of 80 percent provides a lot more flexibility to make a lot of money on a relatively low volume, whereas in an industry with margins of 3 percent, there is very little room for error and a company must sell in huge volumes to make it work.

ANALYZING TECHNICAL FEASIBILITY

During the process of determining market feasibility, it is important to also figure out if the technology being proposed or in development is feasible from a technical standpoint. Two of the biggest problems that product developers face are incorrect product definitions and market changes.[4] Often, a product that met customers' needs in the early stages of design is not correctly translated into final product features and benefits, and the product ends up falling short of customer desires. Moreover, the market does not stand still while the developer is in the product development phase, therefore the developer must continually scan the market for potential shifts in needs and preferences, as well as for competitors that may have entered the market.

Technical feasibility is typically assessed in three stages. The goals of this process are to ensure that customer requirements are met in the final product and to speed the time to market.

STAGE ONE: CONCEPT TESTING

At the concept-testing stage, only customers who understand the technology will be able to comment and provide valuable input to the design. Still, fundamental aspects of the technology can be tested for feasibility using computer modeling software like CAD and SolidWorks.

STAGE TWO: PRIMITIVE PROTOTYPE

It is important to get a physical prototype into the customer's hands as quickly as possible because customers often notice things that engineers never think of. When Gentech Corporation put its earliest physical prototype of an air-compressor/ generator into the hands a customer, it got feedback that saved it an enormous amount of time and money. Gentech's combination air-compressor/generator weighed in at just under 300 pounds, yet it was designed to be portable and had handles that enabled the user to maneuver it with relative ease. As customers began to use the machine, they quickly noted that to grab the handles, they had to bend nearly to the ground; this was not ergonomically sound, and certainly could cause back problems. That feedback caused Gentech to modify the machine, raising the handles to waist height, in the earliest stages of development. Had Gentech waited to receive customer input until it had finalized its design, the product redesign would have been very costly.

The entire product does not need to be ready before customers see it or use it. If a major component of the product is ready and visible to the customer, a mock situation that lets the customer judge the effectiveness of that component can be set up. Software developers have always used an iterative process with primitive prototypes. They get an initial interface out to users to get feedback, then add some functionality and get more feedback. This process continues until the entire prototype is completed. In the biotech industry, feedback at various stages is built into the system through FDA-required clinical trials.

STAGE THREE: NEAR-PRODUCTION QUALITY

Stage three may occur after the market feasibility analysis is completed. Therefore, after this stage has been completed, additional results can be added to the feasibility analysis. If everything was done right in stage two, the customer was able to actually use the product and provide vital feedback on its design, ergonomics, and ease of use, among many other potentially relevant variables. In stage three, the product has reached near-production quality; in other words, it is just about ready to go to market. Production quality means that the device can be replicated in volumes through a defined process. At this point, it is critically important to get the product into the hands of as many customers as possible and ask them to use and abuse it over a more extended period of time and typically at their own sites. In this stage the developer will be attempting to:[5]

- Identify the features and benefits to which the customers respond most strongly.
- Measure the customers' level of acceptance, liking, and intent to purchase.
- Measure how well the product worked in a real user environment over time.
- Judge feelings about price.

It is important that the developer observe how the product is actually being used during these extended tests and that a written agreement from the customer stating that this is a product test is secured.

PRODUCT RISKS AND BENEFITS

Any product has associated risks and benefits that the entrepreneur must weigh prior to investing the time and money in product development. In addition to looking at the technical feasibility of the product, how the product will be developed and manufactured will need to be determined. Effective product development does not happen without planning. There are significant risks in developing a product without considering its ability to be manufactured in quantities or even a way to manufacture it at all. Product development is discussed in more detail in Chapter 4. In addition, protecting new products with patents and trademarks is a critical component of any competitive strategy, as well as a way to create additional revenue streams through licensing those intellectual property rights. Chapters 5 through 7 deal with intellectual property and licensing and suggest ways to analyze a product in terms of potential rights that might be advantageous to acquire and ways to defend those rights against competitors that may try to infringe them.

SOME KEY QUESTIONS TO ANSWER

The following questions should be considered when analyzing a product's risks and benefits:

- What are the features and associated customer benefits of the product or service?
- What product development tasks must be undertaken and what is the timeline for completion?
- Is there potential for intellectual property rights?
- How is the product or service differentiated from others in the market?

MARKET ANALYSIS

Analyzing the market for a product is arguably the most important task to undertake during feasibility analysis. Identifying the product's primary market, those customers that are most likely to purchase first, is critical to determining an entry strategy. The first definition of the primary customer will typically be fairly loose and broad. However, with more research, particularly primary research with customers, that definition will be refined until it is actually useful. Key questions that should be answered by the research are:

- Who is most likely to be the first customer for this product?
- What does this customer typically buy, how do they buy it, and how do they become aware of it?
- How often does this customer buy and what is their buying pattern?
- How can this company meet the customer's needs?

Market research can be done very systematically through a four-step process of evaluating information needs, researching secondary sources, talking with customers, and forecasting demand for the product.

EVALUATING INFORMATION NEEDS

Prior to collecting market information, it's important to decide how the data will be used to assess the feasibility of the new venture. This decision will better ensure that the data collected are actually required. Additionally, the type of data collected determines the types of analyses that can be performed. For example, if the goal is to predict customer demand for the product and statistical tools are used to analyze the data, then the data need to be collected in a form that permits statistical analysis. Most of the analyses that entrepreneurs conduct result in simple, descriptive statistics. It is important to do secondary research of the market first to gain a good understanding of the market before a plan to test the customer with primary research techniques is developed. Some secondary resources for market research are listed at the end of the chapter.

CONDUCTING THE CUSTOMER TEST

Several valuable pieces of information will come out of an effective customer test: a realistic definition of the target market, an estimate of demand, a sense of how willing the customer is to purchase from the company, and an in-depth profile of the customer.

To get that information, a variety of different research techniques will be required—observation, phone surveys, mail surveys, Internet surveys, interviews, and focus groups, among others. Each has advantages and disadvantages, and the choice of technique typically will be based on the entrepreneur's time frame and budget.

Most of the techniques require a representative sample of the population of customers the entrepreneur is interested in. Choosing the sample is a critical part of the process because it determines the validity of the results achieved. For most circumstances, a random sample is appropriate, that is, one where the entrepreneur does not control who is chosen to participate; therefore, the responses are not biased. Because of time and budget constraints, most entrepreneurs end up choosing a convenience sample, which simply means that not everyone in the target market has a chance of being selected, for example, a sample of people attending an industry trade show or conference. Even with a convenience sample, a degree of randomness can be ensured by setting up a system for random selection, for example, choosing every fourth person or using a random-number generator to determine which respondents will be selected. What should not be done is to choose a sample of people known to the entrepreneur. One of the principal reasons for doing a feasibility analysis is to get a real, unbiased idea of whether a product has market potential. Friends and relatives are not always the best source of unbiased information. Moreover, while the surveys and interviews are being conducted, the respondents are forming impressions about the product and the company based on how the entrepreneur deals with them, how she uses the information, and how well she protects their privacy.[6] In the next sections, some of the basic primary research-gathering techniques in their order of effectiveness for inventor-entrepreneurs will be reviewed.

FOCUS GROUPS AND INTERVIEWS

Focus groups bring together a representative sample of customers (and often noncustomers) for a presentation and discussion session. A focus group is really a multi-person interview. When using focus groups, it is important to hire a person, the facilitator, with expertise in group dynamics to facilitate the event and keep the group on track. It is also a good idea to videotape the sessions (with the customers' permission), so that the entrepreneur can take more time to analyze what went on.

Although one-on-one interviews and focus groups can be more time-consuming and expensive than other techniques, they have significant advantages that make them the most effective means of gathering primary data on customers. In a face-to-face setting, there is more opportunity to discuss and clarify questions and responses. Plus, the focus group facilitator or entrepreneur has the advantage of observing the nonverbal communication of the respondents, which is often invaluable in discerning what the respondents really mean to say.

Interviews and focus groups produce the highest response rates of all the research-gathering techniques. They also tend to provide the most valuable responses, because they permit open-ended questions that can lead to an interchange resulting in more in-depth information. In a focus-group setting, the facilitator can observe the interplay of several customers' comments at once while demonstrating the product (if that is possible) and soliciting constructive criticism and suggestions. If appropriate, a blind test might be conducted, giving customers the entrepreneur's product and a competitors' product without labeling them, and then observing their responses and reactions to the products. Software developers and engineers with digitally based products conduct focus groups on the Internet via tech user groups that examine the product and look for potential problems.

SURVEYS: MAIL, PHONE, AND INTERNET

Surveys are a common tool for collecting data when a large sample is required. However, surveys and their associated instrument, the questionnaire, are one of the most misused weapons in the data collection arsenal. People frequently believe that they can throw together a few questions and easily acquire the information they need. However, questionnaire design is much more complicated than it might appear; in fact, there are proven methods of questionnaire construction. Working with a specialist in this area will ensure that the most effective questionnaire for the entrepreneur's needs is developed.

Mail surveys are plagued by a low response rate, and the inability to clarify responses and assure accuracy. Typically, a follow-up mailing will be necessary to achieve an acceptable response rate. Phone surveys improve on response rate, and permit the clarification of questions and responses. However, they do take a lot of time to complete, are prone to surveyor bias due to tone of voice, and the advantage of non-verbal communication feedback is lost. In addition, many potential respondents resist responding to phone surveys because they are regularly bombarded by telemarketing surveys and perceive the entrepreneur to be in that category.

The Internet has helped to reduce the cost of mail surveys by allowing entrepreneurs to secure e-mail distribution lists and conduct mass mailings as easily as the market research firms do.[7] The Internet certainly makes it easier to conduct global surveys, and the response rate to Internet surveys is usually rapid. However, Internet samples are mostly made up of avid Internet users, so there will be non-response bias on the part of non-Internet users. A questionnaire can be posted on the entrepreneur's Web site and potential respondents can be directed to the site through off-line means if the entrepreneur's site is not highly trafficked. Alternatively, a link to the questionnaire can be posted to online user groups or e-mailed to targeted customers. A low response rate may be achieved because like people who receive telemarketer calls, Internet users are barraged by data-gathering mechanisms at every turn and may resist filling out another questionnaire.[8]

CREATING THE CUSTOMER PROFILE

One of the most important outcomes of primary research is an in-depth customer profile that describes the primary customer, whether it is a consumer or another business, in great detail. This profile will form the basis for future marketing efforts, as well as identify specific customers who should review the product in the final assessment of technology feasibility. The customer profile typically contains the following information: age, income level, education, buying habits (when, where, how much), where customers find products like the entrepreneur's, and the way they would like to purchase the product. Of course, this information will vary depending on whether the customer is a consumer or a business. For a business customer, characteristics such as the type of business and its size, primary customers, location, revenues, and so forth are appropriate.

FORECASTING DEMAND

If one of the most important tasks is testing the customer to ascertain demand for the product, one of the most difficult tasks is actually forecasting how much product will be sold over time. This task is particularly challenging if the product is a breakthrough product that has not existed in the market previously. In that case, there are no real benchmarks to go by and the entrepreneur will have to extrapolate data from a similar product. Most entrepreneurs do their own research to come up with numbers from which to derive a forecast. This is at once advantageous and disadvantageous—disadvantageous because the entrepreneur may not have the skills required to do the job effectively, and advantageous because the process will provide a better understanding of the target market and its needs.

Perhaps the best way to arrive at a demand figure is to triangulate from three different points of view: (1) the entrepreneur's own knowledge and customer test information, (2) analogous products, and (3) industry experts. By conducting the customer test, the entrepreneur has a vital piece of the triangle—the customer's point of view. In addition, looking at the sales of a similar product can provide clues as to what results the product might achieve. For example, demand for compact disks was extrapolated from historical demand for cassette tapes because it was logical to assume that acceptance of compact disks might follow patterns similar to those found in the transition from eight-track tapes to cassettes. Studying adoption rates of technology in a particular industry is an excellent way to refine the demand estimate and also develop a realistic timeline so that forecasts are as close to what will actually happen as possible.

Interviewing people who work on a daily basis in the industry in which the new business will reside is another great way to zero in on demand. The numbers derived from distributors, manufacturers, retailers, suppliers, and the like will be some of the most realistic numbers available as they will likely be based on broad-based experience as opposed to the more anecdotal demand estimates secured from customers.

Sometimes the only way to get really accurate estimates of demand is to actually go into limited production in a test market where it is easier to control production volume, marketing, and distribution. If it is a representative test market, it will be an excellent gauge of what numbers might be achieved in a broader market. Many companies use a benchmark figure of 50 percent. If customer preference for the product over substitutes is less than 50 percent, the product may be in trouble. Of course, this assumes that customers have been correctly targeted.

SOME KEY QUESTIONS TO ANSWER

In completing the market analysis, some important questions should be addressed:

- What are the demographics of the target market?
- What is the customer profile? Who is the customer?
- Have conversations with customers occurred?
- What benefits are customers looking for?
- When do they buy and how much do they buy?
- Who are the competitors and how is the new venture differentiated from them?

ANALYZING DISTRIBUTION CHANNEL ALTERNATIVES

A distribution channel is simply the route that a product takes in moving from the producer to the end user. Today, a distribution strategy can make or break a company. With the Internet reducing transactions costs, making supply chains more efficient, and generally changing the way industries function, it is no wonder that distribution has become a significant part of a company's competitive strategy. This Internet effect has moved businesses from marketplace to market space.[9] Distance does not affect products that can be digitized and time does not hamper businesses that locate online. Businesses have used the Internet to transform passive conduits (traditional distribution channels) into interactive conduits. One significant negative outcome of this is that mass marketing and commoditization (competing on price) are common on the Internet. It is an unfortunate fact that the more efficient distribution channels become, the more opportunity there is for commoditization.

Another trend has been the consolidation of small distributors, which reduces or eliminates channel costs.[10] Consolidation occurs when a small number of companies garner the majority of the market share in an industry over a very short period of time. For manufacturers, the consolidation of distribution channels means less competition among distributors and therefore higher prices for manufacturers.

Entrepreneurs have a number of options when looking at distribution channels from a strategic perspective. Where a company is positioned in the channel will determine who its customer is, what kind of business it is, and, in part, how expensive its operations will be. See Figure 3-4 for a depiction of the two basic types of channels: direct and indirect.

Every product has more than one channel option, and the option(s) an entrepreneur chooses is a function of the customers' expectations. Graphing the distribution options and comparing them in a manner similar to that shown in Figure 3-5, lets the entrepreneur judge:

- The time from production to customer or end user based on the lead time needed by each channel member.
- The final retail price based on the markups required by each intermediary to account for the value each has added to the product as it moves through the channel.
- The total costs of marketing the product. Manufacturers, for example, often support the advertising efforts of their distributors and retailers.

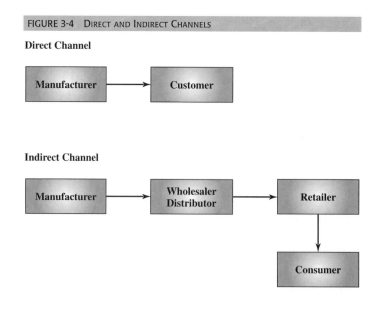

FIGURE 3-4   DIRECT AND INDIRECT CHANNELS

Direct Channel

Manufacturer → Customer

Indirect Channel

Manufacturer → Wholesaler Distributor → Retailer → Consumer

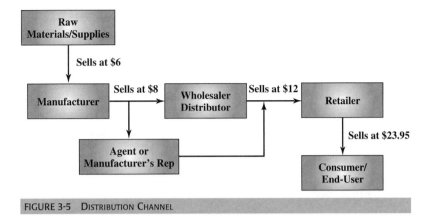

FIGURE 3-5   DISTRIBUTION CHANNEL

Figure 3-5 depicts an example of a distribution channel that shows the value added at each point.

In this channel, the raw materials producer charges the manufacturer $6 per unit; the manufacturer turns this raw material into product and sells it to a distributor for $8 per unit. The manufacturer could also choose to use a manufacturer's sales representative to find outlets for the product and receive a commission on sales achieved. The retailer typically doubles the price to the consumer. In some industries, retailers more than double the price. Notice that the amount of markup generally increases moving downstream through the channel. More risk is incurred and consequently it costs more to do business.

Which distribution channel the entrepreneur chooses will be a function of how satisfied customers will be with it, whether or not it can do what the entrepreneur requires, and whether or not the entrepreneur can make a reasonable profit using that channel. In addition, there are some other factors that should be considered:

- **Costs.** The expenses associated with marketing and distributing the product to the customer must be examined as they will affect the ability to make a profit.
- **Market coverage.** Most new companies rely on intermediaries because they can enter a new market more quickly, which is important when the entrepreneur has limited resources.
- **Control.** Where a company positions itself in the distribution channel dictates the degree of control the entrepreneur will have over the product after it leaves the company. If the company is introducing a product that requires unique marketing tactics to get the attention of the customer, it may not want to use an intermediary that also carries competing products, as its product may not receive the attention it needs to attract sales.
- **Speed and reliability.** If customers expect to get the product quickly, that too must be considered when choosing the channel of distribution. This is why Dell Computers assembles its own products and ships them direct to the customer. Similarly, if reliability is something customers demand (and what customer doesn't?), the entrepreneur will need to have more control over any downstream intermediaries as they are the link to the customer.

The bottom line is that a distribution strategy must be chosen wisely, as it will have a major impact on the business and on the satisfaction of customers.

SOME KEY QUESTIONS TO ANSWER

The following are some key questions to answer regarding the value chain and distribution channel:

- What does the value chain for the new venture look like?
- Which distribution channel alternatives are available and which customers will be served by them?
- Are there ways to innovate in the distribution channel; that is, find new methods of distribution?

ANALYZING THE FOUNDING TEAM

The tradition of the solo entrepreneur held fast for decades. This was the person who succeeded alone—who retained sole ownership of the business, made all the key decisions, and did not have to share the profit with anyone. Small start-up businesses, typically in the service, craft, or artisan areas, are still led by solo entrepreneurs. However, in the 1980s, researchers started to discover that a team effort has a far better chance of achieving a successful start-up than a solo entrepreneur.[11] There are many reasons for this. A business start-up is an intense process requiring huge amounts of time and effort; with a team, the effort can be shared. Moreover, with a team, the scope of expertise expands, and the new venture can go much farther before outside personnel have to be hired. A founding team with a variety of skills and experience also brings a lot of credibility to lenders and investors.

But team requirements reach far beyond the founding team to strategic partnerships with professional advisers, industry players, and others who will be able to help the new venture. These extended networks are invaluable to the entrepreneurial process.[12]

CHOOSING THE FOUNDING TEAM

More often than not, the founding teams of technology ventures consist of scientists and engineers. This is fine during the early stages of product development, but as the team gets closer to commercialization, it is important to fill in the gaps in business knowledge. Investors look first at the management team and then at the technology, because it is the team that will execute the business concept. If the team cannot execute, the business will never get off the ground. One of the reasons that so many dot-com companies failed is that their teams had no expertise or experience in what they were doing. All they had was a compelling product with no realistic execution plan.

Achieving the perfect team in the beginning is a difficult task, but some guidelines will make the task easier:

- At a minimum, the three functional areas of business should be included in the start-up team: finance, marketing, and operations.

- Someone on the team should have experience in the industry in which the company will operate.
- Everyone on the team should have a good credit rating as this will be very important when the team attempts to seek financing for the venture.
- The company should choose people who have a good network of contacts that might help the business.
- The company should choose people who believe in the business concept as much as the founding team does so that they will have a vested interest in seeing the business succeed.
- The company should select people who will devote the required time to the venture and who can endure the financial constraints of the start-up phase.

FILLING IN THE GAPS

Any expertise that might be missing on the team can be gained in a number of ways. The company can outsource noncore functions to another firm or to professional advisors such as attorneys, accountants, bankers, and consultants. Setting up an advisory board or informal panel of experts is a good way to get free advice from people who want to see the business succeed. As part of the feasibility analysis, the entrepreneur will determine the knowledge gaps in the start-up team and develop a plan to fill those gaps. For more details about team building in high-tech ventures, see Chapter 11.

CONSTRUCTING A FEASIBLE BUSINESS MODEL

High-tech ventures have several commercialization alternatives for their technologies, and the business model created will be a function of the alternative chosen. To complete the overview of feasibility analysis, the business model alternatives will be discussed in brief here and in more detail in later chapters as noted.

In general, a business model is the economic value model for the new venture—a plan for how the business will make money and create value for its customers and partners. For most incremental innovations, business models are fairly well established by the industry. As a result, the mistake that many entrepreneurs make is to default to the logical business model—for example, generate revenues off the sales of the product to distributors—without ever considering the many other ways that revenues can be generated off the same technology.

Radical innovators have a more difficult task because typically no established business model exists that would fit their product, and they have to create one simultaneously with the development of the technology. In the 1990s, Monsanto engineered a tomato that was resistant to insect strains that were threatening tomato crops. Monsanto had been in the textiles and specialty chemicals business since the 1970s and, therefore, did not know how to generate income from this breakthrough technology. It was also faced with the reality that this new genetically engineered tomato would hurt its successful pesticide business. Monsanto finally decided to modify its new tomato seed so that it would only reproduce once; as a result, farmers would need to repurchase seeds every 2 years.[13] This is an example of how a business model can dictate the direction of technology development. By its very nature, a radical innovation disrupts current ways of doing things and requires that the innovators create new value chains and new business models.

Depending on the type of technology developed, an entrepreneur has four basic alternatives for commercialization:

- Licensing the technology to third parties
- Selling the technology outright to a third party
- Partnering with a larger company and sharing the technology
- Starting a new venture

These alternatives will be considered in depth in Chapter 8. After deciding on a business model, it is time to consider the capital needs that will be required to execute this model and test it in the market.

No matter how many financial analyses the entrepreneur conducts, it all comes down to cash. Income statements and balance sheets can make a company look successful on paper, but cash pays the bills and funds the growth of the business. The first three commercialization alternatives require financing to get through product development and marketing of the technology to a licensee, a buyer, or a strategic partner. Deciding to start a business to launch the product requires additional start-up and operating capital to take the business to a positive cash flow. For the feasibility analysis, a sales forecast based on the business model will be calculated as well as the timeline for the projected launch of the product. A resource needs assessment that looks at capital requirements will also be required. This topic will be taken up in depth in Chapter 8.

SOME KEY QUESTIONS TO ANSWER

Some of the important questions regarding start-up capital that will need to be answered in the feasibility analysis include:

- What are the start-up capital requirements?
- What are the working capital requirements?
- What are the fixed-cost requirements?
- How long will it take to achieve a positive cash flow?
- What is the break-even point for the business?

SHOULD THE ENTREPRENEUR GO FORWARD?

More than anything else, the feasibility analysis is an internal document that gives the founding team the confidence they need to proceed with commercialization. However, many high-tech ventures can secure funding based solely on a feasibility analysis. In the following section is an outline for a feasibility document that can be prepared for investors and other interested parties.

The feasibility analysis describes what the market says about the business concept. It will also paint a picture of the conditions required for this venture to be successful. The feasibility analysis is not about a go/no go decision. Rather, it is about giving the entrepreneur the information he needs to make an informed decision about going forward. It is rare for an inventor/entrepreneur to get completely through a full-blown feasibility analysis and find a challenge that cannot be surmounted. If there is a fatal flaw in the concept, generally the entrepreneur will find it very early in the process if enough time is spent in the industry and market talking to as many people as possible. The inventor-entrepreneurs who get surprised by fatal flaws at the point of launching the product are those who held their concepts too close to their vests, were afraid to talk to people about them, and who did not do their market research. That is why it is so important to begin the feasibility analysis prior to product development, to find those major challenges to the concept before a lot of time and money has been invested in a product for which there is no market or not a big enough market to make the effort worthwhile.

FEASIBILITY ANALYSIS OUTLINE
COVER FOR THE FEASIBILITY STUDY

EXECUTIVE SUMMARY
Include the most important points from all sections of the feasibility study. *Do not exceed two pages.*
Make sure the first sentence captures the reader's attention and the first paragraph presents the business concept

TITLE PAGE
Name of company, feasibility study title, founding team members' names

TABLE OF CONTENTS

FEASIBILITY DECISION
The decision as to the conditions under which the entrepreneur is willing to go forward with the business concept

THE BUSINESS CONCEPT
What is the business?
Who is the customer?
What is the value proposition or benefit(s) being delivered to the customer?
How will the benefit be delivered (distribution)?
Spin-offs and potential for growth

INDUSTRY/MARKET ANALYSIS
Industry analysis
Target market analysis
Niche
Competitor analysis and competitive advantages (competitive grid)
Customer profile
Distribution channels (alternatives and risk/benefit)
Entry strategies (initial market penetration/first customer)

TECHNICAL FEASIBILITY AND PRODUCT DEVELOPMENT PLAN
Detailed description and unique features of product/service
Current status of product development
Tasks and timeline to completion
Intellectual property acquisition
Plan for prototyping and testing

FOUNDING TEAM
Qualifications of founding team
How critical tasks will be covered
Gap analysis (professional advisors, board of directors, independent contractors)

FINANCIAL PLAN
Summary of key points on which financial feasibility is based
Assumptions or premises for resource needs assessment
Resource needs assessment
Pro forma income statement (1 to 3 years) by month or quarter
Break-even analysis

TIMELINE TO LAUNCH
Tasks that will need to be accomplished up to the date of launch in the order of
   their completion

BIBLIOGRAPHY OR ENDNOTES (FOOTNOTES MAY BE SUBSTITUTED)

APPENDIX (A, B, C, ETC.)
Questionnaires, maps, forms, resumes, etc.

❖ SUMMARY

Discovering an opportunity is an exciting process; developing a feasible concept for a business is a much more difficult task. How effectively the entrepreneur defines the customer, the value of the benefits that will be delivered to that customer, and the distribution channel that will be used to reach the customer will determine the success of the commercialization effort. To effectively judge the feasibility of a business concept, the entrepreneur will undertake a variety of analyses, beginning in the broadest sense with the industry. Using both primary and secondary research techniques the entrepreneur will study the nature of the industry, its place in the industry life cycle, the competitive landscape, trends, and the direction in which the industry is moving. From there, the entrepreneur will move to looking at the market in which the primary customer for the technology will be found. It is the customer who will provide the vital information as to whether there is a market for the product, how big that market is, and whether customers will buy from the entrepreneur's company. It is also from customer information that the entrepreneur can begin to look in depth at the applications of the technology and the features and benefits most valued by customers. Intellectual property protections for the core technology will be considered as well as any applications that will be developed. Analyzing and choosing a distribution channel is a far more complex undertaking today because there are so many choices and because effective distribution has become a significant competitive advantage for all types of businesses. Determining the best channel for the product will again depend on what the customers expect as well as the type of business the entrepreneur wishes to have. All the effort put into the commercialization of the product can still result in failure if the entrepreneur does not have the right team to manage the development process and execute the plan for the business. The founding team is arguably the most important thing to investors. If the new venture does not have an experienced and talented founding team, it will not be able to make the business a success. Finding creative ways to fill the gaps in expertise will be one of the important analyses to do in preparing to commercialize the technology. Lastly, an appropriate business model should be developed and the start-up costs for this venture calculated. When the results of all the analyses are in, the entrepreneur will have a clear picture of the conditions necessary to make this venture a success and will be able to go forward confident that he has reduced a significant portion of the risk of commercialization.

❖ DISCUSSION QUESTIONS

1. Why is it important to define the business broadly but focus the business concept?
2. You have developed a new software product that more effectively performs natural language searches through databases using voice recognition technology. What would your plan be for testing this product with customers?
3. Based on the product in question 2, what would you want to know about the industry to feel confident that you could enter it with a new venture? Be specific.
4. What are some ways that you can fill in the gaps in expertise and experience in the founding team?
5. Suppose you determine that there are not enough customers for the new product. What could you do, short of abandoning the product?

❖ RESOURCES

Berinstein, Paula, ed. *Finding Statistics Online*. Medford, NJ: Information Today, Inc., 1998.

Hague, Paul, and Peter Jackson. *Market Research: A Guide to Planning, Methodology and Research*. London: Kogan Page LTD, 1999.

Levinson, J. C. *Guerrilla Marketing*. Boston: Houghton Mifflin, 1984.

McQuarrie, Edward F. *Customer Visits: Building a Better Market Focus*. Thousand Oaks, CA: Sage Publications, 1998.

Miller, Jerry P. *Millennium Intelligence*. Medford, NJ: CyberAge Books, 2000.

Porter, M. *Competitive Strategy: Techniques for Analyzing Industries and Competitors*. New York: Free Press, 1980.

Porter, M. *Competitive Advantage*. New York: Free Press, 1985.

❖ INTERNET RESOURCES

American Demographics
www.demographics.com/directory
A site to help you learn how to target your marketing efforts

American Marketing Association
www.marketingpower.com
Web site focusing on services provided by the American Marketing Association

CEO Express
www.ceoexpress.com
A guide to business resources on the Internet

Department of Commerce
www.doc.gov
Links to many sites of interest to business owners

EntreWorld.org
www.entreworld.org/Default.cfm
Articles and help on issues related to evaluating a business opportunity

Federal Web Locator
www.infoctr.edu/fwl/
Links to economic news, export information, legislative trends, and more

IndustryLink
www.industrylink.com/
Offers links to sites of interest to people in a number of different industries

Mediamark Research
www.mediamark.com
Provides general Internet statistics

PR Newswire
www.prnewswire.com/
Good source of news on corporations worldwide

OneSource
www.onesource.com
A comprehensive source of industry information

Quirks Marketing Research Review
www.quirks.com/
One-stop source for information on marketing research. Includes case studies

ResearchInfo.com
www.researchinfo.com/
A source of free resources on market research topics

Securities and Exchange Commission
www.sec.gov/
Good source of financial information on specific industries

SEC Edgar Database
www.sec.gov/edgarhp.htm
Contains documents that publicly traded companies must submit to the SEC

The Competitive Intelligence Guide
www.fuld.com
Provides advice on how to seek competitive intelligence and links to specific industries

Thomas Register
www.thomasregister.com/
The online version of the Thomas Register of American Manufacturers. Contains information about products, services, and companies

Understanding Your Market
www.sbaonline.sba.gov
Web site of the Small Business Administration. Provides information on market and customer analysis

ZONDIGO: CHAOS IN THE WIRELESS WORLD

Wireless communications technologies have evolved to the point that there are tremendous opportunities for businesses to reduce costs and generate additional revenues by implementing wireless solutions. However, even with these technological advancements, the adoption rate of wireless solutions has been anemic. Businesses face numerous complexities and uncertainties when integrating the endless number of devices, network protocols, and back-end business systems to cost-effectively develop and scale wireless solutions. With the overwhelming number of new wireless hardware, software, and network technologies being developed, a business's wireless application may become obsolete within months. Additionally, the costs associated with creating wireless solutions, given their complexity, can be exorbitant. Scalability also becomes an uncertainty, due to the constant struggle required in upgrading applications to be compatible with new wireless technologies.

THE SOLUTION: ZCORE

Zondigo is a software company that was founded to make it easy and cost-effective for businesses to create and scale wireless solutions. Zondigo's core product, Zcore, is a software operating engine and open development environment that bridges the languages, technologies, and protocols required to communicate with wireless devices, applications, and networks.

Without this technology, wireless Web content must be created specifically for the device it will be displayed on, even if it already exists in the standard Web format, HTML. If content is destined for multiple wireless devices, it generally must be reworked to suit the idiosyncrasies of each device—screen size, screen resolution,

data rate, memory limitation, etc. Zondigo's goal is to enable developers to create the content once, then distribute it to any and all types of devices. Figure 3-6 depicts this relationship.

Zcore serves as the central wireless technology "hub" for all devices, network protocols, and back-end database systems. Through partnerships with leading third-party wireless technology companies, Zondigo builds connectors to proprietary wireless systems and applications, giving greater control and flexibility to businesses, allowing them to choose the systems and applications they need. Zcore also consists of back-end system access modules that integrate easily with existing business systems. By continually integrating new connectors and access modules, Zcore provides businesses with a long-term, scalable solution as an alternative to the ad hoc systems that exist today. Zcore has been developed using a transaction engine that has been proven to scale to and support over 30 billion transactions per month (or over 10,000 per second). The engine was developed and proven by Zondigo's CEO at L90, which he also cofounded.

Zcore currently supports the most common wireless technologies for digital phones, voice systems, and handheld devices. New wireless technology advancements are continually being added to the Zcore engine. Examples of the currently supported technologies are:

- **Voice.** Voice recognition, text-to-speech, interactive voice response
- **Digital phones and pagers.** One-way SMS messaging, two-way SMS messaging, WAP, iMode
- **Handheld device operating systems.** PalmOS, RIM, PocketPC

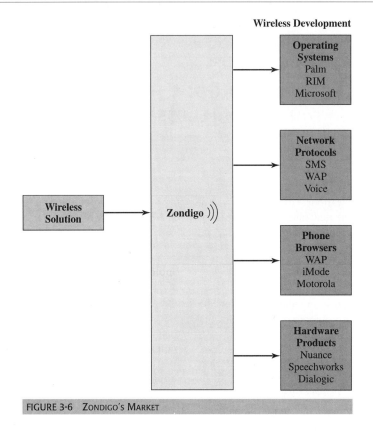

FIGURE 3-6   ZONDIGO'S MARKET

THE TEAM

Frank Addante, the Chief Executive Officer and founder of Zondigo, is a technologist with prior start-up experience. He was the Chief Technology Officer (CTO) and founder of the technology division of L90, Inc., (NASDAQ: LNTY), a leading Internet marketing and software company. Addante created L90's proprietary technology platform, which currently performs over 5 billion transactions per month and reaches over 50 percent of all Internet users. He has licensed this core technology back from the company he cofounded in order to get a 12- to 18-month head start on development and a major competitive advantage.

Addante has surrounded himself with a solid team that includes Zondigo cofounders Frederick Lowe (CTO) and Rekha Ravindra (Vice President of Product Development). Members of the management team have significant management experience with leading technology and consumer companies. The Advisory Board also includes an impressive list of executives from companies such as AT&T, Exodus, Akamai, and NetZero. These participants are highly focused on marketing and technology. This should help Zondigo gain access to potential clients.

CUSTOMERS AND APPLICATIONS

On the sales front, Zondigo has built a beta application for Intel that is currently in use. They have built four other beta test applications for potential customers and have an active prospect list of companies that are evaluating the Zondigo offerings. They also have signed an integration contract with an original equipment manufacturer (OEM) customer and launched Zcore on webMillion.com, the seventh-stickiest site on the Internet,[14] to prove their concept. These early successes have helped the management team prove their concept and develop a three-phase sales and marketing strategy that defines the customers and applications served by Zondigo and explains how the company will segment the market.

Phase I

Primary Markets

- **Sales force automation.** Mobile solutions allow enterprises to dramatically increase worker productivity and overall operating efficiencies. Zondigo will leverage its expertise in identification-based systems and back-end systems integration to become a leader within this market.
- **Transportation- and travel-related services.** Zondigo believes that wireless solutions for the travel industry are compelling given the time sensitivity and benefits associated with conducting mobile transactions while traveling.
- **Wireless companies.** Zondigo will provide its Zcore product to empower wireless solutions providers with the core technology necessary to implement scalable wireless applications that can interact with other wireless technologies. Zondigo recognizes that these customers will be smaller in size in the short term. However, management believes that this market will grow quickly, and as the market grows, so will revenues from these customers.

Phase II

As industry participants continue to adopt wireless voice and data technologies, Zondigo will be well positioned to capitalize on the enormous growth of m-commerce (mobile commerce) and v-commerce (voice commerce). The release of location-based services will be a key driver of these services. Zondigo will deploy additional products and services in Phase I target markets and leverage this position into broader markets through direct sales channels, OEM relationships, and strategic partnerships. In addition, the Company will begin to deploy its Zcore technology in European markets where the adoption rate of wireless technologies has outpaced domestic markets.

Primary Markets

- **Enterprise companies.** Zondigo believes that technological advancements and sub-

scriber adoption rates will continue to accelerate by the fourth quarter of 2001 and will drive m-commerce and v-commerce revenues for enterprises.
- **Advertising companies.** Through its strategic relationship with L90, a premier technology marketing company, Zondigo is well positioned to become the technology solution of choice for companies wishing to deploy wireless advertising initiatives.

Phase III

As wireless and voice technologies continue to evolve, driven by 3G and packet data technologies, Zondigo will continue to add functionality to Zcore, including location-based, multimedia, and video conferencing technologies. These technology offerings will "piggyback" on solutions implemented in Phases I and II of Zondigo's business strategy. Zondigo will continue to deploy its technologies internationally.

COMPANY BACKGROUND

While Frank Addante was the Chief Technology Officer of L90, Inc., he deployed one of the very first wireless solutions at a sales and technology conference. It received enormous amounts of attention from many companies. From this initial wireless solution, it became evident that the amount of energy and resources to build and support a wireless infrastructure were exorbitant. The costs for individual companies to build a wireless solution were clearly not worth the return.

Addante and his cofounders started Zondigo in October 2000 based on the need for wireless solutions to support companies' broader scale needs. They planned to allow customers to come to one company for all their wireless needs. In November 2000, Zondigo received its first round of financing through a strategic investment from L90, Inc. The companies arranged a cross-license agreement of their respective technologies for future use. Zondigo's license agreement of L90's technology gave Zondigo a major head start from a research and development perspective. Zondigo started with an infrastructure that could support up to 40 billion transactions per month. This instantly put 2 million lines of code under the company's belt, something that took Frank and his team several years to develop at L90. Since raising the first round of financing, Zondigo has developed and deployed Zcore version 1.0, negotiated five key technology infrastructure partner relationships, set up and deployed three U.S. Data Center hosting facilities, and integrated the best wireless technology networks and services. As of this writing, Zondigo was raising its next round of financing to allow it to execute its sales and marketing strategy, as outlined earlier.

INDUSTRY OVERVIEW

The term "wireless" has become a buzzword. During the dot-com bubble, many technology start-ups focused on wireless technologies and applications. Some simply added the word "wireless" to their name or company description in hopes of associating themselves with this high-growth sector. Due to unrealistic predictions of relentless, explosive growth, expectations and valuations of wireless companies reached extraordinary levels in 1999 and early 2001. In the wake of the crash of the technology sector between April of 2000 and April of 2001, wireless and other hot technology sectors have endured a backlash against expectations and valuations. But somewhere in between lies the reality—that wireless technologies represent a solid long-term growth opportunity with many new applications to come. "Classic" or "old-economy" companies and their workforces will be increasingly empowered by wireless technologies that empower faster action and decision making by making real-time enterprise data more accessible.

Wireless technologies are making real-time information and communications available any time, almost anywhere. Wireless also has the power to disrupt entire industries, as fixed wireless (or Wireless Local Loop) technologies will very soon allow CLECs or wireless service providers to "totally circumvent the incumbent telecommunications providers."[15] No longer will carriers who own wires in the last mile be able to exclude competitors from offering better, faster, and cheaper technology to homes and businesses. Wireless technologies, therefore, "empower the end user, and have the power to change the economics of existing businesses."[16]

Many entrepreneurs and companies have recognized this potential, creating a flood of wireless technologies, devices, protocols, and compa-nies in the last 2 years. As most of them are in the early stages of commercializing their technology, most will not endure in the long run. "The market will not likely support a great number of incompatible technologies, devices, and protocols."[17] Too many different technologies, devices, and protocols create incompatibility, which creates confusion and slows progress in the industry. Industry analysts believe that this is the reason why wireless telephone technology in the United States is relatively far behind that of the rest of the world, especially Europe. European governments declared GSM the cross-border standard for wireless technologies in the early 1990s, so device makers and service providers were forced to innovate to differentiate themselves from the competition. In the United States, on the other hand, no standard was set. As a result, we have a hodge-podge of competing incompatible standards, including CDMA, GSM, AMPS, and TDMA.[18]

This totally laissez-faire stance on the deployment of wireless services has not turned out to be the best approach for consumers. Multiple, overlapping wireless networks have been deployed across the United States, creating a massive duplication of efforts several times over. Instead of thoroughly covering the country with the base stations necessary for ubiquitous service, multiple service providers put their competing base stations in the same areas, and often left "holes" in their service in many other areas. The high cost of deploying these redundant networks means that each service provider has to recoup their own costs, "keeping service fees higher and the number of features and the quality of calls lower" than in Europe.[19]

OPPORTUNITIES FROM CHAOS

This wireless chaos has created great opportunity for those who believe they have a solution. One important potential solution is Software Radio. This means that instead of a base station with relatively simple hardware that transmits and receives one standard, "a base station with a flexible, software-based transceiver could be programmed for any or all standards."[20] The promise of Software Radio is that, instead of multiple incompatible wireless base stations and handsets, a single base station or handset would operate on any service provider's network, using any protocol (CDMA, GSM, AMPS, etc.). Each device could also be instantly upgraded to support a new standard, even wirelessly!

The same concept applies to wireless phones (handsets) and computers. Instead of a phone that only has the hardware to work on one carrier's network, a Software-Radio-based handset would be able to work on any network. New network "protocols" could easily be downloaded into the phone, even spontaneously when a user steps off of a plane into a foreign country. The handset would simply "announce" itself to the network, and then download whatever protocol it needs to operate there. The phone would work on any network, anywhere—almost instantly. For that matter, the handset could be used to access a corporate or home network on the fly. This might be useful to a corporate traveler visiting one of their company's offices in another city or country. If that office or division uses a different wireless networking standard, the user's handset or laptop could instantly "learn" what it needs to access that wireless LAN.

The same fragmented state of the wireless industry that makes Software Radio a great opportunity also makes the transfer of data and content between incompatible systems a potentially "lucrative opportunity. The trick is to provide a platform that will allow developers to port the all-important ingredient—content—to any of the approximately 100 different and incompatible wireless/handheld devices available on the market today."[21] This is the opportunity being addressed by Zondigo and the Zcore platform. That would make Zondigo a software company. It might also make it an infrastructure company. In fact, the CEO, Frank Addante, would say it is both. He breaks the wireless industry into four groups: infrastructure companies, end user technologies, professional services, and software.

Addante believes that Zondigo straddles all of these categories, which is one of their key differentiators. This allows Zondigo to offer a complete solution to their customers that gives users greater power, control, and flexibility in creating and extending their enterprise applications.

CHALLENGES

In any high-growth market with new technologies there are numerous challenges. First and foremost, proving the market for wireless solutions seems to be the main challenge faced by Zondigo and others in their space. Addante believes that with the introduction of location-based services, 2002 will be the next major inflection point that the wireless industry will continue to accelerate from. In the meantime, Addante and his team must prove this market one day at a time by continuing to win paying customers. Second, differentiating Zondigo from wireless software companies will also be critical to their success. Zondigo believes that there are many wireless companies out there that say they are doing everything, claiming to offer a single-source solution needed by companies that want to drive business via wireless communications. But those competitive companies often provide a software application that is proprietary and inflexible while making bold claims. Therefore, these same companies may make it more difficult for customers and investors to understand the value that Zondigo truly provides, which are summarized in the following list.

Key Benefits of Zcore	
Cost savings	This reduces upfront and ongoing development costs.
Development control	Zcore and its accompanying software development kit enable application development using any language(s) or service(s).
Simplicity	Provides easy-to-use development interface and integration into existing systems.
Adaptability	Solutions deployed with Zcore are continually compatible with new wireless technologies.

The third major challenge faced by Zondigo is that there are many businesses that see the need for wireless solutions but are not ready to move forward with an action plan. This is the result of the aforementioned 100+ competing and incompatible standards that have created confusion and trepidation in the market. Early adopters have jumped into the fray. However, "most companies are sitting on the sidelines, not convinced they need this technology,"[22] or if they are convinced, they are not sure how to go about it. Getting companies to understand the strength of wireless and its opportunities for their businesses is another critical element to the success of wireless companies such as Zondigo. Addante and his team need to be advocates not just for Zondigo's products and services, but also for wireless technologies in general. ■

Source: This case was written by Lucrezia Bickerton and Casey Horton, MBA 2001, as a basis for classroom discussion, April 17, 2001, University of Southern California. Used by permission of Casey Horton.

❖ BIBLIOGRAPHY

Zondigo Company Press Release. "Zondigo's New Software Product Energizes Wireless Development." Los Angeles, CA, April 2, 2001.

Zondigo Company Press Release. "L90, Zondigo Forge Wireless Partnership." Los Angeles, CA, January 29, 2001.

Zondigo Company Press Release. "Zondigo Selects MobileSys' Wireless Messaging Services for MobileTrack, Its SMS-to-Voice Transaction Platform." Los Angeles, CA, January 29, 2001.

Zondigo Company Press Release. "L90, Inc. Announces Strategic Partnership with Zondigo, Inc. to Prepare Marketing Technology for a Wireless World," Los Angeles, CA, January 16, 2001.

Zondigo Company Press Release "Zondigo Appoints Seven High-Profile Board Members." Los Angeles, CA, December 18, 2000.

❖ WEB SITES

www.zondigo.com

www.L90.com

www.microsoft.com

www.aethersystems.com

www.voxeo.com

www.brience.com

www.tellme.com

www.ztango.com

❖ NOTES

1. Mike Hofman, "The Razor's Edge," *Inc.* (March 1, 2000) *www.inc.com.*
2. Michael E. Porter, *Competitive Strategy: Techniques for Analyzing Industries and Competitors* (New York: The Free Press, 1980): 3.
3. Larry Downes and Chunka Mui, *Unleashing the Killer App: Digital Strategies for Market Dominance* (Boston: Harvard University Press, 1997): 59–60.
4. Robert G. Cooper, *Winning at New Products*, 3d ed. (Cambridge, MA: Perseus Publishing, 2001): 50–53.
5. Ibid., 260.
6. Douglas R. Pruden, "Customer Research, Not Marketing Research," *Marketing Research* (Summer 2000).
7. Robert Gray, "The Relentless Rise of Online Research," *Marketing* (May 18, 2000).
8. Mick P. Couper, "Web Surveys: A Review of Issues and Approaches," *Public Opinion Quarterly* 64, no. 4 (Winter 2000): 464–494.
9. J. F. Rayport and J. J. Sviokla, "Managing in the Market-Space," *Harvard Business Review* (November–December 1994): 141–150.
10. Adam J. Fein, "Manage Consolidation in the Distribution Channel," *Sloan Management Review* (Fall 1999) *www.findarticles.com.*

11. A. H. Van de Ven, R. Hudson, and D. M. Schroeder, "Designing New Business Start-Ups," *Journal of Management* 10 (1984).

12. Paola Dubini and Howard Aldrich, "Personal and Extended Networks Are Central to the Entrepreneurial Process," *Journal of Business Venturing* 6 (1991): 305–313.

13. Richard Leifer, Christopher M. McDermott, Gina Colarelli O'Connor, Lois S. Peters, Mark Rice, and Robert W. Veryzer, *Radical Innovation* (Boston: Harvard Business School Press, 2000): 94–95.

14. Frank Addante, Zondigo Wireless, interview by Lucrezia Bickerton and Casey Horton, Los Angeles, CA, April 3, 2001.

15. Y. Pathak, Wireless Technologies, interview by Lucrezia Bickerton and Casey Horton, Irvine, CA, April 11, 2001.

16. George Gilder, "Gilder Technology Report," 6, no. 3 (2001).

17. Jeffrey Hines, "The New W.W.W. (Web Without Wires)," Deutsche Banc, Alex. Brown Equity Research, New York, May 2000.

18. Brian Modoff, "Wireless Web Goes Wild," Deutsche Banc, Alex. Brown Equity Research, San Francisco, CA, June 2000.

19. Ibid.

20. Joseph Mitola, III, *Software Radio Architecture* (New York: John Wiley & Sons, 2000).

21. John H. Hill, "M-Powering Wireless Network Convergence," Solomon Smith Barney, San Francisco, CA, January 18, 2001.

22. Edward Snyder, "Outlook & Opportunities for the New Millennium," Chase H&Q Equity Research, San Francisco, CA, January 6, 2000.

4

HIGH TECHNOLOGY PRODUCT DEVELOPMENT STRATEGIES

OVERVIEW

This chapter will examine

❖ the new product development process

❖ metrics for product development

❖ the outsourcing of technology innovation

INTRODUCTION

A definite shift in R&D strategy has been taking place over the past few years. The Industrial Research Institute[1] reports four major changes taking place: (1) a new emphasis on business growth through R&D, (2) market capitalization based on intangible assets, (3) more R&D time and capital being allocated to new business projects and new business models with concrete results instead of to basic research, and (4) companies increasing the number of strategic alliances and acquiring more technology through mergers and acquisitions. Another trend is an increase in the licensing out of technology to other companies and the acquisition of technology through in-licensing.

Intangible assets are quickly becoming the basis for market capitalization. A 1997 study by Coopers & Lybrand (now merged with PriceWaterhouse) discovered that two-thirds of the $7 trillion market value of publicly traded companies in 1997 did not appear on their balance sheets because it was in intangible assets such as intellectual property.[2] In the software industry, intangibles can account for as much as 98 percent of a company's assets. Today, more start-ups and corporate spin-offs are being built to flip rather than to exist for the long term; in other words, they are built for a 12-to-24-month life, whereupon they are sold. WebTV was built to flip. It had 35 critical patents for the delivery of Internet content over TV when Microsoft acquired it in 1997 to gain access to those intangible assets. These built-to-flip companies are typically more flexible and lean than most corporate R&D departments, so they present a real source of competition for companies that do not take advantage of this structure. Licensing has also become a critical strategy for companies with intangible assets, particularly for those patents that are noncore to the business's strategy. In 1980, licensing amounted to about $3 billion in revenues; in 2001, it had grown to over $110 billion.[3] Finally, the degree to which a company can execute its R&D and commercialization processes more rapidly than its competitors will determine its ultimate success. The challenge is to develop superior products faster and at less cost.[4] This need for speed has resulted in more strategic alliances and more in-licensing of noncore technology.

PRIMARY CAUSES OF NEW PRODUCT FAILURE

In a booming economy, it makes sense that companies might consider taking a risk on new product development (NPD), but in a slower economy, businesses automatically start retrenching, and NPD falls to the wayside. However, it is often a good strategy to undertake NPD in slow economic times. When product development is finished and the product launched, there will probably be fewer competitors to contend with. The company will be able to enjoy the large margins and temporary monopoly that new products bring, and distribution channel partners who have been looking for something to spark their slumping sales will be revitalized. Most importantly, when things are booming again, the company will have already established its place in the market and others will have to meet its standards to successfully compete. Many highly successful companies launched in slow economic times, for example, Microsoft Corp. in 1975 and Federal Express Corp. in 1973.

However, not all product launches are successful. The statistics on new product success are not encouraging. Given that companies spend an average of 46 percent of their resources on designing, developing, and launching a new product, and given that one in every four projects started never sees the marketplace, it is easy to see why firms are looking for ways to improve their success rate.[5] The only way to do that is to consider why companies fail at NPD. The Conference Board has conducted the most thorough research on new product failures and these early results are confirmed by the recent work of R.G. Cooper and others. The results are summarized in Table 4-1.[6]

From the table, it is clear that lack of good market analysis was the downfall of many product efforts. Scientists and engineers often assume that because the product works well in the laboratory, customers will naturally like it—the "build it and they will come" syndrome. However, that is not often the case. The only way to effectively read customer needs is to talk with them.

The second biggest cause of new product failure was technical problems. Going from the research laboratory to production and then to final product offers many challenges and chances for missteps. Very often these problems stem from moving too rapidly through the design and early prototyping phase where most of these problems could have been caught. When all the causes of new product failure are considered, it is clear that most of them resulted from failure to understand the market and the customer.

TABLE 4-1   Primary Causes of New Product Failure

Cause of Failure	Percentage of Total Cause of Failure	Approximate Percentage of Companies Responding
Poor market analysis	24	45
Product defects	16	28
Weak marketing effort	14	25
NPD costs too high	10	18
Strong competitor reaction	9	16
Poor timing of product launch	8	14
Production problems	6	12
Other causes	13	23

Source: Hopkins, D. S. *New Product Winners and Losers*, Conference Board Report #773, 1980; and Hopkins, D. S. and E. L. Bailey, "New Product Pressures," *Conference Board Record 8* (1971): 16–24.

IDENTIFYING WINNERS

So, what is the good news? Some of the primary causes of NPD failure have been discussed, however, NPD success requires more than just doing what the failures did not do. Many of the product failures have some of the same characteristics as the successes. Several research studies have explored this issue in an effort to uncover the factors that distinguish the successes from the failures. Robert Cooper studied 102 companies—102 new product successes and 93 failures—and was able to identify three key factors to product success: (1) the customer perceived that the product was a unique and superior product in terms of benefits and value, (2) the company had a strong market orientation and conducted in-depth market research before proceeding with the new product, and (3) the company leveraged its technology competency and executed well.[7] The Stanford Innovation Project, a study of high-tech electronics firms, yielded similar results in that they found that effective execution of the market launch was a critical factor to success and that winning products were generally technically superior to losers.[8] Additionally, it found that the winning products produced high gross margins and a high performance-to-cost ratio.[9] Moreover, successful products were introduced ahead of competitors' products and had the full support of top management.[10]

An internal Hewlett-Packard study identified 10 critical factors in predicting new product success.[11] More recently, Cooper's work has produced eight success measures.[12] These two lists have been combined to produce the following list of 12 critical success determinants:

1. The team creates a superior product with unique benefits and value for the customer.
2. The company chooses an attractive market where there is a great need for what the company is offering.
3. The development team understands the customer's needs because it conducts an in-depth market analysis. From those needs, it creates a well-defined product prior to beginning the NPD process.
4. The goals of the NPD project are aligned with the company's strategic goals.
5. The team has a thorough understanding of how competitors do or do not meet customers' needs.

6. All regulatory and intellectual property issues are identified and addressed.
7. Project decision criteria, such as manufacturing cost and time to market, are identified and prioritized.
8. The project leverages the company's technical capabilities.
9. The company positions the product correctly.
10. The most effective distribution channel is chosen, and the company leverages its marketing expertise.
11. Upper management endorses and supports the project and supplies sufficient resources to all aspects of the project.
12. The company executes the NPD process with high levels of quality.

Later the chapter demonstrates how these factors are incorporated into a new NPD model.

THE NEW PRODUCT DEVELOPMENT PROCESS

Which factors positively affect the product development outcome has been the source of much discussion in the research literature. Brown and Eisenhardt propose that process efficiency and product effectiveness are a function of various agents: team members, project leaders, senior managers, customers, and suppliers.[13] However, Iansiti and Clark contend that a company's ability to perform is dependent on its capabilities.[14] Capabilities are used to deploy and coordinate various resources[15] and are composed of the knowledge within the organization.[16] Technological capabilities such as R&D and manufacturing routines are arguably the first important driver of product development success.[17] Accumulated technological knowledge from previous experience[18] and knowledge of product architecture, aesthetics, and ergonomics are complementary to these capabilities.[19] Market knowledge is also a critical factor in product development success.[20]

For many decades the product development cycle was thought of as a linear process, consisting of a series of activities that took place in a vacuum. Today, the need for rapid cycle development and flexibility has made NPD a team effort with many tasks going on simultaneously. Product development has often been framed in terms of traditional S-curve theory, which speculates that early stage technologies display a relatively slow rate of progress in performance. However, as the technology is better understood and diffused into many small markets, the rate of performance improvement will escalate. Later, when the technology reaches a mature stage, it reaches an upper limit of performance such that to achieve any improvement requires additional, costly engineering. The pattern of this escalation and decline resembles the letter S.[21] Understanding this pattern makes it possible to design a product development strategy that introduces succeeding technology at the appropriate moment so as to not lose the momentum achieved in the middle stage.

Figure 4-1 presents a graphical depiction of the commercialization process. It incorporates and adapts the concepts from Cooper's stage-gate research[22] and the platform development projects of Miller and Morris.[23] In essence, the graphic divides

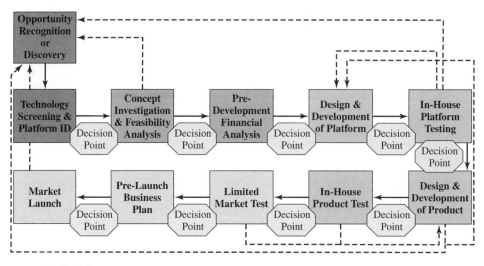

- - - - Feedback Loops

FIGURE 4-1   FROM IDEA TO MARKET

the process into phases, tasks, and decision points, with feedback loops to indicate that the process is iterative in many respects. The phases are distinguished by their shaded gradations. Listed within each phase are the activities that are conducted concurrently in an effort to gather enough information to move the project to the next phase. The decision points, similar to Cooper's "stage-gates," are where predefined outcomes are achieved and measured against a set of criteria to determine if the project should move forward. These decision points also reflect the informal networks inside companies and project teams that often accomplish these activities outside of formal structures. The decision points are critical to the product development process as they protect the company from potential errors that may not have been caught had a formal decision point not been established. Note that for projects that are not developing platform technologies, the process moves from predevelopment financial analysis to the design and development of the product. In the next sections, the various activities in the NPD process will be discussed.

PHASE 1: OPPORTUNITY RECOGNITION OR DISCOVERY

Phase 1 activities are primarily conceptual in nature and require that the team be able to see the big picture—to match opportunities with company goals and present a view to the future. Chapter 2 pointed out that opportunity recognition can be stimulated in a variety of ways—a call from management for new ideas, a need expressed or implied by customers, or a serendipitous discovery. In his groundbreaking book *Innovation and Entrepreneurship*, Peter Drucker proposed that there are 12 sources of future opportunity.[24]

1. The unexpected success
2. The unexpected failure
3. The unexpected outside event

4. Inconsistent economic events

5. Inconsistency between reality and our assumptions about reality

6. Inconsistency between our perceptions and actual customer expectations

7. Inconsistency within the logic of a process

8. Process need

9. Industry and market structures

10. Demographics

11. Changes in perception

12. New knowledge

Each of these sources of opportunity holds clues about the future and should be examined against long-held assumptions.

It is important to distinguish between platform projects or basic research and new product projects. Platform projects build a new core technology from which many products can be developed. Particularly with a new company, platform projects are not often identified as such in the beginning, but are later identified as platform projects after experience with an initial product suggests that a certain technology could be reused in other products. Platform projects are different from research projects, the outcome of which is new knowledge and the advancement of the field, not necessarily an application of that knowledge.

PHASE 1: TECHNOLOGY SCREENING AND PLATFORM IDENTIFICATION

Determining whether or not to develop a particular project is a combination of technical and market considerations. Typically, the technical screening comes first. This is a relatively simple task if the independent inventor who recognized the opportunity is considering the project, as it is not a matter of choosing among a number of opportunities; in most cases, the inventor has been working on a particular path of research and that becomes the project. However, in an established company, there are many scientists and engineers, all looking for new projects. The company cannot put its limited resources toward every project that comes along, it must weigh the choices and decide on one or two to evaluate—whatever its budget will permit. The problem is that most screening decisions take place without any formal criteria and without the input of a multidisciplinary team.

All potential technologies should be subjected to careful scrutiny. The following sections discuss some of the areas that need to be addressed and the pertinent questions that should be answered when evaluating the potential success of a new technology.

THE ROLE OF THE CUSTOMER

The following questions address the role of the customer:

1. How will customers use the product?

2. Will customers see this product as a continuation of previous technology—an improvement—or as discontinuous, a product that will make previous technology obsolete?

3. Will installation be required? If so, what form will it take?

4. How much learning is involved on the part of the customer?

5. How will customers purchase the product?
6. Are there customers beyond the initial targeted customers? Who are they and why will they buy the product?
7. What will it take to create customer awareness and stimulate the desire to purchase?
8. What is the potential of this market assuming the success of the product?

THE ROLE OF EXISTING ARCHITECTURE AND COMPANY CAPABILITIES

The following questions address the role of existing architecture and company capabilities:

1. Does this technology extend a current S-curve or begin a new one?
2. If the company does not choose to go ahead with the development of this technology, will someone else develop it?
3. What technical requirements does this project have and does the company have those capabilities?
4. What are the biggest technical risks?
5. Is the product capable of being manufactured? Can the company do it or will it have to outsource that capability?
6. Does the company have unique capabilities that make it imperative that it be the one to develop this technology?
7. Do competitors have technology that better meets customer needs?
8. Does the company's technology reflect real customer needs? In what way?
9. Does the company have the capabilities to execute this project well?
10. If the company must invest in new capabilities, can it justify a return on investment sufficient to make it worthwhile?
11. Can a platform of products be built off this technology? Is it sustainable for the long term?

THE ROLE OF BUSINESS DEVELOPMENT

The following questions address the role of business development.

1. How can an effective job of market research be ensured?
2. How long will the research take and who will be responsible for it?
3. How will customer input be incorporated?
4. What will happen if the research points to an insufficient market or to product failure?
5. What are the intellectual property and regulatory issues associated with this project? Is the technology patentable?

IMPACT OF THE PROJECT

The following questions address the impact of the project:

1. How will this project affect the company? Employees? Facilities? Equipment? Shareholders?
2. What impact will this project have on our suppliers and other strategic partners?
3. Are new people with different skills required?
4. Will this project be perceived positively internally and externally?

Answering these questions will provide the organization with a tremendous learning experience and will help to minimize some of the risk associated with any new undertaking. Screening opportunities in this phase is the most liberal of all the decision points for two reasons. First, the entrepreneur does not have all the information required to determine that an opportunity is not feasible and it's important not to prematurely exclude an opportunity. Second, although it is not really possible to conduct a financial assessment at this point, little capital has been expended, therefore the financial risk of going further is relatively small.

Note that some of the questions concern platform development of incremental and disruptive innovations. Incremental innovation is based on an existing platform and presents fewer product development issues than disruptive innovation, which has no precedent. With incremental innovation, it is often possible to conduct concurrent engineering or parallel processing in this phase as well as in Phase 3. However, for disruptive innovations, the learning curve is steep, and it is often more advantageous to follow a more sequential process.[25]

In addition to the questions given earlier, a more structured approach to evaluating and selecting projects should be considered. Three common approaches are discussed in the following sections.

BENEFIT MEASUREMENT

Benefit measurement[26] is a useful evaluation tool in this phase because it does not require the financial data that is so often used to measure the value of a project. Instead, it employs strategic variables, such as the product's fit with corporate goals, market attractiveness, and competitive advantage. The principle disadvantage of this technique is that it deals with the project in a vacuum; in other words, it does not consider the project as part of a system where what happens in one area of the project affects every other area. A variety of approaches to benefit measurement are available. The Q-Sort method is a simple way to rank order a set of project ideas and is particularly well suited for this early screening phase. Each member of the team is given a deck of cards with one idea on each card. They are then asked to categorize the ideas based on some specified criterion such as feasible/not feasible or high to low in perceived value. After several rounds of ranking and debating the results, the team will usually arrive at a consensus of the best projects.

The checklist method is another way to screen several new product ideas. Start with a list of yes/no questions that predict a good project. Out of the total number of questions, determine how many yes answers it will take to qualify as a good project. Evaluate each idea against these criteria. Surprisingly, when the questions are well thought out and cover all the critical points for project success, this simple procedure has been shown to accurately predict a good project. A more elaborate version of the checklist involves using interval scales instead of yes or no responses. This provides a rating scheme where scores can be calculated to arrive at the best project.

ECONOMIC MODELS

Under traditional economic models, techniques such as break-even analysis, return on investment, and discounted cash flow can be used to evaluate the potential success of a product. These are the most popular methods for making decisions on projects, but unfortunately, the entrepreneur doesn't have reliable financial data with which to do these analyses until late in the process. Nevertheless, calculating the time to payback on the investment in a new project is a useful exercise that involves figuring the time from project start to market launch and the time from launch to recovery of all expenses related to the new product development. A more complex and rigorous approach is to compute a discounted cash flow (DCF), which takes future earnings from the project and discounts them to the present in recognition of the time value of money. (A dollar today is worth more than a dollar 5 years from now, thus projects with lengthy development periods are penalized.) Project expenses are subtracted from the DCF to arrive at the net present value (NPV). If NPV is positive, the project has overcome a significant challenge. In addition to calculating the DCF, it is wise to conduct a sensitivity analysis where certain assumptions are tested, for example, what if production costs exceed estimates by 20 percent? What if revenue initially is 80 percent of predicted revenue? DCF analysis is discussed in Chapter 8 where the valuation of technology is also addressed.

Another economic evaluation approach, options pricing theory, recognizes that management can kill the project at any decision point along the way. When project risks and costs are both high and the probability of technical success is low, the DCF/NPV method will substantially understate the value of the project; the options approach, called Economic Commercial Value (ECV),will yield a much higher valuation. ECV uses a decision tree and considers future earnings, the probabilities of commercial and technical success, and the costs of development and market launch.[27] Table 4-2 provides a comparison of values derived from DCF/NPV and ECV analyses. Note that because ECV gives the higher valuation, using this technique will permit more potential projects to pass this level of screening.

TABLE 4-2 Valuation with DCF/NPV and ECV	
Premises	
Discounted income stream to present value (DCF)	$45 M
Development costs	$8 M
Commercialization or market launch costs	$6 M
Probability of commercial success if product is launched	50%
Overall probability of successful development and commercialization	30%
Net Present Value ($45 − $8 − $6)	**$31 M**
NPV with Probabilities	
Probability of success × payoff minus the probability of failure × costs of failure (.30 × $31) − (.70 × $14)	($0.5)
ECV = {[(45 × .5) − 6] × .5} − 8	$0.25

Formula used: $ECV = [(PV{*}P_{cs} - C){*}P_{ts} - D]$. Where ECV = Expected commercial value of the project; P_{ts} = probability of technical success (yes/no = 50%); P_{cs} = probability of commercial success given technical success has occurred; D = development costs remaining in the project; C = commercialization costs; PV = present value of future earnings discounted to the present.
Source: Adapted from R. G. Cooper, S. J. Edgett, and E. J. Kleinschmidt, *Portfolio Management for New Products* (Reading, MA: Perseus Books, 1998).

PHASE 2: CONCEPT INVESTIGATION

In Phase 2, the business concept is assessed against the company's capabilities and the technology platform on which products will be based is further refined. This is accomplished through a preliminary investigation of the market to determine whether the product already exists in some form, whether there appears to be a market for the product, how much it might cost to produce the product, and what the timeline to market launch should be. If the technology has the potential to be patented, a preliminary patent search might reveal some prior art that could affect the ability to patent the invention. (For more information on patents, see Chapter 5). In addition, the research described in the feasibility analysis in Chapter 3 should be undertaken. Certainly, an in-depth evaluation of the industry would be valuable at this point, as would a preliminary examination of the market, customer needs, and potential demand. The feasibility analysis will be revised and updated throughout the NPD process as new information from the developers becomes available. Although there is a decision point at the end of this phase, the reality is that concept investigation is a continuing process that runs concurrently with subsequent phases and activities.

PHASE 2: PREDEVELOPMENT FINANCIAL ANALYSIS

Recall the discussion of Monsanto at the beginning of Chapter 3. Had Monsanto not considered a business model for their new technology for insect-resistant tomatoes while it was in development, they would have never found a way to make the product consumable (i.e., customers have to repurchase seeds every 2 years). By making the technology consumable, Monsanto created a renewable revenue stream. Most companies conduct a financial analysis of a project under development. When conducting such an analysis, it is important to input all of the functions that will be involved in the project—finance, marketing, sales, manufacturing, and so forth—in order to get the most accurate financial estimate possible. In this phase, a business model is built that essentially defines how the company intends to make money on this project and also looks at the return on the investment. This business model is, in effect, a financial justification for the project. A company does not want to spend $15 million in development costs for a $5 million market.

PHASE 2: DESIGN, DEVELOPMENT, PLATFORM TESTING

The platform is basically the core technology from which multiple products and applications can be developed. Frequently, it is in the form of a basic product so that the underlying technology can be demonstrated. In this phase, much time should be spent creating iterative prototypes that can be quickly tested by stakeholders and customers in a real-world environment. As this technology is the basis for all the subsequent applications, it must be well designed and thoroughly tested in order to reduce the possibility of errors in future applications based on the technology. As the prototypes become more refined, manufacturing needs can be determined based on the input of vendors, manufacturers (internal and external), and customers. Once this phase is complete, the project will have passed what Miller and Morris refer to as the "wall of invention."[28]

From this point on, the company will no longer conduct basic research on the core technology, but will begin the business portion of the commercialization process.

PHASE 3: DESIGN AND DEVELOPMENT OF THE PRODUCT FAMILY

Phase 3 activities require technical skills in product development and prototyping. This stage includes the actual development of products based on the platform, from design to functional prototype. Three aspects of this stage reflect changes that have taken place in the product development process: designing right the first time, reducing time to market, and the importance of rapid prototyping.

DESIGNING RIGHT

Designing right the first time has been the mantra of product developers for years as developers recognized that it was the quickest way to reduce the cost of developing a product. Typically, design represents about 8 percent of the product development budget, but it accounts for 80 percent of the final cost of the product. When errors in design are discovered well into the product development process—at the prototyping stage and beyond—it means costly redesign and reworking of the prototype. If this happens several times, it can lead to a final design whose costs will take much longer to recoup.

In some industries, such as electronics and chip manufacturing, the probability of getting the design right the first time is close to zero. Ironically, the rapid-cycle product development landscape dictates that if the product was actually designed right the first time, it probably took too long to do it. Nevertheless, one of the keys to designing right is getting customers involved early in the design process. Cadence Design Systems, Inc., a San Jose, California, developer of electronic design automation (EDA) software, believes in codevelopment with customers. When it began the design of its virtual component codesign (VCC) software tool, it brought in 12 customers, chip and systems companies that would be using the product. This customer team was active throughout the entire product development process, from specifications reviews to testing code. The VCC product was such a success that this method of development has become the norm for Cadence.[29]

REDUCING TIME TO MARKET

In biotech and other science-based industries, long development cycles are the norm, typically measured in years. Inefficiencies and delays abound in the industry, costing companies thousands of dollars a day in profits. Reducing time to market can have a significant impact on market success and bottom-line profit.

Table 4-3 shows the development process for pharmaceuticals and the challenges to getting through the process in a timely fashion. It has been estimated that a clinical cycle has 204 discrete activities that must be completed to produce the clinical report.[30] The secret to reducing product development time lies in better coordination of all the development activities. Some specific ways to reduce cycle time in any industry include:

- **Document the workflow associated with the product development process.** Every new product development process consists of a number of tasks, many of which are interrelated or sequential. Creating a flowchart of these activities will help uncover duplicated efforts, potential bottlenecks, and other problems that could slow the development process.

TABLE 4-3 The Pharmaceutical Development Process and Its Challenges	
The Process	*Loss of Time in the Process*
1. Discovery of a pharmacologically active chemical entity	• Determining the test protocol • Identifying a site for the investigation
2. Toxicology testing	• Preparing the test product • Testing the clinical product for stability
3. Formulation of the drug	• Filing an Investigative New Drug application with the FDA
4. Clinical development	• Creating and publishing case reports • Gathering data from the investigative site • Developing computer programs to record data • Analyzing the data • Summarizing the findings • Coordinating investigators and contractors

Source: Adapted from R. W. Boggs, Linda M. Bayuk, and David A. McCamey, "Speeding Development Cycles," *Industrial Research Institute* (September–October 1999): 33–38.

- **Set goals for completion times.** An interesting phenomenon occurs when team members work together over a long period of time. The time it takes to complete a task actually increases because inefficient routines become internalized. To break out of old routines and increase the speed at which tasks are completed requires setting new performance goals that everyone buys into. These goals should be just beyond the logical reach of the team, causing the team to look for innovative ways to increase their performance. Focusing on reducing cycle times has allowed Procter & Gamble to reduce its 80–week drug research cycle to just under 15 weeks.[31]
- **Make the team accountable for its performance.** All the planning and design will go for naught if no one is accountable for implementing the plan. It is important to find ways to measure improvement and provide incentives for achieving goals.

USING COMBINATORIAL RESEARCH TO REDUCE CYCLE TIME

In the biotech industry, where pharmaceutical companies depend on R&D to produce a continual stream of new drugs, combinatorial research methods allow researchers to produce and screen thousands of compounds at a time through an automated process. Combinatorial analysis results in better compounds because thousands of variables can be tested virtually instantaneously. It also achieves faster time to market, produces more market launches, and permits the use of premium pricing, all of which increase the value of R&D.[32]

Combinatorial research is useful in other industries as well. The research of John Busch provides an example in the area of materials R&D. In the plastics industry, a new concept will typically take 3 to 4 years of R&D, another 1 to 2 years of pilot testing to scale out the operation, and then a full-scale launch that will not return a profit for at least 5 years. Part of the reason for this extended time to launch is the time it takes to conduct all the experiments to arrive at the most effective material compound. Combinatorial methods can produce at least a 10-fold increase in R&D productivity, reducing the time in R&D from

4 years to 3 and the time in the pilot test from 3 years to 2. Bringing the new product to market earlier also permits a 15 percent price premium on the asking price. The financial consequences of all this are to increase the value of such a development program from $10 million to $37 million taking into account the up-front costs of the combinatorial facility.[33]

USING COMPUTER-AIDED SYSTEMS TO SPEED TIME TO MARKET

The biotech industry is not the only one that faces challenges to accelerating its idea-to-market process. Major manufacturers of consumer and business products must aggressively strive to more rapidly produce new generations of products that are superior in quality to their predecessors. Many of these companies, such as Ford Motor Co., Lexmark, and Boeing Corp., depend on design software to speed product development. Structural Dynamics Research Corp. (SDRC) is a software provider whose goal is to eliminate the prototype stage and perform all product testing on the computer. If all the changes to a product are made while it is still in the virtual stage, the company will save enormous amounts of money and time, not incremental amounts, but literally halve the amount of money and time required.

As any change in design is systemic, that is, it affects other parts of the product, there must be a way to track those changes and ensure that the appropriate modifications are made in all affected areas. SDRC's software creates a master model, which is a digital database containing all of the product information. Anyone can access the model and test modifications, but only one person may make permanent changes. This means that everyone knows what everyone else is doing and systemic effects are accounted for, making the whole process go more quickly.

IN-HOUSE PRODUCT TESTING

Most products enter a period of in-house testing after the development phase has ended. The fact that the testing occurs in-house rather than in the marketplace does not mean that customers are not involved. The customer is a vital part of the in-house testing process. Customers should have leeway to use the product in the environment in which it was intended to be used and given the opportunity to provide feedback in a way that is helpful to the development team. Based on the customer feedback, the development team may have to modify the product.

PHASE 4: LIMITED MARKET TRIAL

Phase 4 activities move the new product from the internal environment of the laboratory to the real world, shifting the development team's focus to the market and how the company will interface with it. Unfortunately, limited market trials are rarely conducted during NPD. When done correctly, however, selling the product in a limited geographic area or to a small group of customers permits the company to test all of the business activities related to selling the product—customer service, billing, marketing, etc. Limited market trials also allow the company to ensure that the product and the manufacturing system are reliable and that all product "bugs" have been resolved. It is much less costly in time and money, not to mention the company's reputation, to find and solve these glitches in a limited market setting than it would be during a national rollout. It is important to develop a means of recording and analyzing the results of the limited rollout so that changes can be made before a full market launch is undertaken.

PHASE 4: PRELAUNCH BUSINESS PLAN

With all the data gathered from the development process and the in-house and limited trial tests of the product and market, the information needed to take the feasibility analysis and turn it into a working business plan is in place. The business plan is the blueprint for the operations of the business, as well as a statement of the company's vision, mission, and goals. The business plan will also contain the marketing plan. The marketing plan will detail how the company will create customer awareness for the new product and build brand recognition and customer loyalty.

PHASE FOUR: MARKET LAUNCH TO FULL OPERATION

The final phase is the actual launch of the product into the market. This stage includes production ramp up and a significant marketing effort, as well as the transition to full operations in the areas of distribution, sales, and support. Chapter 12 discusses the unique issues related to marketing high technology products.

The scenario for product development just described assumes that a company has been formed to execute this process. In many cases, as with smaller companies or independent inventors, many activities will be outsourced to third parties with the capabilities the company might lack. Furthermore, the company will need to consider pre-development issues (during feasibility analysis) and determine whether it will license the technology, sell it, or produce it. These commercialization decisions are depicted in Figure 1-1 in Chapter 1.

METRICS FOR PRODUCT DEVELOPMENT SUCCESS

A number of models for measuring product development success have been proposed over the past decade: voice of the customer, time-based competition, and maximizing reuse, to name a few. Companies have rushed to adopt these measures as their ace-in-the-hole for success. However, mixed results from the use of these models indicate that no one model used alone can ensure product development success. Recent research has found that organizations that are rated high in R&D effectiveness by their R&D directors are significantly more capable than their less effective counterparts in nearly every area. Moreover, they are far better prepared for fast-cycle product development and are better at developing strategic alliances, understanding customer needs, and commercializing their technology.[34]

Some of the characteristics of these effective organizations include:

- Encouragement of experimentation and risk-taking
- Learn from mistakes and incorporate that knowledge into next-generation products[35]
- Tolerance of failure
- View R&D as a vital contributor to overall business performance
- Senior management gets involved early in the product development process
- Market pioneers with the ability to adapt to changing markets and technologies[36]

Firms that were rated as less effective face several challenges. These firms are unable to accelerate their product development process and achieve a faster time to market. They are also not able to overcome the "not invented here" syndrome, which keeps them from taking advantage of strategic alliances. They are not effective at comprehending the needs of the customer before the customer has even identified those needs. Finally, they do not have the mechanisms in place to convert basic technology to market applications.

MANAGING THE RISK OF R&D

Product development occurs at the intersection of engineering or science and market research in an effort to provide something that customers want. As most product development involves software, hardware, tooling, prototyping, or clinical trials, the risks associated with product development are derived from investment and project management.[37] Each of these will be considered separately.

INVESTMENT RISK

R&D is one of the most expensive aspects of technology commercialization. When a company plans to allocate a large portion of its budget to R&D or an outside investor considers investing in a company's R&D, the decision to do so is based on assumptions the company has made about the market and the customer. If those assumptions come from outdated or secondary sources of information, the risk of error increases. Some of the questions that any company or investor should ask prior to considering an R&D opportunity include the following:

- Is the purpose for undertaking R&D consistent with the firm's business goals?
- Are the data upon which decisions will be based current and from reliable sources?
- Has the company collected primary data from potential customers?
- How realistic are the initial estimates of volume, price, and cost?
- What is the opportunity cost of this project?
- Why should this project be done over others?

PROJECT MANAGEMENT RISK

It is the job of the project manager to achieve a balance among three resource constraints: time, funds, and product requirements.[38] Some of the questions appropriate to judging the risk associated with resource constraints include:

- What compromises, if any, must be made to deal with cost, quality, safety, and the environment?
- What risks are inherent in this product development process and how will they be handled?
- How will volume, price, and costs be forecast?
- How will the company respond to competitor actions?
- How will the company anticipate technological changes and estimate the product life?
- How will product obsolescence be identified and measured?
- What will be the impact of this technology on other products in the market?

- How will the firm determine if it has met customer needs?
- What are the plans for product launch to the market, including design and documentation release, supply chain management, and process documentation for manufacturing, installation, and service?[39]

UNIQUE RISKS ASSOCIATED WITH PHARMACEUTICAL DEVELOPMENT

The pharmaceutical industry faces additional risks that do not impede product developers in other industries. A survey conducted in 1999 by the editors of *Drug Discovery & Development* found that, in general, clinical trials and FDA approval were the biggest time delays experienced by researchers.[40] But when asked to identify specific tasks that slow the development process, researchers cited writing reports and proposals (50 percent of respondents), management duties (35 percent), and testing too many compounds that would never be used to make drugs (35 percent).[41]

The recent increase in the global consolidation of pharmaceutical companies has posed another risk to product development. It is well known that pharmaceutical development is a lengthy process that requires a long-term commitment on the part of the people involved. Recent mergers within the industry threaten that commitment and have sparked an environment that some have described as "short-term turf building." The long-term impact of this new environment could be devastating to the industry.

INCREASING R&D EFFECTIVENESS

Recognizing that R&D is an expensive proposition for any company, but also realizing that it is a vital component in a company's competitive strategy, it is important to find ways to increase the effectiveness of R&D in those areas that have a significant impact on overall business performance. Research has uncovered the key areas that organizations should focus on to increase the effectiveness of their R&D programs.

FORM INTERNAL LINKS BETWEEN TECHNICAL AND NONTECHNICAL GROUPS

In general, R&D and technology personnel are not involved in the nontechnology functions of the business.[42] The tendency in most organizations is to work apart rather collaboratively, to guard information rather than share it. Business owners and CEOs need to bridge the gap between the tech and nontech sides of the business by involving each in the other's activities. The most successful firms place business people on product development teams early in the product development process. Similarly, they place technology staff inside functional groups such as marketing and finance so that the technology people can understand the nature of business problems and business goals and find ways to facilitate them with technology. The case study on IDEO at the end of the chapter is a good example of a company that integrates all the various disciplines represented in its organization.

INVOLVE CUSTOMERS AND SUPPLIERS IN THE BUSINESS

The most effective firms have open and frequent communication between R&D, manufacturing, marketing, suppliers, and customers.[43] The earlier discussion of Cadence Design Systems demonstrates how having customers and suppliers on the product development team can create a very intense relationship. Cadence can recall 5-day, 10-hour-a-day meetings to work out disagreements, but the resulting success of their products proved to them that the additional effort to put customers and suppliers on the team was well worth it.

MEASURING R&D EFFECTIVENESS

John R. Hauser, Research Director at MIT's Center for Innovation in Product Development (CIPD), has developed a mathematical model for "weighing and balancing a range of strategic priorities in order to gain the greatest degree of leverage and maximize the bottom line."[44] The model looks at risk, costs, rewards, and profits and calculates a number that represents the relative, current value of a given strategic priority. In this way, a company knows when it has achieved tangible benefits from a particular strategic focus. A positive number indicates a competitive advantage for the firm, whereas a negative number points to an overemphasis on a particular strategy. Hauser likens the model to a thermostat that keeps a room at a continuous level of comfort despite outside conditions. Understanding the model means comprehending what a company measures versus what it rewards. Thus, if your priority is time to market, then the person in charge of production should be rewarded based on how quickly the new product goes from design to prototype to market readiness. This sounds like common sense, but it is not often practiced. Hauser proposes that a company is what it measures. A set of priorities and appropriate rewards must be established such that when the product developers act, they maximize their rewards, as well as the rewards to the company.

OUTSOURCING TECHNOLOGY INNOVATION

Today's fast-paced innovation and shorter windows of opportunity require resources that few companies have in-house. It is unlikely that one company, acting alone, can sustain a technological advantage for very long relying solely on its own creative talent and capital resources. More and more companies are seeking technology from external sources, from about 20 percent of their total technological base in the 1980s to over 50 percent in the 1990s.[45] Fortunately, several forces have come together to make the outsourcing of innovation possible and even more cost-effective than doing it in-house. First, economists report that the gross national product in the largest world economies is doubling every 14 to 16 years.[46] This environment has spawned hundreds of new, focused niches of sufficient size to invite innovation. Second, the number of technologists and knowledge specialists has increased at an exponential rate. The knowledge products they have developed have made it possible for small businesses to compete alongside large companies. The software-based communication, analytical, and modeling tools they have created have inspired new products and services in fields as diverse as biotech and food services. Finally, entrepreneurs are encouraged to develop and exploit new technologies because of the availability of investment capital and the lower capital requirements to start new technology ventures.

Today, technology companies reduce risk, lower costs, and decrease cycle times by factors of 60 to 90 percent through the strategic outsourcing of innovation.[47]

Moreover, outsourcing provides a firm with a network of expertise that it could not afford to hire in-house. Consider industries dependent on software, for example manufacturing, where 15 sequences of programming can be combined in 10 million ways, each producing the potential for a new product or process. It is difficult to conceive of a company that could fully exploit all of those possibilities using in-house resources.[48] Cisco Systems is an excellent example of a company that has successfully outsourced its innovation and manufacturing, allowing it to maintain its 100 percent growth rate in the 1990s. Today, Cisco has over 30 vendors and service providers that develop new technology for their routers and improve performance in their hosted applications.

Many businesses have achieved high returns on outsourcing business process innovation and focusing on their core business—product development. Some of the business processes that lend themselves to outsourcing include logistics, accounting, software systems for enterprise management, and energy systems. Third-party vendors can apply their expertise to specific areas of the business to reduce costs and produce more efficient operations.[49] Many firms have discovered innovative marketing solutions by outsourcing to firms that specialize in customer relations. For example, HP Medical Products develops relationships with hospitals such that it is able to plant observers inside the hospital to find and solve problems that hospital personnel, such as trauma care physicians, do not see while they are performing their duties.[50]

MAKING OUTSOURCING WORK

Prior to the Internet, doing product development in-house was the norm, and certainly an important success factor in rapid product development. When people work next to each other on a daily basis, communication and information transfer are rich and frequent. This informal association helps to build a company culture, which is an important competitive advantage. However, doing product development in-house has some weighty disadvantages that can actually slow the product development process. These disadvantages include the following:

- Daily familiarity often distorts priorities and goals.
- Internal groups often want to protect their turf, and therefore resist going outside the company for product development skills.
- Informal discussions are often not formalized in writing, and are consequently forgotten or not implemented.
- With the constant flow of ideas, the tendency to continually add new features and improvements may delay product development milestones.
- Face-to-face meetings are cancelled more often than electronic meetings.

Today, product development teams have the option of being "cowired," that is, connected electronically. Cowiring offers a number of advantages:

- It is easier to meet more frequently electronically, and more frequent communication is facilitated.
- Virtual collaboration software lets a team automatically record and track meetings. Notes from the meetings are archived and made available to any team member.
- An entrepreneur can take advantage of expertise in any part of the world and communicate not only in real time, but also in non-real-time threaded discussions.

Using a cowired approach to communication may actually shorten time to market and time-to-volume manufacturing. A combination of face-to-face meetings and electronic communication is probably most effective for product development. Team-building meetings are best held face-to-face or at least through videoconferencing. Other types of communication, such as technical meetings, can occur via the Internet or e-mail. For example, Hewlett Packard's DeskJet printers are developed by cowired teams located on three continents. HP Washington is the lead team, but the printers are simultaneously produced in Singapore, Barcelona, and San Diego. In addition, more than 150 suppliers and partners are also involved in product development. HP chose the cowired approach as designers were frequently traveling abroad because language and cultural differences made it difficult to communicate by phone. They now use an application called OneSpace, which lets all the teams see the same three-dimensional mechanical model at the same time.

CREATING SUCCESSFUL PARTNERSHIPS

The possibilities for partnering for innovation are endless, and the examples of successful partnerships are many, but to achieve that positive result, a company must find partners who, first and foremost, share the same goals and values, and second, understand that although the partnership is interdependent in its purpose, the companies involved in the partnership remain independent in their ability to accomplish their own specific goals.[51] MCI places about 20 times more of its technical people inside its partners' firms than in its own offices. This strategy provides its partners with a constant interface to the company and stimulates its partner software and service innovators to develop new products that work with the MCI system.[52] This strategy facilitates feedback and quick failures that are essential in a fast-paced innovation process. MCI also shares gains from improved performance with its partners, thus encouraging them to seek increased levels of innovation.

Research has found that companies with successful partnerships rely on three points of contact.[53] The first point is top-level managers who screen opportunities, develop goals, and align company strategy with the new opportunities. The second point of contact involves identifying champions from each of the partners' firms whose careers depend on the success of the partnership. The third contact point consists of the interactions among the various people in the partner firms who will actually carry out the goals of the partnership. One of the keys to successful communication at all three contact points is a common communication software platform.

BENEFITING FROM SUCCESSFUL PARTNERSHIPS

Companies that have effectively outsourced innovation report a variety of benefits to their organizations, including the following:

- The ability to attract the best talent with expertise in very specific areas
- The ability to get to market faster and to be more flexible in the process
- The ability to lower risk of adoption by involving customers from the onset of innovation
- The ability to spread the risk of new product development among several partners
- The ability to share resources and reduce the cost to any one partner

In today's fast-paced world of product development, superior partners must be developed early on and those relationships sustained so that when a company needs help in a particular area, it has someone it can call.

❖ SUMMARY

The product development environment has been changing rapidly. Today, companies are focusing on growth through R&D innovations because they see that intangible assets such as patents and trademarks now form the basis for market capitalization. Companies are allocating more R&D time and capital to new business projects and business models that produce concrete results. Companies are also increasing their use of strategic alliances, as well as acquiring the technology they need through in-licensing and acquisitions. Despite these changes, most new products fail, primarily because the companies that launch them do not do the necessary market research to learn what customers want. Successful companies have customers who perceive a unique and superior product. In addition, successful companies have a strong market orientation and execute their business plans well.

The product development process is nonlinear and iterative. It generally begins with a discovery or recognition of an opportunity. This is followed by a period of technology screening and platform identification to determine which project the company intends to undertake. Once the technology is determined, technical and business activities begin to take place simultaneously. As the business team develops a business concept and investigates the market through feasibility analysis, the technology team is designing, developing, and testing the technology platform and then the product family. Each group is providing the other with feedback and new information. Then comes a period of in-house and limited market testing. If all goes well, preparations for product launch begin with the development of a business plan and marketing strategy. Throughout the product development process, the team employs a number of metrics for measuring product development progress, technical feasibility, and customer feedback. Research has found that forming internal links between technical and nontechnical groups and involving customers and suppliers in the business can enhance the effectiveness of the R&D process. Furthermore, outsourcing aspects of the R&D process and working with strategic partners can make the process more cost-effective.

❖ DISCUSSION QUESTIONS

1. As a product developer, what are the three most important things that should be remembered when formulating a product development strategy?
2. In what ways can a company increase its chances of designing right the first time?
3. Every R&D project carries with it some degree of risk. Suppose an entrepreneur is proposing to develop a wearable PDA that is unobtrusive and responds to voice commands. What are some of the risks in the development of this product? How should they be managed?
4. What are the major advantages and disadvantages of outsourcing innovation?

❖ RESOURCES

Christensen, Clayton. *The Innovator's Dilemma.* Boston: Harvard Business School Press, 1997.

Cooper, Robert G. *Winning at New Products*, 3d ed. Cambridge, MA: Perseus Publishing, 2001.

Katz, Ralph. *The Human Side of Managing Technological Innovation: A Collection of Readings.* New York: Oxford University Press, 1997.

Miller, William L., and Langdon Morris. *Fourth Generation R&D.* New York: John Wiley & Sons, 1999.

Tushman, Michael L., and Charles A. O'Reilly, III. *Winning Through Innovation: A Practical Guide to Leading Organizational Change and Renewal.* Boston: Harvard Business School Press, 1997.

Wheelwright, Steven C., and Kim B. Clark. *Revolutionizing Product Development: Quantum Leaps to Speed, Efficiency, and Quality.* New York: The Free Press, 1993.

❖ INTERNET RESOURCES

The National Technology Transfer Center
www.nttc.edu
This organization helps companies work with federal laboratories to turn their work into technology that businesses can use and sell

Product Development & Management Association
www.pdma.org/
A nonprofit organization dedicated to improving the effectiveness of product development practices

SBA Office of Technology (SBIR)
www.sbaonline.sba.gov/sbir
This site provides information on SBIR technology grants available to inventors

Visions Magazine
www.pdma.org/visions/
The online magazine from the Product Development & Management Association

Worldwide Rapid Prototyping Service Bureau
home.att.net/~castleisland/sb_ci.htm
An up-to-date directory of over 525 locations that provide rapid prototyping capabilities

IDEO: WHERE INNOVATION IS THE CULTURE

If you want to produce over 90 new products a year, try turning your company into a living laboratory. At least that is the approach that IDEO founder David M. Kelley takes. IDEO, based in Palo Alto, California, is one of the most important design companies in the world, with offices in San Francisco, London, and Tokyo. Some of the more familiar products to come out of the company include the PalmV PDA, Crest's "Neat Squeeze" toothpaste container, and Levolor blinds.

Because the world in which Kelley and his employees work is stressful and driven by unreasonable deadlines, Kelley believes that the environment must be flexible and freewheeling. Employees work in project teams for weeks or months at a time and then switch to another project team with different members. The IDEO culture also recognizes differences in tastes and preferences. For example, the younger employees love to play loud music while they work, so Kelley designated a special area for them called the Spunk Space where they will not disturb their more conservative coworkers. It is a noncompetitive environment where the customer is the boss. Their 26–person team of human-factors experts, industrial designers, electronic engineers, interaction designers, mechanical engineers, software programmers, and manufacturing engineers work together to produce smart products. Everyone is expected to be up-to-date in their area of specialty, but employees are also encouraged to explore outside of their disciplines.

IDEO's brainstorming sessions follow five guidelines: (1) stay focused on the topic, (2) encourage wild ideas, (3) defer judgment, (4) build on the ideas of others, and (5) only allow one conversation at a time. Their motto is "fail often to succeed sooner." Consequently,

IDEO constantly builds and tests prototypes, identifying failure points early in the product development cycle. How a company deals with failure is often a sign of how innovative it is. In fact, the biggest reason that more companies do not have a product development culture like IDEO is their fear and disdain of failure. Once they have given a new product idea the go-ahead, everyone is expected to believe in the product and work to make it happen. The problem with this approach is that no one is identifying failure points along the way, so when problems are finally discovered at the end, it is a far more costly process to redesign and rework the product. At IDEO, failure points are identified early and often so that teams can quickly learn from them and move on. IDEO teams also design and test multiple components of a product simultaneously. For example, while they are working on the electrical components of a new product, they will also be testing its waterproof case or testing its circuit board's resistance to heat. For products that require Federal Communications Commission (FCC) certification, testing is done early in the process instead of waiting until the end.

Satisfying customers' needs is the prime directive at IDEO. For example, one health care network was looking for an appliance that would let medical caseworkers monitor elderly patients at home without having to physically visit them each day. IDEO sent its human-factors experts into patients' homes to learn what the important needs were. By doing this, they found out everything they needed to know to give users what they needed, from how the user opens the monitor box to the size of the buttons the user must push to make it work.

AT IDEO, no innovation ever disappears. All ideas, whether they have been used in a product or not, go into a virtual museum called the Tech Box, also called the toy box, which is really a metal filing cabinet with five drawers, each housing a different category of innovation, for example, thermo and optical innovations, manufacturing processes, and amazing materials. In each drawer are a variety of strange gadgets, each one prototyping some innovation. Anyone can take one of these to test it for use on a product that is being developed. The Tech Box has been such a success in inspiring ideas that IDEO has replicated it in 10 other offices, including customer–partner Steelcase, a manufacturer of office furniture. The physical Tech Box is only part of the picture. IDEO has also developed an intranet that links all of its offices, provides everyone with data on each of the 150 materials in the filing cabinets, and connects the user with the person who placed the gadget in the Tech Box.

So successful has IDEO's culture become that major corporations such as Samsung and Steelcase are coming to Kelley to learn how to make their own organizations more creative. Steelcase has been a client of IDEO since 1987, but in 1996 that relationship became much more strategic to Steelcase when it acquired an equity stake in IDEO. The two companies have found strong synergies in the relationship. For Steelcase, the benefit was obvious: to work with the best in R&D to develop state-of-the-art office environments. For IDEO, the benefit came in what Steelcase taught it about the nature of work environments. Steelcase was one of the first to identify the move from the "I" office environment to the "we" environment where space for teamwork dominates the overall space.

IDEO seems to have found the solution to sustaining innovation in a corporate environment by redefining the way R&D looks. Rather than relying on the rigid structure and process orientation of most R&D companies, it has chosen to create an environment where creativity and innovation are natural by-products of the company culture. ∎

Sources: Bill Roberts, "Innovation Quotient," *Electronic Business* (December 2000): *www.e-insite.net/eb mag/.* John Teresko, "R&D Serves Dual Purpose," *Industry Week* (August 21, 2000): *www.industryweek. com/.* Tia O'Brien, "Encourage Wild Ideas," *Fast Company* 2 (April 1996): 83; Paul E. Teague, "A Toy Box for Ideas," *Design News* (January 17, 2000): *www.manufacturing.net/dn/.* Sarah L. Roberts-Witt, "Intranet Marries the Tactile and the Technological," *Internet World* (December 7, 1998): *www.epinions.com/mags Internet_World_1.*

❖ NOTES

1. "R&D Trends Forecast for 2001," *Industrial Research Institute* (November 2000).
2. Kevin G. Rivette and David Kline, *Rembrandts in the Attic.* (Boston: Harvard Business School Press, 2000).
3. Willy Manfroy, "Licensing with Strategic Intent," *Les Nouvelles* (March 2000): 44–47.
4. J. Wind and V. Mahajan, "Issues and Opportunities in New Product Development: An Introduction to the Special Issue," *Journal of Marketing Research* 34 (1997): 1–12.
5. A. Griffith, "Drivers of NPD Success" in *The 1997 PDMA Report* (Chicago: Product Development & Management Association, 1997).
6. D.S. Hopkins, *New Product Winners and Losers,* Conference Board Report #773 (1980); and D.S. Hopkins and E.L. Bailey,

"New Product Pressures," *Conference Board Record* 8 (1971): 16–24.
7. R. G. Cooper, "The Dimensions of Industrial New Product Success and Failure," *Journal of Marketing* 43 (Summer 1979): 93–103.
8. M. S. Maidique and B. J. Zirger, "A Study of Success and Failure in Product Innovation: The Case of the U.S. Electronics Industry," *IEEE Transactions in Engineering Management* 31 (November 1984): 192–203.
9. Ibid., 192–203.
10. Ibid.
11. E. Wilson, *Product Development Process, Product Definition Guide,* Release 1.0, internal Hewlett-Packard document (Palo Alto, CA, 1991).
12. R. G. Cooper, "New Products: What Separates the Winners from the Losers?" In

Milton D. Rosenau, Jr., ed., *PDMA Handbook for New Product Development*, (New York: John Wiley & Sons, 1996).

13. S. L. Brown and K. M. Eisenhardt, "Product Development: Past Research, Present Findings, and Future Directions," *Academy of Management Review* 20 (1995): 343–378.

14. M. Iansiti and K. Clark, "Integration and Dynamic Capability: Evidence from Product Development in Automobiles and Mainframe Computers," *Industrial and Corporate Change* 3 (1994): 557–605.

15. R. Amit and P. Schoemaker, "Strategic Assets and Organizational Rent," *Strategic Management Journal* 14 (1993): 33–46.

16. Iansiti and Clark, "Integration and Dynamic Capability: Evidence from Product Development in Automobiles and Mainframe Computers," 557–605.

17. A. Camuffo and G. Volpato, "Dynamic Capabilities and Manufacturing Automation: Organizational Learning in the Italian Manufacturing Automobile Industry," *Industrial and Corporate Change* 5 (1996): 813–838; R. H. Hayes, G. Pisano, and D. M. Upton, *Strategic Operations: Competing Through Capabilities* (Cambridge, MA: Harvard Business School Press, 1996).

18. C. E. Helfat, "Know-How, Asset Complementarity, and Dynamic Capability Accumulation: The Case of R&D," *Strategic Management Journal* 18 (1997): 339–360.

19. K. T. Ulrich and S. D. Eppinger, *Product Design and Development* (New York: McGraw-Hill, 1995).

20. S. D. Hunt and R. M. Morgan, "The Comparative Advantage Theory of Competition," *Journal of Marketing* 59 (1995): 1–15.

21. Clayton M. Christensen,, "Exploring the Limits of the Technology S-Curve. Part I: Component Technologies," *Production and Operations Management* 1, no. 4 (Fall 1992): 340.

22. R. G. Cooper, "The New Product Process: A Decision Guide for Managers," *Journal of Marketing Management* 3, no. 3 (1988): 238–255; R.G, Cooper "Third-Generation New Product Processes," *Journal of Product Innovation Management* 11 (1994): 3–14.

23. William L. Miller and Langdon Morris, *Fourth Generation R&D* (New York: John Wiley & Sons, 1999).

24. Peter Drucker, *Innovation and Entrepreneurship* (New York: HarperBusiness, 1985).

25. Miller and Morris, *Fourth Generation R&D*, 300.

26. M. R. Baker, "R&D Project Selection Models: An Assessment," *IEEE Transactions on Engineering Management* (November 1974): 165–171.

27. R.G. Cooper, *Winning at New Products* (Cambridge, MA: Perseus Publishing, 2001): 228–229.

28. W.L. Miller and L. Morris, Fourth Generation R&D, New York: John Wiley & Sons, 1999, 306.

29. Bill Roberts, "Innovation Quotient," *Electronic Business*, (December. 2000).

30. R.W. Boggs, Linda M. Bayuk, and David A. McCamey. "Speeding Development Cycles," *Industrial Research Institute*, (September–October, 1999), 33–38.

31. Ibid., 38.

32. John V. Busch, "Combinatorial Analysis—How Much Is It Worth?" *Research-Technology Management* 44, no. 2 (March–April 2001): 38–45.

33. Ibid.

34. A. K. Gupta, D. Wilemon, and K. Atuahene-Gima, "Excelling in R&D," *Research-Technology Management* (May–June 2000) *www.iriinc.org/webiri/index.ctm*.

35. A. K. Gupta and D. Wilemon, "Changing Patterns in Industrial R&D Management," *Journal of Product Innovation Management* 13, no. 6 (1996): 497–511.

36. Gerard Tells and Peter Golder, "First to Market, First to Fail? Real Causes of Enduring Market Leadership," *Sloan Management Review* 37, no. 2 (1996).

37. Barry S. Leithhead, "Product Development Risks," *Internal Auditor* (October 2000): 59–61.

38. Ibid.

39. Ibid.

40. Tim Studt, "Drug Development Bottlenecks Not Cured by Technology Alone," *R&D Magazine* (January 1999): 40.

41. Ibid.

42. Gupta and Wilemon, "Changing Patterns in Industrial R&D Management," 497–511.

43. Gupta, Wilemon, and Atuahene-Gima, "Excelling in R&D," *Research-Technology Management* (May–June 2000).

44. "How Do We Know We're Measuring the Right Things?" *Product Development Best Practices Report.* (The Management Roundtable, 2001).

45. Gene Slowinski, Susan A. Stanton, John C. Tao, Wayne Miller, and Donald P. McConnell, "Acquiring External Technology," *Research-Technology Management* 43, no. 5 (September–October 2000): 29–35.

46. United Nations, Statistical Yearbook (New York: 1998), *www.un.org/Depts/unsd/sd_databases.htm.*

47. James Brian Quinn, "Outsourcing Innovation: The New Engine of Growth," *Sloan Management Review* (Summer 2000) *www.findarticles.com.*

48. James Brian Quinn, "Strategic Outsourcing: Leveraging Knowledge Capabilities," *Sloan Management Review* 40 (Summer 1999): 9–21.

49. Ibid.

50. W. Grimson, R. Kikinis, and F. Jolesz, "Image Guided Surgery," *Scientific American* 280 (June 1999): 62–69.

51. K. Zien and S. Buckler, "From Experience: Dreams to Market: Creating a Culture of Innovation," *Journal of Product Innovation Management* 14 (July 1997): 274–287.

52. Rivette and Klein, *Rembrandts in the Attic*, Boston, MA: Harvard Business School Press, 2000.

53. Ibid.

THE CONCEPT OF INTELLECTUAL PROPERTY

OVERVIEW

This chapter will examine

- ❖ the theory of intellectual property
- ❖ trade secrets
- ❖ copyrights
- ❖ trademarks
- ❖ patents

INTRODUCTION

Never before has the concept of intellectual property captured the imagination and interest of companies, large and small, with such intensity as it does today. Intellectual property refers to that group of legal rights associated with patents, trademarks, and copyrights. These rights give their holder the right to exclude others from making, selling, or distributing the protected asset. Today, companies are scrambling to secure as much intellectual property as possible to gain a competitive advantage and to create multiple revenue streams from licensing those rights to others. Large companies with huge patent portfolios are mining those portfolios for any intellectual property that might allow them to sue their competitors for patent infringement.

Autodesk, the world's fourth-largest software developer, is a good example of these new strategies of intellectual property management. Autodesk has been under attack from large systems companies demanding royalties, and it has found that it must acquire a significant patent portfolio just to protect itself. Though it will take years to build, a large patent portfolio will give Autodesk the ability to cross-license and save on huge royalty payments. For Autodesk, acquiring patents is a necessary defensive tactic.[1] Intellectual property strategies like these will be discussed in Chapter 7.

Determining the type of intellectual property protection needed and able to be acquired is not always straightforward. For example, utility patents protect functional works such as machines and devices, whereas copyrights protect expressive works such as books and musical compositions. However, software is both functional (driving a process or change) and expressive (a literary work). Even the courts have had difficulty in deciding which legal form to apply. Software can always be copyrighted but it must meet the strict requirements of patentability to achieve that level of protection. In addition, intellectual property rights are often confused with material property rights. Intellectual property rights are actually temporary rights to exploit an invention or idea; they do not convey ownership in the material property sense. This distinction is most clearly understood in the biotechnology arena. A scientist may acquire a patent for a genetic process that produces a new life-form, but that scientist does not own the right to the life-form itself.[2] This chapter covers the fundamentals of intellectual property rights, how to determine which ones can be acquired under what circumstances, and how to acquire them.

THE THEORY BEHIND INTELLECTUAL PROPERTY PROTECTIONS

The rationale behind intellectual property protection and the resulting creation of a limited monopoly for the inventor originates from several economic theories.[3] In general, these theories speak to the activities that intellectual property protection encourages, which include incentives to invent, disclose, and commercialize.[4]

INCENTIVES TO INVENT

The incentive-to-invent theory posits that without the temporary monopoly created by intellectual property protections, an invention is easily stolen and produced, often at a lower price, before the original inventor can recoup the costs of research and development. In this situation, the commercial advantage logically goes to the second mover who does not have to incur the high cost of product development and, therefore, can introduce the product at a lower cost, effectively putting the original inventor out of business. With patent protection, however, inventors have an incentive to invest money and time in new inventions with the realization that they will have a "quiet" period in which to sell the product at a high enough price to recoup their R&D costs before competitors enter the market. Although research conducted in the 1970s and 1980s found that patents were not an incentive to innovate, more recent research has suggested that intellectual property rights play a significant role in the innovation process, particularly in volatile industries such as the pharmaceutical, software, and telecommunications industries.[5]

INCENTIVES TO DISCLOSE

With formal and legal intellectual property protections, inventors are able to disclose their inventions publicly without fear of losing legal rights or risking loss of value. Furthermore, disclosure adds to the knowledge base in the field, preventing the duplication of research efforts. Without legal protections, inventors would likely keep their inventions as trade secrets in order to maintain their value. Unfortunately, trade secrets are difficult to sell or license, because once the secret is disclosed, it loses its proprietary value.

INCENTIVES TO COMMERCIALIZE

In addition to the economic risk of R&D, there are commercial risks for strategic partners, such as manufacturers who must incur the expenses of setting up for manufacture, seeking resources, and producing the product. Manufacturers benefit from the inventor's temporary monopoly. They enjoy a quiet period to produce and distribute the product at a fair price, given their higher initial costs of manufacture, before they must find a way to lower costs to compete with other manufacturers who have entered the market.

THE DISINCENTIVES OF INTELLECTUAL PROPERTY

There are four arguments that counter the idea that intellectual protections provide an incentive to invent. The first argument claims that intellectual property protections actually hurt consumers and end users because consumers must pay higher prices for patented products than for nonpatented products during the time that the inventor is enjoying a monopoly. The second argument claims that if the patent holder does not permit other companies to develop improvements and derivative innovations off the original patent, the patent will never realize its full profit potential. In fact, it is rare that any single inventor has the foresight to recognize all the potential applications and derivatives of his or her invention. By preventing others from accessing the invention's technology, the inventor is really making it more difficult for the technology to achieve mass-market acceptance quickly enough to begin to make money from it. The third argument is that the original inventor often does not reap the biggest financial rewards from the commercialization of the intellectual property. More often, the second mover, who did not have to incur the onerous costs of R&D, achieves profitability much more quickly. The final argument is that patents affect the direction of research by creating incentives for the development of substitutes for the original invention rather than complementary ones. One study found that 60 percent of patented innovations were imitated within 4 years of their patents and for two-thirds the original innovation's cost.[6] Despite these arguments against intellectual protections, the general consensus is that their benefits to society outweigh any disadvantages. Moreover, most of the disadvantages or disincentives can be overcome through a solid intellectual property strategy.

In the following sections, the various forms of intellectual property are addressed. Figure 5-1 depicts the intellectual property pyramid. Trade secrets are the base from

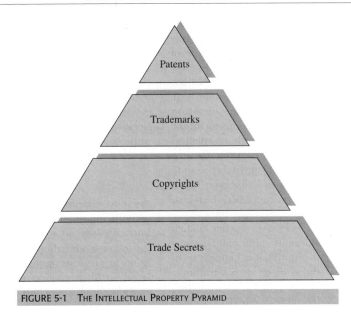

FIGURE 5-1 THE INTELLECTUAL PROPERTY PYRAMID

which all other intellectual property protections derive. As one moves up the pyramid, the strength of the intellectual property protection increases, with patents providing the strongest form of protection.

TRADE SECRETS

Trade secret law is the foundation upon which all intellectual property law rests. The Uniform Trade Secrets Act defines trade secrets as

> . . . information including a formula, pattern, compilation, program, device, method, technique or process that derives independent economic value, actual or potential, from not being generally known to, and not being readily ascertainable by proper means by, other persons . . .

Trade secrets include:

- Novel and useful inventions for which the company chooses not to seek patent protection
- Computer source code
- Manufacturing processes
- Designs and drawings
- Technical know-how
- Business information such as customer lists, vendors, supply sources, marketing plans, and in-house talent

Consider the case of Hewlett-Packard, a company that regularly maintains many inventions for internal use only. In general, these inventions enhance Hewlett-

Packard's manufacturing processes, giving them a competitive advantage in production capability. Because patents are disclosed to the public once they are issued, patenting these inventions would effectively give competitors access to Hewlett-Packard's technology. Competitors could adopt and modify the Hewlett-Packard technology for use in their manufacturing processes and technically not violate Hewlett-Packard's patents if they held it as a trade secret. Protecting the inventions as trade secrets rather than patenting them prevents this from happening.

Any information that is commonly known or in common use or any information that is easily reproduced from known data cannot be treated as a trade secret. Thus, standard industry manufacturing processes cannot be protected as trade secrets. Furthermore, a skill developed by an employee during the course of employment can not be considered as a trade secret.[7]

Trade secrets convey some rights to their holders. The holder of a trade secret can prevent specific groups of people from copying, using, and benefiting from the trade secret or disclosing it without permission.[8] These specific groups include:

- Anyone bound by a duty of confidentiality, such as employees
- Anyone who acquires a trade secret through illegal means, such as theft
- Anyone who obtains a trade secret from someone who did not have permission to reveal it
- Anyone who learns about a trade secret accidentally if it is reasonable to assume that person should have known it was a trade secret
- Anyone who has signed a nondisclosure or confidentiality agreement

One caveat: Anyone who uncovers a trade secret independently without using illegal means (such as reverse engineering a competitor's product) is not barred from using the information. For example, if a competitor has developed a new formula for cleaning oil from concrete and the company purchases the product and uncovers its composition in its own lab, the company can legally use this information to develop its own version of the formula and market it.

Unlike patents and trademarks, trade secrets are not public, they do not need to be registered with any governmental agency, and they are easy to obtain. The only requirement for a trade secret is that there must be documentation that establishes the existence of the protected information and proves that the company produced it. Consequently, although trade secrets are easy to obtain, they are difficult to value. The true ownership and value of trade secrets can often only be determined through litigation.[9] This becomes important when a company is considering its intellectual property strategy, a topic that will be discussed in Chapter 7. Nondisclosure agreements are a common way to protect trade secrets, and those agreements are discussed in the next section.

NONDISCLOSURE AGREEMENTS

The nondisclosure agreement, or NDA, has become an important document in the information age. Today, if an idea is shared without proof that it was shared in confidence, the trade secret holder may have inadvertently given up trade secret rights. Not only that, but if the idea involved a potentially patentable invention, the disclosure may have started the clock on the 1-year requirement for filing a patent application after publication; in addition rights to file for foreign patents may have been lost, An NDA is a contract between the inventor and another party that prohibits that party from disclosing information provided in confidence. Although standard NDA forms are available, it is important to note that no one NDA fits all situations. To be legally binding, an NDA must contain the following:

- It must provide for consideration, which is what is exchanged for the promise to do something or refrain from doing something. For example, if the entrepreneur shows the business plan to a potential manufacturer, the entrepreneur is giving up proprietary information and the manufacturer is giving up the right to disclose or use that confidential information in exchange for the potential to do business with the entrepreneur.
- It must define what is confidential by specifying what is being protected so that the other party cannot claim they did not know what was confidential.
- It must identify how the other party will be using the information, for example, to secure a manufacturer, seek start-up capital, or find a new member of the management team.
- It must designate what is to be done with any materials exchanged, for example, destroying documents or returning them to the owner.

An interesting area of trade secret law is what happens to technical knowledge when an IT worker moves to a new job. Amazon.com hired 10 former IT employees of Wal-Mart Stores, Inc., and Wal-Mart sued, alleging that the employees had stolen trade secrets about its valuable data warehousing technology. The parties eventually settled the case out of court because Wal-Mart's case was weak. Apparently, Wal-Mart had failed to explain to its workers what it considered to be trade secret information.[10] In such cases, the courts tend to side with the worker if the employer cannot prove that the worker misused the trade secret.

Anyone with whom confidential information is shared should sign an NDA, but the NDA is only as good as the people who sign it. The NDA gives the right to defend trade secrets in a court of law, and it serves as documentation of the existence of the trade secrets.

COPYRIGHTS

Copyrights protect the original works of authors, composers, screenwriters, computer programmers, and the developers of other creative works. Contrary to common belief, copyrights do not protect ideas, but rather the form in which they appear. For example, an author can write about business communications, but that author cannot copyright the *idea* of business communications. This is why several authors can write about the same topic without violating a copyright.

A copyright gives the holder the right to exclude others from reproducing the work, preparing derivative works, distributing copies of the work, and displaying the work in public. Copyrights last for the life of the holder plus 70 years, after which they go into public domain; however, under the Sonny Bono Copyright Extension Act of 1998, no expired copyrights will enter the public domain until 2019. Works for hire and works published anonymously now have copyrights of 95 years. To secure copyright protection and give the author the ability to sue an infringer, the author must put the work in a tangible form, one that can be seen or heard. Although it is not required by law, a copyright notice should also be affixed so that someone who violates the copyright cannot claim that they did not have notice. The notice should appear as follows:

© Copyright 2002 by Kathleen Allen

To obtain the full protection of the law, the copyright should be registered at the Copyright Office of the Library of Congress in Washington, D.C. A complete copy of an unpublished work or two complete copies of a published work must also be submitted.

The courts have proclaimed, "The purpose of the copyright law is to create the most efficient and productive balance between protection (incentive) and dissemination of information (disclosure), to promote learning, culture, and development."[11] Certainly, copyright law and the whole issue of dissemination of information are undergoing their most strenuous test in the information economy. The Digital Millennium Copyright Act is one outcome of the new economy.

THE DIGITAL MILLENNIUM COPYRIGHT ACT

One of the biggest challenges associated with delivering products and information over the Internet is the ease with which others can infringe on another's rights. For example, recording companies and music distributors continually fight against the disruption of their business models by Internet users who digitize, copy, and distribute copyrighted music over the Internet. The Digital Millennium Copyright Act (DCMA) was signed into law in 1998 in response to the threat of the Internet to the works of authors and artists. This law makes it illegal to "manufacture, import, distribute, or provide products or services that are primarily designed or produced for the purpose of circumventing technological measures, such as encryption, scrambling, or other methods, used by copyright owners to protect their works."[12] The law also contains a safe harbor clause to protect Internet service providers from damages if they unknowingly infringe on someone's rights by transmitting or storing infringing material or by linking users to sites containing infringing material. The most famous case to be affected by the new law was the one involving Napster, the Internet company that developed a technology to allow users to share and download music for free using its software program, which temporarily turned the user's computer into a server for the purpose of swapping MP3 files. Napster did not qualify as an Internet service provider, and although it did not host or share copyrighted material directly, virtually all of the content available at the Napster site (*www.napster.com*) was copyrighted material. As of July 2001, Napster was enjoined against distributing copyrighted music and was in the process of developing a new copyright friendly service.[13]

FAIR USE

Fair use is a concept that applies limits to copyright protections in that it permits someone to use another's works without permission. For example, using someone's words for criticism, education, or scholarship is acceptable as long as the original author or artist is credited. However, using another's work to endorse a commercial product is not acceptable. The Internet has created some challenges to the concept of fair use. For example, if a message is posted to a public e-mail list, a receiver can, by implication, forward or archive that message without obtaining permission from its original author as long as the original meaning of the message is not changed.

TRADEMARKS

An invention that cannot be patented can be marked with a brand or trademark that indicates that the inventor originated the idea. A trademark is a symbol, logo, word, sound, color, design, or other device that is used to identify a business or a product. Essentially, it is a *brand*. The term *trademark* is regularly used to refer to both trademarks and service marks, which identify services or intangible activities "performed by one person for the benefit of a person or persons other than himself, either for pay or otherwise."[14] There are other classifications of trademarks, but they generally are not in common use. These classifications can be found at the U.S. Patent and Trademark Office (USPTO) Web site (*www.uspto.gov*). Under the terms of the Lanham Act (1946) and its various amendments, three requirements must be met for a trademark to be valid:[15]

- The mark must consist of a device, symbol, name, work, or combination thereof that the USPTO has defined as valid.
- A manufacturer or merchant must adopt and use the mark.
- The mark must distinguish goods sold or manufactured by one party from another.

The trademarking of a color presents some interesting issues. The 1995 Supreme Court case *Qualitex Co. v. Jacobson Products Co.*, 115 S.Ct. 1300 (1995), held that the green-gold color of a dry cleaning press pad could be trademarked. To trademark a color, it must be demonstrated that the color possesses a secondary meaning and that people actually associate the color with the particular product. Owens-Corning registered pink as a color for fiberglass insulation, which was upheld on legal challenge because pink had always been associated with insulation. However, trademarking a color is not as easy as trademarking a name. Color must meet the trademark requirements of secondary meaning, absence of functionality, and the color depletion theory, which has been the biggest reason courts have denied trademarks for color. The underlying argument is that the granting of trademarks on color would eventually deplete the reservoir of colors available to the public [*Id.* In *Qualitex*, 115 S. Ct. 1300, 1304 (1995)].

The holder of a trademark has the right to exclude others from using confusingly similar marks. In general a trademark can be protected against:

- Counterfeiting and misappropriation, that is, using a mark that is basically indistinguishable from another mark
- Infringement when a mark is likely to cause confusion, that is, when it is too similar to another mark.
- Dilution, that is, when the use of the same or similar mark, even in a noncompetitive situation, reduces the value of the mark to its owner

The case of *American Express v. American Express Limousine Service*, 771F. Supp 729 (E.D.N.Y. 1991), presents a good example of a situation where the owner of a famous mark experiences dilution because another company uses its mark for its service. In this case, a limousine service used the American Express mark for its business. Although the two companies were not in competition with one another, the court found that the defendant limousine company's use of the mark would have a deleterious effect on American Express, the financial services company.

The key to trademarks is that the holder must show *intent to use* or that the trademark is actually in use in interstate commerce. A potential trademark applicant is not required to search for potentially conflicting marks prior to filing an application, but this is easily done on the USPTO public search library at *www.uspto.gov*. Searching for conflicting marks will save time and protect against having to change the mark later in the process. A search for conflicting marks can be accomplished by doing a "knock-out" search on the Internet using a search engine such as AltaVista. Trademarks can be checked against state and federal registers. This can be done on the USPTO Web site. Before a trademark is registered, an intent-to-use application is filed and ™ (or ᔆᴹ for services) is placed after the name or logo. After the trademark is registered, the symbol ®, which means it is a registered trademark, is used. To apply for a trademark, a drawing of the mark and the appropriate fee, which starts at $325 per class of product or service in which the trademark is used, should be submitted. Some of the categories into which trademarks can be classified include:

- 02   Human beings
- 03   Animals
- 04   Supernatural beings, mythological or legendary beings
- 05   Plants
- 08   Foodstuff
- 09   Textiles

There are some marks that cannot be trademarked. These include:

- Immoral or deceptive marks
- Marks that use official symbols of the United States or any state or municipality, such as a state flag
- Marks that use a person's name or likeness without permission

The USPTO determines whether a mark can be registered. If it rejects the application, the applicant has 6 months to respond. In theory, once someone owns a trademark, they can own it forever if they follow the post registration formalities and the mark remains in commercial use. Trademarks actually become more valuable with age as the amount of goodwill they create increases. For many businesses, trademarks are the most important assets of the business because they are the means by which the business is known and distinguished from its competitors.

Under the General Agreement of Tariffs and Trade (GATT), the United States has assumed the obligation for registering trademarks internationally under Section 44(b) of the Trademark Act 15 U.S.C. §1126. Consequently, all countries that are party to the agreement respect these trademarks.

TRADEMARKS AND THE INTERNET

The Internet has spawned a number of new trademark-related legal issues that arise out of technologies used on the Internet. One of the most common areas for dispute is domain names.

Domain names, the addresses for Web sites, have created many problems because under federal trademark law, similar businesses may have similar names if they do business in different geographic regions (15 U.S.C. sec. 1057c, 111565-6). However, the Internet does not have geographic boundaries, and simply registering a domain name does not constitute use under the rules of the Lanham Act, which prevents trademark uses that might cause confusion in the marketplace.[16] For example, under trademark law, General Motors and General Mills can both exist because they are in different industries, but the Domain Name System (DNS) allows only one *general.com*. Similarly, a generic name cannot be registered as a trademark, but a generic domain name such as *business.com* can be registered.

The problem of cybersquatting, the registration of domain names with the purpose of attempting to sell them back to companies that might use them, is far less rampant now that the courts have sided with companies that have preexisting trademarks registered prior to the domain name registration. One frequently cited case is that of a 12-year-old boy with the nickname "Pokey" who was given the domain name "*pokey.org*" as a birthday present, and this became his home page on the Internet. Shortly thereafter he began receiving cease-and-desist notices from Prema Toy, the owners of the characters Pokey and Gumby. Fortunately, the case did not go to trial because the original creator of the characters insisted that the domain name be returned to the boy.[17]

The issue of cybersquatting is further exacerbated by the fact that not all domain names are registered through one organization. In fact, there are about 200 domain name registrars, and they do not all follow the same rules. Thus, a well-known domain name may be registered in another country under a different top-level domain (e.g., .ma for Mauritania or .gr for Greece), and unless the original company discovers it, customers could easily be diverted from their site. In 1999, Amazon.com filed a lawsuit against its counterpart in Greece, amazon.gr, [*Amazon.com v. CITI Services,* (1999) No. 990543 (D.Delaware. August 18)] for using its name and selling books through the site. Ultimately, a Greek court issued an injunction against CITI prohibiting the use of the name *Amazon* because it found that simply substituting .gr for .com would not decrease confusion.

PATENTS

The most powerful form of protection for intellectual property is the patent, which grants the holder the right to *exclude others from making, using, or selling the invention during the term of the patent*. In other words, a patent grants defensive rights, not offensive rights—it does not give the patent holder the right to make and distribute the invention, but it does allow the holder to prevent others from doing so. It is important that the patent holder defend the patent or risk losing it.

The U.S. patent system, as we know it today, was designed over 200 years ago by Thomas Jefferson. He designed it with the express purpose of providing the independent inventor with a brief legal monopoly during which to get the invention into the market and recoup development costs before facing competition. The first patent was issued in 1790, and more than 5 million U.S. patents have been granted to date. Curiously, the mousetrap has received more patents than any other invention. Still manufactured by the Woodstream Corporation of Pennsylvania, it goes by the trade-marked name Victor. Since it was first patented in 1903, the mousetrap has been the source of at least 40 patent applications a year. However, only 24 of the total 4,400 patents for mousetraps have actually made money. With so many applications, the USPTO has divided mousetrap inventions into nine categories, including smiting, choking, squeezing, electrocuting, and exploding.

The number of patent applications is increasing at a faster rate than at any other time in history (see Figure 5-2). Of course, not all patent applications result in the issuing of a patent. In 1999, 270,187 utility patent applications were filed with the USPTO. Of those, 153,493, or 56.8 percent, ultimately received patents. That was a 4 percent increase over the previous year. Because of rising demand for its services, the USPTO is now a performance-based organization that is required to:

- Process all inventions within 12 months (to be achieved by 2003)
- Offer electronic filing and electronically process patent and trademark applications

Today, about 80 percent of all U.S. patents derive from large corporations, and most inventors work in the research departments of large companies. However, the USPTO is mindful of the special needs and limited resources of independent inventors and has recently created the Office of the Independent Inventor to serve them. In addition, the courts have generally sided with independent inventors in cases where large corporations have infringed on their interests. See Chapter 7 for more information on patent infringement.

WHAT CONSTITUTES A PATENTABLE INVENTION?

Even though it may appear that virtually anything can be patented, the truth is that the USPTO has four specific criteria for determining the patentability of an invention:

- It must fit into one of the five classes established by Congress
- It must have utility
- It must not contain prior art
- It must be nonobvious

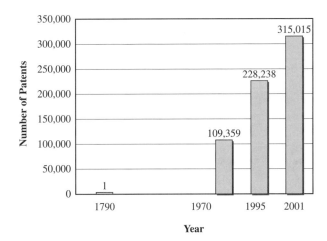

FIGURE 5-2   GROWTH IN PATENT APPLICATIONS

Source: USPTO: TAP Products and Services Brochure, *www. uspto.gov/web/offices/ac/ido/oeip/ tap/brochure.htm.*

THE FIVE CATEGORIES OF PATENTS

The U.S. Congress has established five categories of patentable inventions.

- Machine or something with moving parts or circuitry (e.g., fax, rocket, photo-copier, laser, electronic circuit)
- Process or method for producing a useful and tangible result (e.g., chemical reaction, method for producing products, business model)
- Article of manufacture (e.g., furniture, transistor, diskette, toy)
- Composition of matter (e.g., gasoline, food additive, drug, genetically altered life-form)
- A new use or improvement of something from the first four categories

If it appears that an invention might fit into more than one category, the inventor is not required to determine in which categories the invention should rightfully be included. Indeed, the Supreme Court of the United States has declared that "anything under the sun that is made by man" falls into the statutory subject matter (*Diamond v. Chakrabarty*, 1980).[18] This statement is not meant to suggest that anything is patentable; there are some very specific exclusions to a patent filing, for example, laws and phenomena of nature, naturally occurring substances, abstract mathematical formulas, and ideas. However, if the inventor alters something found in nature, as in the case of genetically altered tomatoes, the inventor may file for a patent. In *Diamond v. Chakrabarty*, Chakrabarty engineered a bacterium that broke down components of crude oil. No such bacterium existed in nature; thus, the Court ruled that this bacterium was the product of human ingenuity and could be patented. It is important to note that if the inventor obtains a patent on an improvement of one of the first four categories, he may not be entitled to manufacture the whole device without risking infringement of the original inventor's patent.

UTILITY

An invention must have utility; that is, it must be useful and real, not mere speculation. The utility must be described in the patent application such that the USPTO will not find the invention to be merely whimsical. Having said that, the USPTO has issued patents on fairly questionable inventions, such as a laser beam to motivate cats to exercise (Patent No. 5,443,036, August 22, 1995). Not to be outdone by the inventors who seek patents from it, on January 5, 1999, the USPTO issued a patent on its spiral office building (No. 5,885,098).

NO PRIOR ART

Prior art refers to knowledge that is publicly available or published prior to the date of invention, which is designated as the date of patent application. In other words, the invention must be new or novel in some important respect. The USPTO has said that an invention cannot be patented if it was known or used by others, previously patented, or described in a printed publication before an application was submitted. All inventions are subject to the "no-sale bar," which means that the invention must not be published or made available for sale more than 1 year prior to filing the patent application. The purpose of this rule is to ensure that the invention is still novel at the time of application.

Novelty is composed of physical differences, new combinations of components, or new uses. Two challenges to novelty exist: statutory and anticipatory. For example, if an invention is published or used in an unconcealed manner, whether in the United States or another country, the inventor is statutorily barred from seeking a patent because the invention is no longer novel. Moreover, if the invention is substantially similar to an existing patent that is still in force, the inventor may not seek patent protection because the patent was anticipated, that is there was prior art, and therefore the invention is not novel.

NONOBVIOUSNESS

The invention cannot be obvious to someone with ordinary skills in the particular field of the invention. In other words, it must contain new and unexpected results and not be the next logical step in a development process. The lack of nonobviousness has frequently precipitated the rejection of a patent application.

TYPES OF PATENTS

The USPTO offers three basic types of patents: utility, design, and plant. Of the three, the utility patent is the most commonly sought and is the source of the bulk of the growth in the number of patents granted in the information age. In particular, utility patents on software make up a large portion of this increase. Manufacturers now protect their investments in software development of test functions, test methods, and failure-analysis systems through patents.[19] In addition to utility, design, and plant patents, the business method patent has been a rapidly growing subcategory of utility process patents.

UTILITY PATENTS

Utility patents protect the functional part of a machine or process. A mathematical formula that describes the launch trajectory of a rocket may not be entitled to patent protection, but the software that actually makes the rocket leave the launch pad may be entitled to patent protection.[20] Gene patents also fall into this category. The first gene patents were issued in the 1970s, but since then, more than 1,000 genes have been patented, and thousands more await patent approval. In many cases, the company applying for the patent has no idea what specific purpose the gene sequence that is being claimed will serve. Human Genome Sciences has been filing for patents since 1994 and currently holds 112 patents on human gene sequences. However, their efforts cannot compare with those of Celera, which began decoding DNA in 1999 and now has filed patent claims on at least 6,500 gene sequences.[21] It is important to remember that scientists can patent laboratory-generated gene sequences and alterations of human genes, but they cannot patent individual human genes occurring in nature. Utility patents endure for 20 years from the date of application with the USPTO.

DESIGN PATENTS

A design patent protects the "visual ornamental characteristics embodied in, or applied to an article of manufacture" but not its structure or utilitarian features.[22] A protected design has no function but is simply part of the tangible item with which it is associated. The design cannot be hidden or offensive in any way, nor can it simulate a well-known or naturally occurring object or person. Examples of design patents include eyeglasses, a design on a vase, or the design of a door handle. A design patent application may only have a single claim (37 CFR §1.153). A separate application must be filed for each independent design, as multiple designs cannot be supported by a single patent claim. (Claims are discussed in the section on the patent process.) Design patents are valid for 14 years from the date of application.

It is important to note the existence of Invention Development Organizations (IDOs), which are consulting and marketing businesses that claim to help inventors bring their inventions to market. Some of these organizations are legitimate, but, unfortunately, most are not. They often encourage the inventor to pursue a design patent without considering the merits or the market feasibility of the invention. The design patent protects only the appearance of an article of manufacture, not its functionality. So once an inventor gets a design patent, someone else can create the same article of manufacture, alter the design, use the same functionality, and also receive a patent. It is wiser to seek the counsel of a qualified intellectual property attorney than to work with an IDO.

PLANT PATENTS

Plant patents protect new and distinct varieties of asexually reproducing plants. The plant for which a patent is being sought must be uniquely different from any plant existing naturally in nature. This patent is good for 20 years from the date of application.

BUSINESS METHOD PATENTS

Traditionally, U.S. courts have held that an invention must involve a physical transformation to be patented, drawing from various courts' interpretations that laws of nature, natural phenomenon, and abstract ideas are not patentable. However, in 1994, the Federal Circuit Court ruled that abstract ideas could be patented if, when reduced to practice, they produced a "useful, concrete and tangible result" [*In re Alappat*, 33 F. 3d 1526 (C.A.F.C. 1994)]. Accordingly, the USPTO revised its guidelines and opened the door to what is now known as the business method patent.

The business method patent is actually a type of a utility patent, and involves the classification of a process. The flood of business method patent applications began with *State Street Bank & Trust Co. v. Signature Financial Group*, 149 F.3d 1360, in 1998. Signature Financial Group applied for a patent on its proprietary application software designed to automate its portfolio management system. State Street Bank wanted to license the application, but when negotiations failed, it sued Signature on the grounds that the patent violated the business method patent eligibility requirements. The Federal Circuit Court ultimately upheld Signature's patent rights. The *State Street Bank* case served to expand the concept of what constitutes physical transformation as a requirement for patentability to include manipulations of electronically stored data. It also eliminated the business method exception to patentability.

Priceline.com's patent on its reverse-auction process and Amazon.com's application on its one-click method (U.S. Patent No. 5,960,411; "method and system for placing a purchase order via a communications network") quickly followed the Signature patent application. Amazon.com defended its new patent with an infringement suit against Barnes & Noble [*Amazon.com v. Barnesandnoble.com,* 73F. Supp. 2 1228 (W.D. Wash. 1999)] to stop it from using the one-click technology. In February 2001, a federal appeals court overturned the lower court's ruling because it "raised substantial questions as to the validity" of Amazon.com's patent.[23] Based on the discovery of prior art during litigation, both companies may now face litigation for some time to come.

The term *business method* is used to describe various process claims, and to this date the courts have not defined what differentiates a business method claim from a process claim.[24] The USPTO issued a statement on March 29, 2000, declaring that the business method patent will only apply to fundamentally different ways of doing business, and the embedded process must produce a useful, tangible, and concrete result.[25]

FILING FOR A PATENT

The USPTO Web site clearly describes the patent application process, but any inventor should still consult with an intellectual property attorney when applying for a patent because much of the USPTO's decision on whether to grant the patent depends on how the claims are worded. Claims are statements about the portions of the invention the inventor believes to be novel. In the United States, only the original inventor or inventors have the right to apply for a patent. However, the original inventor may subsequently assign the patent to a company or individual. If a patent has joint owners, any single owner can make, use, or sell the invention without consulting with or obtaining permission from the other owners. Therefore, if two inventors jointly apply for a patent, they should have a written agreement that discusses the distribution of equity in the patent and potential proceeds from royalties or sale.

It is always wise to conduct a preliminary patent search or seek the services of a patent attorney or firm that specializes in patent searches. As most patents are not commercialized, it will be difficult to know for sure if the invention is novel without doing a patent search.

THE DISCLOSURE DOCUMENT PROGRAM

Inventors often protect their inventions in the earliest stages of development by taking advantage of the USPTO's Disclosure Document Program. The disclosure document merely serves as evidence of the date of conception of an invention; it does not grant any rights like those granted by patents, and it does not take the place of a formal patent application. The disclosure statement could become an important document should two inventors find themselves working on the same idea at the same time. The inventor who filed the disclosure statement could be in a stronger position to be declared the one who can file for a patent. It is important to note, however, that the date of receipt of the disclosure document is not the effective filing date for a patent application.[26] Furthermore, the disclosure document does not substitute for a conventional, permanently bound, witnessed, and notarized laboratory notebook or record.[27]

The disclosure document should contain a detailed description of the invention and its uses so that an ordinary person skilled in the art could make and use the device.[28] The document will be kept in confidence for 2 years, after which the USPTO will consider it abandoned if no patent application is filed. Under no circumstances should the inventor use the tactic of mailing a disclosure statement regarding the invention in a sealed envelope addressed to the inventor. It has no value to the USPTO.

THE PROVISIONAL PATENT

The provisional patent allows an inventor to complete a first patent filing in the United States at a much lower cost than that required for a formal patent application. This approach should definitely be considered as it is legally more powerful than a disclosure document and permits the inventor to label the invention as *patent pending*. The purpose of the provisional patent is to give inventors an opportunity to speak with manufacturers and others about producing the invention without fear that they will take the invention as their own. It does not, however, take the place of a formal, non-provisional patent application. The inventor is given only 12 months from the date of filing the provisional patent application to file a formal patent application, and that time period cannot be extended. During the 12 months, the inventor must use due diligence to complete a formal application for a nonprovisional patent. Another advantage of the provisional patent is that the 12 months do not count toward the 20-year life of the nonprovisional patent, so that the patent life effectively becomes 21 years. Like the disclosure document, if the inventor does not file for a nonprovisional patent within the 12-month period, the patent will be considered abandoned and the inventor will lose the opportunity to declare the provisional patent filing date as the date of invention.

NONPROVISIONAL PATENT

To secure a patent, the inventor must file a nonprovisional patent application that contains a comprehensive description of the invention, what its uses are, and how it is uniquely different from anything currently patented. In filing for a patent, the inventor will want to stake out as broad an area of claim as possible. The application will require a technical description, known as the disclosure of the invention. It must contain enough detail for an ordinary person skilled in the relevant technology to make and use the invention. Although it does not need to include blueprints or original source code, it should use flowcharts and text to describe each step of the process of making the invention.

The claims in the application serve to define the scope of the protection requested. Every patent application must contain at least one claim of novelty, utility, and nonobviousness. The attorney will word the claims so that they are broad enough to cover all the potential applications of the technology, but specific enough to demonstrate uniqueness. For example, inventor Bill Nelson applied for protection on a device that permits the user to run both electrical and pneumatic tools. The claim that deals with how the machine is controlled remotely, that is, how it starts and stops, would be defined narrowly if the claim said that pulling the trigger of an electrical or pneumatic hand tool controls the start/stop function of the machine. In this scenario, another inventor could conceivably discover a different way to control the start/stop function from the tool without violating the remote start/stop claim itself. That is the danger of a narrow claim. Instead, Nelson claimed more broadly that the remote start/stop function is controlled from the tool without specifying that the trigger must be pulled. This is a broader claim and more difficult to circumvent. Again, it is important to emphasize that drafting a claim is an art that should be undertaken by an intellectual property attorney. However, engineering or scientific expertise is vital to an effective technical description. That is why many patent attorneys have engineering or science backgrounds.

The cost of the patent process depends on the type and complexity of the invention. The USPTO provides a fee schedule on its Web site. Those who can prove that they are "small" inventors (as opposed to inventors inside a large corporation), may be entitled to lower fees.

When the patent application is received by the USPTO, it conducts a search of its patent records for prior art. It then issues an office action that normally includes objections to the claims contained in the application. This office action can take place any time between 6 months and 3 years from the date the application is filed.[29] In the unlikely event that the inventor receives an initial office action that all the claims are allowable, the inventor should be concerned. It could quite possibly mean that the inventor did not seek enough in the claims. During this time, the patent application is described as "patent applied for," which establishes the claim and dates relative to prior art; the patent application is not available to the public. It is very common for the USPTO to reject one or more claims on the first pass, frequently because of prior art or nonobviousness. Several communications between the inventor's attorney and the USPTO examiner assigned to the patent application will argue the merits of any claims that may have been rejected by the examiner. Normally, the inventor's attorney will need to modify the wording of the original claims to rectify any problems that the patent examiner may have indicated. Once the USPTO accepts the revised claims, it issues a notice of allowance that announces that the patent will be issued. The inventor may market and sell the invention during this process, but must clearly label it *patent pending* and provide the number assigned to the patent application. Once the patent is issued, it becomes public record and anyone can view it.

If the patent is rejected, even after modifications, the inventor may appeal to a Board of Patent Appeals within the USPTO. Failing to overturn the rejection here, the inventor may appeal to the U.S. Court of Appeals for the Federal Circuit. As this process may take years, an inventor may want to weigh the cost of undertaking the appeal against the value of getting the invention to market without a patent. The inventor may abandon a patent application even after the first office action rejecting some or all of the claims. This might be a wise decision if the inventor believed that the potential value of the invention is low when weighed against the cost of appealing, maintaining, and enforcing the patent.

There are maintenance fees associated with patents that many inventors fail to understand. These fees are paid at $3\frac{1}{2}$, $7\frac{1}{2}$, and $11\frac{1}{2}$ years from the date the patent was granted or risk expiration of the patent. The fee schedule is found on the USPTO Web site. The bottom line is that inventions are much easier to patent than they are to sell. It's probably wise not to patent an invention for which there is no market or the market is too small to allow the inventor to make a profit.

There are four recommended contact points with the USPTO during the patent application process:

- The Office of Independent Inventor Programs (OIIP)
- The Patent Assistance Center (PAC)
- The Technology Center Customer Service Center
- The patent examiner assigned to the application

FOREIGN PATENTS

U.S. patent rights extend only to the borders of the United States. They are not valid in other countries, as every country has its own laws regarding intellectual property. However, several international agreements have clarified many of the issues regarding the patenting of inventions in foreign countries. With the Paris Convention of 1967, the clock stops for a year if an inventor files a patent application in any member country.[30] This means that the second country in which the inventor files a patent will treat that application as though it were filed on the initial date of application in the first country, giving the inventor the earliest date of invention.

The Patent Cooperation Treaty of 1970 (PCT) permits an inventor to file a PCT document or blanket application in his or her home country and then designate the countries in which the patent is requested.[31] The inventor has 30 months to begin the process of filing a formal patent application in every country they have listed in the PCT. Similarly, the European Patent Convention (EPC) offers a blanket application and grants an inventor rights in all member countries. However, enforcement of patent rights is still on a country-by-country basis.

There are two important differences between international and U.S. procedures in patent filing. The EPC gives patent rights to the first person to file for the patent, whether or not that person is the original inventor. The United States permits only the original inventor the right to file an application. Furthermore, in the United States, an inventor can make an invention available for sale up to 1 year before filing a patent application. This is not the case in other countries, where publication or availability for sale before the date of filing will bar the right to apply. In addition, most countries other than the United States require that the invention be manufactured in that country within 3 years of receiving the foreign patent.

It is very important to consult with an intellectual property attorney with experience in foreign patents. The attorney can help the inventor determine if the time and expense of foreign patents is essential to the success of the potential business. Frequently, businesses instead choose to develop partnerships with companies in the countries in which they want to do business so as to take advantage of already existing distribution channels.

❖ SUMMARY

Intellectual property consists of proprietary rights in the form of patents, trademarks, copyrights, and trade secrets, which are granted by the U.S. Patent and Trademark Office and the U.S. Copyright Office or through common law as in the case of trade secrets. These rights give the holder the right to exclude others from making and using the property under protection. Trade secrets are the easiest form of protection to obtain but provide the weakest level of protection. All they require are documents specifying that something is a trade secret that must not be disclosed. These documents often take the form of nondisclosure agreements and contracts. Copyrights protect the original works of authors, artists, musicians, and programmers and last for the life of the holder plus 70 years. To secure copyright protection, the work must be in a tangible form and contain a copyright notice. Trademarks protect symbols, logos, words, sounds, colors, designs, or other devices used to identify a business or a product in commerce. Trademarks must be in commercial use to be valid and are renewable every 17 years. Patents are the most powerful form of protection for intellectual property. They grant the holder the right to exclude others from making, using, or selling the invention during the term of the patent. An invention may qualify for a patent if it fits into one of five classes established by Congress, has utility, does not contain prior art, and is nonobvious.

❖ DISCUSSION QUESTIONS

1. An inventor has just developed a new type of collapsible furniture that will be useful for students in college dormitories where space is limited. What kinds of protections should the inventor consider for this product and the business that would be developed to commercialize it?

2. An inventor has developed a new financial software application. What will determine if the inventor may apply for a patent or seek copyright protection?
3. Why would an inventor choose to file a provisional patent application rather than a disclosure document?
4. For what reasons might an inventor decide not to patent an invention that is clearly patentable?
5. What kinds of things are best protected through trade secrets?

❖ RESOURCES

Ferrera, Gerald R., Margo E. Reder, Ray August, Gerald Ferra, Stephen D. Lichtenstein, William T. Schiano. *Cyberlaw: Your Rights in Cyberspace.* Mason, OH: South-Western Publishing, 2001.

Goldstein, Paul. *Copyright, Patent, Trademark and Related State Doctrines, Cases and Materials on The Law of Intellectual Property.* 4th ed. New York: Foundation Press, 1999.

Kahin, Brian, and Hal R. Varian. *Internet Publishing and Beyond: The Economics of*

Digital Information and Intellectual Property. Boston: MIT Press, 2000.

Maskus, Keith E., and C. Fred Bergsten. *Intellectual Property Rights in the Global Economy.* Washington, DC: Institute for International Economics, 2000.

Mosely, T. E., Jr. *Marketing Your Invention.* Dover, NH: Upstart Publishing, 1992.

❖ INTERNET RESOURCES

European Patent Office
www.epo.co.at/epo
This is the equivalent of the U.S. Patent Office in Europe

Japanese Patent Office
patent-jp.com/JPS.htm
This is the equivalent of the U.S. Patent Office in Japan

The Digital Dilemma: Intellectual Property in the Information Age
www.nap.edu/books/0309064996/html/
A free online book that presents comprehensive information on protecting digital property

The National Technology Transfer Center
www.nttc.edu
This organization helps companies work with federal laboratories to turn their work into technology that businesses can use and sell

KuesterLaw
www.kuesterlaw.com/
A technology law resource guide

U.S. Copyright Office
lcweb.loc.gov/copyright
This is where authors and others should file for copyright protection

U.S. Patent and Trademark Office
www.uspto.gov
This is where inventors and those applying for trademarks can find information and forms for filing applications

GORDON GOULD:
THE FATHER OF LASER
TECHNOLOGY

When your childhood heroes are Marconi, Bell, and Edison, it is not surprising if you become an inventor. Gordon Gould knew before he entered high school that he would someday be an inventor, but he did more than just wait for that day to come; he prepared for it by studying how things work. As a child, he used to fix his neighbors' clocks. After studying physics in high school, he became fascinated with light and went to Yale in 1941 to study. When World War II broke out, he was forced to quit school and take a job on the Manhattan Project, the project that created the atomic bomb. In 1951, he resumed his studies at Columbia. He was fired from the City College of New York where he had been teaching to support his doctoral research because of his refusal to testify against his colleagues in McCarthy era hearings to root out communists. His faculty advisor for his doctoral work at Columbia then managed to secure a job for Gould in a radiation lab, which turned out to be a fortuitous turn of events.

Gould experienced his "eureka" discovery on November 9, 1957, when he was 37 years old. Another Columbia physicist, Charles H. Townes, had invented a means of amplifying microwave energy, which he called the "maser," but Gould was interested in finding a way to do this same thing with light. The idea for his invention came to him in a rush that evening, and he spent the entire night writing down all his thoughts and designs and potential applications for the invention. The next day he immediately had his notebook notarized. Gould's invention was a way to amplify light and use the resulting light beam to cut and heat substances and to measure distances. Gould realized that this discovery was going to be his life's work.

Gould consulted with a patent attorney, but, unfortunately, he misunderstood what he was told. He thought that he had to build a working prototype of his laser to acquire a patent, but the USPTO only requires that an inventor describe his invention in such a way that a person skilled in the art can replicate it. So excited was Gould to begin work on a laser application that he left the university without finishing his dissertation and took a position with Technical Research Group, Inc., a small New York company. Upon winning a $1 million grant in 1959, he finally filed for an historic patent that disclosed more than a dozen interrelated inventions covering fundamental laser technology. Meanwhile, Charles Townes had already applied for a patent on his optical maser. To make matters worse, the government declared Gould's research top secret, and because he did not have a security clearance as a result of his earlier run-in with the McCarthy panel, his notebooks were confiscated. Fortunately, he had kept copies of them and retained the primary know-how for the project in his mind.

Townes and his partner, Arthur Schawlow, received the patent on their optical maser in 1960 and for the next 17 years, theirs would be the only laser patents on which royalties would be paid. In 1973, Gould received a decision from the Patent Office that declared that his original application had no disclosure of an operable laser technology. This decision also effectively invalidated his pending applications. Gould would not give up; he was battling for his patents, but the cost was becoming unbearable. At one point, Gould was referred to a well-known patent attorney, Richard I. Samuel who, after much investigation, believed that Gould was the true inventor of the laser. His firm agreed to fund Gould's patent fight for up to $300,000 in exchange for 15 percent of future royalties. The firm that had agreed to act as the licensing agent for Gould's patents, REFAC, would take 25 percent of future royalties, leaving Gould with 35 percent.

In May 1977, the patent office announced that it would issue a patent to Gould for a device that amplified light. Over the next few months, Gould filed for several more patents and also filed an infringement suit against Control Laser International Corp., which had been paying royalties to Townes for the maser patent for nearly 17 years. On the strength of the first patent, in 1979, Gould and his attorney won enough financial backing from private investors to start Patlex Corp., which they later took public. What was unusual about this new company was that its primary asset was its equity stake in the outcome of various lawsuits. Gould and Samuel had filed suits against about 90 percent of the laser companies in existence at that time.

What followed were years of battles with the USPTO and the various companies Patlex had sued. In many instances, the Patent Office behaved in rather unusual ways, because, as it claimed, any Gould patents could potentially be enforced against the government as well. Still, the Patent Office is supposed to be an independent body, not an advocate, and this atypical behavior in the end worked in Gould's favor. On December 19, 1985, the court stated that the Patent Office had made many errors in evaluating Gould's patent claims and ruled in his favor. That ruling started an avalanche of rulings in Gould's favor. In the end, more than 100 laser makers signed licensing agreements with Patlex, including such giants as Ford, General Electric, and National Semiconductor. Gould was finally recognized for his historic invention. ■

Sources: Erik Larson, "Patent Pending," *Inc.* (March 1, 1989): online Mike Hofmann, "Patent Fending," *Inc.* (December 1, 1997); *ld v. General Photonics Corp.* 534 F.Supp. 399 (N.D. Cal. 1982); *Gould v. Mossinghoff,* 229 U.S.P.Q. 1 (D.D.C. 1985).

❖ NOTES

1. Bill Roberts, "Patent Strategies," *Electronic Business* (October 1999): 79–84.
2. Evdokia Moise, "Intellectual Property: Rights and Wrongs," *Observer*, no. 216 (March 1999): 35–38.
3. R. S. Eisenberg, "Patents and the Progress of Science," *University of Chicago Law Review* 50 (1989): 1,017–1,086; E. W. Kitch, "The Nature and Function of the Patent System," *Journal of Law and Economics* 20 (1977): 265–290; R. P. Merges and R. R. Nelson, "On the Complex Economics of Patent Scope," *Columbia Law Review* 90 (1990): 839–916.
4. Jap P. Kesan, "Intellectual Property and Agricultural Biotechnology," *American Behavioral Scientist* 44, no. 3 (November 2000): 464.
5. Wesley Cohen, Richard Nelson, and John Walsh, "Protecting Their Intellectual Assets: Appropriability Conditions and Why U.S. Manufacturing Firms Patent (or Not)," working paper 7552, National Bureau of Economic Research, Washington, DC, 2000;

Scott Stern, Michael Porter, and Jeffrey Furman, "The Determinants of National Innovative Capacity," working paper 7876, National Bureau of Economic Research, Washington, DC, 2000.
6. Edwin Mansfield, Mark Schwartz, and Samuel Wagner, "Imitation Costs and Patents: An Empirical Study," *The Economic Journal* 91 (December 1981): 908–918.
7. C. J. Berger, "How to Protect Trade Secrets," *Real Estate Weekly*, March 1, 2000. Online Source
8. Stephen Fishman and Rich Stim, "Trade Secret Basics," *NOLO Law for All.* (February 4, 2002) *www.nolo.com/encyclopedia/articles/pts/trade_secrets.html.*
9. Ibid.
10. Steve Alexander, "Intellectual Property," *Computerworld* 34, no.1 (January 3, 2000): 98.
11. *Whelan v. Jaslow*, 797 F.2d 1222; 21 Fed. R. Evid. Serv. (Callaghan) 571: U.S. Court of Appeals for the Third Circuit, March 3, 1986, Argued, August 4, 1986, Filed.

12. U.S. Copyright Office, *Summary of the Digital Millennium Copyright Act of 1998* (Washington, DC: December 1998): 4.

13. Brian Hiatt, "With Napster Weakened, RIAA Hopes to Settle Landmark Lawsuit," *www.MTV.com* (July 27, 2001).

14. 15 U.S.C. §1127.

15. Steven W. Kopp and Tracy A. Suter, "Trademark Strategies Online: Implications for Intellectual Property Protection," *Journal of Public Policy & Marketing* 19, no. 1, (Spring 2000): 119–131.

16. Jennifer Doviak Brown and John E. Prescott, "Product of the Mind: Assessment and Protection of Intellectual Property," *Competitive Intelligence Review* 11, no. 3 (2000): 60.

17. "This Pokey Isn't That Pokey," *USA Today* (May 13, 1998): 6D.

18. *Diamond v. Chakrabarty,* 447 U.S. 303 (1980).

19. Kevin Klughart, "Protect Your Intellectual Property," *Test & Measurement World* (July 1999): 15–22.

20. "Qualifying for a Patent," *NOLO Law for All. www.nolo.com/encyclopedia/articles/pts/pct3.html#FAQ-294.*

21. "Human Gene Patents Defended," *BBC News,* (October 27, 1999, 10:53 GMT).

22. U.S. Patent and Trademark Office: Design Patents. *www.uspto.gov/web/offices/pac/doc/general/design.html.*

23. Steven Bonisteel, "Bounty Hunters Get Bonus for Effort on Amazon Patent," *Newsbytes* (March 14, 2001).

24. *State Street Bank & Trust v. Signature Financial Group Inc.,* 149 F.3d 1368, 47 USPQ2d 1596 (Fed. Cir. 1998).

25. John J. Love and Wynn W. Coggins, "Successfully Preparing and Prosecuting a Business Method Patent Application." Paper presented at annual meeting of AIPLA, (2001), *www.uspto.gov/web/menu/pbmethod/aiplapaper.rtf.*

26. U.S. Patent and Trademark Office *www.uspto.gov/web/offices/pac/disdo.html.*

27. U.S. Patent and Trademark Office: Disclosure Document Program *www.uspto.gov/web/offices/com/sol/notices/disdo.html.*

28. Ibid.

29. Klughart, "Protect Your Intellectual Property," 15–22.

30. Paris Convention for the Protection of Industrial Property, 21 U.S.T. 1,583,828 U.N.T.S. 305 (1967).

31. Patent Cooperation Treaty, 28 U.S.T. 7645 No. 8733 (1970).

6

LICENSING INTELLECTUAL PROPERTY

OVERVIEW

This chapter will examine

❖ the licensor's view of licensing

❖ the licensee's view of licensing

❖ the license agreement

❖ a company's licensing strategy

INTRODUCTION

Although intellectual property has long been a source of competitive advantage to businesses, it was not until the 1980s that companies began looking at intellectual property as a way of creating wealth. Since that time, rising R&D and production costs, increased competition, and an uncertain economy have spurred companies to diversify their revenue streams so as not to rely solely on revenues from sales.[1] Licensing is a $95 billion a year industry in the United States, $170 billion worldwide.[2] Although the largest dollar volumes from licensing go to large corporations such as IBM, which was granted over 3,000 patents in 2000, most licensors and licensees are smaller companies that realize that royalty revenues provide a significantly higher return on investment than other sources of revenue.[3,4] It is often more profitable for the owner of a technology to become a licensor of that invention than to try to develop and market all the possible applications of the invention. Licensing to others speeds the adoption of the technology and stimulates further innovation.[5] Moreover, in a much broader context, the majority of industrialized economies depend on technology created outside their borders. Only in Japan, the United States, and West Germany are more than 90 percent of the patents domestic patents.[6] In the United States, manufacturing is the largest recipient of royalty income, at about 76 percent of the country's total royalty income. This is not surprising when one considers that about 73 percent of all R&D is performed by manufacturing businesses. However, nonmanufacturing royalties are increasing, particularly in the areas of communication services, computer programming and related businesses, and testing services.[7]

There are also nonfinancial reasons to have a licensing strategy in place. Many software companies prefer to have another company handle distribution. They do this by licensing their core software product to developers who can then customize it to meet the needs of particular customers. This allows the original software manufacturer to enjoy the benefits of reaching multiple markets without the expense of setting up distribution channels.

THE LICENSOR'S VIEW OF THE LICENSING PROCESS

A successful licensing process will include a number of steps that should be followed to ensure that the needs of both the licensor and the licensee, who will depend on each other during the term of the agreement, are met in a mutually satisfactory way. This process will be examined from the point of view of the licensor as depicted in Figure 6-1.

DECIDE WHAT WILL BE LICENSED

A product, process, know-how, right to manufacture, right to market and distribute, or the right to use a product in the production of another product can be licensed. Every situation is different; therefore, the best combination of rights for the technology the entrepreneur wishes to license must be determined so that the highest value possible can be achieved. Some entrepreneurs choose to license noncore or core technology when they need to expand their companies into diverse markets and do not have the capability to do so alone. Others may decide to hold technologies captive for internal use by the organization, usually for an operational advantage.

DEFINE THE BENEFITS TO THE LICENSEE

As with any purchase, buyers or licensees will be purchasing benefits that they need. Those benefits need to be identified; in other words, what makes the license valuable to the buyer? The licensor's ability to achieve the highest value for a technology is a function of the benefits the customer perceives to be associated with the technology, as well as the attendant benefits of any know-how that is transferred with the technology. These benefits are easily defined from the licensor's perspective, but it is equally important to get the customer's perspective as well.

CONDUCT MARKET RESEARCH

It is important to make certain that the potential market into which the licensee will take the product is sufficiently large to ensure a reasonable profit from the effort. If the licensor's technology is new, that is, not well known, the licensor will have to build a case for the feasibility of the market to attract potential licensees. Potential licensees will have conducted their own research, and that will be presented to the licensor as

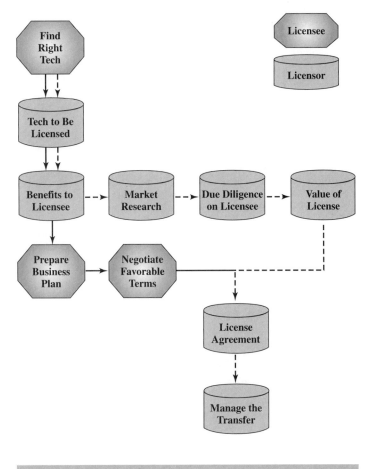

FIGURE 6-1   THE LICENSING PROCESS

part of their negotiating strategy, but it is always wise for the licensor to do their own research as well. As licensees are trying to make a case for the market they have chosen, they may avoid bringing up negatives. Therefore, the licensor will want to find out for himself what those negatives might be and if they can be overcome.

UNDERTAKE DUE DILIGENCE ON THE LICENSEE

As license agreements usually extend for several years, it is vitally important to ensure that any potential licensee possesses the resources, knowledge, and skills to fulfill the terms and conditions of the license agreement and successfully commercialize the technology. Any potential licensee candidates should provide contact information for previous license agreements they may have had. The licensor should then follow-up on those contacts to find out if the candidate was reliable in the payment of royalties and achieved performance targets. This will be a good indication of how the licensee will behave under a new license agreement.

DETERMINE THE VALUE OF THE LICENSE AGREEMENT

Intellectual property in the form of patents is perhaps the most undervalued of all assets. In 2000, IBM earned in excess of $1.3 billion in licensing revenues; Texas Instruments earns more than $400 million annually from licensing, and Stanford University earns $200 million annually.[8] Several factors determine the ultimate value of a license agreement:

- The economic life of the intellectual property, that is, how long it provides a revenue stream to the company
- The potential for direct competition by companies that design around the intellectual property
- The potential for government legislation or regulation that might damage the marketability of the intellectual property
- Changes in market conditions that might render the intellectual property devoid of value

Valuation of intellectual property will be the subject of Chapter 8. For now, once these four factors have been considered, the ultimate value of the intellectual property is determined by a negotiation in good faith between the parties.

TRANSFER PRICING

When the rights to technology are licensed to another party, the licensor charges a price that is reasonable for the transaction. Reasonable is usually defined as an "arm's length" price or fair market price. When a company licenses to another company, the assumption is that this is an arm's length deal. However, when technology is transferred from one entity to another *inside* the same company, the Internal Revenue Service requires a transfer pricing analysis to ensure that the licensor company is not merely shifting income from one entity to another to avoid taxation. Licensors should consult with a qualified accountant to learn the best method of transfer pricing for their companies.

Licensors should also ask for a refundable evaluation fee from prospective licensees to screen out less-than-serious candidates. In addition, an up-front commitment fee that ensures that the licensee has a financial stake in the venture is wise. Finally, a running royalty, typically based on a percentage of gross sales, is charged over the life of the license agreement. The question of whether to issue an exclusive or a nonexclusive license is tricky. A significantly higher royalty rate can be commanded with an exclusive license that gives the licensee the advantage of a temporary monopoly in which to establish the new product. Licensors who grant exclusive licenses typically do so only to an established industry player, as it will be in the best position to pay the higher royalty rate. It is important to grant exclusive licenses only in fields in which the licensee has a demonstrated capability and global rights only to companies that have global experience. Nonexclusive licenses are most appropriate for technologies that have broad applications in many areas such that no one company could possibly cover them all. Genetic therapy is one example of a field where nonexclusive licensing or exclusive licensing in one industry is advantageous because at this early stage of the technology, it is nearly impossible to predict all of its possible applications in medicine, agriculture, and the chemical industry.

UNDERSTAND THE LICENSING PROCESS

It is important to develop a strategy to effectively manage the transfer of technology so that the intellectual property can be protected until the licensor is sure that the deal is secure. The following sections present some guidelines for managing the transfer of technology.

MANAGING THE TRANSFER

Upon receiving an inquiry from a potential licensee about a licensor's technology and a request to schedule a potential visit, the licensor should perform the tasks described in the following sections to ensure the effectiveness of the meeting.

Preparing for the First Meeting   Before the first meeting with a potential licensee the licensor should:

- Provide the potential licensee with a comprehensive nonconfidential disclosure about the technology that is available for licensing.
- Elicit additional information from the licensee candidate about their company's capacity, staffing plans, technical capabilities, and financial strength.
- Highlight the benefits of the technology and facilities.
- Prepare a secrecy agreement for the licensee candidate.
- Prepare employees for the visit, its purpose, and the need for nondisclosure of certain elements of the technology.
- Do due diligence on the licensee before the meeting.

The First Meeting   The following suggestions should be kept in mind during the first meeting with a potential licensee:

- The first meeting should take place at the licensor's site so that the licensor maintains control of the discussion and disclosure.
- The licensor should present a professional presence and avoid unprepared remarks. If language is a problem, an interpreter will ensure that the parties understand each other correctly.
- The licensor should make clear that any technology advancements undertaken by the licensee are granted back to the licensor. In addition, license payments must be tied to performance and the impact of secrecy obligations, which could compromise the licensee's work, should be discussed.

SECRECY AND NEGOTIATION

The licensor should define the plans for disclosure of the technology to the licensee. Typically, this is done in stages until the agreement is signed. During this period the licensee may designate a "Typhoid Mary" in her organization who receives the technology disclosure information but is contractually constrained (in effect, quarantined) from revealing it for a period of time.

The bottom line is that the license agreement is a negotiated document, and the party who wields the most clout is a function of the importance of what they bring to the agreement. Licensors possess the power when they own a radical technology that no one else has. Licensees hold the power when the innovation is so radical that there are few, if any, potential licensees willing to take the risk of developing and commercializing it. To entice the first licensee, the licensor may have to provide preferential treatment in the form of a lower royalty rate, a lower upfront fee, and the first right of refusal on new markets. To effectively negotiate with the licensee in this or any other scenario, the licensor needs to understand the other party's decision-making processes, as this will affect the time line for transfer of the technology and its ultimate commercialization in the marketplace.

DURING THE TERM OF THE AGREEMENT

The licensor should establish a point of contact with the licensee's business and assign someone in the company as the licensee's point of contact to reduce the probability of communication problems. It is likely that the licensor will also need to provide some in-house tech support over the term of the agreement. Companies often place one of their own employees inside the licensee's company during the development phase to oversee and facilitate a smooth transfer of the technology.

THE LICENSEE'S VIEW OF THE LICENSING PROCESS

With more and more companies acquiring technology to speed up their R&D processes and remain competitive, in-licensing has become big business. However, the very speed that has induced companies to acquire technology rather than develop it themselves has made the due diligence requirement that much more important. The licensee must investigate the licensor's track record. Has the licensor successfully executed other license agreements? What has been the company's success rate with new products? What kind of relationship has the company had with its licensees?

Potential licensees should insist on direct access to the owner/CEO of the company with which they intend to do business. The owner/CEO represents the vision of the company and embodies its culture and attitudes. If the licensee does not have good feelings about this person, chances are she will not enjoy working with the company. Two clues to the potential success or failure with the licensor are whether or not the owner/CEO prepared for the meeting and their attitude at that meeting. A lack of preparation could signal that the company is not familiar with the licensing process or it does not take the licensee seriously. If the licensing company employs a full-time licensing professional with expertise in tech transfer, the whole process will go more smoothly.

SEARCHING FOR THE RIGHT TECHNOLOGY

Evaluating the technology being considered for a license agreement is critically important because the consequences will be long-term and any mistakes will be costly. Some of the questions that should be answered when evaluating a technology are:

- Does the technology work in the way the licensor claims?
- On what measures are the performance data calculated? Watch out for data based solely on lab performance, because there is usually a decline in performance from the laboratory to the real world.
- Is the technology completely owned by the licensor or does the licensee also have to be concerned about another party and their role in the process?
- Will the licensor provide any guarantees of the technology's performance?

LICENSE EXCHANGES

To add order to the often chaotic world of licensing, some companies, such as Yet2.com, have started license exchanges, which are matchmaking sites for licensors and potential licensees. Yet2.com believes that most companies exploit only about 20 percent of their R&D ideas because they cannot find value in the remainder.[9] Another company, perhaps in a different industry, may have a commercial application for that archived technology. The problem is that most companies rely on the grapevine to find licensees, and that technique is often not very fruitful. For example, 3M has the patent on a polymer that they use in adhesives. They know that the polymer could also be used in chromatography, but 3M does not do work in that area, so they do not know any potential licensing candidates. By putting the patent on a license exchange, 3M might be able to find a company that can use it. Yet2.com places anonymous descriptions of licensors' technologies on its site. The licensors pay a modest fee per entry, and the potential licensees view the descriptions for free. If they would like to view more complete descriptions, earlier uses of the technology, patent status, and licensing forms, they pay a small fee. To go to the next level of access, the potential licensee must pay an earnest fee and then the licensor is revealed to them. If a deal is brokered and a license agreement executed, Yet2.com receives a 10 percent royalty up to a $50,000 maximum.

PREPARING A BUSINESS PLAN

The licensor will want to know that the licensee has studied the market and has a plan for how to commercialize the technology. The licensee will be asked to provide a business plan that demonstrates her company's ability to execute, in other words, that the company has the resources—human, financial, knowledge, and facilities—to commercialize the technology. Information about how to construct this business plan can be found in Chapter 15.

NEGOTIATING FAVORABLE TERMS

From the licensee's perspective, the technology for which the licensee is seeking rights should be uncoupled from the business itself. Only the value added by the new product associated with the license agreement should be paid for. Licensees generally do not benefit from a nonexclusive license that gives all competitors the same advantage. With a nonexclusive license, only the licensor and the customers of the licensee benefit. An exclusive license, even for just one industry, is preferable to a nonexclusive license for products in several industries.

THE LICENSE AGREEMENT

It is important to consult an attorney with experience in license agreements to draw up an agreement that defines the terms and conditions between the licensor and the licensee. The following sections describe some of the clauses typically found in license agreements. A qualified attorney will structure the agreement with the appropriate clauses for the particular situation.

GRANT CLAUSE

The grant clause describes what is being delivered to the licensee through the license agreement, that is, the right to manufacture, distribute, use, and such. To accomplish the transfer of the technology, the clause will grant the licensee the right to practice the technology and the right to the knowledge and know-how of the licensor. These may be transferred via design sessions, training, and so forth. The grant clause also states whether the license is exclusive, which gives the specified rights only to the licensee, or nonexclusive, which means that others may enjoy these rights as well. It may contain an immunity-from-infringement clause to protect the licensee from potential patent infringement by the original inventor. The agreement will also specify if the licensee has the right to grant rights to sublicensees.

PERFORMANCE CLAUSE

A performance clause states the dates by which the licensee should have achieved certain agreed-upon goals, such as development of the commercial application of the technology, first customer, or sales targets. Performance clauses are like preventive medicine. They help the licensor avoid a situation where the licensee ties up a technology in an exclusive agreement but never actually commercializes it or does not achieve the expected sales levels.

SECRECY CLAUSE

A secrecy or confidentiality clause restricts disclosure and use of the information being transferred and specifies who may know the details of the intellectual property and for what period of time. It also spells out when and under what conditions the person may share the details with others in the licensee's business and for how long. Typically a secrecy obligation lasts for between 5 and 10 years.

PAYMENT CLAUSE

The payment clause discusses the method of payment for the license—upfront fee, lump sum paid in installments based on performance, running royalty based on a percentage of net sales price, etc. If the license agreement involves a foreign licensee, this clause will also designate the currency in which royalties will be paid. U.S. licensors typically want payment made in U.S. dollars, but sometimes the licensor and licensee agree on a combination of both currencies. Because foreign currency fluctuates over the life of the agreement, royalty payments will vary as well, which could result in more or less income for the licensor, as well as higher or lower payments for the licensee. These factors should all be taken into consideration when structuring the royalty portion of the agreement.

GRANTBACK CLAUSE

A grantback clause is sometimes called an improvement clause. It permits the licensee to improve on the product with the stipulation that the rights to any improvements are granted back to the licensor. The agreement may also have a grantforward clause, which gives the licensee the right to use improvements made by the licensor or original inventor.

TERM

Every license agreement, like every contract, must specify a term for its existence at the end of which the agreement no longer binds the parties. It is possible to specify in the agreement that the license agreement may be renewed or extended by mutual agreement of the parties.

ADDITIONAL CLAUSES

Some license agreements involve equity instead of royalties or a combination of the two. Some will entail cross-licensing between the two firms party to the agreement. In other situations, the agreement will contain a "most favorable licensee" clause where the first licensee of a new technology will receive additional benefits for the risk of being the pioneer and more favorable financial terms than those given to subsequent licensees.

More and more software companies are including escrow clauses in their licensing agreements. The software companies place their source code into escrow with a neutral third party to serve as documentation if there is an intellectual property lawsuit and to protect themselves and customers should the company go bankrupt. In fact, recently, one of four business software licenses has an escrow clause in it.[10] One Internet company had its entire Web site copied by a foreign competitor. Fortunately, the company had placed the text, photos, and graphics in an escrow account, so when the case gets to court, they will be in a better position to prove that theirs was the original site.

LICENSING STRATEGY

A licensing strategy should be part of any technology company's overall goal to diversify its revenue streams and sustain a competitive advantage, but any licensing strategy must also meet other company goals and core values. Is the company willing to cross-license with competitors? Can it license without hurting its current products? These are the kinds of questions that must be asked when developing a licensing strategy. In addition, the following items should be accomplished:

- **Secure the support of everyone in the company.** When a technology is licensed to another firm, the licensor is essentially creating a partnership with that firm. Licensing takes time, upfront capital, and the commitment of everyone to see it through. It also requires a plan for how to defend the licensor's patents against infringers in order to protect the investment of the licensee.
- **Conduct an intellectual property search.** A small start-up company is probably not going to have a lot of intellectual property to track, but over time an innovative company will acquire a fairly large patent portfolio. It is important to look at existing patents as well as technology that has patent potential to see whether it is strategic to the company's core competency or capable of being licensed. If it is

strategic, then whether to patent the technology or retain it as a trade secret for internal use must be decided. Once these decisions are made, the technologies will need to be valued. Unfortunately, no formula can perfectly determine the value of a license agreement, as each deal is unique. Issues such as whether to license on a percentage of gross sales basis or on a use basis will affect value. Whether or not geographic exclusivity is important will also affect the structure of the deal. Valuation of technology is discussed in more detail in Chapter 8.

- **Identify licensee candidates.** Because the licensor/licensee relationship is a long-term one, it is important to select that licensee carefully. The licensee's track record in business and their capability to further develop the technology into marketable applications will be vital assets to the licensor.

❖ SUMMARY

Rising R&D and production costs, increased competition, and an uncertain economy have spurred companies to diversify their revenue streams so as not to rely solely on revenues from sales. Licensors need to decide which of their technologies they want to license. Then they must define the benefits of the technology to the licensee and conduct market research to determine if what the potential licensee says about the market for the technology is reliable. Conducting due diligence on the licensee is important to ensure that the licensee has the resources, knowledge, and skills needed to fulfill the terms and conditions of the license agreement and successfully commercialize the technology. Valuing the license agreement is a difficult task that is based on the economic life of the intellectual property, the potential for direct competition, the potential for government legislation, and changes in market conditions that could affect the value of the technology. The licensee, on the other hand, will want to do a comprehensive search for technology that will fit with their company and then prepare a business plan that will be shared with the licensor to demonstrate the licensee's understanding of the market and what is required to successfully commercialize the technology. Every company should have a licensing strategy that is supported by everyone in the organization, that contains a plan for managing the company's intellectual property, and that allows the company to identify the best licensees.

❖ DISCUSSION QUESTIONS

1. Why is it important today for any technology company to have a licensing strategy?
2. From the licensor's perspective, what would be important to have in place prior to speaking to potential licensees?
3. Suppose you have found a core technology that you want to license to develop and sell applications in your industry. In addition to the technology, what would you want to have transferred under the license agreement?
4. Under what circumstances might a technology company not want to license technology it owns?
5. Why is it important to have a performance clause in the license agreement?

❖ RESOURCES

Parr, Russell L., and Patrick H. Sullivan.
*Technology Licensing: Corporate Strategies for
Maximizing Value.* New York: John Wiley &
Sons, 1996.

Raugust, Karen. *The Licensing Business
Handbook.* New York: EPM Communications,
Inc., 2000.

Sherman, Andrew J. *Franchising & Licensing:
Two Ways to Build Your Business.* New York:
AMACOM, 1999.

❖ INTERNET RESOURCES

Yet2.com
www.yet2.com
Web site where inventors can post their
patents to a database. Potential licensees can
browse by keyword search or category

Intellectual Property Technology Exchange, Inc.
www.techex.com
A license exchange for licensing and research
professionals in the biomedical industry

The Patent & License Exchange
www.Pl-x.com
Web site where inventors can post their

patents to a database and evaluate their intellectual property holdings

PricewaterhouseCoopers
www.pwcglobal.com/
Includes a variety of reports on intellectual
property. Search on keywords "intellectual
property"

IP Marketplace
www.ipmarketplace.com
This site auctions all types of intellectual
properties

P&G: FINDING THE VALUE OF THE LICENSING NETWORK

Large companies are at a distinct disadvantage when it comes to innovation for several reasons: (1) if they are successful, they often suffer from inertia, the fear of doing something different that might jeopardize their success; (2) they often become insular, that is, they resist change and mistrust anyone outside the organization; and (3) they rely on incremental innovations and shun anything that changes their product platform. Procter & Gamble (P&G) fits this profile perfectly. P&G had not launched a new brand since 1983, going 15 years without a new product. When P&G finally did introduce a new brand, the fat substitute Olestra, it was a disappointing failure. In the late 1990s, however, P&G finally broke through its dormant period, introducing six new products at one time. One, the Swiffer mop, was enormously successful, but the cost of the market launch of six brands simultaneously put P&G in a financially precarious position, and it once again backed off from developing new products.

With more at stake on each new product, P&G finally realized that it could no longer isolate itself from the outside world and hope to be innovative enough to compete. P&G holds about 27,000 patents, but it uses less than 10 percent of them in its current product portfolio. Although it is common for information technology and biotech firms to license their technologies and reap multiple streams of revenues from them, it has not been as common in less-high-tech fields such as consumer products and services. The world views P&G as a consumer products company, but it sees itself as a technology company. Its signature product, Tide, is not simply a laundry detergent; it is a highly technical product with a lot of science behind it. That science is proprietary and can be licensed to other companies to stimulate the development of new products.

In 1996, P&G formed a licensing group with the intent of sharing its intellectual property with other companies. Jeff Weedman was put in charge of this effort. He knew that for the licensing initiative to succeed, P&G had to be willing to license its best intellectual property, not just the pieces for which they no longer had any use. He also knew that he had to create an incentive system that would encourage his team to work with companies on the outside. After all, why would a scientist work long and hard on a new technology only to see it licensed to another company. Unfortunately, P&G was not receptive to Weedman's ideas in the beginning. Not only did it keep the group from tapping into the patent portfolio of valuable P&G intellectual property, any license revenue the group managed to generate did not go back to the group that invented it, but went to the company's general fund. It seemed as though Weedman's concept would never fly. Finally, in 1998, Weedman found a champion in the CEO, Durk Jager, who believed that it was time for P&G to accelerate its rate of innovation. They decided to make any patent that had been in the portfolio for at least 5 years or used in a product for 3 years available for licensing. For example, P&G's food and beverage division had developed a formula that helped the body to absorb supplementary calcium. P&G used this technology in one product—Sunny Delight. With Weedman's encouragement, the division began licensing the technology to other beverage companies, including Tropicana. The rationale for this decision was that if you do not license a beneficial technology to your competitor, that competitor will find a way to design around your patent and compete directly. If you license it to the competitor, you are ahead of the game because the competitor is paying you for the use of the patent rights. To date, P&G has completed a few dozen deals, and the number is growing. In June 2001, P&G announced a licensing agreement with Newell Rubbermaid's Goody division to produce a line of hair accessories. In another partnership with Changing Paradigms, a private-label manufacturer, it is expanding its baby-care Dreft brand detergent with stain remover.

Sometimes the real value of a project goes well beyond the financial rewards. If P&G brings in $1 billion a year in additional revenues from licensing (only IBM has managed to achieve that figure), that amount will represent only about 2 percent of P&G's total revenues. More important than the new revenue is the change in culture at the industry giant and the recognition that it must share its technology if it is to continue to grow. The company's new goal is to have half of all of its innovations come from outside the company through licenses and partnerships. ◼

Sources: Ron Lieber, "P&G Has Something to Smile About," *Fast Company* (August 2001); Ron Lieber, "P&G's Not-So-Secret Agent," *Fast Company* (July 2001); Christine Bittar, "P&G Signs Cover Girl, Dreft Deals," *Brandweek Online* (June 11, 2001) *www.brandweek.com/brandweek/index.jsp.*

❖ NOTES

1. Goodwin Procter LLP "Patent Licensing: Another Way to Enhance Return on Investment," *IP/Tech Advisor* (July 1, 2001) Vol. 1, no. 3.
2. Charles M. Riotto, president, New York-based International Licensing Industry Merchandisers' Association, *www.licensing. org.*
3. Shiara M. Davila, "Rent-a-Brand," *The Advisor* (July–August 2001): 34–36.
4. Goodwin Procter LLP "Patent Licensing: Another Way to Enhance Return on Investment."
5. William J. Baumol, "Licensing Proprietary Technology Is a Profit Opportunity, Not a Threat," *Research-Technology Management* 42, no. 6 (November–December 1999): 10–11.
6. Ibid.
7. Stephen A. Degnan, "The Licensing Payoff from U.S. R&D," *Research-Technology Management* 42, no. 2 (March–April 1999): 22–25.
8. Paul Germeraad, "The Changing Role of R&D, *Research Technology Management* 44, no. 2, (March–April, 2001): 15–20.
9. John Pullin, "Ideas Exchange in Site," *Professional Engineering* 13, no. 6 (March 22, 2000): 28–29.
10. Bill Roberts, "Safe Keeping," *Electronic Business* 26, no. 2 (February 1, 2000): 44.

INTELLECTUAL PROPERTY STRATEGY

OVERVIEW

This chapter will examine

❖ developing a patent strategy

❖ creating a trademark strategy

❖ issues in intellectual property strategy

INTRODUCTION

Intellectual property is a source of wealth for companies and also a source of risk. Sixty percent of all intellectual property litigation involves patents. However, even if a company has no patents, it is still at risk of litigation over trademarks, copyrights, and trade secrets. The size of the company does not matter; every company has some exposure to risk. If it participates in joint ventures, does an IPO, merges with another company, or creates a licensing agreement, it is at risk for intellectual property litigation. If employees leave (and that is occurring with greater frequency), a company is exposed to potential litigation over intellectual property such as trade secrets.

Today, it is unlikely that a company will be able to protect a product with a single intellectual property vehicle (patent, trademark, copyright, or trade secret). The competitive, global environment requires a barrier of protection to safeguard a product from those who would seek to co-opt it for their own market. The barriers that companies create have become large and complex. Figure 7-1 shows some of the intellectual property barriers that may need to be constructed to protect an integrated circuit invention and its potential applications. If the inventor of the integrated circuit does not define its application claim broadly enough, it is conceivable that a competitor could patent an application not accounted for in the inventor's original application and then demand royalties from the original inventor's customers.[1]

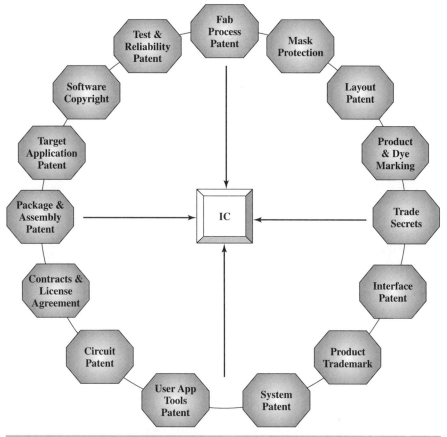

FIGURE 7-1   PROTECTION NET FOR AN INTEGRATED CIRCUIT

However, an aggressive patent strategy that shuts out competitors can backfire on a company that is not producing superior and reliable products. Such was the case for Affymetrix, a microarray chip producer with over 400 patents, which limited licensees to only making arrays that contain about a tenth as many genetic probes as the Affymetrix chip.[2] With these gene chips, a tissue sample, and a scanner, a researcher can study the cells in a tissue to learn which are active and which are dormant. However, for 5 years, Affymetrix's customers complained that the chips they were receiving produced false results and were often delivered long after the promised delivery date. They began to file lawsuits against Affymetrix and sought to develop their own patents on different microarray designs in an attempt to circumvent Affymetrix.

Today, the risks to a company's intellectual assets are far more serious than those to physical assets, and an increasing part of that risk involves things that cannot be controlled—people, partners, and environments.[3] Some of the new risks to intellectual assets include:

- **Brand.** One misstep can have a dramatic impact on a company's brand and revenues. Coca-Cola learned that lesson when a bad batch of carbon dioxide made some children sick in Belgium in the summer of 1999. Coca-Cola's operating income dropped $205 million, in addition to the $103 million in costs that the bottler incurred.[4]

- **Business model.** Successful business models are ripe for replication. When AutoNation demonstrated that it could sell more than $1 billion in cars online, it inspired numerous clones.
- **Intellectual property.** The interesting dilemma about intellectual property is that the greater the risk an entrepreneur takes in creating a new intellectual property, the greater the chance that the entrepreneur will experience a huge breakthrough. Today, it is important to balance very risky projects with safer ones, continue with incremental innovation, and interrupt that incremental innovation from time to time with breakthrough innovation.
- **Human capital.** More important than how many talented people a company has on staff is how many it can keep. Employee turnover and brain drain are pervasive and costly to technology businesses. Unfortunately, when businesses face financial problems, the first place they cut is their human capital, as it is the quickest way to improve the bottom line; it is also the quickest way to lose your competitive advantage.
- **Network.** More and more companies are outsourcing noncore competencies in an effort to speed up cycle times and achieve faster time to market. However, outsourcing also leaves them vulnerable to those companies for critical components of their business.

In the past, many companies cross-licensed intellectual property to avoid patent infringement claims. Today, although cross-licensing is still a viable strategy and essential in some industries, such as information systems, fewer of these cross-licensing agreements are being seen as companies are focusing more and more on recognizing the real value of their intellectual property.[5] In particular, software companies are seeking patents in ever increasing numbers to ward off industry giants such as IBM and Texas Instruments and to gain legal footing, as the courts tend to favor patent holders. Moreover, damage awards have skyrocketed, making the cost of acquiring a patent reasonable by comparison. In today's marketplace, not only strong defensive strategies, but also equally strong offensive strategies are in evidence. Like any other strategy, a patent strategy requires buy-in from the top down and incentives to keep everyone committed.

DEVELOPING A PATENT STRATEGY

Patents carry the strongest proprietary rights, and therefore result in the most defensible strategies. Just a few years ago, patents were considered merely cost centers in a company. This was because the financial systems of most companies were based on historical cost accounting. Unless a company purchased intellectual property from another company, intellectual property did not show up on the company's balance sheet. In fact, patent mismanagement was rampant. Perhaps the best example of patent mismanagement was Kodak's development of a line of instant cameras to compete with Polaroid. Kodak completely disregarded the patent barriers that Polaroid had erected around its technology, and the courts found Kodak guilty of infringement. Kodak was required to pay Polaroid $925 million in damages, shut down its $1.5 billion manufacturing plant, lay off 700 workers, and buy back the 16 million cameras it had sold for approximately $500 million. The 14-year infringement battle also cost Kodak

$100 million in legal expenditures. Another reason patent mismanagement has been so common is that many companies do not know what intellectual property they have, particularly if they have merged with or acquired another company. A classic example of this occurred in the 1960s and 1970s when Xerox's Palo Alto Research Center (PARC) developed the mouse and the graphical user interface, fundamental aspects of today's computing environment. Xerox did not see itself as being in the computer business, so it never successfully commercialized these technologies.[6]

Few companies have recognized the value of their patent portfolios to produce revenues. One company that has is IBM. In 1990, IBM began an aggressive strategy to maximize the value of its patent portfolio. It increased its licensing royalties from $30 million in 1990 to over $1 billion in 2000, an astronomical 3,300 percent increase.[7] This new revenue stream now accounts for over one-ninth of IBM's pretax profits.[8] IBM would have to sell an additional $20 billion in products each year to produce the same revenue stream.

SUCCESS AND PATENT STRATEGY

As most companies have become better at managing tangible resources, this skill is no longer a differentiating factor. Today, companies are differentiated based on technology and intangible assets such as trademarks, patents, and trade secrets. An effective patent strategy will improve a company's chances for success in three ways: providing a temporary monopoly, enhancing financial performance, and increasing competitiveness.[9]

ESTABLISH A TEMPORARY MONOPOLY

The most important benefit of a patent is that it lets a company take advantage of a first-mover strategy in a market with no competitors; that is, it allows it to stake out a temporary monopoly. It also helps protect core technologies and leverage them to create a family of branded products. Xerox had a monopoly on the copier market for almost 20 years before it was forced by a federal court to license the technology. So important is patent strategy that some firms choose their R&D efforts based on where they can gain the strongest patent protection.

IMPROVE FINANCIAL PERFORMANCE

Today, the bulk of a company's assets reside in intellectual property, and most of these assets are underutilized, undervalued, and do not generate revenues to their owners. Although patents are important as a protection mechanism for a company's products, they are equally important as revenue generators and leverage for partnerships and cross-licensing agreements. Annual maintenance costs and taxes can be eliminated by getting rid of worthless patents or donating unneeded patents to universities and other nonprofits.

INCREASE COMPETITIVENESS

Patents are intelligence-gathering tools that provide a wealth of information about a competitor's strategy. In 1998, a small, graphic-chip design firm, S3, saw that it was very quickly going to run into Intel's patent wall. Using an anonymous bid, it acquired the patents of a chipmaker that had filed for bankruptcy. Having done its homework, S3 knew that within that portfolio of patents was the patent that predated the Intel Merced chip patent. Now S3 was in a position to hold Intel hostage. Instead, it chose to reveal itself to Intel and demand that Intel cross-license its patents in exchange for the vital patent it had acquired.[10] The strategy was successful.

UNDERSTANDING PATENT INFRINGEMENT

Patent infringement occurs when a party other than the inventor holding the patent or a legal licensee makes and sells a product that contains every one of the elements of a claim. The issuance of a patent gives the holder the right to defend that patent against infringers in a federal court. In fact, an inventor must defend a patent or risk losing it in a challenge from a competitor. If a patent holder is successful in prosecuting the infringer, he or she may receive a reasonable royalty and an injunction to prevent further manufacture and use of the infringing product. If the infringer refuses to pay the required royalty, the inventor can enjoin or close down the infringer's operation. Alternatively, the court may choose to mediate an agreement between the parties that allows the infringer to pay an agreed-upon royalty in exchange for permission to use the patented invention.

Surprisingly, it is difficult to prove that a patent is invalid, as the courts generally side with the USPTO, assuming that it made the proper decision.[11] This means that defendants in an infringement suit bear the burden of proving with "clear and convincing" evidence that the patent is not valid. This is a much higher burden of proof than the typical "preponderance of evidence" found in civil litigation. Furthermore, the U.S. Supreme Court created the "doctrine of equivalents," which says that a product will infringe an existing patent claim even if it lacks a component listed in the claim if it contains a similar component that is "insubstantially different." This was done to prevent infringers from using insignificant differences to circumvent a patent. However, the federal circuit court has recently defined the doctrine more narrowly, saying that if the component was added after the original filing of the patent application (and that is often the case), that component is not entitled to protection under the doctrine of equivalents [*Festo Corp. v. Shoketsu Kinzoku Kogyo Kabushiki Co.* 187 F.3d 1381,1381–82, 51 USPQ2d 1959, 1959–60 (Fed. Cir. 1999)].

Patent infringement actions are costly and very difficult to prosecute, primarily because the infringer often makes the case that the patent was invalid in the first place. The average cost of patent litigation today is $2.5 million and growing.[12] In addition, many companies regularly challenge their competitors' patents in court as a business strategy to drain their competitor's resources and make it difficult for the patent holder to compete. A patent infringement warning which generally comes in the form of a strong letter from the patent owner's attorney, should never be ignored. It's important to consult with an attorney and determine if infringement is actually taking place. If a company finds that it is infringing, it should take immediate steps to stop the infringement and seek a resolution from the owner.[13] If, on the other hand, a company's patent has been infringed upon, it may recover damages for a period of only up to 6 years before it files the suit. If the company waits too long to file a suit, it may be barred from filing at all, because it is presumed that if it knew about the infringement and did nothing, it probably was unable to defend its patent.

The courts tend to favor the inventor and often file injunctions against alleged infringers even before the case is tried. They can also triple the damages if they determine that the infringement was willful (see sidebar). Enormous awards in the hundreds of millions of dollars are not uncommon. In 1996, independent inventor Gilbert Hyatt received a patent on the basic microprocessor, astonishing the semiconductor industry. He then assigned his rights to Phillips Petroleum Co., which will help him collect $100 million in licensing fees from the computer industry.[14] Gilbert had fought for this patent for 20 years.

❖ **Settling Patent Infringement Can Be Lucrative**

Jerome Lemelson was one of the most prolific inventors in U.S. history, but his fame comes from the rewards he reaped from aggressively defending his patents against major corporations. In 1989, he received his first favorable verdict when a jury awarded him $24.8 million against the toy manufacturer Mattel, Inc., which had infringed on his patent for a flexible toy racetrack. The judge later raised the amount to $71 million because he believed that Mattel had willfully infringed on the patent, but in 1992, an appeals court overturned the ruling. That did not stop Lemelson, who went on to file lawsuits and threaten companies such as Motorola, Eastman Kodak, and Apple. By the time of his death in October 1997, he had received about $200 million in settlement compensation. In an effort to support the efforts of independent inventors and to encourage people to invent, Lemelson established a foundation to "stimulate the U.S. economy and secure its position in the global marketplace by creating the next generation of inventors, innovators, and entrepreneurs."[15]

PATENTS AS A COMPETITIVE ADVANTAGE

In the world of intellectual property, patents provide the strongest competitive advantage because they enable a first-mover position, provide a temporary monopoly, allow the company to initially price at a premium to recoup the costs of R&D, and may even serve to create a new industry, as with the laser. Xerox dominated the copier market for 20 years with high margins and rapid growth due to its patents. Genetics Institute, a biotech firm, determines which drug to develop based on the results of clinical trials and on the potential strength of the patent.[16]

However, companies do not rely solely on patents for competitive advantage. Research has found that companies build an arsenal of weapons that includes secrecy, first-to-market and integrated product/process strategies, and supply chain control strategies, all of which are designed to strengthen the patent position and put up barriers wherever a competitor tries to go.[17] The need for a diversified portfolio of strategies comes from the very nature of competitive advantage in high technology. Original inventors often lose their competitive advantage once a dominant design has emerged. With a dominant design in place setting the standard, firms in the industry typically shift their focus from product development to process innovations to remain competitive.[18]

CREATING A PATENT WALL

Companies with consumer products that are easy to design around often attempt to create a patent wall, a barrier of multiple, interlocking patents that prevent another company from duplicating the product. Gillette, the shaver company, has taken this strategy to new heights. It has surrounded its Sensor shaver with 22 interlocking patents that cover everything from the twin, independently moving blades to the design of the handle. It even patented the container in which it comes because it gives off a masculine sound and feel when the package is ripped open.

A similar strategy is *bracketing,* which is when subsequent inventions effectively lock a competitor out of the market. For example, suppose a competitor has developed an innovative high-intensity light and has patented the filament. Now suppose that the filament requires a more durable glass bulb and socket housing to absorb the additional heat from the high-intensity bulb and special packaging because the bulbs are vulnerable to the oil on human hands. The competitor has the patent on the filament, but if another company patents the socket housing, the glass bulb, and the packaging, it has effectively locked this competitor out of the market unless the competitor goes through that company.[19]

A well-constructed patent strategy can gain a company access to a new market that they might not have been able to tackle without including patents in their strategy. For example, in 1994, Avery Dennison Corporation, the label company, developed a new film for use in product labeling and already had its first customer, Procter & Gamble. When Avery looked at some of the patent activity taking place, it found that a huge company, Dow Chemical, was beginning its foray into the same market space. Avery had an important strategic decision to make: Should it continue to invest considerable resources in this film technology when faced with such a formidable competitor? Fortunately, Avery had patents on fundamental aspects of the film technology, and it strengthened its position by filing for additional patents. Avery then used that patent stronghold to prevent Dow Chemical from making its film product.[20]

Unfortunately, the small inventor often does not have the resources to fight the large contender. Consider the following situation: A small company obtains a patent for a new technology. Big companies respond by "wallpapering" around it through a series of closely related patents. Then the large company sues the small company for patent infringement. The small company cannot afford to fight a multimillion-dollar battle with its limited resources, so it backs off and agrees to license the technology to the big company for less money than it rightfully should have gotten.[21]

The independent inventor with a small company needs to carefully consider whether filing for a patent is worth it. The only right that is gained from a patent is the right to sue an infringer, and the small company may not have the financial wherewithal to do so. If the company holds critical know-how that is essential to the implementation of the invention, it may decide not to patent it and retain the invention as a trade secret. It will be very difficult, even for a large company, to duplicate that knowledge. If, on the other hand, a patent is absolutely necessary, the inventing company should consider partnering with a larger company looking for new technology. The chances of actually getting the technology to market without having to deal with infringement lawsuits will be much higher.

RUNNING

If a company sets up a barrier, a competitor will eventually find a way around it, or at least that is the premise of the run strategy. Inventors who sit behind their barriers in a defensive posture give their competitors time to catch up and overcome the barriers. The concept of running is to introduce a constant stream of innovation, always staying at least one step ahead of the competitor. By doing so, the inventor gains first-mover advantage and a greater degree of control over the competitive environment.[22] Hewlett-Packard and Intel are two examples of companies that employ the running strategy by decreasing the cycle time on next-generation products.

BUILDING A COALITION

A strategy that runs counterintuitive to traditional thinking is when a company lowers barriers to entry and invites competitors to use its technology, creating a coalition of companies all using the same technology. Innovators have chosen this approach for several reasons: (1) to increase the likelihood that their technology becomes the dominant design because more companies are developing applications and using it, 2) to increase demand from distributors and end-users, (3) to enhance the company's current capabilities, (4) to take advantage of the network effects of more people using the technology, and (5) to enter markets that were previously unattainable.[23] These coalitions are often created through licensing. In the 1970s, Intel licensed its microprocessor to several semiconductor companies in an effort to ensure that customers had an adequate supply of microprocessors and system support. In turn, these licensees then developed complementary chips, which worked to ensure that Intel retained the dominant design. Once Intel's design was established as the dominant technology, Intel kept future generations of chips proprietary.

MAINTAINING PATENTS

When companies do not pay the required maintenance fees on their patents, those patents can expire and become available for others to use. When one company acquires another, the due diligence team may have overlooked this point, and the reason the acquirer sought the company in the first place—for its patent portfolio—may suddenly evaporate because it did not ask whether the patents were all in force and when they would expire. It is also important to determine if the pending patents are strong, that is, that the company will not experience problems with prior art and improper claims.

IMPROVING THE COMPANY'S FINANCIAL POSITION

Today, the greatest asset value in most manufacturing companies is not in tangible assets such as machinery or facilities, but in intangible assets, specifically, intellectual property. This is true of most companies. However, in general, these firms are not exploiting those assets to their competitive advantage. They are not realizing new revenue streams from existing patents; in fact, most are letting those patents sit untapped in their portfolios where they actually cost the company in patent maintenance fees and lost opportunity. Doing an audit of the patent portfolio can yield a veritable treasure trove of potential revenues and cost savings. Companies such as DuPont are taking multimillion-dollar write-offs on patents they donate to universities, while at the same time relieving themselves of maintenance fees.

CONDUCTING A PATENT AUDIT

It is important with any patent strategy to do some due diligence, not only on the company's existing patent portfolio, but also on any patents the company intends to license or acquire. The following are some actions that should be taken during a patent audit:

- Map the patents in the portfolio to determine expiration dates, maintenance fee schedules, strength of patents, and interrelationships among patents.
- Determine if there is access to the know-how associated with the patent either in the form of documents or the original inventor(s).
- Check how often other companies cite these patents or patents targeted for acquisition. If those citations are declining in number, it may mean that the patent is becoming obsolete and the pace of innovation in that area has slowed.
- Evaluate the financial worth of the patents. This can be accomplished by separating the patents into critical and noncritical patents according to their effect on company goals. Those that are critical typically involve core technologies used in

the company's current and future products. Noncritical patents represent technologies that will be licensed and are not used in current or future products.

WHAT HAPPENS WHEN THE PATENT RUNS OUT

What happens when a company produces one of the world's biggest-selling drugs, with annual sales of $2.6 billion, and its patent is about to expire? That was the situation facing Eli Lilly Co., whose wonder drug, Prozac, reached the end of its patent protection in the United States. Lilly had some understanding of what would happen, because in 2000, Lilly's patent in the United Kingdom expired, resulting in an 80 percent drop in sales when patients switched to less expensive clones.[24] In 2001, Barr Laboratories was poised to launch the first generic version of Prozac and profit immensely during the 180-day exclusivity period, which U.S. regulations give the first generic to reach the market. By the end of 2001, Eli Lilly was estimating the worst loss in the history of a blockbuster drug,[25] and in January 2002, the Supreme Court rejected Eli Lilly's appeal of a lower court decision that allowed Barr Laboratories to begin marketing its generic version of Prozac.[26]

SPOTTING INVALID PATENTS

With the deluge of patent applications and technology changing at an ever-increasing rate, the USPTO has not always done a thorough job of investigating prior art. As a result, many patents are issued that are later declared invalid because the technology has already been invented or they do not meet the patent law requirements. The consequence of all these junk patents is that companies are spending millions of dollars in licensing fees that they should not have to spend. Two companies have been founded to try to solve this problem: BountyQuest and IP.com. These two companies try to stop patents before they are granted or invalidate them after the fact.

The two companies work in different ways. IP.com provides a service where an inventor with an issued patent registers that patent in the public domain on IP.com's site. It then becomes part of a worldwide database of patents. The USPTO and the European Patent Offices have agreed to include IP.com in their prior art searches. BountyQuest takes a different approach. Its business model is based on the concept of the bounty hunter who captured at-large fugitives to collect a reward. BountyQuest encourages scientists, engineers, academics, and others to find prior art and challenge a new patent. In February 2001, BountyQuest awarded money in amounts of $10,000 and up for 4 out of 19 attempts to challenge the validity of patents in the areas of single-chip network routers, databases, and online music. One of the most stunning finds was that someone had patented downloadable digital audio in 1996; the original inventor, Perry Leopold, had actually patented it in the late 1980s.[27]

DEVELOPING A TRADEMARK STRATEGY

Trademark infringement is taking on epidemic proportions in the United States, with over 14,000 lawsuits filed in U.S. district courts in the past decade alone.[28] Companies are now taking greater care in protecting their trademarks, because trademarks are more than simply a way to distinguish one company or one product from another. They can actually bestow inimitable associations and meanings to a product that set it apart from competitors. Therefore, the standard for judging infringement is the likelihood of confusion.[29] Similarity between trademarks is the most common cause of trademark infringement cases.[30] The similarity can extend to sound and meaning. Trademarks cause confusion if they result in the same connotation in the minds of consumers, for example, the confusion between Play-Doh versus Fundough (*Kenner Parker Toys Inc. v. Rose Art Industries Inc.*), or when one trademark looks like it is parallel to another, suggesting that they come from the same source, for example, Roach Inn versus Roach Motel insect killers (*American Home Products Corp. v. Johnson Chemical Co., Inc.*).[31]

The growth of the Internet has made the protection of trademarks much more challenging. In 1998, MARQUES, the European association of trademark-owning companies, surveyed 350 intellectual property specialists to examine the issue of trademark infringement on the Internet. In just 3 weeks, it received 60 responses and found the following:[32]

- At least 85 percent of companies had experienced intellectual property infringement, 78 percent had suffered domain name infringement, and 40 percent had experienced copyright infringement.
- At least 80 percent of respondents wanted special measures to protect famous and well-known trademarks on the Internet.
- About 98 percent of respondents believe that the protection of names on the Internet is very important.

Domain name infringement is not the only problem facing trademarks. Other abuses arise out of a Supreme Court ruling that gives free speech on the Internet the highest level of protection. For example, Netscape Communications, Chase Manhattan, and Bally Total Fitness have all threatened legal action against the entrepreneurs who founded the "sucks500.com" top-level domain name so that it can attack these companies via sites such as *netscapesucks500.com*. The company has survived because using a trademark in a parody as a way to express an opinion is protected under the First Amendment.[33] A new type of domain name infringement is *typosquatting*. With typosquatting, the infringer locates the most trafficked Web sites, then registers a domain name made up of the most commonly made typographical errors. For example, one typosquatter registered "*wwwpainewebber.com*." The courts later determined that PaineWebber is a famous mark and that the defendant's domain name diluted the value of the mark [*PaineWebber, Inc. v. WWWPainewebber.com*, 1999 U.S. Dist. Lexis 6552 (E.D. Va., April 9, 1999)].

Other types of trademark infringement include the following:[34] Metatags (key words) and word stuffing; burying the name of a competitor into the source of a Web site or burying black text on a black background so that it can only be seen when the area is highlighted.

- Theft of images, text, and audio.
- Theft of a celebrity's name for use in an adult content site.

These are discussed in the next section.

FRAMING, LINKING, AND METATAGS

The ease with which information can be captured or linked on the Internet also makes it easier to violate the copyrights and trademarks of other companies. The first case to address the issue of infringement based on Internet linking was *Washington Post Co. et al. v. TotalNews* (1997) 97 Civ. 1190 S.D.N.Y. TotalNews.com did not publish its own news gathered by its reporters, but simply linked to news articles from other sources and displayed them in its frames so that they appeared to belong to TotalNews.com. The case was finally settled out of court and TotalNews.com agreed to stop framing the other Web sites. However, it was still permitted to link to the other sites through hyper-links using the names of the linked sites in plain text.[35]

When metatags are embedded in the pages of a Web site, the user cannot see them, but search engines use them to quickly find key words without searching an entire Web document. Infringers have used this technology to embed trademarked domain names of well-known companies in their sites so that their site comes up near the top on a keyword search. In a high-profile case, *Playboy Enterprises Inc. v. Calvin Designer Label* (1997) 985 F. Supp. 1220, Playboy accused Calvin Designer of trademark infringement because it was using the Playboy trademark in the machine-readable code on its Web pages. The court found in the plaintiff's favor and declared that the action constituted trademark infringement and unfair competition.

TRADEMARK STRATEGIES

So how does a company protect its trademark against infringement? The World Intellectual Property Organization (WIPO; *www.wipo.int*) suggests the following tactics:

- Conduct an Internet audit of domain names and trademarks on the Web using an Internet search engine such as AltaVista. Examining UseNet (user groups) and the company's e-mail system to learn the extent of infringement is also important.
- Monitor the company's domain name portfolio on a monthly basis; that is, check every site or record the company owns to make certain that it is accurate. Be sure to renew domain name registrations promptly.
- Perform a monthly audit of the Web, UseNet, and any other areas where infringers are likely to operate. Systems can be purchased that will do these searches and provide reports on a daily basis.
- Check to make sure that appropriate trademark and copyright notices are posted.
- Make certain that the company is entitled to use any images or content that appear on the Web site and that it has appropriate permissions where required.

PROTECTING AND DEFENDING TRADE SECRETS

Relegated for years to the background, trade secrets have finally achieved their well-deserved status in the information age. The sheer breadth of business and technical situations covered by trade secrets makes them an important part of any commercialization strategy. Trade secrets protect the vast majority of research and nonpatentable inventions that companies undertake. Without trade secret protection, much of the proprietary information developed by companies could easily be transported to a competitor and used against the company that owns it.

Still, trade secrets are not as strong a defense as patents for several reasons. Because they are not registered with a governmental entity, their validity can only be proven in a court of law, and that typically only occurs during litigation. They do not carry the weight of patents in an infringement situation. For example, if a company is accused of infringing on another company's patent, it will not be able to respond with trade secrets as an equivalent proprietary right. Moreover, trade secrets are difficult to value and equally difficult to protect.

Companies can protect their trade secrets in a number of ways. For example, Coca-Cola keeps the recipe for Coke in a bank vault in Atlanta. Only through unanimous agreement by the board of directors can the vault be opened. Only two employees know the formula at any one time. This is an extreme example. Most businesses mark documents as confidential and keep them locked up when they are not being used, encrypt confidential documents that reside on computers, and require anyone who comes in contact with the trade secret to sign a nondisclosure agreement.

To protect trade secrets, it must be proven that they are in fact secrets and that the company has taken measures to preserve their secrecy. If someone steals or reveals trade secrets, the company that holds them has the right to ask the court to issue an injunction to prevent further disclosure. For example, suppose an employee e-mails the code for the latest version of encryption software his company developed to a competitor and further suppose that his company had made it clear and in writing that the code was a trade secret. His company can go to court and attempt to seek an injunction preventing that competitor from using that code. Moreover, it can also seek damages for any economic harm from the illicit use of the software. To receive relief from the court, the company must prove that what was stolen or disclosed was actually a trade secret (an executed confidentiality agreement helps here).

It is important to note that the intentional theft of trade secrets is a crime under federal and state law. The Economic Espionage Act of 1996 (18 U.S.C., Sections 1831 to 1839) gives the U.S. Attorney General the power to prosecute anyone involved in trade secret misappropriation. In all cases, a qualified attorney specializing in intellectual property and trade secrets specifically should be engaged to help the company protect and defend its IP assets.

ISSUES IN INTELLECTUAL PROPERTY STRATEGY

Many inventions result from a combination of processes and components, some of which are in common use and therefore considered to be "off-the-shelf," in other words, any company can use or modify them to suit its purposes. When a patent is issued, all of the processes and components of the invention become available to the public, and it is often easy for competitors to look at the patent and devise ways around it. For example, in the manufacture of semiconductor devices, a process that includes growing a crystalline cylinder, masking and etching the wafer, and testing the final finished die, there are more than a thousand different small processes. Some of these processes may produce unique outcomes, whereas others are simply commonly used processes in the industry. Consequently, semiconductor companies protect some of their processes with patents and others with trade secrets.[36]

Patents provide the right to exclude others from making and distributing the invention for 20 years from the date of application, but trade secrets can theoretically last forever. However, trade secrets do not provide exclusivity. If someone is able to reverse engineer a product to discover how it is made or an employee reveals a trade secret, it is no longer a trade secret unless the person who has learned the secret maintains it in confidence as well. It is important to note that the person who discovers the secret may have the ability to apply for a patent on it should it be a patentable invention and not previously patented (see Chapter 5). In that case, the USPTO may not consider the original inventor's work as prior art, because it was concealed and not disclosed to the USPTO. This is an inherent risk to businesses that choose to hold patentable inventions as trade secrets.

However, there have been cases where, because of the existence of a contract between an inventor and a licensee prior to the filing of a patent, essentially creating a trade secret, the licensee can be bound to a royalty payment beyond the life of the patent. For example, the heirs to the Listerine fortune continued to receive royalties on the patent 25 years after the patent had expired due to an agreement with the licensee to reveal the secret formula early as a trade secret (*WarnerLambert Pharmaceutical Company, Inc. v. John J. Reynolds, Inc.* 178F Supp 655 SDNY 1959). This situation produces what is called a *hybrid license,* with rights deriving from both patents and trade secrets.

APPLYING PROTECTION TO A TECHNOLOGY OR PRODUCT/PROCESS

Determining the level and type of intellectual protection required should begin early during the product development cycle and recur at various stages during that cycle. Using the integrated circuit example in Figure 7-1, the final test depends on several special tests that occur earlier in the process. Placing patent protection on the special tests required for the final test can help erect a barrier around the technology that competitors will have difficulty overcoming, as they will not be allowed to use the proprietary tests to manufacture the integrated circuit.[37] Oftentimes, companies fail to protect the value of the processes associated with patented technology. Processes are an important part of a competitive advantage and should be protected as patents or trade secrets.

COMMERCIALIZATION PRIOR TO PATENT PROTECTION

In some instances, the market demands that a company commercialize its technology prior to seeking or achieving patent protection. During the feasibility analysis portion of the commercialization process, the entrepreneur investigates the market to determine if the business concept developed around the technology has merit. This process takes time, money, and effort, but is an important task to undertake prior to spending substantially more time and money developing a prototype and completing the commercialization process. This feasibility analysis will also likely determine if it makes sense to apply for a patent. The courts have specifically prevented inventors from putting their inventions in public use or on sale more than a year prior to filing for a patent (35 USC 102b). However, what constitutes "on sale" is subject to question, and what bars a patent application depends on clarification of (1) the minimum type of activity that comprises "on sale" and (2) identification of the point at which a process becomes an invention.[38]

As to the first requirement, the federal circuit court has required a definite sale or offer to sell more than 1 year prior to the date of patent application. The court has had a more difficult time with the second requirement, because it depends on how *invention is defined.* Whether invention is merely a concept or whether it necessitates a reduction to practice (demonstrable prototype) can make a difference in determining if the inventor has voided the right to apply for a patent. For example, in *Seal-Flex, Inc. v. Athletic Track and Court Construction*, 98 F 3d 1218, 1324 (Fed Cir 1996), the court determined that an on-sale bar starts "when a completed invention is offered for sale." In this case, *completed,* means reduced to practice. However, another case, *Micro Chemical, Inc. v. Great Plains Chemical Co.*, 103 F 3e 1538, 1545 (Fed Cir 1997), found that an on-sale bar was valid when an invention was substantially complete and offered for sale, in other words, when the invention "would work for its intended purpose upon completion."

Finally, in 1998, the Supreme Court ruled that *invention* refers to "a concept that is complete" that does not require a reduction to practice (119 S CT 304, 310, 1998). According to the Supreme Court, an on-sale bar applies when (1) an invention (as defined here) is offered for sale and (2) the invention is ready for patenting.

This ruling overturned the lower court's ruling in *Pfaff v. Wells Electronics*, 124 F 3d 1429 (Fed Cir 1997). In this case, Texas Instruments requested that the inventor, Pfaff, develop a socket. When the designs were complete, the inventor sent them with instructions and specifications to a socket manufacturer. Soon after, Texas Instruments gave the inventor a written purchase order for 30,100 units, which it had previously requested in a verbal agreement. All of this took place prior to the critical date, the 1 year prior to patent application, so the court ruled that the on-sale bar applied. The only exception to the *Pfaff* ruling is if an inventor can show that the offer for sale was done for purposes of experimentation to prove that it would do what it was supposed to do.

CHOOSING NOT TO PATENT

Sometimes choosing not to patent an invention is the best strategy. Consider a situation where a company has no significant competition and its R&D costs represent less than 2 percent of the selling price of its product. The company would incur little risk in simply forgoing the expensive patent process in favor of building its brand quickly in the marketplace. In contrast, consider a company that has a huge R&D expense to recoup from its initial sales. It needs time to do that, and, if it has a successful product, competitors will flock to replicate it. In this case, the company might be wise to seek patent protection.

Another instance where choosing not to patent might make sense is where there is no way to create an impenetrable patent barrier or doing so would be costly and time-consuming. Again, the better strategy may be to get the product to market quickly and keep improving it to stay ahead of follow-on competitors. In general, in situations where the real life span of the patent is uncertain because of market fluctuations, and the profit potential is also uncertain, it may not make sense to spend the time and money filing for a patent. Likewise, choosing whether to file for foreign patents is also a function of how strong the patent would be and whether the geographic territory it covered was worth the expense.

AVOIDING LITIGATION

Most businesses experience some form of litigation in their lifetime, however, it is possible to reduce the probability of being sued for patent infringement with an understanding of where the potential pitfalls are. Most start-ups outsource capabilities to other firms or independent contractors, particularly in the technical and engineering areas. Every time a company hires or fires someone, it exposes itself to liability for infringement, for example, a new employee who brings trade secrets from a previous employer or an employee who was laid off and who takes proprietary information on a patent application the company has just filed to a new place of employment. When a company is growing, management often does not take the time to ensure that the company is protected from the movement of employees or independent contractors. Strategic alliances where licensing or cross-licensing occurs are particularly ripe for issues of liability. Again, the company exposes itself to trade secret and patent infringement liability if the partnership does not work out.

All inventors should be aware that the USPTO has speeded its processing of software and process patents. These are areas where insufficient prior art exists and where the USPTO often has little experience because innovation is taking place at such a rapid pace.[39] Unfortunately, unscrupulous inventors and patent factories often attempt to take advantage of the USPTO's lack of prior art in the area, securing what are known as "junk" patents, then using them to blackmail start-up companies. Moreover, competitors in some industries time their infringement suits to coincide with a company's initial public offering to negatively affect that company's stock price.[40] It is clear that patents today are used in ways never foreseen by Thomas Jefferson when patent protection came into being.

COLLABORATING ON INVENTIONS

Today, more than ever before, scientists and engineers are collaborating on inventions. This has occurred because of a growing demand for specialization, the pressure of a global marketplace, the rise of the Internet as a collaborative tool, and the broadening of the scope of intellectual property law.[41] In complex fields such as biotechnology, it is nearly impossible for one person to have all the knowledge required to develop a new technology. It takes collaboration to move a field of investigation forward. Amgen, for example, minimized its development risk for Epoetin alfa, a drug used to treat anemia, by putting together a 50-50 joint venture with Kirin Brewery to provide Amgen with the manufacturing and distribution expertise that it lacked. R&D costs are increasing at exponential rates, making it essential that an inventor collaborate to share the costs of product development. Typically, these collaborations are transient, as it is more cost effective to hire expertise on an as-needed basis. Economists have provided the term *social capital* to describe the concept that to achieve innovation requires not only physical capital, human capital, and financing, but also an understanding of how those individuals and institutions work with each other to use the resources needed for production.

Despite its benefits, collaboration also raises legal issues and concerns about the protection of intellectual property. Surprisingly, collaboration has not received much attention in the intellectual property literature.[42] Traditionally, scientists and engineers have preferred to handle their own collaborative difficulties, relying only on the intervention of their universities, journals, and funders.[43] This belief has produced the notion that as long as rights are clearly defined, collaborations should occur freely. The reality is often much different. It is not uncommon for collaborators to have difficulty identifying who can claim invention rights, who holds rights to royalties, and who is entitled to further develop the work that was created. Some participants in a team project ultimately learn that their work was never acknowledged when the research is published, and that any use of the published material could constitute plagiarism. Problems of this type have many ramifications, not only for the researchers, but also for the university and society at large. When collaborative efforts run into trouble, society is unable to access the benefits of that research, which is one of the principal tenets of intellectual property law.

Collaboration has produced another challenge, that of misconduct. Collaboration diminishes individual responsibility, and, as a result, there is growing evidence of the falsification or fabrication of research results.[44] This has financial effects on the project and also tarnishes the reputation of those involved, as reflected in the quality of the work and its accessibility. Intellectual property law in its current form does not deal well with these issues. Several actions should be taken to ensure that collaborative research and development protects the rights of the inventors and encourages individual responsibility. These actions are discussed in the following sections.

DISCUSSING POTENTIAL ISSUES AT THE OUTSET

The invention team must meet at the initiation of the research to define roles and discuss potential issues that might arise. An intellectual property attorney who can point out potential issues the technologists do not see should facilitate this discussion. Of course, the attorney may identify so many potential legal issues that the team will not see a way to effectively work together, but the probability of that occurring is typically far less likely than the surfacing of serious and compelling issues later in the project that could stop the effort entirely. Furthermore, if these issues are dealt with in the beginning when the participants are often in equal bargaining positions, it is more likely that they will reach an agreement that is satisfactory to everyone. At this point, no one has invested time, effort, and financial capital that are not recoverable.

One example of this situation is found with blocking patents. A blocking patent challenge comes about when a single technology is protected by more than one patent, and a different inventor owns each of the patents. As a result, no one can make and use the technology without the permission of each of the other inventors. Someone who is not an inventor can use the technology only if they obtain agreements from all the relevant inventors.[45] In this situation, the solution has been patent pooling, which is a series of agreements on how rights will be licensed to pool members, as well as procedures in the event that new intellectual property is developed.[46] Patent pools that are negotiated without the help of outside expertise or mediation result in low transaction costs. Members in a patent pool must understand that it will be difficult, if not impossible, to accurately assess the value of a license agreement, but that on average, returns to the members reflect their contributions to the pool.[47] In addition to returns, members of patent pools typically experience better information flow and create strategic alliances that lead to further opportunity.

Many collaborations do not succeed; in fact, many potential projects never get off the ground because of disagreements about how the collaboration will work. The failures are now well known because the implications to the reputations of the participants and their ability to collaborate in the future are at stake. One classic example of the challenges collaboration can bring was the dispute between two renowned scientists, Robert Gallo of the National Cancer Institute and Luc Montagnier of the Pasteur Institute. As part of their research, the two scientists exchanged virus samples. The unintended consequence of this collaboration was the identification of the AIDS virus. Each claimed the discovery and the right to patent, when in fact the discovery was most probably the result of cross-contamination. Their battle for patent rights stalled the research and damaged the relationship between two prestigious institutes.[48] One thing that makes it difficult to achieve agreement before a project begins is that, unlike other types of agreements, the objectives of research agreements are often not seen in advance. When scientists begin working in a particular area, they sometimes undertake a process of exploration without a particular outcome in mind.

DEALING WITH TRADE SECRET ISSUES IN THE LAB

In some areas of research, trade secrets are essential to the patenting of a discovery or invention. One of the areas where this is particularly true is in the use of mice in biotech laboratories. Once a mouse is genetically altered in a research project, anyone conducting further research in the same area will require access to the genetically altered mice. However, the scientist who originally bred that strain of mice, a difficult and costly process, needs a period of exclusivity to complete the research. Journals in the biotech field are now recognizing this right and according the breeder a 2-year period of exclusivity, after which that strain of mice becomes public domain and must be made available to other scientists.[49] Living organisms such as mice cannot be patented, so a trade secret becomes the intellectual property of choice.

THE BASICS OF INTELLECTUAL PROPERTY MANAGEMENT

In large part, the Japanese technology explosion resulted from good intellectual property management. Over 45 percent of Japanese companies seek patents with the express purpose of blocking the development and sale of "look-alike" products.[50] Another 41 percent file for patents as defensive measures, that is, not to commercialize them, but to prevent others from doing so. Typically, about 65 percent of Japanese technologies are not commercialized immediately.

The primary purpose of patents is to contribute to the company's profits. Patent management has become a profit center instead of a cost center. In Japan, for example, Hitachi has been the company that has earned the most from the management of its patents, earning well over $364 million from patents in 1996.[51] From its very founding, Hitachi believed that inventions would be its lifeblood and encouraged its engineers to continually innovate. After World War II, Hitachi began to acquire foreign technology in such areas as semiconductor manufacture, computer production, television, and nuclear power generation. In the 1970s, Hitachi's goal was to file as many patents as possible. In 1970 alone, it filed 20,000 patent applications. Because the company was losing money on its patents, paying out $95 million in licensing fees on $5 million in revenues, it decided to make its technology available to other companies.[52] As a result, it became the first Japanese company to provide its patents to other companies and to recognize the competitive advantage of strategic patents. In 1985, it finally began to make money on its patents.

As a company becomes more innovative and begins acquiring many forms of intellectual property, it is important to have a mechanism for managing intellectual property so that opportunities to create revenue streams are not missed and so that the company can better defend its intellectual property against assault by an infringer. The following sections offer some guidelines for developing an intellectual property management strategy.

START WITH ORGANIZATION

It is not possible to design a plan to effectively manage technology if a company does not know what it has, and, considering that it must also manage what its competitors are doing, this planning and management can become an overwhelming task. Fortunately, technology has produced tools that make it easier for businesses to track and maintain intellectual property. Some of the information that needs to be tracked includes:[53]

- Types of patents by technology and company project
- Value of the patents: which ones have licensing potential, which have high value and should be defended, and which should be abandoned
- The number of competitor patents that relate to a specific technology field
- The technical fields that the USPTO has assigned to the patents
- Time remaining on a patent
- Maintenance fee schedule

Figure 7-2 displays a radar diagram example of an analysis of one company's intellectual property. Some of the software now available for this kind of organizing includes Intellectual Property Asset Management (IPAM) software at *www.aurigin.com* and DR-LINK software at *www.mnis.com*.

LEARN WHAT'S OUT THERE

The best way to find out who has done what and what technologies are out there that are similar is to conduct a database search with patent-searching software that uses keywords. Then create a map that shows the relationships among materials, processes, and applications of the technology, in addition to identifying which companies own pieces of the landscape.[54]

Citation trees, which are graphical depictions of patent history, can also be constructed. The USPTO requires that this be done for a patent application, citing all previous and related patents. Furthermore, if citations are color coded by company and country, it's easy to see which company dominates a specific area and which countries are filing which patents.

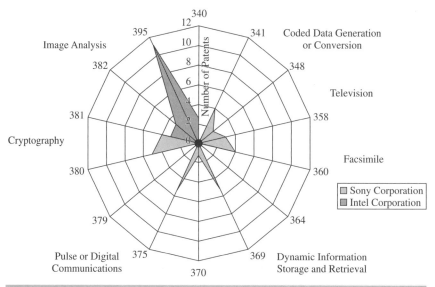

FIGURE 7-2   RADAR DIAGRAM ANALYSIS OF INTELLECTUAL PROPERTY

Source: Paul Germeraad, "Intellectual Property in a Time of Change," *Research-Technology Management* 42, no. 6, (November-December 1999): 34.

PUTTING IP KNOWLEDGE TO USE

A database and topographic maps can be used as sources of inspiration for new innovations or to find solutions to customers' problems. They are also a good way to think about whether there are potential partners in any of these companies and tech-

---

❖ **Guidelines for Ensuring a Successful Patent Application**

With the speed of change, inventors and entrepreneurs who file for patents need to make certain that they do things the right way. Here are a number of guidelines that are worth considering (in addition to those suggested by the USPTO):

- Use flow charts to depict the steps in a business method patent.
- Clearly state what the commercial embodiment of the business method claims, that is, how the invention will appear to the potential customer or end-user.
- Make sure that a thorough search of the prior art is conducted so that time is not wasted filing claims that will be denied.
- Try to predict who potential infringers might be and design claim sets so that they are difficult, if not impossible, to design around.
- Cite nonpatent literature in the application to find prior art that may not appear in the patent literature.
- Take advantage of examiner interviews.

nologies that have been uncovered. Similarly, the research will identify companies that are working in the same competitive space.

❖ SUMMARY

Intellectual property is increasingly a source of wealth and risk for companies. The potential for new revenue streams from patents developed and never commercialized is enormous. At the same time, the need to defend intellectual property against infringers has never been greater. An effective patent strategy will provide a temporary monopoly, enhance financial performance, and increase competitiveness, all of which contribute to a company's success. However, successful companies do not rely solely on patents for their competitive advantage. Rather, they build an arsenal of weapons such as secrecy, first-to-market and integrated product/process strategies, and supply chain control strategies, all of which are designed to strengthen the patent position and put up barriers for competitors. As with a patent strategy, a trademark strategy can build a strong brand and protect it. More than 85 percent of companies have experienced infringement of their trademark rights. It is vitally important to regularly audit domain names and trademarks to make sure that rights are not being violated. Trade secrets are also an important part of any commercialization strategy. They protect research and nonpatentable inventions, but as they do not carry the weight of patents in an infringement situation, care must be used in protecting them. A company needs to label trade secrets as such and take measures to preserve their secrecy. In the course of developing an intellectual property strategy, the level and type of protection required will be determined. If a company is collaborating on an invention or outsourcing an innovation effort, it will need to take extra precautions to preserve and protect its intellectual property.

❖ DISCUSSION QUESTIONS

1. In what ways can an effective patent strategy contribute to the success of a technology venture?
2. What is the value of developing a trademark strategy?
3. What issues need to be considered when outsourcing innovation or collaborating on inventions?
4. What steps should a company take if it suspects that an infringer is violating its patent?

❖ RESOURCES

Dobrusin, Eric N., and Katherine E. White. *Intellectual Property Litigation: Pretrial Practice.* 2d ed. New York: Aspen Publishers, 1999.

Holzmann, Richard T. *Infringement of the United States Patent Right.* Westport, CT: Quorum Books, 1995.

Knight, H. Jackson. *Patent Strategy for Researchers and Research Managers.* New York: John Wiley & Sons, 2001.

Paradise, Paul R. *Trademark Counterfeiting, Product Piracy, and the Billion Dollar Threat to the U.S. Economy.* Westport, CT: Greenwood Publishing Group, 1999.

❖ **INTERNET RESOURCES**

International Trademark Association
www.inta.org/
A nonprofit organization dedicated to the protection and advancement of trademarks as essential elements of international commerce

Patent and Trademark Depository Library Program
www.uspto.gov/web/offices/ac/ido/ptdl/index.html
Program administers a nationwide network of public, state, and academic libraries that have been designated as Patent and Trademark Depositories; libraries provide patent information to the public

The Trademark Center
www.tmcenter.com/
A leading provider of trademark research and protection. Services include free trademark searches and access to trademark information

The Patent and License Exchange
www.pl-x.com/
Financially oriented intellectual property management tools and services

Yet2.com
www.yet2.com
A marketplace for licensors and licensees

ROBOTIC SURGERY
TO THE RESCUE

What is the possibility that someday a surgeon will perform a surgery thousands of miles away from the patient? Based on recent advancements in robotic surgery, this will soon be reality. Today, a heart surgeon can use a surgical robot to perform a bypass operation on a patient without opening the patient's chest beyond five tiny incisions and while the heart is still beating.[55] The surgeon sits at a computer console several feet away from the operating table and uses two control instruments and a color video monitor to perform the procedure.

The benefits of robotic surgery to the patient are less trauma and faster recovery time. The primary benefits to the surgeon are less stress and fatigue, which are common in lengthy surgical procedures. Should fatigue cause tremors in the physician's hand during the procedure, the robot's "virtual stillness" technology filters it out. Another benefit is the ability to see anatomical structures in precise detail, something not possible with traditional surgical techniques.

Currently, there are more than 50 advanced robotic systems in hospitals around the world. Two systems in use in the United States are the Zeus Robotic Surgical System, manufactured by Computer Motion, and the da Vinci, produced by Intuitive Surgical. Both of the U.S. robotics companies have their technologies in clinical trials, but only da Vinci has received FDA approval for thoracoscopic and laparoscopic procedures. The day after the FDA announcement, the first non-clinical-trial use of robotic surgery for gallbladder removal was performed at Doctors' Hospital in Richmond, Virginia, on patient Kimberly Briggs. Less than 4 hours after the surgery, she faced a press conference and claimed that she felt "great."

Being a pioneer is not always easy; Computer Motion and Intuitive Surgical have faced off in an effort to be declared the preeminent robotic system. In May 2000, Computer Motion filed a lawsuit against Intuitive for infringing on seven of its patents, initiating a flurry of legal papers. Computer Motion holds a valid patent (#6063095) on critical hand tremor elimination technology, which is essential for use during minimally invasive surgery. The lawsuit claims that the da Vinci system uses their technology and is infringing. Therefore, it has added this patent to the other seven in the claim of infringement. Meanwhile, Computer Motion has an additional 45 patents pending.

Both companies' systems have been approved for use in Europe, but only da Vinci has received FDA approval for non-cardiac thoracoscopic and laparoscopic surgery in the United States. This means that Intuitive is the only company that can sell its robotic system in the United States. Despite patent litigation, FDA approval has given Intuitive a first-mover advantage in the United States. In addition, the FDA determined that future submissions of devices and clinical indications could be expedited in about 90 days. The standard approval process often takes up to a year to complete. This gives Intuitive another competitive advantage.

On February 7, 2001, the U.S. District Court for the Central District of California stayed all proceedings in the patent litigation between the two companies to allow the U.S. Patent Office time to resolve the interferences between them. An interference is a proceeding where the USPTO resolves a dispute between inventors claiming the same invention. In this case, the USPTO found interferences between a patent owned by SRI International and licensed in an exclusive agreement to Intuitive and three Computer Motion patents. During the proceedings, the USPTO will have to decide if, in fact, the subject of the patent is patentable and then who invented it first. Because SRI filed its application in January 1992, it is considered the senior party.

Computer Motion, which filed 7 months after SRI, must prove that it should keep its patents. Some observers believe that the only way to resolve the intellectual property issues here, given what is at stake, is for the two companies to merge and work together to set the standard for robotic surgery. ■

Sources: "Intuitive Surgical Announces Status of Patent Litigation," *Business Wire* (February 7, 2001.) "Intuitive Surgical's da Vinci System Cleared by FDA to Perform Robotic Chest Surgery in the United States," *Business Wire* (March 5, 2001.) David Noonan, "Next Frontiers: The Ultimate Remote Control," *Newsweek* 137, no. 26 (June 25, 2001): 70–76; "Battle of the Robosurgeons," *Business Week Online*, *www. businessweek.com/*, June 14, 2001); Steve Ditlea, "RoboSurgeons," *Technology Review* (November– December 2000) *www.techreview.com/*.

❖ NOTES

1. Kevin Klughart, "Protect Your Intellectual Property," *Test & Measurement World* (July 1999): 15–22.

2. W. Wayt Gibbs, "Patently Inefficient," *Scientific American* (February 2001) *www.sciam.com/index.cfm*.

3. Thomas A. Stewart, "Managing Risk in the 21st Century," *Fortune* 141, no. 3 (February 7, 2000): 202–206.

4. Ibid.

5. Bill Roberts, "Patent Strategies," *Electronic Business* (October 1999): 79–84.

6. Alberto Torres, "Unlocking the Value of Intellectual Assets," *McKinsey Quarterly* no. 4, (1999): 28–37.

7. Kevin G. Rivette and David Kline, "Discovering New Value in Intellectual Property," *Harvard Business Review* 78, no. 1 (January–February 2000): 54.

8. Ibid.

9. Ibid.

10. Ibid.

11. Marc E. Brown, "U.S. Patents to Be More Narrowly Interpreted," *Electronic Business* (February 2001) *www.e-insite.net/eb-mag/*.

12. Judith Pearson, Stephen Nickson, and Sean Marvel, "Court in Session: Intellectual Property at Risk," *Risk Management* 48, no. 2 (February 2001): 10–15.

13. Ralph A. Mittelberger, "Patents: What Every Engineer Should Know," *Civil Engineering* 71, no. 6 (June 2001): 58–63.

14. Mike Hofman, "Patent Fending," *Inc.* 19, no. 18 (December 1997): 111–114.

15. Lemelson Foundation Web Site *www.lemel son.org/*, April 13, 2002.

16. Rivette and Kline, "Discovering New Value in Intellectual Property," 54.

17. Wesley Cohen, Richard Nelson, and John Walsh, "Protecting Their Intellectual Assets: Appropriability Conditions and Why U.S. Manufacturing Firms Patent (or Not)," working paper no. 7552, National Bureau of Economic Research, Washington, DC, 2000.

18. Allen Afuah, "Strategies to Turn Adversity into Profits," *Sloan Management Review*, 40 no. 2 (1999): 99–109.

19. Rivette and Kline, "Discovering New Value in Intellectual Property," 54.

20. Ibid.

21. Brad Mead, "Patents: An Idea Whose Time Has Gone?" *Inc.* (March 2001): 43–44.

22. Afuah, "Strategies to Turn Adversity into Profits," 99–109.

23. Ibid.

24. Mark Court, "Eli Lilly Poised to Lose Patent on Prozac," *The Times*, July 30, 2001, *www.thetimes.co.uk/ /*.

25. "Lilly Updates Estimates on Prozac Loss," *Chemical Market Reporter,* October 8, 2001. *www.findarticles.com/cf_0/m0FVP/13_260/ 79250331/p1/article.jhtml?term=Eli+Lilly+ AND+Prozac.*

26. "Supreme Court Rejects Lilly's Appeal," *Chemical Market Reporter,* January 21, 2002. *www.findarticles.com/cf_0/m0FVP/ 3_261/82297625/p1/article.jhtml?term=Eli+ Lilly+AND+Prozac.*

27. Lisa Moskowitz, "Flimsy Patents Beware: There's a Bounty on Your Head," *MIT Technology Review* (February 2, 2001) *www.techreview.com.*

28. Daniel J. Howard, Roger A. Kerin, and Charles Gengler, "The Effects of Brand Name Similarity on Brand Source Confusion: Implications for Trademark Infringement," *Journal of Public Policy & Marketing* 19, no. 2 (Fall 2000): 250–264.

29. Michael J. Allen, "Who Must Be Confused and When? The Scope of Confusion Actionable Under Trademark Law," *Trademark Reporter* 81, no. 2 (1991): 209–259.

30. Ellen R. Foxman, Philip W. Berger, and Joseph A. Cote, "Consumer Brand Confusion: A Conceptual Framework," *Psychology and Marketing* 9 (March–April 1992): 123–141.

31. Richard C. Kirkpatrick, *Likelihood of Confusion in Trademark Law* (New York: Practicing Law Institute, 1998); *Knorr-Nahrmittel A.G. v. Reese Finer Foods, Inc.* (1988), 695 F. Supp. 787 (D.N.J.).

32. Nicholas Wood, "Protecting Intellectual Property on the Internet. Experience and Strategies of Trademark Owners in a Time of Chance," *International Review of Law Computers & Technology* 13, no. 1 (1999): 21–28.

33. Ibid.

34. Ibid.

35. Steven W. Kopp and Tracy A. Suter, "Trademark Strategies Online: Implications for Intellectual Property Protection," *Journal of Public Policy & Marketing* 19 no. 1, (Spring 2000): 119–131.

36. Jim Pooley and Walt Bratic, "The Value of Trade Secrets," *Managing Intellectual Property* (October 1999).

37. Klughart, "Protect Your Intellectual Property," 15–22.

38. Ed Poplawski, "Setting the Clock for Forfeiting Patent Protection," *Managing Intellectual Property, Patent Yearbook* (1999): 63–66.

39. W. Scott Petty, "Patent Office Retools to Examine Business Model Patents," *Intellectual Property Today* (September 2000): 36.

40. Alvin Lim, "How Business Model Patents Will Affect Your Start-up Model," unpublished paper, University of Southern California, San Diego, CA, December 7, 2000.

41. Rochelle Cooper Dreyfuss, "Collaborative Research: Conflicts on Authorship, Ownership, and Accountability," *Vanderbilt Law Review* 53, no. 4 (May 2000): 1,161–1,232.

42. Ibid, 1161-1232.

43. Jon Cohen, "Share and Share Alike Isn't Always the Rule in Science," *Science* 268 (1995): 1,715–1,718; Paul M. Rowe, "Encouraging Good Scientific Conduct," *The Lancet* 343 (1994): 1,627.

44. Richard Stone, "Baltimore Defends Paper at Center of Misconduct Case," *Science* 269 (1995): 157.

45. Nancy Morawetz, "Bargaining, Class Representation, and Fairness," *The Ohio State Law Journal* 54 (1993): 1, 2–3

46. Robert P. Merges, "Contracting into Liability Rules: Intellectual Property Rights and Collective Rights Organizations," *California Law Review* 84 (1996): 1,293.

47. Dreyfuss, "Collaborative Research: Conflicts on Authorship, Ownership, and Accountability," 1161-1232.

48. Lawrence K. Altman, "The Doctor's World: Cooperation vs. Competition," *New York Times*, April 14, 1987, C2

49. Lawrence K. Altman, "French Sue U.S. Over AIDS Virus Discovery," *New York Times*, December 14, 1985, Section 1; Philip J. Hilts, "D.S. Drops Misconduct Case Against an AIDS Researcher," *New York Times,* November 13, 1993.

50. "The Facts Behind Japan's Technology Explosion," *Managing Intellectual Property* 99 (May 2000): 19.

51. Ibid.

52. Ibid.

53. Paul Germeraad, "Intellectual Property in a Time of Change," *Research-Technology Management* 42, no. 6 (November–December 1999): 34.

54. Ibid.

55. David Noonan, "Next Frontiers: The Ultimate Remote Control," *Newsweek* 137 no. 26 (June 25, 2001): 70–76.

CHAPTER

8

BUILDING AND VALUING THE BUSINESS MODEL

OVERVIEW

This chapter will examine

❖ radical innovation business models

❖ the drivers of value

❖ financial models for assessing value

INTRODUCTION

Scientists and engineers often are focused like a laser beam on the technology they are developing with hardly a thought to its business potential. However, today more and more of these technologists are attempting to address the important issue of how to make money from the technology they have developed, and, more specifically, how the technology and the company that launches it will create value for its shareholders, investors, customers, and value chain partners. This is the process of building a business model, and this process has taken on additional importance as businesses realize the value and necessity of a unique business model that provides a real competitive advantage. As new models surface with increasing regularity, the real challenge is how to sustain the efficacy of the business model over time and protect it from imitation that could dilute it and turn it into a commodity.[1] An innovative business model is an important contributor to the value of a business.

The marketplace for technology in the United States began in 1946 when a Harvard professor and some Boston-area bankers and industrialists founded ADR, the first U.S. venture capital firm. With start-up funds of less than $5 million, they began data mining the technology around Harvard and MIT. Their biggest success came when they met a young MIT researcher named Ken Olson. They invested $70,000 in his Digital Equipment Corporation, and, by 1971, the investment had grown almost 5,000 times the original amount.[2] From that point on, technology firm investment became a staple of growth portfolios. Another major event contributing to the importance of technology as an investment was the 1980 IPO of Genentech, the biotech firm that at the time had no single salable product, only the prospect of losing money for several years. Despite that dismal picture, in 1980 Genentech went public in one of the largest stock run-ups in the history of the market: $35 to $88 in less than an hour and reaching a market cap that exceeded that of the American Can Company, a *Fortune* 100 company with over 100 years of operating history.[3]

The task of valuing a company is made more difficult today by the fact that companies now typically hold intangible assets over tangible assets by a factor of 4:1.[4] There are four primary classes of intangible assets: intellectual property, brands, publishing rights, and licenses, and each adds value to the company. Many efforts are being made to develop reliable methods for valuing companies whose assets are principally intangible. Some early studies point to a ratio of $18.70 in earnings for every dollar spent on R&D to develop these intangible assets.[5] These earnings are derived from licensing revenues, as opposed to actually making the product and selling it. But can a ratio like this be applied to a new technology company? In the case of new companies, arriving at an appropriate valuation of the technology or the company is challenging at best. With established companies, comparison firms can be used as a guide to valuation and price/earnings ratios can be applied to arrive at value. Valuation can also be based on a proven track record, experienced product lines, and an established customer and supplier base. However, with a new company, future earnings that are not based on a past track record are merely speculative.

The tools that will be described in this chapter will help the user arrive at a range of values, as no one tool takes into account all that must be considered when valuing a technology or a company. Ultimately, the valuation process comes down to a negotiation between buyer and seller that reflects each one's perception of the company's market value and their understanding of the assumptions on which the valuation was based. The chapter will begin with business models and then move into valuation.

RADICAL INNOVATION BUSINESS MODELS

Incremental innovation projects rarely struggle to find a business model because they provide improvements to existing technology. Thus, the value chain is well established, customers are familiar with the product, and ways to make money are fairly standardized. This does not mean that the teams producing these incremental innovations should not look for radically new models; they should, but building a business model is not difficult when there are lots of examples already in the market. In fact, case studies of successful innovations in business modeling have generally involved evolutionary, rather than revolutionary or radical models, suggesting that the best strategy might be to constantly revisit and revise a business model so that it never becomes stagnant.[6]

The case is quite different, however, for radical innovation projects for which there are no precedents in the market. In this case, the team will need to study business models in other industries to see if there are ways to extrapolate them to their industry or derive a business model from a customer need. The fiber-optic industry is a good example of the difficulty in predicting a viable model. There is no industry agreement on which applications will drive optical networking technology in the future, and that disagreement is reflected in the business models. Wholesale fiber backbone carriers and ISPs believe that Internet protocol will dominate and services will be implemented over the Internet, so their business models involve paying for information and services on the Internet. On the other hand, telecommunications providers are still betting on copper-based services, but the convergence of voice and data could threaten these businesses and decrease the profitability of business models dependent on voice traffic. Defense contractor Hughes's original business model focused on selling and servicing satellites for government and industry clients. Upon seeing that defense budgets were dwindling, Hughes realized that it must come up with a new business model to make up for the loss of defense contracts. In the early 1990s, Hughes started its DIRECTV division to pioneer a new direct-to-consumer business, sending out cable channels and movies to consumers' home satellite dishes for a monthly fee.[7] The timing was right, and profits from this division soon comprised 77 percent of Hughes' overall profits by 2001. This is a good example of how new business models emerge out of situations where businesses have to find a way to do more with what they have. Developing a business model begins with considering how the company intends to position itself in the value chain.

STRATEGIC POSITIONING IN THE VALUE CHAIN

The first step in developing a business model is to identify the value chain for the technology being developed. Upstream from a business are all the suppliers, OEMs, and producers; downstream are all of those intermediaries, such as distributors and retailers, that stand between the producer and the ultimate end user. Where a company is located on that value chain is a function of its capabilities, whether technology is licensed or forms the basis of a new venture and what kind of business the entrepreneur wants to operate. The goal should be to find a location that will allow the business to make a profit, sustain the company over the long term, and create strategic alliances that will add value to the company and help it achieve its goals.

Independent DSL providers have traditionally been wholesalers on the value chain, and that business model has been their demise. For example, one independent DSL provider, Northpoint Communications, filed for bankruptcy protection in February 2001 and was removed from the NASDAQ listing when its stock price fell to just 25 cents. The problem with the DSL business model is that as wholesalers, they must share their revenues with ISP resellers that provide them with customers and with telecom carriers from which they must lease copper lines and colocation space. If they could sell direct and get rid of the ISP intermediaries, they might have a better chance of becoming profitable. However, that approach has not been successful. DSL provider Rhythms NetConnections, for example, had an 80 percent retail direct base of customers, but on August 1, 2001, it filed for reorganization under Chapter 11 of the bankruptcy code. As a result of all the failures in the DSL and ISP areas, Covad Communications, the leading DSL provider, restructured its business model to serve customers who are in distress because of loss of connection with their ISPs. The new model is called "The Safety Net Program" and creates a stress-free way to transition to a new service with minimal disruption. DSL is essentially a commodity, so in the volatile world of telecommunications, having the flexibility to change a business model to adapt to the environment and provide value-added services is not just good business practice, it is a matter of survival.

Once the business is located in the value chain, it's important to figure out who pays whom, and the kind of pricing involved. Several iterations of the business model will probably be tested before arriving at the model that yields the best results, not only for the entrepreneur's company, but also for everyone else in the value chain. A company often establishes a price based solely on its cost to produce and does not consider what the market is willing to pay. Both figures should be tested early during the feasibility analysis of the project (see Chapter 3), because discovering that a price that the market will tolerate will not allow the company to cover its costs and make a profit may cause the entrepreneur to decide not to pursue the project. After all, customers ultimately determine if there is a business or not, so how they respond to a proposed price is critical to the business's success.

It will also be important to determine whether the business model chosen will force customers to change the way they use a particular product, assuming an incremental innovation. Will that change be worth it to them? For example, Texas Instruments is producing a new digital technology for the distribution of films to movie theaters via fiber-optic cable or satellite. This technology would require theaters to purchase expensive new equipment. Although it is clear that cost savings would accrue to the studios distributing the films, it is not clear how the theater owners would benefit; and until Texas Instruments can demonstrate a benefit to theater owners, the technology will not become mainstream in the market.

RADICAL INNOVATION IN AN INCREMENTAL ENVIRONMENT

The research of Leifer et al., presented in their book *Radical Innovation,* found that mainstream businesses producing incremental innovations face several challenges. Because they have enjoyed relative success, these companies mistakenly assume that what they are doing must be correct. However, research has demonstrated that they face the following issues:[8]

- How will they prevent the cannibalization of their current products?
- How do they overcome customer resistance to new technology where switching costs are relatively high?
- How do they avoid the inertia of the current business model?

This last question is perhaps the most significant. Established firms need to find ways to radically disrupt their current business models with new products, services, and business practices that create opportunity for growth.

CREATING MULTIPLE REVENUE STREAMS

Scientists often recognize that they need to license a technology to reach all the potential markets for that technology. For example, suppose an inventor/licensor synthesizes a new molecule and is able to obtain a patent. The new molecule has the potential to become the basis for a drug, a pesticide, or perhaps a food additive.[9] If the inventor has wisely invited people from different industries to learn about the technology, the inventor will quickly see that the technology can be licensed in these three different industries to achieve three distinct revenue streams without ever having to leave the laboratory and form a company.

An excellent example of the importance of creating multiple revenue streams is the research that Scott Shane did in 1998 on three-dimensional printing technology at MIT.[10] MIT filed for a patent on the Three Dimensional Printing Process (3DP) on behalf of four MIT researchers. The 3DP process produces layers of bonded powder material to form a specified component. Not unlike most researchers, the four were motivated by the pursuit of knowledge and had no intention of starting a company. Consequently, the MIT Technology Licensing Office was charged with finding suitable licensees for the technology. Over the 9 years that this technology was available for licensing, eight teams of entrepreneurs investigated its properties and considered ventures to exploit the technology. They found applications in everything from rapid prototyping and three-dimensional forming of replacement bones to time-release drugs and personal sculptures. In all, eight distinct applications were identified that were not recognized by the original inventors. Some of the lessons to be gained from this example are:

- Opportunities usually arise out of industry experience, so it's important to expose a technology to a number of people in different industries.
- Understand and protect the value of the core technology so that it can be licensed for a variety of applications.
- Go beyond the original invention team to find new applications.
- License applications outside the company's core competency to gain critical mass so that the technology might become the standard or dominant technology in its field.

CONSTRUCTING THE MOST EFFECTIVE BUSINESS MODEL

Building the most effective business model for a business will be a function of many factors:[11]

- **An understanding of the value chain and how it works.** Launching a radical innovation or even an incremental one requires a systems approach because any new technology will have a significant impact on all the partners in the chain. Therefore, a new entrant must be prepared to identify how it creates value, not just for itself, but for every member of the value chain.
- **Where the company is positioned in the value chain.** It's important to find the place in the value chain where the most value can be created. Potential strong partners and those companies that may threaten the company's performance must also be identified. If the value chain partner is inadequate, the chain will need to be modified or the company will need to acquire skills it does not currently have so that a weak partner cannot hurt the business.
- **The company's ability to experiment, learn, and critically evaluate.** Whenever a company is dealing with uncertainty—and every technology venture is facing uncer-

TABLE 8-1 Sources of Opportunity for New Business Models	
Reposition on the value chain	Look for unserved or underserved niches and customer dissatisfaction.
Reinvent the value chain	Tear apart what currently exists and create a whole new value chain. Extrapolating from other industries is often the inspiration for a reinvented value chain in an industry.
Redefine value-added	If, for example, competitors in the industry seek out contracts for work from customers, a company may choose instead to learn what customers typically want, do the work first, and then sell it to them in a turn-key package. It is then selling convenience. This is what J.D. Powers & Associates did in the market research industry.
Redefine distribution	Think about where customers spend a lot of their time and put a product there. If customers typically are at the end of a long chain of intermediaries, consider selling direct.

tainty in some regard—it needs to test the waters: evaluate, modify, and retest on a continual basis. By doing so, it will learn how to most effectively compete in the marketplace and sustain itself as a company. This process works best when a company is out in the marketplace talking to customers, suppliers, and anyone else who affects the business.

- **The company's ability to defend what it is doing.** When a company introduces a radical technology, by definition it is putting someone out of business, so it should not expect an easy path to success. Knowing in advance that competitors will attack every front, the company needs to be proactive rather than reactive. It needs to be prepared to prove to its value chain partners why their futures lie with this company and the technology it has created.

Table 8-1 summarizes some of the areas in which a new business model can be found.

THE DRIVERS OF VALUE

Many variables, both tangible and intangible, affect the valuation at each stage of the company's development: R&D, intellectual property, added growth, and the technology portfolio. Investors will look at market risk, technology risk, and management team risk. As the perceived risk increases, so does the required rate of return on the investment. Some of the critical risk factors that investors consider include the following:

- The size of the market and its readiness to adopt the technology
- The competitive advantage of the firm and its ability to sustain that advantage
- The skills, experience, and track record of the management team
- The upside potential of the venture
- The downside potential of the venture
- An appropriate exit time for the investors
- The current state of the economy and the industry in which the venture will operate

The primary drivers of technology value will be considered first and then the valuation process itself.

THE VALUE OF ADDED GROWTH

To grow, a company must invest in fixed assets, intangible assets, and working capital by using its free cash flow, which is the cash that is not being used to grow the business. The rate at which the business grows is then the return on capital invested multiplied by the investment rate. For example, to achieve 5 percent growth, a company must have an investment rate of 25 percent of operating income (20% $\times$ 25% = 5%).[12] To grow at a faster rate, it must invest more of its free cash flow. To achieve a high rate of growth, say 20 percent, a company would need to invest 100 percent of its free cash flow. It's easy to see why companies have to finance rapid growth through debt or equity vehicles. Furthermore, finding opportunities to invest with a 20 percent return or even any return above the cost of capital is not easy. However, R&D can provide that kind of return. The problem is that many companies do not have the staying power to wait long enough to reap the value added by R&D. Add the cost of investing in R&D to the cost of supporting the rapid growth that results from R&D, and it's easy to see why the company will likely experience negative cash flow for several years. In the long run, however, if the company can sustain a high rate of growth, the business becomes more valuable. And, as the rate of return on invested capital increases, each 1 percent of added growth produces a higher dollar value.[13] On the other hand, if a company merely earns back its cost of capital, it will never grow in value. Logically then, if the rate of return is less than the cost of capital, the company will actually lose value.

It is difficult for a company to sustain a high rate of growth over a long period of time due to all the variables that affect the value of technology in the marketplace and the company's ability to consistently achieve rates of return greater than its cost of capital. The issue of growth is dealt with in Chapter 13.

There are other ways to create value through growth. Table 8-2 summarizes these methods and explores their sustainability over time.

THE VALUE OF A NEW APPLICATION

With shrinking product life cycles and decreasing time to market, more and more companies are recognizing the value and need for intellectual property as a competitive advantage. Courts have been favoring the patent holder and new opportunities have emerged to use intellectual property to control and manage competition.

Building the business model for an emerging technology is a precursor to any valuation of technological intellectual property (IP) assets. The IP being valued must be identifiable and distinguished from other company assets. It must also be intangible and capable of producing future economic benefits. Intellectual property creates value for the company because it can be sold many times over in the form of licensing royalties. Dell Computer Corp. used its business method patents in 1999 to create a $16 billion cross-licensing deal with IBM that gives Dell lower-cost components and frees it from millions of dollars in royalty payments to IBM. Revenues from the licensing of U.S. patent rights alone have soared from $15 billion in 1990 to more than $110 billion in 2000.[14] It is predicted that these revenues could exceed a half trillion dollars in 10 years.

TABLE 8-2   Other Sources of Value Through Growth

Source of Growth	Comments
Highly Sustainable	
Market growth	Established businesses grow at rates comparable to the growth of the GDP. Other markets experience 5 to 10 percent annual growth rates over long periods of time. Positioning in a growth market can create value.
Market penetration	R&D often plays a role in this value creation strategy in the form of new technology that makes old technology obsolete, assuming there are no significant customer-switching costs. Regular development of breakthrough products is necessary to sustain growth.
Market share	To sustain a market growth strategy, the market share captured must also be retained. This is accomplished through continual improvement in all areas of the business, but particularly in R&D.
Not Sustainable in Long Term	
Price	High prices are sustainable only as long as the technology is new and free from competition. Competing on price is not sustainable because eventually the price goes below cost and the ability to increase volume to offset declines.
Manufacturing cost reduction	Value can be created for a time by reducing manufacturing costs, but eventually the company hits a wall. Only proprietary processes have sustainability for the length of the rights granted for them.
Overhead cost reduction	Reducing overhead is similar to reducing manufacturing costs, but this strategy has the further disadvantage that it is not positively affected by R&D expenditures.

The valuation of intellectual property generally begins with a technical assessment, which defines the invention, its scope and theoretical basis, and potential applications of the technology. Valuation then moves to an assessment of the invention's patentability and the ability of the inventor company to defend the patent once it is obtained. In the case of a new application, there is no precedent, so comparative approaches are not satisfactory. It is not known if customers will purchase the technology or when they will purchase it. In the 1930s, the U.S. Department of Agriculture developed the Adoption-Diffusion (A-D) model to understand why farmers were reluctant to adopt demonstrably superior technologies. The A-D model classifies end-users into five categories based on how they respond to new technology.

1. **Innovators.** People who are very comfortable with change and demonstrate an eagerness to adopt new technologies well before their colleagues. They understand that the product will not be perfect; in fact, they enjoy discovering the imperfections and reporting them to the inventing company.
2. **Early adopters.** People who are also very interested in trying new products, but who shy away from being the first to do so.

3. **Early majority.** People who observe the response of the early adopters to a new technology until they feel comfortable taking the risk to adopt. They want to know that the product works as intended.
4. **Late majority.** Once half of the market has adopted the technology, the late majority enters. These are people who want to make sure that the technology is well tested and proven and has been on the market for some time.
5. **Laggards.** These are the most conservative of buyers and usually are the last to give in and adopt a technology. They also are more focused on price.

The Technology Marketing Group Inc. (TMG) of Acton, Massachusetts, applied this model to the chemical industry with surprising results.[15] The firm they describe had developed a technology for use in pharmaceutical research, development, and production. Before going into product development, the firm wanted to place a value on the technology to learn if it made sense to go forward. The firm assumed that since pharmaceutical companies are usually on the cutting edge of innovation, they would at a minimum fall into the early adopter category. After many discussions with pharmaceutical firms, TMG discovered that the actual lag time for adoption of this new technology would be 5 years. Given that the innovators in the industry had not yet adopted the technology, it was estimated that it would be 10 years before the firm could sell sufficient volumes of the product. Ultimately, the calculated return on investment (ROI) over that length of time resulted in a decision not to pursue the technology. This example demonstrates the importance of estimating adoption times for each of the five categories of adopters and not assuming a value based solely on the initial adopters or innovators.

THE VALUE OF A BALANCED PORTFOLIO

Established companies may be able to enjoy the benefits and competitive advantage provided by a diversified portfolio of R&D and company investments. For example, there may be one product that is already a cash cow, another that is growing steadily and does not require additional influxes of capital, and yet another that is in the final stages of R&D that has incurred significant development costs, which it will not recover for several years. If the R&D project was the only one the company had, it would be faced with seeking outside sources of financing to launch this product. However, with a balanced portfolio and one project generating a lot of free cash flow, it may be able to fund the launch of the new product from that cash flow. A diversified and balanced portfolio provides a lot of flexibility. In terms of value to the company, the overall portfolio is strong and will increase as the new project begins to provide a return on the investment.

THE VALUE OF A LICENSE AGREEMENT

The licensing of technology proves that value can be created even without an operating business. Licensing also produces a market where technologies can be freely bought and sold, and is, therefore, another benchmark for the valuation of technology.[16] The value of a license agreement is the result of a negotiation between the licensor and the licensee and is a function of the rights being granted to the licensee. It has nothing to do with past costs of development of the technology; these costs are irrelevant. If more than one party is interested in the license and the license is exclusive, there may be a bid-up of the value. Because license agreements are essentially partnerships between the licensor and the licensee, there is every incentive to ensure that the agreement is a win-win for both parties so that the value is maximized for both.

Boer has suggested that licensing scenarios fall into two broad categories: proven technologies and unproven or partially proven technologies.[17] With proven technologies, setting the correct royalty rate is the result of striking a fine balance between technology gains and market forces. Industry examples and precedents on which to base the decision are usually available. With unproven technologies, however, the royalty is generally less because the licensee is assuming a great deal of risk in developing and proving the technology in the marketplace. In effect, the licensee is becoming an inventor and reducing some of the risk for the licensor. Normally, the licensee will have to invest some of its own capital and recover the cost of acquiring the money, along with a reasonable premium for the risk taken, from the return on its investment. Algebraically, this can be expressed as

$$\text{(Capital Investment + R\&D Investment)}$$
$$\times \text{(ROI} - \text{Weighted Average Cost of Capital)} + \text{License Fees}$$

In this scenario, licensing revenues increase profits after taxes are paid.

Most industries have established royalty rates from which licsensors don't deviate if they hope to acquire licensees. The rates can vary from 2 to 3 percent in some industries to 15 percent in others. In addition, the one-quarter rule of thumb suggests that pretax profits from the invention be divided in the following manner: 25 percent to the inventor, 25 percent to the developer, 25 percent to the manufacturer, and 25 percent to the distributor. If the invention represents only a small part of the value of the total product, however, the royalty rate may be discounted to reflect this. By applying the royalty rate to the size of the market and capitalizing it, a rough estimate of the value of the technology can be achieved. But how is a discount rate chosen? The licensee will probably want a rate that is equal to the actual cost of capital if the risk is not more than a person would normally take in the day-to-day business. However, if the risk is substantially greater, the discount rate would be equivalently higher. The cost of any alternative means to achieving goals, such as the cost of inventing around the patent or the cost of delay in product development should also be considered. Other factors that affect the royalty rate and the value of the license to the licensee include:

- The nature and scope of intellectual property protection
- The nature and size of the market
- The stage of development of the technology
- The significance of the technology
- The scope of applications for the technology
- The patentability of the technology
- The lag time for substantial adoption (the A-D model)
- The existence and nature of competing technologies
- The amount of investment required to develop and commercialize the technology

As a licensor, it is important to charge potential licensees a refundable evaluation fee so that those candidates who are just looking can be screened out and time and effort can be focused on serious candidates. If the negotiation moves forward and a license agreement is drafted, the licensor should also ask for an upfront payment, particularly if an exclusive license is involved. Paying an upfront fee is a way for the licensee to show their commitment to the technology. To ensure that the licensee progresses in a diligent fashion, it's a good idea to ask for minimum royalties, that is, a minimum amount that must be paid annually to continue the license agreement. However, this tactic requires some flexibility on the part of the licensor, because if the licensee encounters difficulties in the development of the technology, it is likely that the licensee will not be able to meet those minimums for a time. A typical license agreement also contains running royalties, which are pegged to sales revenues. This can be in the form of a flat percentage or a variable percent based on volume achieved or other appropriate measure.

WHEN VALUE IS DISCOUNTED

Just as certain factors serve to enhance the market value of a technology company, other factors cause that value to be discounted. Investors charge a control premium, which is essentially the discount or penalty they apply to a company that is poorly managed. The degree to which the value is discounted is a function of the amount of financial leverage the company has, the nature and magnitude of the nonoperating assets, and the opportunity cost of not exploiting available business opportunities.[18] Investors also discount for lack of marketability, that is, the size and dollar value of the stock interest acquired, the financial stability of the company, whether the shares available are a controlling or minority interest, and the size of the underlying assets and equity in the company, among other things.

A VALUATION PROCESS EXAMPLE

Figure 8-1 depicts the valuation process as an investor might see it.[19] It uses a hypothetical technology company called Trojan Haptics, a new media company that is working on technology to enable the blind to use the Internet through the sense of touch.

STAGE 1

Trojan's founders, a team of three engineers, have thus far invested $1 million in the company for initial research. An early round of friendly capital provided an additional $3 million. At this stage, investors apply what is called a *step-up ratio,* which is a type of multiplier that is negotiated between the seed-round investors and the founders. Generally, it is determined by typical industry ratios for similar deals. A ratio of 4 is considered mid-range for initial financing rounds. With this in mind, the value of the company—postmoney valuation—is found through the following formula:

$$(\text{Cumulative R \& D Dollars} \times \text{Step-up Ratio}) + \text{Financing}$$
$$= \text{Postmoney Valuation } (\$1M \times 4) + \$3M = \$7M$$

The $4 million in premoney valuation was created through a process of risk reduction. When the team first started, they estimated that they had a 40 percent chance of making $1 million in research funds meet the conditions necessary to advance the technology to the feasibility stage of R&D. They met that goal with the $3 million in friendly money; thus, their probability of reaching the next goal is now 100 percent. That is what the seed-stage investors saw.

Stage 1: Seed Capital

Trojan Haptics

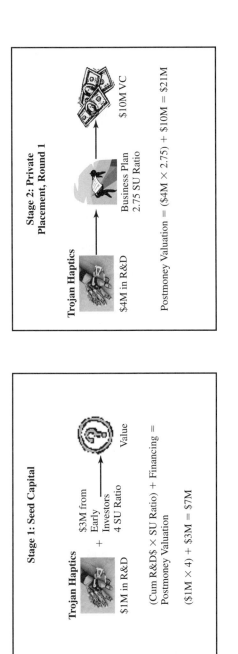

$3M from
+ Early
  Investors
  4 SU Ratio

Value

$1M in R&D

(Cum R&D$ × SU Ratio) + Financing =
Postmoney Valuation

($1M × 4) + $3M = $7M

**Stage 2: Private
Placement, Round 1**

Trojan Haptics

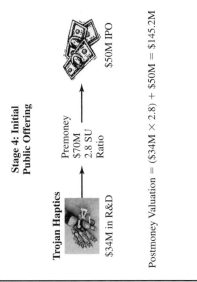

$4M in R&D

Business Plan
2.75 SU Ratio

$10M VC

Postmoney Valuation = ($4M × 2.75) + $10M = $21M

**Stage 3: Private
Placement, Second or
Mezzanine Round**

Trojan Haptics

Premoney
$30M
3.57 SU
Ratio

$20M VC

$14M in R&D

Postmoney Valuation = ($14M × 3.57) + $20M = $70M

**Stage 4: Initial
Public Offering**

Trojan Haptics

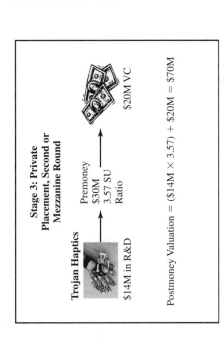

Premoney
$70M
2.8 SU
Ratio

$50M IPO

$34M in R&D

Postmoney Valuation = ($34M × 2.8) + $50M = $145.2M

FIGURE 8-1   THE VALUATION PROCESS

Source: The Valuation Process from "R&D Productivity and Value (in $ millions)" from Peter F. Boer (1999) Technology Valuation
New York: John Wiley & Sons, exhibit 6.6, p. 136. This material is used with permission of John Wiley & Sons, Inc.

STAGE 2

The company needs funding to carry it through the early stages of its business when income is negative. The term *burn rate* applies here. Burn rate is the rate at which a company goes through its cash. If a start-up company has $10 million in funding and an annual burn rate of $4 million, it will be out of cash and back for a new round of funding in 2.5 years. In Trojan's case, its cumulative R&D expenditures have grown to $4 million. The company's R&D progress in the feasibility stage has been very encouraging, and a business plan has been developed. However, these events are not nearly as exciting as the original discovery in the seed stage that quadrupled the investor's original return. The investors and the company have negotiated a premoney valuation of $11 million, which equates to a step-up ratio of 2.75. Added to the $10 million the investors have agreed to put into the company, this gives a postmoney valuation of $21 million.

STAGE 3

It is quite common for technology start-ups to go through several rounds of private placement and also engage in other financing activities, such as joint ventures with other companies or the creation of other start-up ventures. In this example, it is assumed that these types of activities are not occurring. Trojan has proven the feasibility of the concept and the technology and achieves a premoney valuation of $50 million on a step-up ratio of 3.57. It has now spent $14 million in R&D. Trojan is receiving increasingly larger sums, but it is also growing rapidly and its burn rate has increased. At this point, Trojan receives $20 million in mezzanine financing, which is the financing used to prepare for an initial public offering. That money brings the company to a $70 million postmoney valuation.

$$\text{Postmoney Valuation} = (\$14M \times 3.57) + \$20M = \$70M$$

STAGE 4

At the time of the IPO, Trojan Haptics has successfully tested the market and found widespread acceptance of its technology. It now plans to do an IPO to secure enough funding to rapidly expand in the market. It has expended a total of $34 million in R&D and is seeking $50 million in an IPO. Based on a step-up of 2.8, that would bring Trojan's postmoney valuation to $145.2 million.

$$\text{Postmoney Valuation} = (\$34M \times 2.8) + \$50M = \$145.2M$$

One of the unusual things about technology start-ups is that even without an operating company, they can enjoy step-ups in valuation of over 100 percent between the first and second rounds of financing, another 80 percent in the third round, and 35 percent at the IPO.[20] Of course, this will depend on the strength of the IPO market at the time.

FINANCIAL MODELS FOR ASSESSING VALUE

In general, all financial valuation methods are based on an analysis of a market at some point in the future under the assumption that the company is a "going concern;" that is, still in business. The only purpose for calculating book or liquidation value is to establish a floor for the valuation, but in technology ventures, even this becomes problematic because the assets of most technology ventures are principally intangible. Furthermore, it is inappropriate to apply price/earnings (P/E) ratios to new and early-stage companies because then the new company's value is based on the valuations of established public companies. Nevertheless, P/E ratios are one of the primary tools of the venture capital community and will be discussed in a later section.

Valuations are based on three assumptions:

1. **Existing use.** The value that comes from present operations, marketing, and financial strategies.
2. **Market value.** The price obtainable in the open market.
3. **Liquidation value.** The actual value of assets when the business closes.

In the case of new ventures, market value is probably the most appropriate assumption.

In the following sections, various financial models for assessing the value of intangible assets are considered. No matter what type of valuation method is chosen, there are several factors that should be addressed:

- The economic life of the intellectual property
- The economic life of the technology
- Transfer capability of the technology
- Restrictions on commercialization
- The cost of developing a substitute product
- The return on investment commensurate with this type of technology

VALUATIONS BASED ON COST

Cost-based valuations rely on calculating the actual cost of the investment in intellectual property in addition to accounting for inflation and the rate of return an investor might require. This might seem simple enough, but research indicates that there is no correlation between the amount of money spent on researching and developing a new technology, for example, and what the actual market value of that technology is. If the technology fails or has no commercial potential, then all of the money spent to develop it is lost and not recoverable. A cost-based valuation can be used as a hurdle rate, but it must be coupled with other methods to provide a more accurate valuation.

INTELLECTUAL CAPITAL MANAGEMENT

Intellectual capital is an intangible asset that is made up of human capital, such as employee know-how, capabilities, skills, and expertise; organizational capital, such as patents, process, and management systems; and customer capital, such as loyalty, goodwill, and supplier relations.[21] The most well-known predictor of intellectual capital value is market-to-book value, which is based on the assumption that intellectual capital is best represented by the difference between the market value and book value. If a company's market value is $100 million (number of shares times share price) and its book value is $60 million, then the difference, $40 million, represents the value of the company's intellectual capital. It should be noted that the intellectual capital management (ICM) method has been attacked as simplistic and vulnerable to changes in the marketplace that affect investors' perceptions of the market value of the company.

THE PRO FORMA DISCOUNTED CASH FLOW MODEL

The most commonly used tool for valuing early stage companies, R&D projects, or securities is the discounted cash flow (DCF) model. This model calculates the present value of the company's projected cash flow for a period of 3 to 5 years. Typically the period of time is a function of when the company expects to do an IPO or experience some other type of liquidity event. The cash flow is based on sales revenues less operating costs and debt repayment (it does not include interest), plus an estimate of the company's residual value at the end of the period. All this is discounted back to the present using a risk-adjusted, weighted-average cost of capital. This method is superior to other methods because it is based on a true economic measure of value—cash flow. There are four basic components to the DCF model.

- **Assumptions for the DCF model.** The assumptions are really the critical part of any model as they detail the basis on which the model was constructed. Those assumptions should be based on industry practices, current economic conditions, the cost of R&D, working capital requirements, market strategy, and projected revenue based on sales. The specific considerations under each of these are discussed in more depth in Chapter 9, where we consider the financial plan for the business.
- **Forecast period.** In general, investors like to see projections of 3 to 5 years, as that is typically the maximum amount of time they will hold an investment. Moreover, projections beyond 5 years are inaccurate at best in a rapidly changing environment, and discounting projections beyond 5 years has little or no effect on valuation.
- **Residual value.** This is the "going concern" value that is applied to the company at the end of the forecast period to account for the fact that the business is expected to keep operating. This residual value is not the same as the terminal value, which is based on the book or liquidation value, because it is assumed that the business will continue. To figure residual value, income capitalization and market multiple techniques can be used. Under the income capitalization approach, the company's earnings in the last year of the forecast are divided by the discount rate or cost of capital required to sustain the earnings into the future. The market multiple approach is often used when the company under consideration is planning an IPO or acquisition at the end of the forecast period. With this method, the earnings are multiplied by the appropriate P/E ratio of similar public companies. Both methods are subject to a lot of uncertainty, and the income capitalization method is particularly affected by the accuracy of the earnings forecasts.
- **Discount rate.** One of the most critical components of the DCF model is the discount rate, which determines the net present value of the projected cash flows. The discount rate is the expected return on investment or cost of capital. As the discount rate increases, the present value of the company decreases. One of the most commonly used tools for producing the discount rate is the Capital Asset Pricing Model (CAPM), which calculates the rate based on two factors: (1) the cost of risk-free debt and (2) a risk premium related to the type of business. This method typically generates discount rates from 10 to 20 percent. However, it should be noted that most venture capitalists do not use it. See the Venture Capital Methods section for more information on venture capital methods of valuation.

For an example of an in-depth DCF model, see Boer's *The Valuation of Technology* listed at the end of the chapter.

THE ROYALTY METHOD

The royalty method assumes a hypothetical license agreement with a royalty stream. The intellectual property is valued by capitalizing the projected post-tax royalty stream that is paid to the licensor for use of the intellectual property rights. This method makes sense in industries where license agreements are common.

THE REAL OPTIONS MODEL

Given the "irrational exuberance" of the investment community in assigning huge multiples of revenues or projected revenues to new technology companies during the period from 1997 to 2000, and the subsequent devaluation of technology stocks after the dot-com implosion of April 2000, many investors are now looking more seriously at the real options approach to valuing technology.[22] Real options are analogous to financial options applied to securities, currencies, and commodities. In this case, they are applied to business situations where management options are considered under changing circumstances.[23]

Boer uses the example of the petroleum industry and the decision to undertake new exploration.[24] When geologists identify a geological structure that holds the promise of a petroleum discovery, they must estimate the probability that the hole is dry; they must also estimate the probable size of the reservoir and the cost of building the structure to exploit it.[25] Traditional discounted cash flow analysis could likely yield a negative net present value in this scenario, and the project would probably be killed. With a real options approach, the investment is looked at as the purchase of a call on an option to produce. In this scenario, the strike price—the price at which the option will be exercised—is the cost of the production facility. The value of the underlying security is equal to the value of the oil produced less the cost of getting it out of the ground. So, if the cost of exploration is $1 million (the cost of the option), and the cost of the production facility is $5 million, the future cost of oil must be better than these figures. If the cost of oil achieves a high enough level, the decision could be made to invest the $5 million in the facility and begin the production of oil. The initial decision to invest the $1 million for exploration will be based on the estimated probability of finding oil and the probability that the price of oil will reach a level that makes the construction of facilities feasible. The first risk is called "unique risk," and this is the risk that the hole will be dry or smaller than projected. This kind of risk can be reduced using industry-specific tools to analyze the geological structure against industry benchmarks. The higher the unique risk, the lower the value of the venture. The second risk is called "market risk," and this is the volatility of the market—the risk that the oil price will be low or high. Market risk raises the value of the venture.

VENTURE CAPITAL METHODS

Venture capital methods of valuing a technology or a company are often determined by the requirements of the portfolios they manage. Typically, depending on the business and the risk involved, they will seek to multiply their investment three times in

5 years (compounded annual ROI of 71 percent) or 10 times in 5 years (58 percent). These rates drop as the company matures, so where the venture capital firm may seek a return greater than 40 percent for a start-up company, it may only need 25 to 30 percent for a company that is about to launch an IPO, because the risk of the investment has been substantially reduced. In the following sections, some commonly used venture capital valuation techniques are examined.

THE HOCKEY STICK APPROACH

With the hockey stick approach, the venture capital firm determines at the outset what return on investment is required during the holding period; it then applies a P/E ratio to earnings at the end of the defined period to calculate the market value of the company. The term *hockey stick* comes from the fact that when graphed, this method produces a curve that represents no earnings in the early stages and then rapid growth. The venture capital firm figures the percentage ownership required using the following formula:

$$(\text{Initial Investment} \times \text{Expected Payoff})/$$
$$(\text{After-Tax Earnings} \times \text{Comparable P/E}) = \text{Percent Ownership}$$

Suppose a company required an investment of $1 million over 3 years. The investor expects a return of five times the investment. The company's after-tax earnings in the third year are forecasted to be $1.2 million, and the investor has determined that the appropriate P/E ratio based on comparables in the public market is 14. Using the ownership formula, the investor would expect to acquire 29.8 percent of the equity in the company.

$$(\$1M \times 5)/(\$1.2M \times 14) = 29.8 \text{ percent Ownership}$$

THE MARKET COMPARISON AND COMPARABLE TRANSACTION METHODS

With the market comparison method, public companies are studied and their multiples in transactions are compared to the company in question. With the comparable transaction method, recent transactions of similar businesses are considered and their actual multiples are used to devise the appropriate multiple of earnings for the current transaction. The effectiveness of this method is a function of the accuracy of the company figures and their compatibility with the firm in question.

❖ SUMMARY

As important as the technology itself is the issue of how to make money and create value for shareholders, investors, customers, and value chain partners. New business models appear daily, and the challenge has become how to sustain the efficacy of the model over time and protect it from imitation that could ultimately dilute it and turn it into a commodity. A business model is not static, but dynamic and evolutionary. The first step in developing a model is to identify the value chain and the company's place in it, with the goal being to find a location that lets the company make a sustainable profit. Any effective business model should provide for multiple streams of revenues. The business model will ultimately affect the valuation of the technology and the company. When investors consider the valuation of a technology company, they look at a number of factors, including the size of the market and its readiness to adopt the technology, the sustainable competitive advantage, and the skills and track record of the management team. Growth, new applications of a technology, a balanced portfolio of technologies, and license agreements drive value. Poor management, high financial leverage, the magnitude of nonoperating assets, and the opportunity cost of not exploiting the technology are discounted from the value of a technology. There are a variety of financial models for assessing value, including cost-based valuations, intellectual capital management, the pro forma discounted cash flow model, royalty methods, real options, and a variety of venture capital methods.

❖ DISCUSSION QUESTIONS

1. What should an effective business model accomplish?
2. How do the drivers of value integrate with the business model?
3. Which of the financial models for assessing value are most appropriate for a new technology venture? Why?
4. What is the primary disadvantage of cost-based valuation and how can it be rectified?

❖ RESOURCES

Boer, Peter F. *The Valuation of Technology: Business and Financial Issues in R&D*. New York: John Wiley & Sons, 1999.

Copeland, Tom, Tim Koller, and Jack Murrin. *Valuation: Measuring and Managing the Value of Companies*. 3d ed. New York: John Wiley & Sons, 2000.

Pratt, Shannon P., Robert F. Reilly, and Robert P. Schweihs. *Valuing a Business: The Analysis and Appraisal of Closely Held Companies*. 4th ed. New York: McGraw-Hill Professional Publishing, 2000.

Razgaitis, Richard. *Early-Stage Technologies: Valuation and Pricing*. New York: John Wiley & Sons, 1999.

❖ INTERNET RESOURCES

Valuation Resources
www.valuationresources.com
A clearinghouse for publications and other resources on the valuation of technology

The Valuation of Technology
www.boer.org/
The home page for Peter Boer's research and book on the valuation of technologys

PIXSTREAM INC.: THE VALUE OF INTANGIBLE ASSETS

Today, as the value of intangible assets is increasing in proportion to the value of most companies' tangible assets, CEOs face the difficult task of educating and convincing shareholders and investors of the value of intellectual property. This case discusses how a knowledge company, PixStream Inc., dealt with this challenge.

When PixStream was incorporated in 1996 in Waterloo, Ontario, Canada, it had over 90 employees and was a leading developer of video networking solutions. Its founders, Brad Siim, Marc Morin, and Steve Bacso, had all graduated from the University of Waterloo with engineering degrees, and while working at Hewlett-Packard developing high-speed hardware and embedded software, they determined that the growth in broadband networks and computing power would facilitate the use of video. They formed PixStream to explore how they could use broadband networks to provide new video applications.

PixStream's technology provided real-time video processing from a variety of audio and video inputs (direct broadcast satellites, local channel feeds, and video servers) and adapted it to any type of network. PixStream saw several applications of this technology, from video-conferencing to TV content redistribution. PixStream was particularly enthusiastic about the ability to offer TV services to subscribers over existing telephone lines. When the founders secured a million-dollar contract in 1996, they quit their jobs and moved PixStream to a converted basement. In December 1997, with several significant contracts secured, they moved into new office space. By February 2000, PixStream had completed four rounds of equity financing worth $55 million. In February 2000, it secured a $35 million special warrant round.

In 1999, PixStream was considering an IPO offering within the next 2 years. Whenever you are planning to do an IPO, you must make sure that your accounting processes correctly depict the financial status of the company, and you usually want to show a history of earnings. One of PixStream's policies from its inception was to expense all of its R&D costs when they were incurred. Since 1996, the company had expensed more than $8 million in R&D costs, as it was under no pressure to produce earnings. Expensing R&D understates asset and equity values, but the CFO and acting CEO Tim Jackson reasoned that if PixStream capitalized its R&D, it would actually be creating assets that would have to be amortized over a long period of time. That approach would serve to increase the company's profits in the short term. Now Jackson was concerned that the policy of expensing R&D was actually making the company appear less valuable to outsiders because it was showing little or no earnings. R&D costs are reasonably considered an investment in the future of the company. Writing them off as an expense when they are incurred is like saying that they will produce no value in the future. Moreover, it is possible that expensing R&D can produce information asymmetry, that is, when company management knows more than outside investors, which can result in a higher cost of capital to the company.

PixStream had not yet faced this issue because it had relied on friendly capital to fund its activities. However, an IPO would throw the company into a whole new ballgame, and Jackson would most likely not know his investors. Therefore, it was vital to determine the full value of the company. What PixStream did not know was that it would never do its IPO because a turn of events took the company in a different direction.

In early 2000, PixStream was looking for a major partner to integrate its technology and speed up its market expansion. It approached Cisco Systems about a partnership, but the network giant was only interested in acquiring the tiny company for $369 million. The founders were convinced that the offering price was substantially more than they could ever achieve in an IPO, so in December 2000, the founders of PixStream sold their company to Cisco Systems for $369 million on revenues of $73 million, the fifth highest price of an acquisition of a private technology company in Canada. It was an all-stock deal that gave the PixStream founders a 20 percent stake in Cisco, which was valued at $74 million. At that time, PixStream had over 200 employees who would be staying on after the sale. Everything went smoothly for 4 months, but then Cisco, whose revenues were declining in the wake of the technology stock devaluation, laid off 8,500 workers, and in April 2001, it shelved the PixStream technology for the foreseeable future and laid off 170 of PixStream's workers.

The difficult part of this story for the founders was that PixStream was very successful prior to being taken over by Cisco, and the technology held great promise. The questions now are, will Cisco ever commercialize the technology, and what is the technology's value under the present circumstances? ■

Sources: Jacqueline Murphy, Claude Lanfranconi, Michel Magnan, James E. Tobin, "PixStream Inc.: Disclosing and Valuing Intangible Assets," *Ivey Business Journal* 65, no. 4 (March–April 2001): 48–57; Andrew Wahl, "PixStream's Waterloo," *Canadian Business* 74, no. 10 (May 28, 2001): 54–56.

❖ NOTES

1. Robert B. Tucker, "Strategy Innovation Takes Imagination," *The Journal of Business Strategy* 22, no. 3 (May–June 2001): 23–27.
2. Jeffrey Young. *Forbes Greatest Technology Stories.* (New York: John Wiley & Sons, Inc, 1998).
3. Genentech's Web site: *www.gene.com/gene/about_genentech/history/.*
4. Paul Germeraad, "The Changing Role of R&D," *Research Technology Management,* 44, no.2. (March-April 2001): pp. 15–20.
5. C. Young, "CEO Alert: Minefields Lie Ahead Regarding Intellectual Property, Patent Law, Competitive Strategy, and the Internet," *InSide Gartner Group* 21 (June 2000), *www3.gartner.com/Init.*
6. Tucker, "Strategy Innovation Takes Imagination," 24.
7. Ibid.
8. Richard Leifer, Christopher M. McDermott, Gina Colarelli O'Connor, Lois S. Peters, Mark Rice, and Robert W. Veryzer, *Radical Innovation* (Boston: Harvard Business School Press, 2000): 100–101.
9. F. Peter Boer, *The Valuation of Technology* (New York: John Wiley & Sons, 1999): 266.
10. Scott Shane, "Three Dimensional Printing," a case study prepared at the Darden Graduate School of Management, University of Virginia, 1999.
11. Leifer et al., *Radical Innovation,* 107.
12. Tom Copeland, Tim Koller, and Jack Murrin, *Valuation: Measuring and Managing the Value of Companies* (New York: John Wiley & Sons, 1995): 143.
13. Boer, *The Valuation of Technology,* 129.
14. Kevin G. Rivette and David Kline, "Discovering New Value in Intellectual Property," *Harvard Business Review* 78, no. 1 (January–February 2000): 54.
15. Mike Hruby and Mark Lutz, "Valuing Technology in New Applications," (Acton, MA: Technology Marketing Group Inc.,) *www.technology-marketing.com/index.html* accessed April 21, 2002.
16. Robert C. Megantz, *How to License Technology* (New York: John Wiley & Sons, 1996): 55–69.
17. Boer, *The Valuation of Technology,* 264.
18. Thanks to Scott Adelson, Houlihan Lokey Howard & Zukin, Los Angeles, CA.
19. Boer, *The Valuation of Technology,* 256–261. For a more in-depth look at the valuation of

technology, see John L. Nesheim, *High Tech Start Up.* (Saratoga, CA: J.L. Nesheim, 1997).

20. Boer, *The Valuation of Technology*, 261–262.

21. Ramona Dzinkowski, "The Value of Intellectual Capital," *The Journal of Business Strategy* 21, no. 4 (July–August 2000): 3.

22. M. Amram and N. Kulatilaka, *Real Options; Managing Strategic Investment in an Uncertain World* (Boston: Harvard Business School Press, 1999); L. Trigeorgis, *Real Options; Managerial Flexibility and Strategy in Resource Allocation* (Cambridge, MA: The MIT Press, 1998).

23. F. Peter Boer, "Valuation of Technology Using "Real Options," *www.boer.org/files/RTMOptions2.doc*, January 17, 2000.

24. Ibid.

25. Ibid.

CHAPTER

9

FUNDING THE TECHNOLOGY START-UP

OVERVIEW

This chapter will examine

❖ start-up risks and stages of financing

❖ seed capital

❖ early stage capital

❖ government funding sources

❖ the cost of raising capital

INTRODUCTION

One of the biggest challenges to starting a new technology venture is building a resource base that will allow the company to survive over the long term.[1] The challenge is particularly daunting when the business concept involves a new, unproven technology. Technology start-ups are dynamic organizations characterized by inexperienced management, lack of commitment on the part of employees, immature systems and controls, and inconsistent quality. These perils and others constitute what researchers have called the "liability of newness," and it is compounded by the nature of new technology ventures.[2] Technology ventures often require far more resources early in the commercialization process and face more complex problems than traditional ventures.

Resources are broadly defined as physical assets, intellectual property, human capital, or financial capital. Research suggests that a unique bundle of resources can produce a significant competitive advantage for a new venture.[3] Entrepreneurs may seek resource partners from any part of the value chain—suppliers, distributors, customers, and investors. Suppliers provide entrepreneurs with credit lines that help to ensure the start-up venture's cash flow. They may also partner with the new venture in the design and development of a new product. Distributors help entrepreneurs avoid the added start-up expense of warehousing and distribution. Customers may want a new product enough to pay a deposit to cover the costs to produce it, and investors supply additional funding to help the company grow.

Resource partners are very aware of the risks involved in high-tech start-ups. For this reason, a partner will often not want to be the first to make a commitment to the new venture, so the challenge for the entrepreneur becomes one of optimal sequencing; that is, which potential partner should the entrepreneur approach first in order to ensure that they can get the second partner, and so on. This situation often requires that the entrepreneur achieve at least a conditional commitment from the first partner in order to entice the second to come on board. Unfortunately, resource partners are often chosen based on their willingness to be the first to invest in the company; however, this approach does not maximize the value of the new venture. Any resource decision involves trade-offs of efficiency, urgency, and bargaining power. Entrepreneurs will not always make the best decision and choose the partner that provides the greatest value. Instead, they will often accept a less efficient partner in exchange for retaining more of the equity of their company.[4]

The retain-as-much-equity-as-possible approach works if the company has the luxury of growing slowly, but in today's volatile marketplace, this is a luxury that most high-tech ventures do not have. Ideally, an entrepreneur moves sequentially from one partner to the next, and partners make commitments conditional on the other partners' acceptance. If no partner is willing to be the first to commit, the entrepreneur may end up shuttling back and forth between partners in an attempt to achieve an agreement until the window of opportunity disappears.

One of the primary reasons that high-tech entrepreneurs have difficulty getting that first commitment is that they often are unable to adequately express the value of the technology to interested parties. Because their companies are new and have little clout, they may even find it difficult to gain the attention of resource providers.[5] Furthermore, without external validation through partnerships or boards of directors, they often cannot convince potential funding sources of the value of their proposition. This is a catch-22 situation for entrepreneurs. The case study at the end of the chapter shows how the team that founded ConneXus got commitment for their venture.

This chapter looks at the financing of a start-up technology venture and the various sources of funding available at the seed and early start-up stages.

START-UP RISKS AND STAGES OF FINANCING

Nothing affects the ability of a high-tech venture to obtain seed and start-up capital more than information asymmetry. When entrepreneurs possess more information about their ventures than the potential funding resources do, conflicts arise that can affect the willingness of investors and lenders to deal with the new venture.[6] At no time in the life of a business is information asymmetry greater than at the seed stage of a high-tech venture. At this early stage, the technology has not yet been proven; therefore, it is difficult to assess the market for the technology. In fact, for a radical innovation, the market may not yet exist, but must be created. The risk at this stage is intolerable for most investors, which explains why so much early stage product development is funded by government grants. The staged development of many high-tech companies presents additional risks for investors, as failure to sufficiently finance any stage of the new venture could cause it to fail. Biotech ventures are especially subject to this risk because they typically have far longer development periods that may last as long as 10 to 15 years.

Every technology venture faces several risk points. The type of risk determines the type of investor the company can realistically expect to attract and the amount of equity it will have to give up for that investment. Figure 9-1 depicts the various risks facing an entrepreneurial venture from pre-start-up to initial public offering. It also includes the types of equity investors that will be interested in the venture at each point.

The seed capital stage occurs during pre-start-up and generally involves product development and preparation for the business launch. In this stage, the risks are related to the technical feasibility of the technology and the risk that an effective and efficient means of manufacturing will not be found. The focus of the entrepreneur is on product development and testing and feasibility analysis of the business concept.

Early stage or start-up funding is needed when the company obtains its first customer and is officially in business. Once this occurs, the focus of the entrepreneur shifts to the market and the risks associated with entering the market and capturing enough customers to create critical mass for product acceptance.

During late-stage or growth funding, the entrepreneur's focus shifts to management issues. The need to professionally manage the growth of the company and incorporate systems and controls to handle growth becomes critical. It is often necessary to

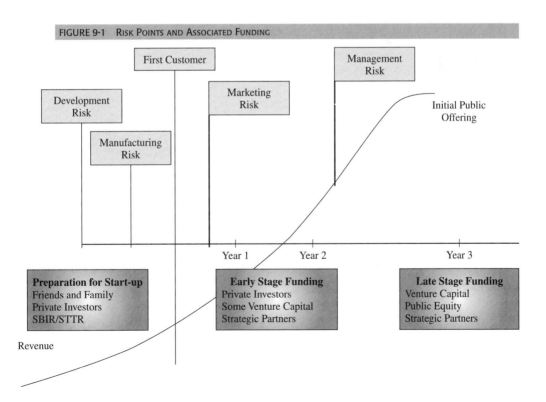

FIGURE 9-1 RISK POINTS AND ASSOCIATED FUNDING

bring in a management team with experience in growing a technology company to take a leadership role. The topic of funding growth will be taken up in Chapter 10.

SEED CAPITAL

The most risky stage of financing is the seed capital stage, that is, when the company is still in product development. The reason for this high risk relates to the risk/reward curve. Most investors want to minimize their risk and maximize their reward for investing in a technology venture. The highest risk is certainly during the development of the technology, whereas the lowest risk is when the company is established and customers accept the technology.

Because of the high risk involved, funding at this stage usually comes from friends, family, and those who believe in the business opportunity. For a new venture to make it past this stage and be in a position to access a wider variety of financing sources, it needs to quickly achieve an operating mode and launch products and services that will provide rapid cash flow and an early break-even. At this stage, overhead must be kept to a minimum, and the company should not bring expensive management talent on board. If the company will eventually need outside capital from angel investors or venture capitalists, it is best to reduce as much of the perceived risk as early as possible by proving the technology and the market. These actions will put the venture in a stronger bargaining position with investors.

FRIENDLY MONEY

Because first-time entrepreneurs often have little experience, no collateral, and few resources, they tend to resort to friends and family who believe in them to secure start-up capital. Although it may be easier to obtain this type of funding than others, in the long run it may be the most expensive money ever obtained; as some have said, "you pay for it the rest of your life." The entrepreneur should approach close friends and family with caution, recognizing the unique challenges of doing so. It is unfortunate but true that some entrepreneurs find it easier to not repay a loan from a family member than they would from another source because they believe they will not be sued. Consequently, money taken from friends and family can often result in hurt feelings and weakened relationships. When entrepreneurs plan to approach friends and family, they often consider exchanging equity for cash rather than asking for a loan. In that way, should the company be successful, the friendly investor will benefit from that success. However, it is important that these friendly investors understand the goals for the company so that they do not demand extraordinary returns in a short period of time. Should the company fail, however, friends and family, as equity stakeholders with common stock, typically will fall to the back of the line in terms of recouping their investment. One way to avoid such a situation is to structure a convertible debt deal where the lender receives interest payments on the amount lent and has the right to convert the debt to equity at a specified time in the future, once the company is successful. This type of deal should not be structured unless the company generates enough cash flow to easily make the interest payments. An attorney should be involved in this type of funding.

To help ensure a successful experience for the company and its friendly investors, the following guidelines should be considered:[7]

- If a friendly investor says no to the offer, do not persist, particularly if the relationship is important.
- Provide full disclosure. An entrepreneur must be completely honest with friends and family and not oversell the business concept, because if the company cannot perform to their expectations, it may damage those relationships. All risks should be disclosed so that friendly investors can make informed decisions.
- Do not take more money than a friendly investor can afford to lose. In other words, if the business should fail, the investor will suffer a loss but will still be financially whole.
- Put all financial agreements in writing. Even though these investors may be friends and family, this transaction is a business deal and should be structured as such to protect all the parties involved.
- Know the investors and how they will act. Understand whether a particular investor will be a silent investor or an active investor who is on the phone daily to learn the status of their investment.

CREDIT CARDS AND OTHER DEBT

Many entrepreneurs have funded the start-up of their businesses with credit cards, especially in industries other than biotech. Credit card funding is expensive, but when there are no other choices, it may be better than not starting the business at all. Today, credit card companies such as Visa and American Express offer unsecured credit lines to small businesses, and the cap on these can often be increased once the entrepreneur has demonstrated the ability to pay down the credit line. Entrepreneurs can also find lenders through online search engines. The best Web sites do not charge an upfront fee and have a good track record of matching small businesses with lenders. An example of such a search engine is *www.getsmart.com*, which is affiliated with 17 banking and non-banking lenders, including American Express. They have been successful enough to attract 1,700 small business applications a month.

Some entrepreneurs have used asset sales to secure funding from friends and family. The way this works is that the entrepreneur sells a company asset to a friend or family member and then leases it back from them. The person holding the asset (the lessor) gets a tax deduction and the entrepreneur gets an infusion of capital and perhaps better terms than could have been achieved in the commercial market.

EQUITY ARRANGEMENTS

Exchanging equity for cash is a common arrangement for early stage companies, but entrepreneurs also trade equity for other things as well, such as professional services, management expertise, and so forth. When a new company is starving for cash, it is tempting to give equity and, as a consequence, the founders may suffer significant dilution in later funding stages. It is important to reserve a certain percentage of the issued stock for such a purpose, as well as to attract future talent to the organization, but in the early stages, the entrepreneurial team should retain as much equity as possible. Later, when they have created significant value in the company, they will not have to give up as much equity for the same ownership stake in the company. One approach that not only attracts investors but is beneficial to the entrepreneur as well is the claw-back technique. With this technique, the deal begins with terms that give the equity investor a certain percentage of stock in exchange for a specific amount of capital. The terms then change depending on how the company performs relative to specified milestones. If performance is good or exceeds the milestones, the entrepreneur regains some of the equity given in the beginning. This approach works well in uncertain times. Another technique appropriate for volatile times is redeemable preferred stock, which gives investors preferred standing in case of a bankruptcy.

In environments where public equity offerings are not always a sure thing, working with an investment bank or underwriting firm affiliated with a commercial bank can protect the company's short-term interests. That way, the entrepreneur can prepare for a situation that could go either way. If an IPO is not feasible, the banker can issue a bridge loan while the deal is on hold.

STRATEGIC PARTNERSHIPS AND OTHER INTERMEDIARIES

Investors and strategic parties can gather two types of information on new technology ventures: (1) the track record and experience of the venture and its founding team and (2) the number and quality of network partners (suppliers, customer, distributors, and so forth). The number of patents a firm has obtained can be a measure of the track record and experience level of a new technology venture. The existence of several patents suggests that the firm has significant technical capabilities and quality scientific and engineering staffs.[8] Because the experience level of a new venture rarely is sufficient and without gaps, investors consider the network of contacts and alliances the firm has formed to fill those gaps. The halo effect of being associated with successful, reputable partners cannot be overstated.

Aldrich and Fiol have identified three social mechanisms that investors might rely on when considering the potential success of a new venture.[9] When two companies form a relationship, there are reciprocal benefits and risks. For example, the failure of a small business might damage the larger partner's reputation. In contrast, the smaller company generally benefits from the association with the larger firm. Reciprocal relationships are the first of Aldrich and Fiol's three mechanisms. The second mechanism is quality assessment, which holds that the prominent partner is usually able to discern quality under conditions of uncertainty.[10] If a prominent company associates with and transacts with a start-up company, it effectively puts its stamp of approval on the smaller company. The third mechanism is reliability. If a small firm gains a partnership with a large, prominent firm, it can be assumed that the large firm believes that the smaller firm is reliable. Consequently, when a small technology start-up manages to gain a prominent partner in a larger firm, the small company gains a more prominent reputation and a higher perceived level of quality and reliability by association.

For entrepreneurs who do not want to or cannot take advantage of debt and equity sources of capital, taking on a strategic partner can provide an infusion of capital or in-kind expertise and capability. Although cash from strategic partners is generally in smaller amounts than cash from other sources, it can be the cement to a relationship that carries with it long-term benefits for the new company. If the new company's activities take the entrepreneur abroad, strategic partnerships are often the only choice when a banker is nervous about funding high-risk activities. An additional benefit of an overseas strategic partner is that they can serve as a liaison to international bankers and help collect bills from foreign customers.

R&D PARTNERSHIPS

One type of alliance that is of particular interest in the seed capital stage is an R&D partnership where a high-tech venture can share the risk of R&D with a more established company, government laboratory, or government agency. With government entities, these partnerships take the form of cooperative agreements where the federal government works with state or local governments or universities to support or stimulate research. They may also be in the form of a cooperative research and development agreement where a federal laboratory and a nonfederal party, such as a high-tech venture, agree to share personnel, services, facilities, or equipment to conduct joint research in a particular area or an agreement whereby the company pays for the right to use government facilities, such as laboratories.

Strategic alliances are often the best way to rapidly move a new technology out of R&D and into the marketplace. VORAD Safety Systems, a developer and manufacturer of on-board radar systems for vehicles, partnered with Eaton Corporation, an $8 billion diversified industrial manufacturer that leads the field in fluid power and intelligent truck systems. Eaton was interested in VORAD's technology but did not have the internal capability to develop it. M/A Com, a microwave manufacturer, and AllState Insurance in Chicago also joined the partnership. The founders of the company retained a 35 percent interest and gained the necessary clout to enter the market from a position of strength. Strategic alliances are discussed as a strategy for growth in Chapter 13.

EARLY STAGE CAPITAL

Once a new venture has completed product development and confirmed the feasibility of its business concept, it is in a stronger position to tap into private investors, venture capital firms, and government resources to launch the venture. Investors generally consider four factors when evaluating a new venture opportunity. The first factor is the degree of uncertainty. New ventures are fraught with ambiguity and uncertainty because there are so many unknowns and the information that the entrepreneurs gather is generally imperfect. Consequently, it is difficult to predict the venture's future. This uncertainty compels investors to carefully consider such as investment, and, if they do decide to invest, they may invest in stages to mitigate some of the risk. The second factor is asymmetric information. In the earliest stages of a new venture, the entrepreneur knows far more about the venture and its potential than the investor. Therefore, it is possible that the entrepreneur might make a decision that adversely affects the investment, and the investor will not be able to immediately observe the effects. This situation puts the investor at risk because they have to make decisions without having critical information. The third characteristic of high-tech start-ups is that their asset base is principally intangible assets—intellectual property, know-how, and so forth. In contrast, firms that have the bulk of their assets in tangible equipment such as buildings, land, and inventory are easier to value and track; investors feel more comfortable investing in these types of firms. When intangible assets are predominant, investors incur a larger risk because these assets are difficult to value and protect. Finally, the markets for high technology also affect a company's ability to obtain venture capital. The supply of capital varies with market conditions and is often erratic. When investors pulled back from investments in e-commerce, it also affected tangential industries such as telecommunications and biotech. In general, venture capital firms have a herd mentality and tend to go where their colleagues go. This fickle behavior is disconcerting to entrepreneurs who find that the timing of their ventures can determine whether they receive adequate funding and can even launch the venture.

ANGEL INVESTORS AND NETWORKS

One of the most overlooked markets for capital for start-up ventures is the angel investor. Although venture capitalists receive all the media attention, angel investors fund the vast majority of all start-ups. Angel investors are essentially private investors who, as a group, invest about $50 billion annually in small, emerging companies. Their funding makes it possible for high-tech companies to move to the stage where they can attract venture capital funding and eventually become publicly traded companies. Angel investors typically fund ventures for $500,000 or less, although in the past couple of years when many professional venture capital firms have grown to billion-dollar funds, angel investors have rushed in to close the gap in the range up to a million dollars or more.

The primary reason that entrepreneurs know so little about angel investors is that they are, for the most part, a low-profile group. With the exception of networks of angels such as the Tech Coast Angels in Los Angeles, they are very private individuals who have usually been successful entrepreneurs in their own right. Although they no longer desire to start their own ventures, they do enjoy the role of entrepreneur, and vicariously become an entrepreneur through the companies in which they invest. Consequently, it is not surprising that angels invest in people first and technology second. Angels must feel confident that the people in whom they are investing are trustworthy, have integrity and experience, and can successfully execute the business concept.

Angel investors are a heterogeneous group, but many have other business activities besides their investments.[11] Like venture capitalists, they tend to have problems identifying sound potential investments and are subject to the same risks of information asymmetry and moral hazard that venture capitalists are. One way that angels seek to mitigate these risks is by becoming more involved in the activities of the business in which they invest. However, although they want to be involved in the business, they do not generally take a controlling interest like many venture capitalists do.

Angels lose money in about 40 to 50 percent of their investments, most probably because their due diligence is generally far less rigorous than that of the venture capitalist. Still, some angels have achieved enormous returns on their investments, as one angel did when he invested $100,000 in Amazon.com, an investment that returned $26 million upon his exit.[12] Unlike venture capitalists, angels tend to hold their investments longer and cash out through a buyout rather than an IPO.

Angels look for investments in industries with which they are familiar. They place a lot of importance on knowing the management team. The company needs to have substantial growth potential, and although the returns that angels require are not as enormous as those of venture capitalists, on average, they seek annual returns in excess of 20 percent. Like venture capitalists, angels need a way to exit the business, either through a sale, a merger, or another round of financing.

Angels bring a mixed bag of emotions to any investment. Because they are usually about 20 years older than the entrepreneurs in whom they invest and have been successful entrepreneurs themselves, angels often want to mentor the entrepreneur. By investing in the young entrepreneur's business, the angel gets to relive the excitement of building a business without having to deal with the day-to-day struggles.

The characteristics of a business that an angel is *not* likely to invest in are listed in Table 9-1. If the entrepreneur's business has any of these characteristics, the business concept should be reconsidered to make it more attractive to a private investor.

The angel investment process has three stages. The first stage is the screening of new venture opportunities, most of which end up being rejected because they do not fit with the angel investor's profile of desired companies. Once an opportunity is identified, however, the second stage begins and the investor will perform a thorough examination of the business plan, the business itself, and the entrepreneur. If the investor decides to proceed, the final stage entails negotiation between the parties to determine the terms and conditions of the investment.

The best way to find angel investors and angel networks is through professional advisors such as attorneys, accountants, consultants, professors, and bankers. Angel investors prefer to receive business plans through people they know, so cold calling a private investor is probably not the best tactic.

VENTURE CAPITAL AT START-UP

The dot-com implosion aside, venture capitalists are often considered to be good predictors of new venture performance because they are in the market constantly evaluating new ventures.[13] Despite their professionalism and the rigor with which they judge ventures, however, nearly 40 percent of all venture-capital-backed start-ups fail to deliver a return on investment to the venture capitalists that backed them.[14] This statistic confirms the uncertainty and risk associated with any business.

Venture capital funds are generally partnerships where approximately 80 percent of the fund is owned by the principal investors, often pension funds and other institutional funds. The portfolio managers control about 20 percent of the fund. The managers are rewarded based on the performance of the portfolio, thus they tend to focus on short-term gains of 3 to 5 years.

TABLE 9-1   An Unlikely Angel Investment

Characteristics Not Favorable to Private Investment by an Angel	
A "me-too" type of product	A poorly defined vision for the company
No intellectual property	No management team, a solo entrepreneur
Business location more than 100 miles away	Weak management team with no experience
Mature or fading industry	Exit time more than 7 years away
Return on investment less than 15 percent	Unfamiliar business or industry
Not enough market research with customer	Minority position with no voting rights
Weak competitive analysis	Too many coinvestors

Venture capitalists drive innovation; when venture capital is plentiful, innovation thrives. However, venture capital, by its need for quick returns, often only stimulates incremental innovation, not breakthrough innovation, which requires much longer time frames. This attitude is clearly manifested in the record-breaking investment venture capitalists made in 3,322 companies during the first half of 2000—$43.39 billion versus $19.28 billion during the same period in 1999.[15] This activity changed the face of investment capital as private investors banded together to compete with venture capitalists for the same early-stage deals. However, after the dot-com bust in April 2000 and the subsequent technology stock crash, venture capital investments were stalled as venture capitalists regrouped, reconfigured their portfolios, and tried to understand what had gone wrong.

From a venture capital perspective, the start-up funding process has slowed significantly. In the fourth quarter of 2000 alone, venture capital deals were about $8 billion less than the first and second quarters of 2000.[16] In the second quarter of 2001, venture capital deals totaled 271, the lowest level in 9 quarters.[17] The largest venture capital firms began pulling back from major investments. For example, J. P. Morgan Partners, with nearly $650 million to invest, made only 10 deals worth $42 million in the first half of 2001.[18] Two reasons explain the current lull in venture capital investment: (1) venture capitalists are taking more time to investigate a new venture after being burned by so many dot-com ventures and (2) the IPO market has virtually halted in its tracks. Venture capital firms are still investing, they are just being more cautious. No matter which sector interests a venture capital firm, they all agree that the focus is on a venture's people—the team and whether that team can execute. See Table 9-2 for a breakdown of the most active venture capital firms at the end of the third quarter of 2001.

Venture capitalists are generally attracted to superstar businesses with a unique technology or the ability to grow quickly and provide a liquidity event such as an IPO. They rarely enter at the seed capital stage of product development, even on technology ventures. Rather, they choose to enter during the marketing and management phases once they know the product can be manufactured and the entrepreneur has reduced some of the highest risk associated with the venture.

Venture capital firms have unique characteristics that distinguish them from other types of financing, in particular, private investors. In general, venture capital is a professionally managed pool of funds that is designed to be "self-liquidating" after 10 to 12 years.[19] The funds seek out firms with rapid growth potential that will give them the supernormal returns over a relatively short period of time that it requires to satisfy its

TABLE 9-2   Most Active Venture Firms—YTD Third Quarter 2001

Firm	Location	Number of Deals
J. P. Morgan Partners	New York, NY	54
Intel Corporation	Santa Clara, CA	51
Bessemer Venture Partners	Wellesley Hills, MA	43
New Enterprise Associates	Menlo Park, CA	42
Austin Ventures	Austin, TX	34
Sequoia Capital	Menlo Park, CA	33

Source: Adapted from PricewaterhouseCoopers Money Tree™ Survey Q3 2001 update. *www.pwcglobal.com.*

investors. Cashing out of the investment comes through a liquidity event such as an initial public offering, a merger, or a buyout. During an economic period where large venture capitalists have pulled back, smaller and less well-known venture capital firms are investing in good deals at better rates than were possible during the heated IPO market of a few years ago.

Venture capital firms play important roles in the ventures in which they invest. They often identify key management needed to grow the firm and regularly serve in a governing role on the board of directors, hiring and firing the principal officers of the corporation and structuring compensation. Their broad network of contacts often provides the new firm with partners and others who can help the firm achieve its goals. Perhaps most importantly, passing the rigorous screening of a venture capital firm and receiving venture capital backing accords the new venture a reputation and credibility that it would not have otherwise had. This reputation makes it easier for the company to find partners, attract key employees, and negotiate contracts with value chain partners.

The initial growth of a technology start-up before it receives venture capital has been found to be a good indicator of future growth.[20] It has traditionally been agreed that venture capital firms consider the business experience and personality of the entrepreneur over the product and market. However, more recent studies have concluded that industry and market factors may in fact be more important than the entrepreneur and the team.[21] In general, venture capital firms look for an optimal combination of a great management team and reasonable product/market factors. One consensus in the literature is that due diligence and high hurdle rates cause venture capital firms to reject approximately 95 percent of all applications submitted to them.

High-tech entrepreneurs often choose venture capital at start-up because venture capital firms provide young companies with many benefits, including mentoring, strategic advice, monitoring, reputation, professionalism, and recruitment of professional management.[22] However, these benefits come at a fairly high cost. Venture capitalists who are deeply involved with the company can present a time-consuming activity for the entrepreneur and may also exert high degrees of control over the actions of the entrepreneur. They also play an active role in corporate governance and have even been known to displace the entrepreneur when they feel that this person is not acting in the best interests of the investors. They certainly have a great deal to say about their exit strategy by ensuring that a liquidity event such as an IPO or a buyout is in the venture's future.

An entrepreneurial venture's strategy is related to its ability to obtain venture capital financing.[23] Innovators or pioneers are more likely to obtain venture capital quickly than noninnovators or followers, which suggests that venture capitalists do not always resist investing in early stage ventures with high risk. Moreover, obtaining venture capital produces faster time to market.

FUNDING BIOTECHNOLOGY

Biotechnology companies face unique issues when seeking start-up funding for a variety of reasons:

- It takes 7 to 9 years to bring a new drug to market at a cost of hundreds of millions of dollars; therefore investing in biotech is definitely a long-term proposition. This means that the venture team is constantly in fund-raising mode, which can detract from its research efforts.

- The technology is typically in the earliest stages of development and has not been proven.
- Most biotechnology is licensed from universities and research institutes and not owned by the company.
- It is very difficult to calculate the value of biotech firms as it is measured by intangibles such as their patent portfolio and the credibility of their scientific team.

SEED STAGE

In general, scientists start biotech companies very early in the development stage of their scientific discovery. At this stage, government grants or major corporations in the industry have funded the basic research. Additional money is required to prove the technology and consider its commercial applications. Therefore, entrepreneurs seek seed capital from angels and venture capitalists based on the strength of the technology and initial market research. Giving up equity at the seed stage is costly, amounting to as much as 49 percent or more of the company, depending on how much risk to the investor has been reduced. With the exception of about 20 percent of the equity, which is retained in a pool to attract professional management, the founders control the remaining equity, at least until the second stage of funding. The team's goal is to create sufficient value in the company before the next round of funding to secure enough capital to take the company through the first phase of FDA approval.[24]

FIRST-ROUND FUNDING: FDA PHASE I TESTING

Phase I FDA testing is designed to assess the safety of the drug, procedure, or other biotechnology and lasts about 18 months. The amount of money required to go through this phase depends on the quality of the seed phase results, but is generally substantially higher than that required in the seed stage, in the range of $15 to $20 million. Value is also added at this stage through the acquisition of intellectual property in the form of patents and know-how.

SECOND-ROUND FUNDING: THE BUSINESS MODEL

Once the company has established the scientific value of the technology, it is time to develop the business model. At this point, the entrepreneurs have access to a wider variety of financing alternatives. Two basic business models are prevalent in biotechnology: the Fully Integrated Pharmaceutical Company (FIPCO) and the licensing model.[25]

The FIPCO Model   The FIPCO model is essentially a start-up venture that takes the technology from discovery to market without using any outside partners. This model is highly capital intensive and has fallen into disfavor in recent years given the speed with which most companies must develop their products and the existence of major pharmaceutical companies that make niche entry difficult. Two companies that have successfully implemented this model are Centocor and NeoRx. This model necessitates an initial public offering to secure enough funding to build manufacturing capabilities and develop marketing and distribution strength. Unfortunately, the amount of money raised in the IPO is rarely enough to sustain the company through FDA Phase III testing and market launch. In 1996, the Boston Consulting Group reported an average cost of $500 million to take a single pharmaceutical from discovery to market; the average amount of capital raised in an IPO in the first quarter of 2000 was $114 million.[26]

Nevertheless, with a public company, the entrepreneurs now have a range of financial options not previously available to them. They can do a secondary IPO to raise additional capital from the market, although this will dilute their outstanding shares. They can also consider convertible bonds, a debt instrument that has become a common method for raising capital in publicly traded biotech companies. The use of bonds is more feasible in the late stages of Phase III testing where FDA approval is imminent. Entrepreneurs should be aware that the recurring interest payments on the bonds could be a drain on the company's cash flow. This approach is far more advantageous to the investor than to the company, because the investor can choose to convert the debt to equity at their option.

The Licensing Model   Under the licensing model, the scientists focus on the development and testing of the technology and then license the development of applications or the applications themselves to large pharmaceutical companies that have existing manufacturing, marketing, and distribution channels. This model requires the least amount of capital to implement, but it has few financing options associated with it. In general, the new company enters into a licensing agreement with a large pharmaceutical company and receives a negotiated royalty on sales. Alternatively, the large pharmaceutical may choose to purchase the small biotech start-up to diversify its portfolio. Yet another approach is for the small biotech firm to outsource the manufacturing and distribution of its technology to a large biotech firm in exchange for retaining a share of the revenues generated.

CORPORATE FUNDING

Corporate venturing is another source of equity financing for technology ventures, particularly in the pharmaceutical and software industries. The actual amount of corporate funding occurring has not been established, but estimates range from $10 to $20 billion annually.[27] During the frantic investment period that preceded the dot-com bust, corporations entered the fray as partners in first-round venture capital deals. Leading high-tech companies saw investing in new ventures as a natural by-product of their businesses. Companies such as Adobe, Dell, and Oracle started venture groups to invest between $2 and $5 million in companies that were complementary to their product offerings. Until the end of 1998, Intel's corporate venture program had invested nearly $1 billion in minority stakes on a global basis.[28]

One of the reasons that high-tech companies invest in new ventures is that corporations operating in the same or similar industry as the new venture understand the nature of that venture better than institutional investors do, so information asymmetries are reduced and the corporation is in a better position to judge the feasibility of a particular investment. Another reason is that large corporations are attempting to diversify their product development with technologies outside their core competencies. This is most easily accomplished via an investment in a small technology company. Moreover, corporate equity investments add tremendous value to the ventures in which they are investing. For example, Microsoft estimates that more than 90 percent of its investments are accompanied by a licensing or distribution agreement with the smaller company.[29]

However, corporate equity does present some unique problems for the start-up venture. Corporate funding designed to move the large company forward can turn out to be a poor relationship for the new venture because the larger company, usually a public company, will tend to emphasize shareholder value of the parent company over the goals of the new venture.

GOVERNMENT FUNDING SOURCES

For start-up technology ventures, particularly those in product development, the government and its agencies have long been a lucrative source of funding. Here we review some of the major sources of government funding available to new technology ventures to help them develop and commercialize their technologies.

SMALL BUSINESS INNOVATION RESEARCH GRANTS

Small Business Innovation Research (SBIR) grants are competitive awards administered by the Small Business Administration (SBA). They are designed to encourage the transfer and commercialization of technologies of U.S. companies with fewer than 500 employees. The government contracts with businesses to find technology solutions for problems it has identified. Any results the company achieves are protected for 4 years after the government contract has ended. For example, Savi Technology Company was awarded a Department of Defense contract to develop a system for tracking equipment and supplies being shipped to U.S. forces during the Persian Gulf War. At the end of the war, Savi was acquired by Texas Instruments, which now markets the technology to companies such as FedEx and Airborne Express.[30]

A recent study of 1,435 firms participating in SBIR programs over a 10-year period found that SBIR awardees enjoyed greater employment and sales growth than nonawardees.[31] They also grew significantly over the period and were more likely to attract venture capital. This result was particularly evident in regions with venture capital activity and in high-tech industries. Some well-known companies began their careers with funding from federal programs, including Apple Computer, Chiron, Compaq, Federal Express, and Intel, to name a few.

Eleven federal agencies participate in the SBIR program: Agriculture, Commerce, Defense, Education, Energy, Health and Human Services, Transportation, EPA, NASA, NSF, and the Nuclear Regulatory Commission. The award process consists of three phases:

Phase I: This phase provides funds to evaluate the technical merit and commercial feasibility of the technology.

Phase II: This phase is by invitation only after a successful Phase I award and continues the evaluation of commercial feasibility.

Phase III: This phase is the commercialization phase and does not include STTR funds. At this point, the company generally seeks other sources of funding, such as private investors and venture capital.

SMALL BUSINESS TECHNOLOGY TRANSFER RESEARCH PROGRAM

The SBA also administers the Small Business Technology Transfer Research (STTR) program, which is designed to promote joint research between nonprofit research institutes and small high-tech companies in the United States with fewer than 500 employees. The small company must submit the request and perform at least

40 percent of the work. The research institute must contribute at least 30 percent of the work. Like the SBIR program, the STTR has three phases:

Phase I: This phase lasts up to one year, during which the technical merit and commercial feasibility of the technology are evaluated.

Phase II: This phase is by invitation only after a successful Phase I award and continues the evaluation of commercial feasibility for a period of up to 2 years.

Phase III: This phase is the commercialization phase and does not include STTR funds. Again, the company will need to seek outside funding.

SMALL BUSINESS INVESTMENT COMPANY PROGRAM

The SBA also backs the Small Business Investment Company (SBIC) program, which provides venture capital to small businesses. Approximately 395 SBICS invested about $5.5 billion in 3,000 small businesses in 2000.[32] A list of these businesses can be found at *www.sba.gov/gopher/Local-Information/Small-Business-Investment-Companies/*. SBICs are private venture capital firms licensed by the SBA. Funds are raised through the sale of securities and debentures to a variety of sophisticated investors such as venture capitalists, corporate pension funds, banks, and individuals. The SBIC functions as a financier to small businesses and can provide long-term loans with a minimum of 5 years independently or in conjunction with a public or private lender. It can also provide equity capital by purchasing the small business's securities. It may not, however, become a general partner in a small business or be liable in any way for the obligations of the business.

THE SMALL BUSINESS ADMINISTRATION

In 2000, the SBA helped 50,000 business owners by backing loans worth $12.5 billion and provided management and technical services to over 1 million businesses at no charge. The SBA loan guarantee program encourages banks to lend to businesses at favorable rates even in times when money is tight. It also provides for longer terms, which helps a young business with its cash flow. The SBA partners with commercial banks and guarantees 75 to 85 percent of the each business loan. In addition, through the SBA, companies can become certified for the SBA 8(a) government contract program, which enables them to seek sole-source contracts under $3 million for services and under $5 million for manufacturing. SBA's online database, PRO-Net, describes its offerings in this area. By law, the SBA is required to offer 23 percent of its government contracts to small businesses. That equates to about $40 billion per year.

THE COST OF RAISING CAPITAL

The cost of raising capital at start-up or for growth is high, both in terms of human and financial capital. Because the process is stressful and pulls the entrepreneur and company employees away from the daily activities of the business at a time when they are most needed, many entrepreneurs decide to start and grow slowly, taking advantage of internal cash flows. However, it is rare that a high-tech company can survive and grow without accessing some outside capital in the form of debt or equity. With that in mind, it is important to understand what is involved in raising capital so that expectations are not set unreasonably high.

Entrepreneurs need to set aside enough time to raise capital and not wait until their company actually needs it to begin the process. It is realistic to expect to spend several months locating the proper financing, to wait a few more months for due diligence to be completed, and then to wait up to 6 more months to actually receive the money. Moreover, in many cases, the first financing source tapped will not end up closing the deal, even after months of courting and negotiations, so it is important to have backups in place so that the process will not have to start again from scratch.

In second-round funding, new investors often will want to buy out the first-round investors, who are typically friends and family, because they do not want to deal with them and believe that they do not contribute anything significant to the company. This can be a very awkward time for entrepreneurs who are caught between a rock and a hard place knowing that the investor can easily walk to another deal if they do not acquiesce.

Some costs associated with raising money must be paid upfront by the entrepreneur. These costs include those involved in the preparation of financial statements, the business plan, and a prospectus or offering document, as well as fees for legal advice and the expenses of marketing the offering. In addition to these upfront costs are the back-end costs of selling securities, which include investment banking fees, legal fees, marketing costs, brokerage fees, and various other fees charged by state and federal authorities. The total cost of raising equity capital can be as high as 25 percent of the total amount raised. Add to that the interest or return on investment paid to the funding source, and it is easy to see why it costs money to raise money.

❖ SUMMARY

Finding and developing the resources needed to start a new technology venture is a challenging task because new technology ventures typically require far more resources early on and face more complex problems than traditional ventures. Furthermore, resource providers are aware of these risks and often find it difficult to commit valuable resources at the earliest stages of a new venture. Before the launch of a new venture, seed capital is required to finish product development, test the business concept, and prepare for product launch. This capital is typically in the form of friendly money and government grants. Once the business is operational, early stage funding is needed to grow the business. Private investors and some forms of venture capital, as well as strategic partners, come into play. In the later stages of the venture, the company has access to venture capital and public equity. Angel investors are individuals or networks of individuals who have usually been successful entrepreneurs themselves and want to help another entrepreneur succeed. Venture capital is a professionally managed pool of funds that invests for high rates of return in relatively short periods of time. Venture capital funding is available to less than 1 percent of all ventures because venture capitalists are generally attracted to superstar businesses with a unique technology or the ability to grow quickly and provide a liquidity event such as an IPO. Biotechnology firms represent a unique scenario in technology commercialization. Many biotech companies license their technology to large pharmaceutical firms as it is much more difficult and costly to start such a venture. In the pharmaceutical and software industries, corporate venturing is another source of equity financing for technology start-ups. Government agencies are yet another source of funding, usually for the product development phase of the venture. Whatever type of funding is chosen, entrepreneurs should be aware that it costs money and time to secure funding, so planning in advance of the actual need is critical.

❖ DISCUSSION QUESTIONS

1. Suppose you want to launch a radical innovation. You have a working prototype and have begun to test the early adopter market. It will take a lot of capital to "cross the chasm" to mainstream adoption. What would your financial strategy be?
2. Compare the roles and goals of angel investors with those of venture capitalists.
3. What are the unique issues related to biotech start-ups that make them different from other high-tech ventures in the start-up stage?
4. What role does the government play in the commercialization of new technology?
5. How can strategic partners be used to speed up the process of innovation and commercialization?

❖ RESOURCES

Brown, Larissa Golden, Martin John Brown, and Judith E. Nichols. *Demystifying Grant Seeking. What You Really Need to Do to Get Grants.* New York: John Wiley & Sons, 2001.

Harmon, Steve. *Zero Gravity: Riding Venture Capital From High-Tech Start-up to Breakout IPO.* New York: Bloomberg Press, 2000.

Lacy, Harold R. *Financing Your Business Dreams With Other People's Money: How and Where to Find Money for Start-up and*

Growing Businesses. Santa Barbara, CA: Rhodes & Easton, 1998.

Levin, Jack S., Ginsburg, Martin, D. and Rocap, Donald E. *Structuring Venture Capital, Private Equity, and Entrepreneurial Transactions.* Frederick, MD: Aspen Publishers, Inc., 2001.

Long, Mark. *Financing the New Venture.* Holbrook, MA: Adams Media Corporation, 2000.

❖ INTERNET RESOURCES

BusinessWeek.com—Your Money
www.businessweek.com
Articles with advice on financing small businesses

Free Government Grants Site
businessgrants.small-large-government.com/
Online grant directories, links, and proposal writing tips

Netpreneur Exchange
www.netpreneur.org
An online community hosted by the Morino Institute that supports entrepreneurial Internet businesses

The SBI Resource Center
www.win-sbir.com/
Tools and services to support SBIR and STTR applicants

Venture Private Equity and Investors' Capital
www.venturepie.com/
In alliance with KPMG, VenturePI matches venture capital finance firms with entrepreneurs seeking financing for technology companies

VentureWire
www.venturewire.com
A daily e-mail newsletter about venture capital funding activity

PREPARE FOR THE MONEY HUNT

When a company has made it through the dot-com implosion and a major company such as Sprint likes what it does and begins to offer its service, it may decide that it has done something right. ConneXus Corp. is that company. In 2001, Sprint PCS signed on to offer *CD (pronounced "start CD"), a ConneXus Corp. service that enables users to identify music playing on the radio and buy it instantaneously through their cell phone. Customers connect to *CD and enter the call signal of the local radio station while the music is playing. They can then choose to purchase it using their credit card and the CD is shipped to them. *CD uses a patented technology to track radio signals 24 hours a day, 7 days a week for 523 radio stations in the top 33 markets in the United States. Before a record company releases a new record, ConneXus obtains a master recording and scans it into its computer to create a digital pattern for that song. Humphrey Chen, ConneXus's co-CEO, claims that the *CD technology is an innovative way to make radio an interactive experience.

What path did partners George Searle and Humphrey Chen take to get their company to this point? The two MBAs graduated from Harvard in 1996 with a business plan but no money to fund the start-up. So Searle took his family back home to Indiana while Chen stayed in New Jersey to seek capital. Chen worked the Harvard network, which paid off when one of his former professors got the duo a meeting with Burr, Egan, Deleage & Co., a large Boston-based venture capital firm. Searle and Chen were only looking for $1 million, which was far less than the well-known venture capital firm usually funded, but their passion for the business inspired the company to inject enough capital into the start-up to allow the partners to build the technology and acquire the necessary equipment to get the business off the ground. With Burr, Egan, Deleage & Co. serving as the lead investor, the fledging company gained instant credibility. ConneXus also arranged for representation in the legal arena by Testa Hurwitz & Thibeault LLP, a highly reputable law firm that agreed to waive its fees until their funding came through.

In the beginning, Searle and Chen were so enthusiastic about the technology that when potential investors asked what the company did, all they could talk about was the technology, which, unfortunately, most investors did not understand. When they realized that they were getting nowhere with this strategy, they changed tactics and focused on the benefits they were providing to the customer—the ability to purchase music when they hear it. This made sense to investors.

Searle and Chen were lucky to have completed and revised their business plan before they began talking to investors. Each time they talked to a potential investor and got them excited about the concept, the investor immediately wanted a copy of the business plan. Searle and Chen knew that if they made the investor wait several weeks while they completed one, they would have lost the investor. Instead, they gave the investor an executive summary and made delivery of the full business plan contingent on a face-to-face meeting. References were another matter. Before meeting with investors, Searle and Chen prepared for the meeting by collecting a contact list of references that they could hand to the investor the moment it was requested.

Searching for money is a never-ending process when you are growing as rapidly as

ConneXus is. It is Searle and Chen's goal to make *CD available to everyone, but they are facing a weak economy and turmoil in the wireless industry. They need to make sure that their strategy for growth fits the times. ■

Sources: Beth Cox, "If M Stands for Music, Then I Love M-Commerce," *MCommerce Times* January 24, 2001:) *www.mcommercetimes.com/*; Sherman Fridman, "Digital Fingerprints Allow Wireless Song ID," *Newsbytes*, June 23, 2000:) *www.newsbytes.com/*; David R. Evanson and Art Beroff, "Ready or Not?" *Entrepreneur Magazine*, August 1999): 56–69.

❖ NOTES

1. Candida G. Brush, Patricia G. Greene, Myra M. Hart, and Harold S. Haller, "From Initial Idea to Unique Advantage: The Entrepreneurial Challenge of Constructing a Resource Base," *The Academy of Management Executive* 15, no. 1 (February 2001): 64–78.

2. Howard E. Aldrich and C. Marlene Fiol, "Fools Rush In? The Institutional Context of Industry Creation," *Academy of Management Review* 19 (1993): 645–670.

3. D. Collis and C. Montgomery, "Competing on Resources: Strategy in the 1990s," *Harvard Business Review* (July–August 1995): 118–128.

4. Thomas Hellmann, "Entrepreneurship and the Process of Obtaining Resource Commitments," working paper, Graduate School of Business, Stanford University, Palo Alto, CA, 2000.

5. Ibid., 18

6. Peter Brierley, "The Financing of Technology-Based Small Firms: A Review of the Literature," *Bank of England Quarterly Bulletin* 41, no. 1 (2001): 64–83.

7. Robert Johnson, "Lending to Family Is a Risky Venture," *The Wall Street Journal,* Interactive Version (*www.startupjournal. com/financing/family/200005160957– johnson.html*).

8. Wesley M. Cohen and Daniel A. Levinthal, "Absorptive Capacity: A New Perspective on Learning and Innovation," *Administrative Science Quarterly* 35 (1990): 128–152.

9. Aldrich and Fiol, "Fools Rush In? The Institutional Context of Industry Creation," 645–670.

10. Toby E. Stuart, "Network Positions and Propensities to Collaborate: An Investigation of Strategic Alliance Formation in a High Technology Industry," *Administrative Science Quarterly* 43 (1998): 668–698.

11. G. Benjamin and W. Sandles, "Angel Investors: Cutting the Waters for Private Equity," *Journal of Private Equity* 1, no. 3 (1998): 41–59.

12. Ibid., 41–59.

13. D. Shepard, R. Ettenson, and A. Crouch, "New Venture Strategy and Profitability: A Venture Capitalist's Assessment," *Journal of Business Venturing* 15 (2000): 450.

14. A. Zacharakis and G. Meyer, "A Lack of Insight: Do Venture Capitalists Really Understand Their Own Decision Process?" *Journal of Business Venturing* 13 (1998): 58.

15. D. Primark, "First-Half Disbursements Continue Venture Capital's Record-Setting Pace," *Venture Capital Journal* 10 (2000): 47.

16. Christopher T. Heun, "Taking Stock of VCs," InformationWeek (January 2, 2001) *www.informationweek.com/home*.

17. Lawrence Aragon, "New VC Deals Are for the Small and Brave," *Red Herring* (October 15, 2001) *www.redherring.com*.

18. Ibid.

19. P. A. Gompers and J. Lerner, *The Venture Capital Cycle* (Cambridge, MA: MIT Press, 1999).

20. A. L. Zacharakis and G. D. Meyer, "The Potential of Actuarial Decision Models: Can They Improve the Venture Capital Investment Decision," *Journal of Business Venturing* 13 (2000): 57–76.

21. Brierley, "The Financing of Technology-Based Small Firms: A Review of the Literature," 64–77.

22. Thomas Hellmann and Manju Puri, "The Interaction Between Product Market and Financing Strategy: The Role of Venture Capital," *The Review of Financial Studies* 13, no. 4 (2000): 959–984.

23. Ibid., 974.

24. Cynthia Robbins-Roth, "From Alchemy to IPO," (Cambridge, MA: Perseus Publishing, March 2000): 117.

25. Brian Laney, "Funding Strategies for Biotechnology Start-Ups," unpublished paper, University of Southern California, San Diego, December 5, 2000.

26. Robbins-Roth, "From Alchemy to IPO," 117.

27. Brierley, "The Financing of Technology-Based Small Firms," 64–77.

28. Klaus Macharzina, "Entrepreneurship on a Global Rise," *Management International Review* 40, no. 3 (2000): 199–202.

29. Neil F. Carlson, "Angels of Silicon Valley," *Strategic Finance* 81, no. 4 (October 1999): 30–34.

30. Peter Weaver, "SBA: More than Loans," *Business Advisor* (July–August 2001): 29–42. *www.business.gov/*.

31. Josh Lerner, "The Government as Venture Capitalist: The Long-run Impact of the SBIR Program," *The Journal of Business* 72, no. 3 (July 1999): 285.

32. Weaver, "SBA: More than Loans," 32.

FUNDING GROWTH

OVERVIEW

This chapter will examine

❖ debt vs equity

❖ financing strategy for growth

❖ venture capital funding

❖ the private offering

❖ the initial public offering

❖ presenting the concept to investors

INTRODUCTION

Rapid growth is an exciting time in the life of a technology venture that can be at once exhilarating and frightening. Frightening because if a new technology achieves mass-market acceptance, demand generally outstrips supply and huge amounts of capital are needed to support the new level of growth. Exhilarating because if a company has achieved its start-up targets and reached a critical mass of customers, new sources of capital will be available to it.

Many factors affect a firm's ability to grow. Research suggests that industry population density or market forces are external forces that dictate how a firm grows.[1] However, internal forces such as capabilities, culture, or strategy also play a critical role.[2] In the case of technology ventures, venture capital investments, and the timing of those investments also affect the growth of a firm.[3] It appears that firms that use venture capital in their funding strategy are fundamentally different from start-ups using traditional financing methods.[4] Venture-capital-funded firms tend to be more innovative in their strategic orientation and experience a more rapid time to market. Furthermore, venture capital firms devote time, energy, and resources to identifying excellent technology opportunities. Once a promising start-up is identified, the venture capital firm provides significant capital and management support, which enhances the probability that the start-up will be successful.

This chapter explores the primary sources of growth capital: venture capital, private offerings, and public offerings. It begins with a discussion of debt versus equity strategies.

DEBT VS EQUITY

When it comes time to seek expansion capital, most entrepreneurs would probably prefer to use debt rather than equity so that they do not have to give up any control of their companies. However, securing debt is not always an option. Today, more and more companies have fewer assets that can be used for collateral against loans, and banks rarely feel comfortable lending to high-risk start-up ventures until they have at least a short track record. The reality is that most entrepreneurs seeking outside capital choose equity sources.

DEBT

Securing debt is advantageous when the returns on the business exceed the cost of borrowing the money, which includes search time, interest, fees, and conditions. With debt, entrepreneurs do not give up control of the company as long as they pay down the debt as required. Entrepreneurs generally achieve a profit sooner with debt because they have to generate cash to service it. However, holding debt does have its downside. If the company does not have collateral in the form of equipment, land, or buildings, it probably will not be able to secure debt financing. If the company is unable to make payments on the loan, the entrepreneur could lose the business. Some lenders ask for equity and convertible debt, meaning that they have the right to convert the principal to common stock, which could dilute the entrepreneur's ownership interest.

To understand lenders' motives, it is important to know that banks derive their profits principally from net interest income, that is, the difference between interest they pay on money they borrow from depositors or other banks and the interest they receive on those same dollars after they lend them to borrowers. The margins are very slim. If a borrower defaults on a loan, the banker must then earn the full net interest margin on more than 33 new loans to recover the loss that now shows on the bank's balance sheet. Bankers generally do not benefit from the upside of a new venture, so they have no interest in sharing the downside on risky, high-tech start-ups.[5] However, a successful start-up with a good chance of long-term growth and an ever-increasing need for capital can provide the banker with a lucrative stream of income.

Lenders want to know the company's time line for growth and what steps have been put into place to achieve that time line. The lenders need to understand how much money is needed, what it is needed for, and what will be accomplished with it. In general, when an entrepreneur comes to a bank for a loan, the banker forms a first impression that is difficult to change, therefore it is important that entrepreneurs prepare for this meeting by thoroughly understanding the financials of the business and the assumptions behind the numbers. Bankers generally work from checklists to conduct a preliminary screen of loan candidates. Two of these checklists, or lending gauges, are The Five Cs and Campari, shown in Table 10-1.[6]

TABLE 10-1   Lending Gauges

The Five Cs	CAMPARI
Character	Character
Capacity to repay	Ability (repay)
Conditions (product, market, economy)	Margin (breakeven for profitability)
Capital	Purpose (of the loan)
Collateral (security against default)	Amount
	Repayment terms
	Insurance (security)

Lenders often request personal guarantees from entrepreneurs to ensure that if the company fails, the borrower can still repay the loan. Lenders also believe that entrepreneurs who have to sign personal guarantees are less likely to walk away from the business and will, in fact, work harder to make that business a success.

Whether or not an entrepreneur chooses to finance with debt, it is important to establish a good working relationship with a banker who has the decision-making power to provide a line of credit the company may want to secure at some point in the future.

EQUITY

Equity, selling shares of stock in a company, also has its share of advantages and disadvantages. Among its disadvantages, the entrepreneur gives up a percentage of the ownership of the company and typically loses some operational control. On the plus side, investors are a support group; they are taking the risk with the entrepreneur, and the entrepreneur does not have to pay the reward until the company is sold or goes public (unless the stockholders' agreement dictates otherwise). When it comes time to seek additional equity capital, the first-round investors may have the contacts needed to find that capital. Using outside investors also is attractive to potential management the company may be trying to bring on board.

A company can issue two types of equity stock: preferred and common. Holders of preferred stock have preferences over common stockholders in the areas of dividends, liquidation, and voting. Upon liquidation, a company pays debt issuers first, then preferred stockholders. Preferred stockholders may also enjoy voting rights based on the number of shares of common stock issued upon conversion from debt to equity.

FINANCING STRATEGY FOR GROWTH

In a perfect world, it would be easy to identify successful companies and investors would not lose money from their investments. However, it is difficult to evaluate the potential of a business in the growth stage (or any other stage for that matter). Hackett Benchmarking & Research and the Stern Stewart consulting firm conducted a study of 60 companies, small and large, in multiple industries to determine how to measure potential success.[7] What they found was startling. The companies were divided into aligned and nonaligned companies. In the aligned companies, managers and shareholders had the same goals; in the nonaligned companies, manager's goals and shareholders' goals were mismatched. This difference was clearly reflected in how the two types of companies responded to the following scenario:

> A company has a hot new product opportunity. Accelerating development of that product will depress earnings for the next few quarters. Should the entrepreneur go after it?

Companies in the aligned group said that they would choose to accelerate development, whereas the nonaligned group said that they definitely would not. A pattern emerged from the study. The nonaligned firms, which performed poorly compared with the aligned group, tended to worry about reported profits, and would even destroy shareholder wealth to achieve them. The superior-performing aligned firms did not rely on reported earnings but rather on economic profit, which is after-tax operating profit minus the real cost of the capital used in the business.[8] The most surprising finding of the study was that 73 percent of the aligned companies did not cap their bonuses, whereas 81 percent of nonaligned companies did. This is significant because the bonus reflects all the other factors; it is where the company demonstrates what it values are and how willing it is to bet that it is right. The bottom line is that outside investors and others will evaluate a firm based on its incentive system because it tells them how aligned management is with shareholder values.

With company goals firmly in place, it is critically important that a technology venture have a financing plan that covers at least a 5-year period. If the company's projections say that it will reach $50 million in revenues by the fifth year, it is important to know how the company intends to accomplish that. Too many entrepreneurs focus on short-term goals—how much money is needed to launch and make it through the first year—and find themselves in trouble when they have not planned for the additional capital needed to extend their growth beyond the first year. If the period between 1997 and 2001 taught entrepreneurs anything, it was that rapid growth too soon and with no systems and controls and no patience can send the business into a tailspin from which it may not recover. An effective financing plan includes the milestones in the entrepreneur's plan for growth: first customer (the primary target market), multiple customers (secondary markets), and multiple products. It also addresses the trigger points, in other words, what must happen to achieve each milestone. The time line includes the amount of money and time needed to achieve each milestone. Growing the business more slowly in the earliest stages permits the company to successfully grow rapidly when it and the market are ready. Some of the questions that should be answered in the financing plan include:

1. Where will the company be in 5 years? Size? Revenues? Markets?
2. Should the company be a public company or remain private? Why?
3. Does the company have a compelling need for significant capital for a specific purpose at each milestone?
4. How many milestones of value creation will be achieved during the 5-year period?
5. How many rounds of funding will it take to reach the 5-year goal?

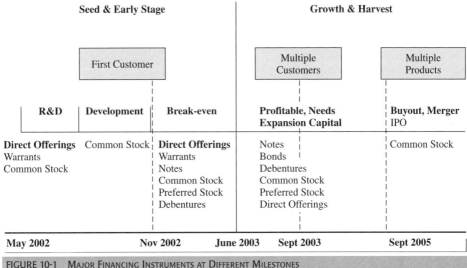

Seed & Early Stage			Growth & Harvest	
	First Customer		Multiple Customers	Multiple Products
R&D	Development	Break-even	Profitable, Needs Expansion Capital	Buyout, Merger IPO
Direct Offerings Warrants Common Stock	Common Stock	Direct Offerings Warrants Notes Common Stock Preferred Stock Debentures	Notes Bonds Debentures Common Stock Preferred Stock Direct Offerings	Common Stock
May 2002		Nov 2002 June 2003	Sept 2003	Sept 2005

FIGURE 10-1   MAJOR FINANCING INSTRUMENTS AT DIFFERENT MILESTONES

6. What sources of funding are most appropriate for this type of business and at which milestones?
7. Which financial instruments are appropriate at which milestones?
8. What is the least amount of money required at each milestone?

Figure 10-1 provides an overview of the various financial instruments typically available to the entrepreneur at particular points in time in the growth of the company. These instruments are defined in Table 10-2.

VENTURE CAPITAL FUNDING

Venture capital funding was introduced in Chapter 9. Here the requirements of venture capital funding are considered in more depth, as the growth phase is more appropriate to the needs of the venture capital firm. Venture capital firms have four fundamental principals under which they operate:[9]

1. **The venture capital firm gets paid first.** Whether by means of a liquidity event or the liquidation of the company in the event of failure, the venture capital firm will get paid first.
2. **Participation in the upside of the venture.** The venture capital firm will benefit from the appreciation in value of the venture over and above the original investment.
3. **Control over critical events.** The venture capitalists will want to have decision rights in matters that vitally affect the business, such as the decision to do an IPO.
4. **Creation of a path to liquidity.** There must be a way for the venture capital firm to cash out of the venture.

TABLE 10-2   Definitions of Common Financing Instruments

Term	Definition
Bonds	A corporate bond is a long-term promissory note where the company pays a percentage of the par value of the note on specified dates and repays the bond principal at maturity. Bondholders are repaid ahead of either common or preferred stockholders.
Common stock	An equity interest in a company that provides voting rights. Common stockholders have pre-emptive rights to buy additional shares when new stock is issued to prevent dilution of their ownership interest.
Debentures	Debentures are unsecured notes with higher interest rates than bonds. Sometimes they are structured as convertible debentures, in which case the holder receives interest payments and can elect to convert the principal to stock at some future date as specified in the agreement.
Direct participation offering (DPO)	The DPO gives the investor a piece of a revenue stream of a product line or unit and is often structured as a royalty participation certificate.
Notes	Notes are promises to pay where the interest rate, payment schedule, due date, and any security are negotiated.
Preferred stock	Preferred stock has a specified dividend rate. Preferred shareholders are paid ahead of common stockholders in the event of liquidation.
Warrants	Warrants give the holder the right to buy securities at a specified price or subscription price. They are long-term financial instruments that are not eligible for dividends.

Venture capitalists invest in companies with excellent management teams and large markets that allow for growth to a minimum of $50 million with pre-tax profit of 20 percent within about 5 to 7 years. A company of this size has the potential for an IPO, which is a liquidity event that venture capitalists need to recoup their investment plus realize a gain. The venture capitalist is generally looking for 10 times their initial investment as a return over 5 years, an annual rate of return of 58 percent.[10]

VENTURE CAPITAL SCREENING CRITERIA

Technology start-ups are dynamic organizations characterized by little experience, lack of commitment on the part of employees, immature systems and controls, and inconsistent quality, which limits their chances of survival.[11] Technology ventures often require far more resources early on and face more complex problems than traditional ventures. For these reasons, they usually need major outside funding. They are attractive investments to venture capital because although they cannot do much to mitigate the liability of newness, they can avoid the continuing liability of smallness through rapid growth, which can mean higher returns for the investor.[12] But technology ventures must be carefully screened.

Traditionally, venture capitalists consider the business experience and personality of the entrepreneur as critical over the product and market. However, more recent studies have concluded that industry and market factors may, in fact, be as important or even more important than the entrepreneur and the team.[13] Other research suggests that venture capitalists look for an optimal combination of a great management team and reasonable product/market factors. Muzyka and Birley found in their investigation of European and U.S. venture capitalists that the top five most important factors that would lead a venture capitalist to invest in a technology venture were related to the management team.[14] The second major group of factors was related to the market. The top five factors were as follows:

1. Leadership potential of the lead entrepreneur
2. Leadership potential of the management team
3. Industry expertise of the management team
4. Track record of the lead entrepreneur
5. Track record of the management team

One area of consensus in the literature is that because of in-depth due diligence and high hurdle rates for return on investment, venture capitalists reject approximately 95 percent of all applications submitted to them.

Investors use four factors to evaluate a new venture opportunity. The first factor is the degree of uncertainty. New ventures are fraught with ambiguity and uncertainty because there are so many unknowns and the information that the entrepreneurs gather is generally imperfect. Consequently, it is difficult to predict the future. This uncertainty compels investors to carefully consider an investment at this early stage, and when they do decide to invest, they invest in stages to mitigate some of the risk. The second factor is asymmetric information, which means that the investor is at a disadvantage in terms of information about the new venture. In the earliest stages of a new venture, the entrepreneur knows far more about the venture and its potential than the investor. Therefore, it is possible that the entrepreneur might make a decision that adversely affects the investment, and the investor will not be able to immediately observe the effects. This situation puts the investor at risk because asymmetric information makes it difficult to make an investment decision. The third factor related to high-tech start-ups is that their asset base is principally in intangible assets—intellectual property, know-how, and so forth. Many investors feel more comfortable investing with firms that have the bulk of their assets in tangibles—equipment, buildings, land, and inventory—that are easier to value and track. Where intangible assets are predominant, investors incur a greater risk because intangible assets are difficult to value and protect. However, today investors in high technology ventures look for valuable intellectual property that will give the company a temporary monopoly in the market. The fourth factor is that the markets for high technology have an impact on a venture's ability to obtain venture capital in the early stages. The supply of capital varies with market conditions and is often erratic. When investors pulled back from investments in e-commerce, it also affected tangential industries such as telecommunications and biotech.

Although every venture fund is different, most venture capital firms follow a three-step evaluation process of due diligence, risk and return analysis, and business valuation when evaluating a technology venture.

DUE DILIGENCE

For the potential investor, due diligence is complicated by the fact that new ventures do not have track records or evidence of previous success. This is why most venture capitalists investigate a venture's founders and the management team so carefully. The venture capital firm conducts background checks, looks at previous ventures in which the founders have been involved, and tries to determine the integrity of the founders and how easy it will be to get along with them. In addition, they are interested in how the founding team got together and whether there is a shared vision for the company.

Estimating the market potential for the venture is another task that takes place in the first stage. For breakthrough innovations, this is a difficult task, as it is difficult to find information from public sources, thus the venture capital firm must rely on the new venture's business plan and its portfolio of contacts in the industry, neither of which are always reliable.[15] In fact, it is not uncommon for the entrepreneurial firm seeking the venture capital funding to present an overly optimistic view of the company's potential and its ability to execute the plan.

RISK AND RETURN ASSESSMENT

It is clear from the research that information asymmetries and potential conflicts of interest between new ventures and their investors affect most investment decisions. Venture capitalists face a conflict based on their principal–agent relationship with the new venture. In the case of the venture capitalist being a principal in the venture, that is, a stakeholder by virtue of the investment, the venture capitalists will require that the new venture provide information on a regular basis so that they can evaluate the situation and determine if more capital is needed. Entrepreneurs typically are not interested in supplying all the required information because they want to be autonomous from the investor. This conflict usually results in the investor requiring stricter terms in the venture capital agreement, which explains why very early stage ventures do not receive venture capital funding. In the second situation, the venture capitalist is an agent who is subject to the risk that if the company into which they have placed investors' capital does not perform, the investors will not return to invest again. To overcome this second scenario, venture capitalists typically impose high hurdle rates, conduct in-depth screening of investments, develop very precise contract specifications, provide incentives, use preferred and/or convertible stock, and closely monitor investments.[16]

The rate of return venture capitalists expect from an investment is directly related to the degree of risk they are taking in making the investment.[17] In general, the required return is a function of the difference between the expected stock market return and the current risk-free interest rate. The type of company and the stage of growth also contribute to the evaluation of risk and reward. In general, the younger the company, the greater the risk, and the greater the return required by the venture capital firm. Figure 10-2 shows the rates of return required by different investors.

Although the returns on investments in seed stage ventures seem astronomical, the reality is that the seed and start-up stages are the most risky, therefore venture capitalists charge more to make up for the nine ventures out of 10 that do not return supernormal profits. At this stage, the entrepreneur may appear to be in a weak position with venture capitalists, but this is only true if the entrepreneur is unprepared and at a point of financial desperation. Although venture capitalists see hundreds of deals every month, they rarely see great deals, so if a great concept is presented, it will get their attention.

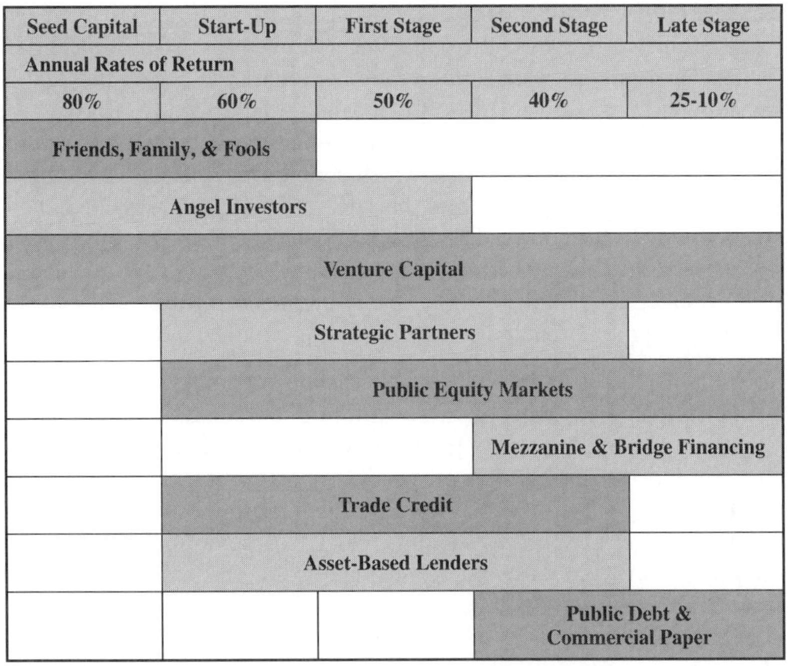

Seed Capital	Start-Up	First Stage	Second Stage	Late Stage
Annual Rates of Return				
80%	60%	50%	40%	25-10%
Friends, Family, & Fools				
Angel Investors				
Venture Capital				
	Strategic Partners			
	Public Equity Markets			
			Mezzanine & Bridge Financing	
	Trade Credit			
	Asset-Based Lenders			
			Public Debt & Commercial Paper	

FIGURE 10-2   STAGES OF FUNDING AND TYPES OF MONEY

Any investment deal has four components that determine its value: (1) the amount of money to be invested, (2) the timing and use of those monies, (3) the return on investment, and (4) the risk level of the investment. Typically, venture capitalists seek both equity and debt from a venture. Equity provides an ownership interest in the business and debt provides an immediate payback in the form of interest payments. Venture capitalists often require redeemable preferred stock or debentures (a debt instrument that converts to common stock), so that if the company does well, they can convert to common stock, and if the company fails, they will be the first to be repaid from the remains of the liquidation. If this strategy is successful, the venture capitalist can receive the entire investment back plus interest and still enjoy capital appreciation in the value of the business as a stockholder.

Venture capitalists will usually demand participating preferred stock, which entitles them to participate in dividends with the common stockholders after receiving the preferred dividend rate. They will also want a liquidation preference that entitles them to receive a specified amount multiplied by the purchase price plus all dividends accrued but unpaid, whether or not they were declared. In other words, the venture capitalists want to have their cake and eat it too! It is easy to see why the terms of a venture capital agreement can be so onerous. Consider the following scenario:

A 2-year-old technology company received a second round of financing from a venture capital firm in the amount of $20 million that it expected would take the company to an IPO in 5 years. Unfortunately, well into the fifth year, the company was still behind in having a marketable application of its technology ready. A compatible company in the same industry saw an opportunity to purchase the struggling company for $30 million and made an offer. The founders were excited as they prepared to accept the deal. The excitement was short-lived, however, when their attorney informed them that their second-round investors were entitled to a two-times-purchase-price return on their preferred stock, which equaled $40 million. The founders would, therefore, receive nothing from the sale of the business. Shocked, the founders were ready to turn down the sale, when their attorney further reminded them that the venture capital firm had redeemable preferred stock, which meant that they could require the company to buy them out of the investment, and were demanding the sale of the company so they could be cashed out.

Unfortunately, this situation is not uncommon. Too many entrepreneurs readily accept investments from venture capitalists without understanding the future ramifications.

Venture capitalists protect their investments in others ways as well. They will frequently require an antidilution provision to ensure that the selling of stock at a later date will not decrease the economic value of their investment. To ensure antidilution, they may require a full-ratchet clause that lets the venture capital firm buy common stock at the lowest rate at which it has been sold. This clause is the most onerous for the company, as it gives the investor a larger equity position in the venture. More common is a weighted average technique (also called fully diluted) based on the amount of shares outstanding, the size of the funding round, and the issuance price. Fully diluted means that all shares, including outstanding options, warrants, and other common stock equivalents are considered.* Furthermore, to overcome having paid too much for an equity stake in the company, the venture capital firm will require a forfeiture provision, which means that if the company does not achieve its projected performance goals, the founders may have to forfeit some of their stock as a penalty to the venture capital firm. This, of course, increases the venture capital firm's equity stake in the company. The entrepreneur can attempt to mitigate this situation by requesting stock bonuses as a reward for meeting or exceeding performance projections. To avoid a scenario where it appears that the liquidity event forecast when the venture capital firm invested will not materialize in the required time frame, the investor typically requires redeemable preferred stock. This means that the company will have to buy back the stock at the negotiated price plus dividends. When this happens, it is not uncommon for the company to be unable to repurchase the stock, which will cause the investor and the entrepreneur to negotiate a decision about the future of the company.

BUSINESS VALUATION

Venture capitalists approach the valuation process from a variety of points of view in an attempt to converge on the best estimate given all the information at hand. In general, there are three types of valuation methods. Accounting methods include the

---

*The weighted average formula is $P + A /P + D$, where P is the number of shares of common stock outstanding prior to the down round (the round of stock sale at a lower price than previously issued); A is the number of shares of common stock that the cash paid in the down round financing would purchase, assuming that the shares were sold at the conversion price of the original preferred stock; and D is the number of shares of common stock issued or issuable upon conversion of the securities issued in the down round.

book value of equity, book value of assets, historic costs, and replacement value. Another set of approaches is based on transaction prices for comparable companies. The approach that comes closest to yielding accurate results for start-up ventures is the discounted cash flow (DCF) method, or net present value. DCF relies on estimating future cash flows and discounting them to the present using a discount factor that reflects the risk of the venture and the cost of capital. DCF methods are not without their own set of problems; principal among them is the difficulty of forecasting into the future when the environment is uncertain.[18] Valuation methods are covered in detail in Chapter 8.

Determining how much of the company the venture capital firm will take is never easy and is certainly a matter of negotiation. Still, the average venture capital firm will want to ensure that the amount of equity taken will produce the expected annual return that it requires. Suppose the venture capital firm is funding a first-stage company and requires a 50 percent annual return on an investment of $3 million. The company is projected to have earnings or net income of $30 million in 5 years, at which time the venture capital firm expects that the company will do an initial public offering. The price to earnings ratio is estimated at 16 based on typical P/E ratios for this industry. In this case, the future value of the company will be $30 million multiplied by 16, or $480 million. If the venture capital firm wants a 60 percent return on investment, the present value of the company is $480,000,000/(1.6)^5, or $10,480,000. Thus, for the investment of $3 million, the venture capital firm would take 29 percent of the company [($3,000,000/$10,480,000) $\times$ 100]. Naturally, these numbers are only estimates. The degree of uncertainty is high in these types of calculations because the company is betting on its future earnings and the venture capital firm is betting that its investment will produce those earnings.

CONTROL RIGHTS

Venture capitalists often overcome the fact that a company in which they are investing may not yet have a product or revenues by exercising control rights. Control rights refer to the allocation of control over the company and its decisions and how that control is divided between the venture capitalists and the entrepreneurs. Control rights typically have three characteristics: (1) venture capitalists normally exercise a disproportionately large share of control over the entrepreneurs;[19] (2) control rights are not static, they are changed and refined over time;[20] and (3) where significant asymmetric information exists, greater control rights are assigned to the venture capitalist.[21]

One way that venture capitalists exercise control to reduce the risk of performance failure is to provide quasi-equity instead of full equity, that is, convertible and/or preferred stock, which enables it to allocate cash flow and have voting, board, and liquidation rights so that it can control the venture over other stockholders.[22] Kaplan and Stromberg conducted a study of 200 venture capital investments in 118 high-tech U.S. companies by 14 venture capital firms over the period 1987 to 1999.[23] Convertible preferred stock was present in 189 out of 200 financing rounds. With convertible preferred stock in early stage situations, if the company performs poorly, the venture capitalists take control. As the company's performance improves, the entrepreneur gains more control. If the company performs with a return of more than 30 percent per year over the 4-year period leading to an IPO, the venture capitalists relinquish their control and liquidation rights, but retain their cash flow rights.

The term sheet is also a way to control the new venture because it typically puts a number of requirements on the venture. These requirements may include audited financial statements, noncompete clauses, stock vesting agreements for employees, limitations on the stock option pool, and limitations on salaries. The term sheet is typically one to two pages and summarizes the structure of the deal with the venture capital firm. It deals with such issues as the number of preferred shares, the price of the shares, the resulting equity distribution between the founders and the venture capitalists, the vesting period, dividend and liquidation terms, redemption rights, and conversion rights, to name a few.

TIMING OF FUNDING

To reduce their risk, venture capitalists also stage the investment and tie funding to achievement milestones. If the entrepreneur achieves the first milestone, which is usually tied to profit and/or revenues, the venture capital firm will release the next stage of funding. If, on the other hand, the entrepreneur fails to reach the milestone as scheduled, the venture capital firm may decide to pull out of the investment and write off the first stage. Another way that venture capitalists reduce risk is to enter the investment with another venture capital firm. In fact, some venture capitalists will not invest in a new venture until another venture capitalist has come on board. Funding is timed to support the potential of the venture and help it achieve a consistent pattern of growth without any stops and starts. In other words, funding should never halt the growth of the company, particularly when speed is critical to a competitive advantage.[24] This means that planning for capital acquisition is essential so that the required funding is available when needed. However, funding does not always happen so easily. One reason is that venture capitalists use their funding to exercise control and create incentives, which may or may not be aligned with a consistent growth path.[25] Furthermore, entrepreneurs often underestimate their growth funding requirements, and growth is therefore slowed by their inability to hire and support increased production. Overestimating the magnitude and timing of revenues and underestimating their costs can cause cash flow problems.[26]

THE AFTERMATH

Once the entrepreneur receives venture capital, the real work begins. Although each venture capital firm has its own particular needs, there are some commonalities among them. The venture capital firm will appoint one person from the firm to act as the lead investor, but often several of the investors in the group will want to be involved in some manner. They will likely expect regular board meetings and have formal financial reporting requirements. These board meetings may take place as often as each month or quarter, and will generally be very structured. It is probable that the lead investor will contact the management team prior to the formal meeting to discuss the strategy for the meeting in private, rather than use a public forum to surprise anyone with an issue. The venture capitalist will also want to make sure that the financial statements are correctly prepared and reflect the company's performance relative to projections. The way that the management team handles the investment capital will largely determine if they will receive additional funding at the next milestone.

Because the stakes are high, conflict may erupt from time to time between the venture capital firm and the new venture on issues relating to where the company is going

TABLE 10-3 Common Problems Between Entrepreneurs and Venture Capitalists	
The Entrepreneurs	*The Venture Capitalists*
Venture capitalists who do not come to the meetings prepared by having read the materials and financial statements provided prior to the meeting.	Entrepreneurs who try to hide the fact that they have not prepared for board meetings by hyping the business in a PowerPoint presentation.
Investors who cannot admit that their advice played a role in a decision that failed.	Entrepreneurs who forget that this is the investor's business as much as it is the entrepreneur's.
Investors who focus on minute details to the exclusion of more important issues.	Entrepreneurs who do not do what they said they would do.
Investors who argue with each other during the board meetings, disrupting the meeting and preventing the discussion of more important issues.	Entrepreneurs who think they are the only ones who understand the business and know what is best for it.
Investors who make strategic decisions about the business without informing the management team or discussing it at the board meeting.	Entrepreneurs who do not understand the importance of board meetings.

and how it will get there. Being able to successfully navigate the land mines that are part of every investment relationship is critical to the continuation of that relationship.

The extent of the venture capitalist's involvement in the new venture will be a function of the stage of the venture, the complexity of the technology, and the performance of the company. Early stage companies require more attention on the part of the venture capitalist, particularly in helping the entrepreneurial team to build their company. High-tech ventures generally require more involvement on the part of venture capitalists because they need to understand the technology and deal with conflicting goals. When a company is performing well, the venture capitalist will probably spend less time on it; however, if the company experiences problems or does not appear to be on target to reach its next milestone, the venture capitalist will most definitely take an active role to turn things around.

Entrepreneurs and venture capitalists understand the importance of their relationship, but each party has complaints about the other. Knowing the issues that can provoke conflict in advance will go a long way toward avoiding stressful situations. See Table 10-3 for some common problems that may occur between entrepreneurs and venture capitalists.

THE PRIVATE OFFERING

The purpose of a private offering is to sell securities in the company to potential investors. Recall that securities consist of common and preferred stock, notes, bonds, debentures, voting-trust-certificates, certificates of deposit, warrants, options, subscription rights, limited partnership shares, and undivided oil or gas interests. Most early stage funding, approximately 80 percent, is accomplished through private offerings that are exempt from federal and state securities laws.

Private placement is a less costly, less time-consuming process than a public offering. In fact, today, many states offer standard forms and offering documents that make it easy for the entrepreneur to complete them. An entrepreneur undertaking a private offering does not need to have a long track record, assets, or significant credit references, as would be needed for bank financing, nor does it have to file with the SEC, as entrepreneurs seeking public offerings are required to do. The venture does have to qualify under the blue-sky laws (securities laws) of its state, which are designed to protect investors against fraud.

The SEC's Regulation D rules provide guidelines for a private placement memorandum, which is the equivalent of an initial registration statement that is filed for a public offering. It contains the same information as a prospectus, but the SEC does not review it. Rule 504 permits an offering with a maximum issue of $1 million in any 12-month period and no limit on investors. Rule 505 permits an offering of up to $5 million with a limit of 35 nonaccredited purchasers and unlimited accredited investors. Rule 506 permits an unlimited offering with 35 nonaccredited purchasers and an unlimited number of accredited purchasers. The nonaccredited purchasers must be sophisticated investors, that is, they must have a net worth of at least $1 million. In all cases, the company cannot advertise the offering, as is the case with a public offering, and there are no SEC reporting requirements unless the company has 500 or more shareholders and $3 million in total assets.

SMALL CORPORATE OFFERING REGISTRATION

Many states have adopted the Small Corporate Offering (SCOR U-7) to make the registration process simpler by providing fill-in-the-blank questions to acquire the company's information. With SCOR U-7, a company can raise up to $1 million by selling common stock directly to the public for at least $5 per share. One major benefit of this is that unless a state specifically prohibits it, the offering can be sold to anyone in amounts as small as $1,000. Moreover, in some states, SCOR companies can trade their common stock on NASDAQ's electronic over-the-counter bulletin board. SCOR permits a variety of securities to be sold, including preferred and common stock, convertible debentures, and debt securities with warrants.

SCOR can also be used to sell securities over the Internet in a "Cyber Public Offering." It should be noted that just because a company can raise seed capital by selling to the public, that does not mean that there is a public market for the stock. Proceeds of a successful offering must be placed in an escrow account until the stated objectives of the company are met. When using this or any other type of offering, it is important to consult with an attorney who will make sure that the company follows all the rules and does not leave itself open to a lawsuit.

DIRECT PUBLIC OFFERING: REGULATION A

Under Regulation A of the SEC, a company may do a direct public offering (DPO), but, unlike SCOR, Regulation A permits an offering of up to $5 million over a period of 12 months. To qualify for a DPO, the company should be able to demonstrate several years of profit under the same management, 3 years of audited financial statements, a compelling business story, a strong and loyal customer base that might be induced to invest, and advisors to help with the management of the DPO.

With a Regulation A offering, the company does not have to file a registration statement with the SEC, but it does need to comply with the antifraud and personal liability provisions of the SEC Act of 1933. The disclosures are the same as those for filing a registration statement for a public offering and include a prospectus that identifies the risk factors, financials, use of proceeds, background of the officers and directors, and the goals of the business. Regulation A does not exempt a company from complying with state securities laws, which can be severe.

THE INITIAL PUBLIC OFFERING

For high-tech companies, the lure of the IPO is real. Despite the sharp drop in IPOs after the technology crash that began in the spring of 2000, most high-tech entrepreneurs see an IPO in their company's future. There are many reasons an entrepreneur would consider an IPO. Once the company is public, it is easy to raise additional cash by doing a secondary offering in the public markets. Public companies can have an unlimited number of investors and enjoy more public exposure both during and after the offering. Jeff Bezos, CEO of Amazon.com, claims that Amazon.com went public not just to raise capital, but also to increase public awareness of the company. Akamai, the Internet content company, also chose an IPO to attract customer and business partner attention.[27] Public companies seem to achieve great credibility almost overnight, making lenders, employees, and customers more likely to do business with them. Once the company is public, investors do not have to invest large amounts of capital to enjoy a stake in the company, as they would have to do in a private offering. Furthermore, stock that is qualified on one of the stock exchanges generally sells at 30 percent more than it would in a private offering.[28]

For all the positives of a public offering, there are significant negatives that should be weighed as well. A public company is just that—public. That means that financial statements, annual reports, and other documents are available to the public, including competitors. The SEC reporting requirements are onerous and typically require a staff to manage them. Ownership is more likely to be diluted from the sale of stock to raise capital. Perhaps the most challenging negative of a public offering is that the entrepreneur must now satisfy shareholders first and foremost. Public companies are under a great deal of pressure to perform in the short term. In contrast, entrepreneurs with private companies can focus on long-term goals while sacrificing short-term profits. Often, with a public company, board of directors meetings focus only on the next quarter's financial reports, how decisions will affect the stock price, and what the stock analysts are going to say about the company. The entrepreneur's original vision for the company may get lost in the morass of quarterly and annual reports. Still, for many high-tech companies, a public offering is the only realistic way to raise sufficient growth capital.

Undertaking an IPO requires that the company have a compelling need to raise a significant amount of capital for a specific purpose. That purpose must be clear to everyone involved with the company. The company must also start acting like a public company well before the IPO process; that is, it must begin to manage the expectations of its investors and improve its ability to accurately forecast earnings on a quarterly basis. It must also develop methods for communicating regularly with stakeholders.

MEASURES OF SUCCESS

With so many IPOs failing to materialize or failing to enhance the value of a company, it is important to identify what it takes to be successful. In an attempt to understand the success factors in an initial public offering, Ernst & Young surveyed more than 150 senior executives from 42 emerging companies representing a wide variety of industries in North America to learn their views on the climate for IPOs.[29] A number of important findings came out of that study that are relevant to any entrepreneur considering an IPO as part of their company's long-term strategy.

- While most IPOs underperform after the public offering, the most successful companies were successful before, during, and after the IPO. What this means is that if a company was not competitive prior to the IPO, the IPO did not necessarily make it more competitive.
- Preparation is a huge contributor to success. The most successful companies began acting like public companies months, and sometimes years, before they did the IPO. They instituted strong systems and controls as well as employee incentive programs.
- More than half of those surveyed believed that developing the business strategy is the biggest leadership challenge for a company contemplating going public.

The bottom line is that a successful IPO is the result of a long process that begins with firm corporate goals and commitment to those goals. The IPO itself is merely the high point of the journey. In the next section, the IPO process is explored.

THE IPO PROCESS

The IPO process is time-consuming and lengthy, with no guarantee that it will be completed. Many a company has reached the end of the road show, designed to sign up institutional investors, only to find itself undersold or sold at a price much below the projected offering price. Before starting the IPO process, it is wise to consult with many people who have gone through the process. By doing so, the entrepreneur can enter the process with full knowledge of what lies ahead.

As everything is dependent on the registration statement with the SEC, a particularly lengthy undertaking, understanding the IPO timetable is valuable. See Table 10-4 for an overview of the IPO timetable. A tool for creating a timetable is available at the Deloitte & Touche Web site (*www.dttus.com/growth/ipotools/timeline.xls*).

The various steps of the IPO process are shown in Figure 10-3. The process starts with the selection of an investment bank, the firm that underwrites the IPO. It is important to select the investment bank as early as possible because it will be the major contact with all the financial interests involved in the IPO. The investment bank sells the securities and essentially guides the company through the IPO process. The large, well-known investment banks—Morgan Stanley Dean Witter, Goldman Sachs, Merrill Lynch, Solomon Smith Barney, and Credite Suisse First Boston—are the dominant players, having a combined share of 72.8 percent of the IPO market from January 1 to March 7, 2000 alone.[30] A very young company that is seeking a public offering before it has achieved at least $50 million in sales will likely have a difficult time attracting one of

TABLE 10-4	Timetable for Completing an IPO
Month	*Task*
Month 0	In months preceding countdown to IPO: • Put systems and controls in place for managing growth • Build a strong team, internally and externally • Choose professional advisors with public company experience • Complete a business plan or update existing one • Prepare complete and current financials • Put at least two outsiders on the board of directors
Month 1	Kick-off meeting Review letter of intent and underwriting fees Draft and revise registration statement and all documents related to under-writing document
Month 2	Complete second and third drafts of registration statement Complete and review questionnaires of officers, directors, and 10–percent shareholders Review management's discussion and analysis of company financial position Board of directors meeting to review offering and authorize filing of registration statement Meet with attorneys and underwriters on all documents Deliver draft of registration statement to printer for printing of "red herring" Prepare audited financial statements Board of directors meeting to review registration statement, authorize blue-sky filings, appoint pricing committee Finalize underwriting documents and registration statement File registration statement and exhibits with SEC
Month 3	Prepare for road show Present road show to underwriters Do road show for investors Respond to SEC comments and make appropriate changes in registration statement Respond to SEC comments on any amendments
Month 4	Pricing committee approves pricing Final amendment with final pricing filed with SEC Final prospectus printed IPO closes

the major investment banking houses, as these firms will find it challenging to sell the company to their major institutional investors. Consequently, a smaller company should consider contacts it might have in the investment banking community or investigate the numerous regional or boutique investment banking firms that often serve small to mid-market companies. It is important to investigate the reputation and track record of the underwriter, particularly in the case of a smaller firm. The industry is highly competitive with the lure of large fees, and these conditions can attract less than scrupulous bankers. An excellent investment banker will provide advice on buying and selling stock and

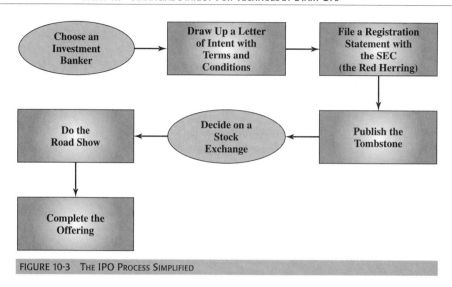

FIGURE 10-3 THE IPO PROCESS SIMPLIFIED

help to create and maintain interest in the stock over a long period of time. Selection of the underwriter also begins a "quiet period" that extends to 25 days after the IPO during which information not included in the registration statement cannot be disclosed.

The underwriter draws up a letter of intent, which spells out the terms and conditions of the agreement between the underwriter and the entrepreneur. It will detail a range of prices for the stock, which is merely an estimate of the price at which the underwriter believes the stock will be sold. The actual going-out price is determined the night before the offering. In general, the going-out price is typically undervalued so that the company shows an upsurge in stock price immediately after the offering hits the market. If the entrepreneur is unhappy with the price the underwriter proposes the night before the offering, their only choice is to cancel the offering. Of course, the entrepreneur still incurs the expenses to date, which can be substantial.

A registration statement is filed with the SEC. This document is referred to as a "red herring," or prospectus, because it details all the potential risks of the investment to anyone interested in investing. It includes biographical material on the officers and directors, the number of shares owned by all insiders, complete financial statements, use of proceeds, and any legal issues related to the company. The prospectus is valid for 9 months, after which any changes must occur through an official amendment. Following the registration, the underwriter places an advertisement, called a tombstone, in the financial press that announces the offering.

One of the major decisions that must be made is on which stock exchange to list the offering. In general, smaller companies list on the American Stock Exchange (AMEX), the National Association of Securities Dealers Automated Quotation (NASDAQ), or one of the regional exchanges. The New York Stock Exchange (NYSE), home to over 80 percent of American securities, has more stringent listing requirements. In general, it requires that a company have 2,000 shareholders of 100 shares or more or total stockholders of 2,200 with average monthly trading volume of 100,000 shares. Alternatively, a company must have 500 total stockholders with an average monthly trading volume of 1 million shares. There are a number of other financial requirements. All of these requirements can be found at *www.nyse.com/listed/ listed.html*. The NASDAQ operates differently than the other exchanges. The NYSE and AMEX are auction markets with securities traded on the floor of the exchange, enabling investors to trade directly with each other. In contrast, the NASDAQ is a floorless exchange that trades on the National Market System through a system of broker-dealers from respected securities firms who compete for orders. Most high-tech companies that are still growing are listed on the NASDAQ.

The culmination of all the preparatory work for the IPO comes with the road show, a two-week whirlwind tour of all the major institutional investors. The purpose of the trip is to make sure that once the registration statement has met all the SEC requirements and the final price of the stock is determined, it can sell in a day. It is also designed to introduce the management team to analysts, brokers, potential investors, and others. How the team responds to questions about its products, business, and competition will determine the ultimate success of the offering. It is no wonder then that the management team spends many hours preparing its road show presentation and practices fielding questions.

WHEN AN IPO FAILS

In 1998, 102 *Inc.* 500 CEOs told *Inc.* magazine that they intended to go public by 2000, but by the middle of 1999, only 8 of the 102 had gone public.[31] The heated economy at that time certainly explains the high expectations of those CEOs, but the reality is that a number of things can derail a company on its way to an IPO.

Optiva Corp., known for its best-selling Sonicare toothbrush, topped the *Inc.* 500 list of fastest-growing private companies in 1997 when it decided that it needed to raise a substantial amount of capital to expand its domestic retail channel and grow in the international market. In May 1998, with Hambrect & Quist and PaineWebber as its underwriters, it filed its S-1 registration statement, with plans to do an IPO later that summer. However, that very summer Gillette announced a surprise lawsuit against Optiva for false advertising against its competing Braun Oral-B product. Optiva was then faced with having to manage both an IPO and a lawsuit. The lawsuit went on for 7 months, stalling the road show. Finally, just before the verdict, Optiva withdrew its registration papers, killing the IPO. Although it lost the lawsuit, its sales continued to increase and in 2001, Optiva announced that Philips Oral Healthcare, Inc., a division of Royal Philips Electronics, was acquiring it.[32]

An even more disappointing situation occurs when a company arrives at the day before the offering, having incurred a million dollars in expenses only to decide to cancel the offering. It was an extraordinarily hard decision for Nick Canitano, the CEO of CCAI, an enterprise resource planning company based in Mayfield Heights, Ohio. It was noon on the last day of the road show. Canitano was expecting the final price per share to be in the $10 to $12 a share range, but the underwriters surprised him with a final offer from the institutional investors of $8 a share, which would reduce the proceeds by millions of dollars. Canitano decided that he did not want to share the upside of his business with investors who only recognized the risk and pulled the offering. Canitano understands why the offering did not go well. First, he was not always able to give good answers to the investors' questions. Second, the industry was in an upheaval at that time and his small company paid the price for others' failures. It is important to understand how fragile an IPO can be, particularly in volatile times such as those seen in the late 1990s and in the early part of the millennium.

PRESENTING THE COMPANY TO INVESTORS

Basically, there are two approaches to seeking growth funding: direct placement or using an intermediary, someone whose job is to raise money for the company. With the direct placement approach, an entrepreneur deals directly with investors, which means that the entrepreneur must have good selling, presentation, and persuasive skills Using an intermediary does not relieve the entrepreneur of acquiring these skills, because the intermediary typically just finds the investor and makes the contact; the entrepreneur must still pitch the concept to the investor. An intermediary is more likely to agree to work with an entrepreneur who has demonstrated the ability to use the direct placement approach. Moreover, the entrepreneur will have to teach the concept and vision of the technology to the intermediary so that the intermediary can be more effective in their initial approach to an investor.

The traditional type of intermediary is an investment-banking firm that raises investment capital for companies in the public markets. Be aware that there are two groups of investment bankers: licensed and nonlicensed. The National Association of Securities Dealers (NASD) regulates licensed money raisers. Any deal involving a NASD licensed broker cannot also involve a nonlicensed broker. Securities dealers are listed in "The Red Book," *Securities Dealers of North America*, published by Standard & Poor's. Investment bankers cultivate their investors over time. These investors range from institutions such as pension funds to individuals. In general, investment banking firms look for deals greater than $5 million in industries they believe hold the greatest potential for return on their investment, and they tend to avoid early stage ventures. One of the investments they seek is bridge financing prior to an IPO because the return on their investment is almost assured within a relatively short period of time.

Reed Taussig, CEO of Callidus Software, decided that he would make the rules when dealing with venture capitalists, and, surprisingly, his strategy has worked. Taussig figures that an investment of 100 hours or more per investor during the due diligence process is necessary and it is important to demand that the venture capitalist be serious about the investment.[33] His company, based in San Jose, California, has been successful in raising $35 million from top-flight investors because of a strategy that he believes works. Here are some of his tips for dealing with venture capitalists:

- It takes approximately 6 months to raise money, so if the senior partners of the venture capital firm show no interest in that amount of time, it is time to move on.
- The venture capitalist should have investment interests in the same space the new venture is in.
- The venture capitalist should not be allowed to talk to the company's customers until the due diligence is completed, and then only a senior partner should do the talking.
- The top people in the venture should not meet the venture capitalist before the investor is qualified as a serious investor capable of providing the required amount of capital.

THE TOOLS OF THE TRADE

There are a variety of supporting documents and other items that are necessary to make a case to a potential investor. These items lend credence to what the entrepreneur is saying and demonstrate that the venture is a serious one. Some of these documents include:

- a business plan
- a Private Placement Memorandum or prospectus in the case of an SEC registered offering
- a company brochure that highlights the vision and mission of the company
- letters from customers and other value chain partners
- company newsletters
- quarterly and annual reports
- press releases and news articles about the company

Many entrepreneurs have secured funding from private investors or venture capitalists on the strength of their presentations. This makes sense because most investors invest in people first and products and markets second. Therefore, the entrepreneurial team must demonstrate that it can execute its strategies.

❖ SUMMARY

Growth is a very exciting time in the life of a new venture, but it also strains the venture's resources because growth requires large amounts of capital. Entrepreneurs raise capital by securing debt or selling equity stakes in their companies. When the returns on the business exceed the cost of borrowing money, debt is a wise choice, but selling shares of stock in the company is the most common way that entrepreneurs raise capital to grow the business. Raising capital requires a well-thought-out plan that identifies milestones and their associated triggers. The plan also details how those milestones will be reached and how much funding each will require. Venture capital funds less than 1 percent of all ventures, but it is an important funding source for technology ventures attempting to grow. Venture capitalists operate under four basic principles: (1) the venture capital firm gets paid first, (2) participation in the upside of the venture, (3) control over critical events, and (4) creation of a path to liquidity. Venture capitalists protect their investment and attempt to reduce their risk through a variety of mechanisms, including control rights, business valuation, and timing of the funding. The private offering is a less-costly way to sell securities in the company to potential investors without being subject to the strict rules of a public offering. Many technology companies plan for an initial public offering in their future. Going public gives the venture more clout in the market and makes it easier to raise additional money, however, the SEC reporting requirements are onerous, the entrepreneur's ownership is likely to be diluted, and the entrepreneur may have to forego a long-held vision to satisfy stockholders in the short term. Companies that were successful before, during, and after the IPO, and that began acting like a public company long before they started the IPO process had the most successful IPOs.

❖ DISCUSSION QUESTIONS

1. When growing a company, why would an entrepreneur choose debt over equity?
2. What elements should an effective financing strategy contain?
3. What is meant by control rights and how do venture capitalists exercise them?
4. What effect does the timing of funding have on a growing venture's success? Why?
5. What important tasks must take place prior to undertaking an IPO?

❖ RESOURCES

Benjamin, Gerald A., and Joel Margulis. *Angel Financing: How to Find and Invest in Private Equity.* New York: John Wiley & Sons, 1999.

Blowers, Stephen C., Peter H. Griffith, Thomas L. Milan. *The Ernst & Young Guide to the IPO Value Journey.* New York: John Wiley & Sons, 1999.

Gompers, Paul A., and Josh Lerner. *The Venture Capital Cycle.* Cambridge, MA: MIT Press, 1999.

Robbins-Roth, Cynthia. *From Alchemy to IPO: The Business of Biotechnology.* Cambridge, MA: Perseus Books, 2001.

❖ INTERNET RESOURCES

Hoover's IPO Central
www.hoovers.com/ipo/0,1334,23,00.html
Records of recent filings and a beginner's guide to IPOs

IPO.com
www.ipo.com/
Comprehensive source of information and resources related to IPOs and venture capital

Red Herring Online
www.redherring.com/
Online home of the well-known journal dedicated to investment and technology

Vfinance.com
www.vfinance.com/
Home of the *Venture Capital Resource Directory*; portal for companies in need of capital and private investors seeking deals

Venture Capital Institute
www.vcinstitute.org/
A foundation for venture and private equity professionals

FROM RICHES TO RAGS AND BACK?: WHEN GOING PUBLIC MAY NOT BE THE RIGHT PATH

In January 1998, 33-year-old Doug Mellinger was on top of the world. Touted as "the next Bill Gates," Mellinger's software programming business, PRT Group, had just completed a successful public offering, and the stock was rising. His own stake in the company was worth $44 million; his family's stake had grown to $112 million. Life was good for this entrepreneur. However, in the space of only a year and a half, the company headed into a tailspin, and Mellinger found himself out on the streets having lost his job as CEO. How could something like this happen in the space of 19 months?

In the early 1990s, PRT was a small software company that provided on-site software engineers to clients. It was a difficult business; software engineers were in short supply and immigration laws prevented companies such as Mellinger's from importing talent in sufficient quantities from places such as India. For a time, Mellinger tried operating off-shore, but most of the countries he investigated were too far away, had inadequate labor, or other problems. Moreover, his clients were not comfortable with the concept of his company operating out of another country. Finally, in 1994, he conceived the idea of creating his own perfect country on the island of Barbados in the Caribbean. He built a village, imported programmers, secured capital, created an infrastructure, and found customers. His goal was to create an environment where programmers were completely taken care of while they spent their days writing code. In essence, Mellinger gave his programmers a turnkey life.

Within a short amount of time, Mellinger had imported 350 employees from 16 countries. Huge companies such as J. P. Morgan and Chase Manhattan were so enthralled with the concept that they gave PRT their business and con-

tributed $12 million to the business's construction needs. Mellinger began creating partnerships with the local government with plans to improve schools and take a nontech country into the technological age. It was a grand vision to solve a real problem.

Riding the crest of a wave of popularity with a great story to tell, Mellinger decided in 1997 that it was time to do a public offering to raise more growth capital. Mellinger was unprepared for the amount of time it would take to do the offering. For 5 months, he sat in meetings with attorneys, investment bankers, and potential investors as they prepared for the offering date. On November 20, 1997, PRT Group went public at $13 a share (NASDAQ: PRTG). By the end of the first day of trading, it listed at $13.25. By February 26, 1998, the stock hit what was to be its high point at $21.63, producing $156 million for Mellinger and his family. PRT was projecting that it would double its revenues in 1998 to $120 million, so Mellinger expanded PRT's programming capability to meet the projected demand. Unfortunately, that demand never materialized, and when several projects dissolved in early 1998, PRT was left with high overhead. Ironically, in 1997, when PRT did not have sufficient programmers to handle the demand, it told its salespeople to slow the pace at which they were attracting new customers.

On March 6, 1998, PRT announced that it would post a first-quarter loss of $3 million rather than the small profit it had originally projected. The result: PRT stock dropped $9.56 in the first hour of trading. Mellinger learned that the concept of shipping custom programming from Barbados did not catch on as quickly as he had thought it would. That, coupled with the fact that custom programming entailed a longer development time and a longer sales cycle, made cash flow a real problem.

The pressure to change the direction of the stock changed the way Mellinger ran the company. Everyone began to panic and reorganization became the norm. By September 1998, a shareholder lawsuit was brought against the company, claiming that PRT falsely portrayed its Y2K capabilities, which caused the stock slump. By then, the stock was trading at $4 a share.

PRT ended 1998 with revenues of $85 million, $35 million below projections. The company had lost 100 employees. Nearly 70 percent of the sales staff had left within the year. Mellinger became the primary salesperson in the organization, but he could not single-handedly develop the sales volume that PRT needed and his sales staff was never properly trained. In May 1999, PRT hired a new president and COO, displacing Mellinger's brother, and he began auditing the company's processes. Changes began to take place, and it was then that Doug Mellinger realized that he was an entrepreneur, not a manager; he did not have the appropriate skills to run a large company. In late June 1999, the COO, Dan Woodward, became the CEO, and Mellinger was no longer an officer of the corporation.

Since June 30, 1999, analysts and others have attempted to understand how something like this could have happened. Logically, it could be attributed to a poor sales force and too much reliance on the selling ability of Mellinger, as well as too much focus on the production side at the expense of marketing. However, many analysts speculate that it was the decision to become a public company that was PRT's undoing. While still a young company, it had the pressure of short-term performance gains that it could not keep up with.

Following Mellinger's departure, the company added a new COO and restructured the company. In a moment of irony, on September 22, 1999, Deloitte & Touche named PRT to its prestigious "Fast 50" program for the New York region, as one of the fastest growing technology companies in the area from 1994 to 1998.

Epilogue: On May 31, 2000, PRT Group Inc. underwent a brand makeover and became Enherent Corp. with a new logo, Web site, and refined strategic direction. At the same time, the company announced that it was moving its headquarters to Dallas, Texas. It retained its Barbados operation, which PRT claims reduces IT application development and management costs for its U.S. clients by 30 to 40 percent. As of November 8, 2001, Enherent's stock was trading at $0.18 share. Although the company is still in business, and some early customers such as J. P. Morgan remain customers, Enherent is not out of the woods yet. Believing in its core competencies, Enherent and CEO Dan Woodward are still seeking the best way to turn the company around. The September 11 catastrophe and the subsequent war on terrorism have slowed its progress, but they have also presented opportunities that the company will need to explore if it is going to become profitable. ■

Sources: "U.S. Firm Brings *Fortune* 500 Clients to Barbados," Enherent Corp. press release, Dallas, TX, May 8, 2001; "PRT Group Evolves to Become Enherent Corp." PRT Group Inc. press release, Windsor, CT, May 31, 2000; Michael S. Hopkins, "Paradise Lost," *Inc.* (November 1, 1999) *www.inc.com*; "PRT Group Inc. Selected as Technology Fast 50 Company by Deloitte & Touche," PRT Group Inc. press release, Windsor, CT, September 22, 1999.

❖ NOTES

1. M. T. Hannon and J. Freeman, *Organizational Ecology* (Cambridge, MA: Harvard University Press, 1989).
2. D. J. Teece, G. Pisano, and A. Shuen, "Dynamic Capabilities and Strategic Management," *Strategic Management Journal* 18, no. 7 (1997): 509–533.
3. Antonio Davila, George Foster, and Mahendra Gupta, "Venture-Capital Financing and the Growth of Start-up Firms," *Research Paper Series*, Graduate School of Business, Stanford University, Palo Alto, CA, November 2000.

4. T. Hellmann and M. Purl, "The Interaction Between Product, Market, and Financing Strategy: The Role of Venture Capital," working paper, Stanford University, Palo Alto, CA, 1999.

5. Jonathan Levie, "Convincing the Cash-Conscious Banker," in Sue Birley and Daniel F. Muzyka, eds., *Financial Times: Mastering Entrepreneurship*, (London: Pearson Education, 2000): 99–100.

6. Ibid., 101.

7. Geoffrey Colvin, "Earnings Aren't Everything," *Fortune* 144, no. 5 (September 17, 2001): 58.

8. Ibid.

9. Brad Weirick, "Introduction to Venture Capital," Presentation at the University of Southern California, San Diego, CA, November 7, 2001.

10. William Bygrave, "How the Venture Capitalists Work Out the Financial Odds," in Sue Birley and Daniel F. Muzyka, eds. *Financial Times: Mastering Entrepreneurship* (London: Pearson Education, 2000): 105–109.

11. G. R. Carroll and M. T. Hannan, *The Demography of Corporations and Industries* (Princeton, NJ: Princeton University Press, 2000).

12. Davila et al., "Venture-Capital Financing and the Growth of Start-up Firms," working paper, Graduate School of Business, Stanford University, Palo Alto, CA, November 2000.

13. Peter Brierley, "The Financing of Technology-based Small Firms: A Review of the Literature," *Bank of England Quarterly Bulletin* 41, no. 1 (Spring 2001): 64–83.

14. Daniel Muzyka and Sue Birley, "What Venture Capitalists Look For," in Sue Birley and Daniel F. Muzyka eds. *Financial Times: Mastering Entrepreneurship* (London: Pearson Education, 2000), 103–105.

15. L. Steir, "Venture Capitalists Relationships in the Deal Structuring and Post-Investment Stages of New Firm Creation," *Journal of Management Studies* 32, no. 2 (1995): 337–357.

16. Brierley, "The Financing of Technology-based Small Firms," 64–83.

17. M. Wright and K. Robbie, "Venture Capitalists, Unquoted Equity Investment Appraisal and the Role of Accounting Information," *Accounting and Business Research* 26, no. 20 (1996): 153–168.

18. T. Luehrman, "What's It Worth? A General Manager's Guide to Valuation," *Harvard Business Review* 75:3 (May–June 1997): 132–145.

19. Paul A. Gompers, "Ownership and Control in Entrepreneurial Firms: An Examination of Convertible Securities in Venture Capital Investments," working paper, Harvard University, Cambridge, MA, 1997; Bernard S. Black and Ronald J. Gilson, "Venture Capital and the Structure of Capital Markets: Banks Versus Stock Markets," *Journal of Financial Economics* 47 (1998): 243–277.

20. Steven N. Kaplan and Per Strombert, "Financial Contracting Theory Meets the Real World: An Empirical Analysis of Venture Capital Projects," working paper, University of Chicago, Chicago, IL, 1999.

21. Andrei A. Kirilenko, "Valuation and Control in Venture Finance," *The Journal of Finance* 56, no. 2 (2001): 565–588.

22. Brierley, "The Financing of Technology-based Small Firms," 64–83.

23. S.N.Kaplan and P. Strombert, "Financial Contracting Theory Meets the Real World: An Empirical Analysis of Venture Capital Projects," working paper. University of Chicago, Chicago, IL, 1999.

24. G. Saloner, A. Shepard, and J. Podolny, *Strategic Management* (New York: Wiley, 2000).

25. Davila et al., "Venture-Capital Financing and the Growth of Start-up Firms," 11.

26. A. L. Zacharakis and G. D. Meyer, "The Potential of Actuarial Decision Models: Can They Improve the Venture Capital Investment Decision?" *Journal of Business Venturing* 15 (2000): 323–346.

27. Jae H. Song, "Maximizing the Financial and Product Market Values of the IPO Opportunity," *Business Horizons* 44:4 (July 2001): 39.

28. Mark Long, *Financing the New Venture* (Holbrook, MA: Adams Media Corporation, 2000), 218.

29. Business Editors, "Entrepreneurs Say
Current IPO Climate is 'Difficult But Not
Impossible,'" *Business Wire*, May 16, 2001,
www.businesswire.com.

30. T. J. Mullaney, "Is the Street Lowballing
IPOs?" *Business Week* (April 3, 2000)
EB112, EB114. *www.businessweek.com.*

31. Susan Greco, "So Near . . . And Yet So Far,"
Inc. (October 15, 1999) *www.inc.com.*

32. Ibid.; "Optiva Corporation Changes Name
to Philips Oral Healthcare Inc.," *www.
sonicare.com/news_offers/news/*, January 8,
2001.

33. Lawrence Aragon, "The Smart VC: Don't
Get Jerked Around," *Red Herring* n/a
(October 24, 2001) *www.redherring.com.*

MOVING FROM R&D TO OPERATIONS

OVERVIEW

This chapter will examine

❖ challenges in transitioning from R&D to operations

❖ organizational models

❖ legal forms of organization

INTRODUCTION

As if the challenges of R&D were not enough, a daunting task awaits the technology team when it is ready to become a company and launch a product. The move from R&D to operations is not an easy transition, because operations require different skills from the technology team. An operating business does not happen overnight; it takes a lot of planning. Lingering technical and market issues continue to emerge, pulling the team in a multitude of directions. If manufacturing processes were not designed in parallel with the development of the product, figuring out how to most efficiently and effectively design those processes could stall the product launch. Furthermore, a late-stage prototype of the product is not the same as a production quality unit, and if the team has not completed the sourcing of all components and raw materials for production, that too could delay the launch.

These issues are only the beginning. Business partners who worked with the team during R&D may not be appropriate partners for a full-scale ramp up of the operations, and the decision becomes whether to continue to outsource some operations to another entity or keep a process in-house and develop it into a core competency. The R&D team does not always understand the objectives of the operations team that is charged with getting the product out and generating revenues. Because the R&D team was focused on design issues, it had the luxury of experimentation, fast failures, and continual improvement; the operations team has none of those luxuries.[1] Instead, it is under pressure to generate cash flow for a business that has been a sinkhole during the entire course of product development. Experience suggests that a transition team should be formed to bridge the gap between the R&D team and the operations team. This chapter will look at the transition from R&D to operations.

CHALLENGES IN TRANSITIONING FROM PROJECT TO OPERATIONS

In their research on high-technology companies, Leifer et al. found a number of issues that regularly plague project teams during the final phases of product development just prior to handing off the project to the operations team to launch the venture.[2] For example, getting customers involved in the design and development of the product is important, but it can also cause a need for changes in the technical specifications of the product and can even result in the identification of a new application and a new customer set that must be studied and addressed. Moreover, manufacturing a prototype typically uses different processes than will likely be used in the final production model. These differences introduce technical and process uncertainty during the transition.

Many project teams enter the transition believing that their technology is the "killer app" that will propel the company forward. Unfortunately, most often it is not. In fact, the early entrant or pioneer usually does not grab the broadest market appeal. Consider the PDA market where the pioneer, Apple's Newton MessagePad, met a lukewarm welcome when customers were frustrated by its inability to correctly interpret their handwriting. Out of the second wave of entrants came products such as Sony's Magic Link and Motorola's Envoy, which were targeted at specific niche markets and had slightly more success built on the now established infrastructure of the industry. It was not until the third wave, which brought the PalmPilot, that a company was able to capture a broad enough market to establish its brand and become successful.

Another concern during this transition period is how applications and markets will develop. The assumptions made during product design and development, even with customer input, often do not hold up when the product is out in the market. Again, the PDA market in 1995 provides a good example. Engineers loaded the units with communications functions because these functions were viewed as the most critical. However, as customers began to use the products, manufacturers learned that the scheduling function was the most critical to the customer and, in fact, the communications functions were not even being used.

CREATING A SUCCESSFUL TRANSITION

A successful transition requires three different groups of individuals: people from the innovation team, people from the operations team, and transition management experts.[3] It is the job of the transition team to finalize the product and its first applications as well as to refine the business model. The transition team will also need to construct a transition plan that details the readiness of the company to launch the product in terms of personnel, systems, and resources. The plan should be a way to measure progress and, therefore, should contain a time line and metrics for measuring that progress. Often the best strategy for a first launch is not to try to guess which application will be the killer app, but attempt to capture several niche market applications that immediately bring in cash flow. Chances are that one of those applications could turn into a killer app.

BUILDING A FIRST-CLASS TEAM

The team that took the new venture through the product development and feasibility stages may not be the same team that is needed to launch the venture and secure the first customer. Particularly in cases where the R&D team was made up of engineers or scientists, the team may not have the skills and experience to suddenly shift gears and begin focusing on the market. Long before the venture is ready for launch, the entrepreneurial team must make sure that it has all of the skills required to deal with the business side of the business. That may mean bringing one or two people on board with management, marketing, and/or financial capabilities. If the team secured first-round funding from private investors and is now seeking venture capital for a second round, the venture capitalists may be able to assist in securing the right management for the company.

Every team needs a leader, and most entrepreneurial teams have a lead entrepreneur who embodies the vision for the company. Whether that lead entrepreneur comes from the technical or the business side of the venture does not matter. What matters is that the lead entrepreneur be the corporate evangelist, the key person driving the company forward through pauses, temporary halts, and every imaginable problem. The leader rallies the troops and serves as a role model for what it takes to create a great company. The lead entrepreneur is also responsible for inspiring the culture of the company, which can become a critical competitive advantage for the new venture.

DEVELOPING THE MISSION

One of the most critical aspects of planning for the operations of a new venture is identifying and communicating the mission of the company. Research has found a positive relationship between a company's mission statement and its performance.[4] Developing a mission statement is a four-part process, as depicted in Figure 11-1. The entrepreneur carries the vision for the business, but to move toward that vision requires discipline, and the mission statement provides that discipline. To construct a mission statement that everyone buys into requires that everyone participate in its formulation, which means including employees and stakeholders, both internal and external.

By communicating with stakeholders during the development of the mission statement, the company can gain a sense of what stakeholders believe they contribute to the performance of the company and how the mission statement is related to company performance. In the second stage, the components of the mission statement are identified. In general, mission statements describe three dimensions of the business: (1) which customer groups are being satisfied, (2) what customer needs are being satisfied, and (3) in what way customer needs are being satisfied.[5] Another approach suggests four components: (1) purpose (why the company exists), (2) strategy (competitive advantage

FIGURE 11-1   DEVELOPING A MISSION STATEMENT

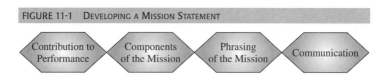

and core competencies), (3) values (what the company believes in), and (4) behavior standards (the behaviors based on the value system).[6]

The third stage of mission development embodies the process by which the mission statement is actually created. A free flow of ideas is appropriate and necessary for the creation of a mission statement that everyone can be proud of. Oftentimes, however, this free exchange of ideas is difficult because the entrepreneur's vision for the company is strong. Consequently, in a new venture, it is likely that the founding team members will actually be the ones to structure the mission statement in such a way that it operationalizes the lead entrepreneur's or the team's vision for the company. In the final stage, the mission statement is communicated to all relevant stakeholders via meetings, the Web site, and by posting it in strategic places in the company's facilities. The following is an example of a mission statement.[7]

> SAIC is a company of people dedicated to delivering best-value services and solutions based on innovative applications of science and technology.
>
> - We commit to exceeding our customers' expectations for quality, responsiveness, and professional excellence while delivering within the agreed price and schedule.
> - We maintain the highest standards of ethical behavior and professional integrity.
> - We employ people of exceptional creativity, expertise, and determination who work closely with one another and with our customers.
> - We pursue technical growth and market diversification to increase value for our customers and opportunity for our employees.
> - We motivate and reward outstanding performance through our employee ownership system.
> - We foster a working environment that encourages technical objectivity, professional and financial growth, and entrepreneurial freedom.

THE ENTRY STRATEGY

The market entry strategy is a key component of the overall move from R&D to operations. Although the entry strategy will be a function of the expectations of the customer, it will also depend on the capabilities of the company at the time of entry. In general, there are three broad entry strategies that entrepreneurs employ: niche, differentiation, and cost superiority. As a general rule, cost superiority is the most difficult and least desirable strategy for a new venture because it entails entering the market farther up the learning curve with operational costs under control and the ability to run the company as if it were well established in the industry. Needless to say, this is a nearly impossible task for an inexperienced new venture with limited resources and lower production volumes. Moreover, this entry strategy is also related to price. It is a common strategy of companies selling commodity products with tiny margins that must lower operational costs to compete.

Most entrepreneurs choose between differentiation and niche strategies for market entry depending on the kind of technology they are developing. The differentiation strategy distinguishes the new company from others in the market through product/process innovation or a unique marketing or distribution strategy. A differentiation strategy is common with incremental innovations where competition is strong and where the new company has developed a process innovation in some aspect of the business or an incremental innovation in the product that allows it to distinguish itself from competitors.

The niche strategy is perhaps the most powerful strategy because the new venture in effect creates a market space that is not currently being served and captures that entire space. This is what Quantum Dot Corporation (see Case Study) did when it took an emerging technology (nanoparticles) and created a new application in the medical diagnostics space. Niche entrepreneurs seek out market disruptions or gaps in the market that allow the company to establish a foothold in the market without going head to head with major companies in the industry. The niche strategy is the most creative and powerful of all the strategies because it permits a new venture to define and target a market space that it can own. Growing in a niche and then tackling additional niches gives the new venture time to develop and gain strength so that in time it can partner with larger, established firms or compete against them in the mainstream market.

ORGANIZATIONAL MODELS

It is estimated that of the millions of ideas for high-tech companies that entrepreneurs consider, only about one in six will ever make it to becoming a public company. A recent study has found that certain organizational models and business practices may enhance the odds of success.[8] The Stanford Project on Emerging Companies has been tracking 167 high-tech companies in Silicon Valley since 1994. Researchers have identified five organizational models: engineering, star, commitment, bureaucracy, and autocracy. These models are depicted in Table 11-1. In the engineering model, the company hires for specific technical or scientific skills, and the peer group is the dominant control mechanism. In the star model, employees are typically selected for their

TABLE 11-1 Results of the Stanford Project on Emerging Companies

	Engineering Model	Star Model	Commitment Model	Bureaucracy Model	Autocracy Model
Percent of companies in study	31%	8%	7%	5%	3%
Characteristics	• Hire for specific skills • Peer-group control	• Employees selected for long-term potential • Little control	• Strong emotional bonds • Informal peer-group control	• Formal control procedures • Challenging work on specific skills	• Motivate with financial rewards • Close personal oversight and specific skills
Failure rate	>13%	>0	0	>13%	13%

Source: Mary Kwak, "Commitment Counts," *MIT Sloan Management Review* 42, no. 4 (Summer 2001): 8–9.

long-term potential in the company and little control is exerted over them. In the commitment model, the informal peer group controls the activities of the organization, and strong emotional bonds are formed within that group. In the bureaucracy model, there are formal control procedures, and employees are hired for specific skills. Finally, in the autocracy model, employees are motivated by financial rewards, there is close personal oversight, and employees are hired for specific skills.

The researchers expected that the star and engineering models would be the most effective models in high-tech ventures seeking a public offering, but, in fact, the commitment model proved to be the best predictor of an initial public offering. What is unusual about this finding is that the commitment model is most often associated with large, stable companies. As of January 1, 2000, the cutoff date for the study, not one of the commitment model businesses had failed or disbanded. The failure rate for the rest of the sample was 13 percent.

THE SILICON VALLEY WAY

Many high-tech start-ups look to Silicon Valley for the model of a successful start-up, but recent events suggest that it may be a model to avoid. The Silicon Valley model has four components: (1) a mobile labor force, (2) independent contractors, (3) signing bonuses and stock options, and (4) draconian working hours.[9] The free agency aspect of the model expects that employees will change positions on a regular basis, resulting in little commitment on the part of employees and the companies that employ them. This makes it difficult for a new venture to develop a sustainable corporate culture, one of the critical competitive advantages of a company. An additional consequence of this model is turnover in the range of 20 to 30 percent annually, resulting in higher costs for recruiting and training, not to mention the costs of productivity disruptions and brain drain. Some companies, such as Cisco Systems (turnover about 8 percent) and SAS Institute (less than 3 percent turnover), have successfully retained employees by displaying an attitude that employees will want to remain with the company for the long-term and treating them in that fashion.

The practice of contracting out every aspect of the business has been popular with technology ventures, and it certainly does make sense for a new venture with limited resources and critical needs that it cannot afford to bring in-house. However, outsourcing has unintended consequences, one of which is that often the core technology or competence of the business—its principal competitive advantage—may be in the hands of an independent contractor who has no long-term loyalty to the contracting company. Furthermore, one study found that most temporary employees or independent contractors, when they realize that they will never become permanent employees, spend the final days of their contracts seeking other work and withholding the tacit knowledge they developed while working for the company.[10] This practice results in significant costs to the company, costs that are not typically reflected in the financial records.

The practice of providing signing bonuses that vest in a relatively short time and stock options that encourage gambling on the part of the recipients also encourages high turnover. Furthermore, this practice does not encourage a sense of ownership in the company or loyalty.

The last practice is expecting employees to work supernormal hours. Unfortunately, there is no research to suggest that a correlation exists between number of hours worked and company performance. In fact, overworked employees generally display higher rates of turnover and burnout. SAS Institute follows a 35-hour work-week, believing that supernormal work hours result in more product defects.[11]

OPERATIONAL STRATEGY

The operational strategy of a company is a plan for defining and coordinating the various processes inside the organization, in particular those that contribute to the manufacture of the product. Research suggests that market success criteria actually serve to define the manufacturing capability of the firm and the resulting infrastructure that must be constructed.[12] The work of Sweeney has identified four basic manufacturing structures:[13]

1. The *caretaker strategy* is used when a company wants to focus on providing efficient production and reliable delivery. Typically, low-cost providers employ this strategy.
2. The *marketer strategy* focuses on customer service to overcome increasing competition. This strategy may take the form of broader product lines, broader distribution, or improved quality.
3. The *reorganizer strategy* is used when companies want to reduce customer delivery lead time and enhance the quality and performance of their products. Generally, this strategy entails developing new production processes for new products and more efficient manufacturing capabilities.
4. The *innovator strategy* is a very aggressive strategy with the goal of outperforming the competition in terms of product performance and customer service. This strategy takes the firm into new and unrelated markets.

The fourth strategy is probably the most relevant to new entrepreneurial ventures that, unlike their established counterparts, have the opportunity to build their operations from scratch with the goal of making superior operations part of their bundle of competitive advantages. Manufacturing adds value to the venture by enabling it to outperform the competition in ways that are not easily visible.[14] Today, entrepreneurial companies no longer consider themselves as merely a collection of products and services, but rather as a collection of unique capabilities that form the basis for their competitive advantage.

PROCESS FLOW

Flexible manufacturing is a response to a dynamic environment that involves forming networks and strategic alliances to exploit core competencies. Flexible manufacturing is made possible by information technology and flexible manufacturing technology, which permits a company to treat customers as individuals, produce orders in arbitrary quantities, and shrink production times.[15]

Achieving optimal agility is a function of several factors, including teamwork among workers, suppliers, and customers; similarity of technology lines within product groupings; commonality of parts, components, and product features to save design time and allow for volume purchases; using off-the-shelf parts whenever possible to save time and money; and letting value chain partners participate in the design and manufacture of products.

An important task that every start-up team needs to undertake when it is in the business-building stage is to map out how the business is going to work. This can be accomplished through a process flow chart or imaginary tour of the business. Figure 11-2 shows two process flow charts for Sudden Presence, a software developer and technology consultant that designs and directly distributes interactive software for consulting clients and character-rich interactive entertainment software for video game publishers. Its value proposition is that it provides peace of mind and confidence to its customers by funding its own software development (something that is not generally done in the industry) and providing products that are innovative, on time, marketable, and cross-licensable. The process flow chart offers a way to visually depict the business and determine personnel and equipment needs, two important pieces of information that will be needed when estimating financial projections for start-up. In Figure 11-2, note that these entrepreneurs have identified business activities, process flow, personnel, and equipment for both the consulting aspect of the business and the software development side. Also note that some capabilities are kept in-house, whereas others are outsourced.

LEGAL FORMS OF ORGANIZATION

Not only do entrepreneurs need to decide on the operational strategy for their new ventures but also the legal form that organizational structure will take. The legal form of organization is a critical decision that will affect the company for a long time. Choosing the most appropriate legal form is a function of three factors: (1) how much liability protection is required, (2) the company's operating requirements, and (3) the company's tax strategy. In the earliest stages of a new venture—R&D and pre-first-customer—liability is minimal and resources are precious, so the least expensive legal form may be appropriate. However, most technology ventures are characterized by high risk, so the founders will typically seek a legal form that offers protection from liability. The operating requirements of the business also come into play in this decision. Whether the business has or requires a centralized management structure or if it is team-based and flexible will need to be taken into consideration. Some legal forms permit more flexibility in the number of owners, for example, or more complexity in organizational structure. The ability to create employee incentives is another operating requirement that must be met by the legal form chosen. The impact of the legal form on the tax strategy of the owners is also important. Some forms allow earnings to be taxed at the owner's personal tax rate, others require that earnings be taxed at the company level. Determination of the best form for tax strategy depends on the expectation of income and losses, the need to distribute profits, exit scenarios, and the ability to convert from one legal form to another.

This section considers legal forms that are appropriate for the R&D and prelaunch stages of technology firms and those that are more appropriate once firms are launched and have customers. In any case, it is wise to consult with an attorney specializing in legal forms of organization to make sure that the right form has been chosen. See Table 11-2 for a comparison of the various legal forms.

CONSULTING GROUP

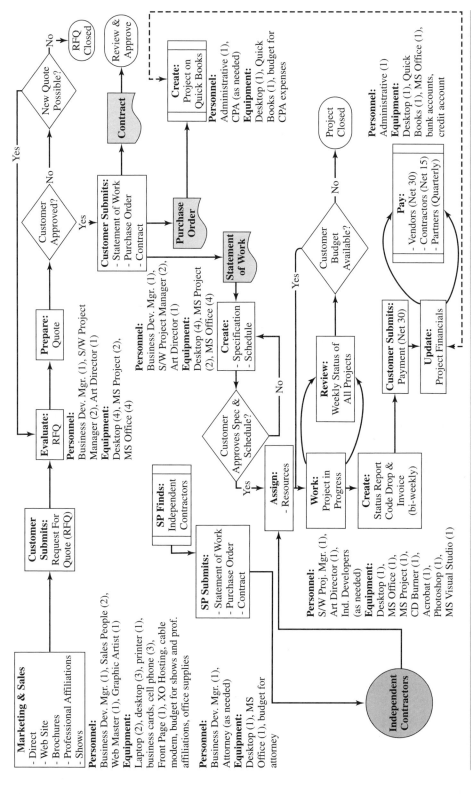

FIGURE 11-2 SUDDEN PRESENCE PROCESS FLOW CHARTS

Source: Contributed with permission of Ara Grigorian, Arman Grigorian and Gary Kirshner, MBA 2000, University of Southern California.

(*CONTINUED*)

PHOBIA LAB (GAME GROUP)

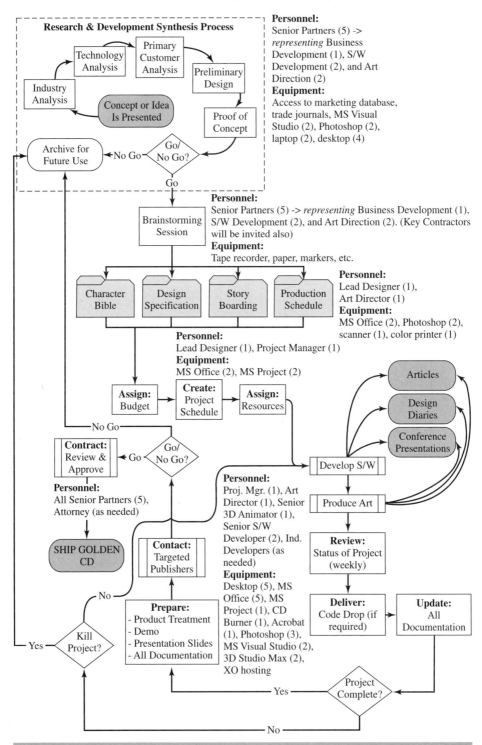

FIGURE 11-2 CONTINUED

TABLE 11-2 Comparative Forms of Legal Organization

Issues	Sole Proprietorship	Partnership	Limited Liability Company	S-Corporation	General Corporation
Number of owners	One	No limit	No limit. Can form with one person in all states but Massachusetts	Limited to 75 shareholders, no foreign investors	No limit on shareholders
Start-up costs	Filing fees for DBA and business license	Filing fees for DBA, attorney fees for partnership agreement	Attorney fees for organization, documents, filing fees	Attorney fees for incorporation documents and filing fees	Attorney fees for incorporation documents, filing fees
Liability	Owner liable for all claims against business, but can overcome liability with insurance	General partners liable for all claims, limited partners only to amount of investment	Members liable as in partnerships	Shareholders liable to amount invested	Shareholders liable to amount invested, officers may be personally liable.
Taxation	Pass-through taxation	Pass-through taxation	Pass-through taxation	Pass-through taxation	Tax-paying entity, taxed on dividends distributed
Continuity of life of business	Dissolution on the death of the owner	Dissolution on the death or separation of a partner unless otherwise specified in the agreement. Not so in the case of limited partners	Most states allow perpetual existence. Unless otherwise stated in Articles of Organization, existence terminates on death or withdrawal of member.	No perpetual life	Perpetual life

R&D AND PRELAUNCH FORMS

Any legal form may be used during the R&D and prelaunch phases of the business, but some forms make more sense than others because they are quick, easy, and inexpensive to set up. Although these easier forms do not protect the owners from liability, they can serve the team well until the point at which it begins to take on liability. The two forms that will be reviewed here are the sole proprietorship and the partnership.

SOLE PROPRIETORSHIPS

The most common legal form of organization in the United States is the sole proprietorship because it is flexible, easy and inexpensive to form, and has minimal regulations. In fact, the company only needs a DBA (Certificate of Doing Business As a Sole Proprietor) if the entrepreneur's name is not the name of the company. From a legal perspective, the sole proprietorship and the owner are one and the same, so the business itself pays no tax. All expenses and earnings pass through the business to the owner; therefore, owners pay taxes on the earnings of the business at their personal tax rates. For all the advantages of a sole proprietorship, the disadvantages weigh heavy, particularly for technology ventures. With a sole proprietorship, it is more difficult to raise capital because of the pass-through aspect, and the sole proprietor has unlimited liability for all claims against the business. Furthermore, the survival of the company depends on the owner and, succession agreements to the contrary, the business ceases with the death of the owner.

Technology companies may attribute the birth of the idea for a technology to a single person but, in reality, most technology companies are started by teams. The partnership legal form best fits this scenario.

PARTNERSHIPS

Section 6 of the Uniform Partnership Act refers to a partnership as "an association of two or more persons to carry on as co-owners a business for profit." Basically, a partnership is equivalent to a sole proprietorship, but with two or more partners. Bringing on a partner is a serious undertaking. The doctrine of ostensible authority holds each partner liable for the acts of the other partner(s) in the course of doing business for the partnership. For example, if one partner enters into a legal agreement with a company on behalf of the partnership, all the partners are bound by the terms of the agreement. This point alone makes clear the importance of choosing partners wisely and drawing up a partnership agreement that spells out the duties and responsibilities of the partners as well as how conflicts will be resolved and how the partnership can be dissolved.

A partnership can be formed by an oral or written agreement or even by implication. For example, the Uniform Partnership Act states that the receipt by a person of a share of the profits of the business is *prima facie* evidence that they are a partner in the business. This means that not only does that partner share proportionately in the profits, but also in the debts of the partnership. The founding team of a new technology venture will most likely all be general partners, which means that they are jointly and severally responsible for the obligations of the partnership. The founding team may decide to take on limited partners, whose liability is limited to their capital investment in the partnership. These limited partners cannot have a say in the management of the partnership or they risk their limited liability status. These types of partners are typically brought in as financial investors.

Like the sole proprietorship, all partnership earnings and losses pass through to the partners, and the partners pay taxes at their personal income tax rates. The partnership does, however, file an informational return with the IRS.

LEGAL FORMS THAT PROTECT THE OWNERS

Most technology ventures choose to use one of the legal forms that protects the owners from liability: the corporation (general and S) or the Limited Liability Company (LLC). It is important to note that while these forms do provide shelter from liability, that limited liability status can be forfeited if the entrepreneur treats corporate assets like personal assets or fails to observe required corporate formalities such as rules for board of directors meetings and the recording of minutes. Personal guarantees on loans will also pierce the "corporate veil" and make the entrepreneur liable. In addition to limited liability status, corporate forms provide more prestige for the company and make it easier to raise capital.

CORPORATIONS

There are two types of corporations: the general corporation and the sub-chapter S corporation. The general corporation is the only form that is a legal entity, that is, it is chartered or registered by a state and survives the death or separation of its owners from the company (perpetual life). As a result, a corporation can sue and be sued, acquire and sell property and other assets, lend money, and pay taxes. The owners of the corporation are its stockholders who, like limited partners, are liable only to the extent of their investment in the corporation.

A corporation is created by filing a certificate of incorporation and articles of incorporation with the state in which the company will be doing business. It also requires a board of directors that hires the company officers who run the business. Many entrepreneurs choose to incorporate in Delaware because that state has an established body of case law on incorporation issues, a judiciary that is favorable to companies, broad indemnification availability, and fewer opportunities for legal problems. The disadvantage is that for purposes of litigation, if the company is physically located in another state, there will be two venues for litigation. Also, the Delaware corporation will need to register as a foreign corporation in the actual state in which the company is located and may have to pay that state's franchise tax.

Corporations enjoy many benefits. These include limited liability, multiple classes of stock that can be issued to meet the various requirements of investors, status, and the benefits of employee incentive plans. However, they also present many disadvantages. They are fairly costly and complex to form and should not be formed without the assistance of an attorney well versed in corporate law. One serious disadvantage arises from the fact that the corporation is a separate entity for tax purposes. If it makes a profit, it must pay taxes on that profit whether or not the profit was ever distributed to the shareholders. Furthermore, after the corporation has paid taxes on the profit, shareholders are taxed again on any dividends distributed. They cannot, however, deduct losses against their personal income tax liability. Another disadvantage is that the entrepreneur gives up some measure of control (unless the corporation is wholly owned) to a board of directors and shareholders. In a public corporation registered on one of the stock exchanges, entrepreneurs are responsible first to the stockholders and second to customers and employees. As the board of directors represents the stockholders, it has the power to remove the entrepreneur as CEO of the corporation.

The S-Corporation attempts to marry the advantages of the general corporation with the advantages of a partnership. The S-Corp is not a tax-paying entity, but a pass-through entity much like a partnership where the earnings are passed through to the partners and taxed at their personal rates. Losses can also be deducted against the owner's personal income tax liability up to the amount invested in the corporation. Businesses most suitable for the S-Corp are those that do not need to retain earnings for growth. The business should also have sufficient cash flow to cover the taxes that the owners will have to pay at their personal rates, otherwise there could be a situation where the company earns a taxable profit but has a negative cash flow, so the owners have to pay the taxes for the company out of their own pockets. S-Corps have strict requirements: they cannot have more than 75 investors, the owners must be U.S. citizens, and the S-Corp cannot issue more than one class of stock. Furthermore, if the company decides to use venture capital or do an IPO, it will need to convert to a general corporation prior to the IPO.

LIMITED LIABILITY COMPANIES

The most recent legal form is the Limited Liability Company (LLC), which offers a flexible alternative to corporations, partnerships, and joint ventures. It combines the limited liability of a corporation with the pass-through tax advantages of a partnership or an S-Corp. It also has the flexibility of a more informal structure. Most LLCs are organized like S-Corporations to take advantage of the pass-through provision. The owners of an LLC are called *members* and their ownership interests are known as *interests*. These terms are equivalent to stockholders and stock. The members create an operating agreement, which is similar to a partnership agreement that spells out the rights and obligations of the members. Members have limited liability unless they have personally guaranteed a debt. Unlike the S-Corp, there is no limitation on the number of members or their status, and the LLC may issue more than one class of stock and have foreign investors. Like the S-Corp, the LLC will need to convert to a general corporation to take on venture capital or do an IPO.

MAKING A DECISION

With an understanding of the various legal forms, it is possible to make a more informed decision about which one is most appropriate. Some of the questions that should be asked as part of that decision-making process include the following:

- Does the team possess all the skills and experience needed to operate this venture? If not, the sole proprietorship will not be a good choice.
- Does the founding team have the capital required to start the business alone or do they need to raise it through equity or debt? Raising capital with a corporation is easier than with other forms.
- Is the team able to run the business and cover its living expenses for the first year? Again, this relates to whether or not the team needs to raise money.
- Is the team willing and able to assume personal liability for any claims against the business? If not, a corporation or LLC must be considered.
- Will the business have initial losses or will it be profitable almost from the beginning? If it will experience significant losses, a pass-through legal form will allow the founding team to write off losses against ordinary income.
- What is the team's harvest strategy? If an IPO is in the company's future, a corporation is the best choice.

The answers to these questions will help to narrow the choices. With the advice of an attorney, the right form should be a fairly straightforward decision. The final question about the team's harvest strategy (sometimes referred to as an exit strategy) is important because the form that is chosen should be one that will not have to be changed or one that can easily shift to another form at the appropriate time. The next section deals with the issue of changing the legal form of organization.

CHANGING LEGAL FORMS

As a company grows and evolves, it may reach the point where the current legal form is no longer appropriate for the company's objectives. For example, say an engineer/inventor decides to set up a laboratory in the garage of his home. His spouse is a corporate executive with a good salary, so he is already covered for medical insurance. He plans to work with two other engineers in a partnership structure until they have something that looks like a viable technology with potential applications in the market. In the beginning, the partnership expects losses as it purchases equipment, builds prototypes, and tests them with customers. Sensing that they have something marketable, the team decides to bring in someone with business expertise and form a company. They know that once they launch the product, they will probably incur continuing losses because of all the expenses of start-up—the promotion of the business, finding space to lease, and hiring employees. The team plans that within a year of introducing the product, they will need to seek venture capital to be able to grow as fast as they expect the market will demand. They also see an IPO in their future.

In the beginning, during product development, a simple partnership is usually sufficient as it conserves the limited resources of the founders and the liability to the team's individual assets is small. However, once the partners take on the responsibilities of a lease and employees, they need to consider insurance or moving to a legal form with limited liability. If the company will continue to experience losses, the team may want to use those losses to shelter personal income, which they could do in an S-Corp or LLC. If the period of loss is not long, it might be more cost effective to go immediately to a general corporation because their future plans include venture capital and an IPO. It should be clear from this example that the legal form of an organization is not a static decision, but is based on the company's needs at a particular stage in its life cycle.

DEALING WITH STOCK

One of the real challenges entrepreneurs face is determining how much a share of stock in their private company is worth. The job is made a little easier at start-up because if the company is not yet in business, it has no book value apart from any initial investment the entrepreneur and the team might have made in the company. In this case, the entrepreneur, with the help of an attorney, sets an initial stock price. An important decision is how many shares to register with the Secretary of State, or *authorize,* and how many shares to transfer to shareholders, or *issue.* How stock is handled determines how much equity the founders retain. Figure 11-3 presents a typical scenario, for which there are many variations. The scenario begins with the company authorizing 100,000 shares of stock and issuing 30,000 to each of the founders. Wanting to diversify their stock holdings, the two founders sell 5,000 shares each to an investor. This brings their equity percentage down from 50 percent to 42 percent, or a total of 84 percent.

Scenario 1

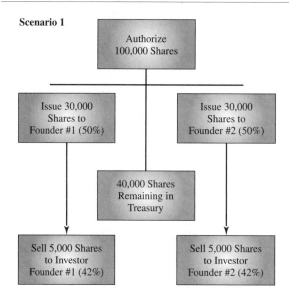

Scenario 2

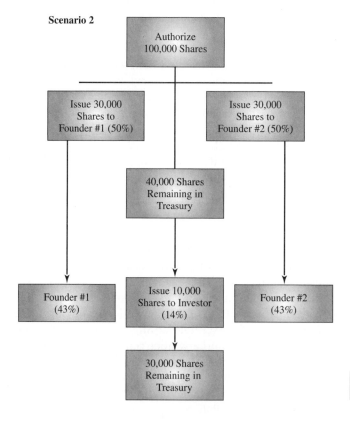

FIGURE 11-3 AUTHORIZING AND ISSUING STOCK

In an alternative scenario, the founders want to hold onto their stock, so they issue 10,000 more shares from the treasury to the investor. This event gives the company 70,000 shares outstanding, and the founders now each hold a 43 percent stake in the company, or a total of 86 percent. The total shares remaining in the treasury stands at 30,000. Many states tie incorporation fees to the number of shares authorized, and attorneys often recommend authorizing the highest possible number for the lowest possible fee. Then the company can issue a small amount to the founder, usually in round numbers so it is easy to calculate percentages.[16] Most investors will accept authorized but unissued stock; however, if the company eventually does a venture capital deal, it will probably have to change its stock structure to meet the venture capital firm's requirements and also amend its corporation documents.

Determining the amount of stock to authorize and issue is generally a function of (1) whether the company intends to raise capital from equity investors; (2) whether the company will deal with estate-planning in the near future, for example, gifting stock to family members; and (3) whether the company intends to provide minority stakes to employees so that it will need a pool of stock reserved for that purpose.

The stock price is a function of what the company plans to do. For example, if it plans to use stock as incentives or give stock to private investors, it will want to use the lowest price possible because the transfer of the stock will trigger a taxable event for the receiver. If, however, the entrepreneur is selling part of the company, it will be important to achieve the highest stock value possible.

❖ SUMMARY

The move from R&D to operations is not an easy transition, as the skills and require-ments of the development team are different from those required for operations. An operating business does not happen overnight; it takes a lot of planning. Lingering technical and market issues continue to emerge, pulling the team in a multitude of directions. A successful transition requires three different groups of individuals: people from the innovation team, people from the operations team, and transition manage-ment experts. It is the job of the transition team to finalize the product and its first applications as well as refine the business model. The transition team will also need to construct a transition plan that details the readiness of the company to launch the product in terms of personnel, systems, and resources. Part of the organizational model is the operational strategy of the company, that is, a plan for defining and coordinating the various processes inside the organization, in particular those that contribute to the manufacture of the product. Research suggests that market success criteria actually serve to define the manufacturing capability of the firm and the resulting infrastruc-ture that must be constructed. The legal form that a new company team decides to use for its venture is a critical decision that will affect the company for a long time. Choosing the most appropriate legal form is a function of three factors: (1) how much liability protection is required, (2) the company's operating requirements, and (3) the company's tax strategy. Most technology ventures choose to use one of the legal forms that protect the owners from liability: the corporation (general and S) or the Limited Liability Company (LLC).

❖ DISCUSSION QUESTIONS

1. What are the key challenges a technology team faces when moving from R&D to operations?
2. Why is developing a mission statement so important to the new venture? What is the strategy for constructing a mission statement?
3. Compare the commitment organizational model with the Silicon Valley model. Which is more effective for a start-up company? Why?
4. Why is the corporate form the most popular for high-tech ventures?

❖ RESOURCES

Bagley, Constance E., and Craig E. Dauchy. *The Entrepreneur's Guide to Business Law.* Mason, OH: South-Western College Publishing, 1998.

Clifford, Dennis, and Ralph E. Warner. *The Partnership Book.* Berkeley, CA: Nolo Press, 1997.

Diamond, Michael R., and Julie L. Williams. *How to Incorporate: A Handbook for Entrepreneurs and Professionals.* New York: John Wiley & Sons, 2000.

Hopkins, Bruce R. *Starting and Managing a Non Profit Organization*, New York: John Wiley & Sons. 2000 .

Whitman, Marina N. *New World, New Rules: The Changing Role of the American Corporation.* Boston: Harvard Business School Press, 1999.

❖ INTERNET RESOURCES

Biz Filings Incorporated
www.bizfilings.com/index.html
Information and guidance for determining a legal form of organization

Findlaw
www.findlaw.com/
Provides a wealth of legal resources, including cases, codes, and forms

Internet Legal Resource Guide
www.ilrg.com/
A comprehensive site containing information on the law and attorneys

NOLO Law for All
www.nolo.com/index.html
A comprehensive site with legal information and tools

QUANTUM DOTS

Starting a new technology company is a challenging task at best, but when the technology is at the cutting edge of a new industry where no one has gone before, there are enormous hurdles to overcome. That was the task that start-up Quantum Dot Corporation took on in 1997 when its founders, Joel Martin and Bala Manian, started the company. They were determined to conquer the field of nanotechnology, manipulating and building materials on the nanometer scale, which is one-billionth of a meter in size. Joel Martin, a physical chemist, and his partner had years of experience in Silicon Valley, having helped launch more than six medical device companies. Institutional Venture Partners supported Martin's notion of finding a technology that would "capture people's imagination" and provided financial backing.

Having money to spend solved only part of the problem. The quest was daunting as most of the technology that Martin found was either "ho-hum" or would require 20 years of development before the market was ready for it. At long last, he found the exciting technology he was looking for in quantum dots. Quantum dots are nanoparticles, semiconducting crystals that are so small that they can only be seen through a microscope. They are governed by the laws of quantum mechanics, which speaks to the behavior of atoms and molecules. The size of a dot determines its wavelength and color of fluorescence. For example, a 2-nanometer particle glows bright green, whereas a 5-nanometer particle produces longer wavelengths that appear as red. What this means is that scientists can use different size dots to produce a broad spectrum of different colors. Although this was interesting science, it had never been translated into a viable business. No one knew what to do with the dots. However, as

scientists began to improve on the dots the colors became brighter and more refined, and it became apparent that they could be used in biological imaging and diagnostics. Nanoparticles could become sensitive probes that would seek out specific biological targets.

About the same time that Martin was looking for a technology to invest in, two scientists at Lawrence Berkeley Laboratory, Paul Alavisatosa and Shimon Weiss, were trying to find a way to exploit the biological potential of quantum dots. Quantum dots are the size of proteins, so it was logical that the two could be compatible. Research in 1998 confirmed that nanoparticles could be used as bioprobes in living systems. One month later, Quantum Dot Corporation was founded, having licensed all the relevant technologies from Lawrence Berkeley Laboratory, MIT, Indiana University, and the University of Melbourne in Australia. Martin basically brought together rival scientists to push Quantum Dot forward. The UC Berkeley Lab also took an equity stake in the company.

The entry strategy was not clear. Martin knew that he did not want to compete with the big diagnostics companies such as Roche, but he also did not want to turn quantum dots into a commodity. Extrapolating from another industry, he settled on Intel's business model. He would make quantum dots an essential element of every diagnostic kit and analytical instrument. The benefit to the customer was that quantum dots would withstand more cycles of excitation and light emission than basic organic molecules, which decompose rapidly, so investigators could track what was happening in cells and tissues for longer intervals of time. Furthermore, quantum dots come in many colors, and those colors are vibrant. The first target market was diagnostic test manufacturers. The second target was instrumentation manufacturers. The company also began work on what it hoped would become its killer app, biological bar codes, which are essentially polymer beads packed with millions of quantum dots. Each bead would have a known color signature instead of the traditional tag, which would be an easier way to recognize gene sequences.

In 2000, the company was experiencing a sense of urgency. It did not yet have a highly successful product despite having raised $7.5 million in the first few months of the business. The company knew that if its killer app was not ready within a couple of years, it would have to find alternatives to support the company financially. At the same time, competitors were nipping at its heels—small companies started by world re-knowned university chemists seeking to capitalize on the growing interest in nanotechnology. By May 2000, the dot-com bust had occurred and solid technology companies were looking better all the time. Quantum Dot was able to complete a $30 million equity round that month with venture capitalists who were not influenced by the extremes of the market and understood the time line of biotech companies. Throughout 2000, with one of the few tangible nanotech products in the marketplace, Quantum Dot received several research grants and began developing strategic partnerships with such giants as GlaxoSmith

Kline, Genentech, and the National Institutes of Health.

"To date, over 100 companies have approached Quantum Dot Corporation to set up collaborations," commented Hingge Hsu, Partner, Schroder Ventures. "These companies see the value and promise of the technology." "We have already inked several deals with both pharma and biotech companies" said Carol Lou, VP Sales and Marketing, QDC. "During 2000, Qdot Nanocrystals will only be available to companies participating in our Technology Access Program or through other collaborations," continued Lou." (Quantum Dot Corp. press release, April 6, 2000).

On May 16, 2001, Quantum Dot Corporation announced that the U.S. Patent and Trademark Office had issued U.S. Patent No. 6,207,392 to the Regents of the University of California for semiconductor nanocrystal probes (Qdot) and their use in biological applications. The technology covered by this patent will accelerate the development of pharmaceuticals and provide a barcode for detecting what is going on in cells. Quantum Dot is at the forefront of nanotechnology. Are they at the cutting edge or the bleeding edge? How long will venture capital support a company that is so early in the market? ■

Sources: A. Paul Alivisatos, "Less is More in Medicine," *Scientific American* 285, no. 3 (September 2001): 66–73; David Rotman, "Quantum Dot Com," *MIT Technology Review* January–February 2000): *www.techreview.com*; "Quantum Dot Corporation Announces Issuance of Patent for Nanocrystal Probes," *BusinessWire* (May 16, 2001): *www.businesswire.com*; Quantum Dots,; Robert L. Whiddon, "Companies Cope with Market Chaos," *IPO Reporter* May 1, 2000): *www.sdponline.com/index.html*; Quantum Dot Corporation, *www.qdots.com/new/homeB.html*.

❖ NOTES

1. Andrew Van de Ven and Douglas Polley, "Learning While Innovating," *Organization Science* 3, no. 1 (February 1992): 92–116.

2. Richard Leifer, Christopher M. McDermott, Gina Colarelli O'Connor, Lois S. Peters, Mark P. Rice, and Robert W. Veryzer, *Radical Innovation* (Boston: Harvard Business School Press, 2000): 134–149.

3. Ibid., 150.

4. R. Germain and M. B. Cooper, "How a Customer Mission Statement Affects Company Performance," *Industrial Marketing Management* 19 (1990): 47–54.

5. D. F. Abel, *Defining the Business: The Starting Point of Strategic Planning* (Upper Saddle River, NJ: Prentice Hall, 1980).

6. S. Shirley, "Corporate Strategy and Entrepreneurial Vision," *Long Range Planning* 22, no. 8 (1989): 107–110.

7. SAIC Web site, *www.saic.com/about/mission.html*.

8. Mary Kwak, "Commitment Counts," *MIT Sloan Management Review* 42, no. 4, (Summer 2001): 8–9.

9. Jeffrey Pfeffer, "What's Wrong with Management Practices in Silicon Valley? A Lot," *MIT Sloan Management Review* 42, no. 3 (Spring 2001): 101–102.

10. Ibid.

11 Ibid, pp. 101–102.

12. M. T. Sweeney, "Towards a Unified Theory of Strategic Manufacturing Management," *International Journal of Operations and Production Management* 11, no. 8 (1991): 6–23.

13. Ibid.

14. David Walters, "Marketing and Operations Management: An Integrated Approach to New Ways of Delivering Value," *Management Decision* 37, no. 3 (1999): 248–258.

15. Kathleen Allen, *Growing and Managing Entrepreneurial Businesses* (Boston: Houghton-Mifflin Company, 1999), 271.

16. Jill Andresky Fraser, "Private Company Stock," *Inc.* (May 2000): 171–174. *www.inc.com*

12

MARKETING HIGH TECHNOLOGY

OVERVIEW

This chapter will examine

❖ the characteristics of technology markets

❖ key decisions for technology-intensive markets

❖ understanding customer needs

❖ collecting market intelligence

❖ pricing high-technology products

❖ developing a marketing plan

❖ promoting high-technology products

INTRODUCTION

Traditional marketing strategy has been changed inexorably by the new context in which businesses operate today. The shift from a product focus to a customer focus has precipitated major changes in marketing theory and practice. For example, as market diversity increases, it creates fragmented markets that make segmentation less effective and efficient.[1] Diversity, which is found in location, lifestyle, ethnicity, income, age, and other factors, refocuses marketing efforts toward satisfying the needs and wants of individual customers rather than mass markets or market segments.[2] It is a more efficient approach to marketing because it focuses on profitable customers and takes advantage of technology to find the right customers for the right products. Customers drive transactions, so marketing today is less concentrated on influencing or inducing people to buy and more focused on responding to demand.

High-technology markets are unique in that they display a great degree of uncertainty in customers, technology, and competitors.[3] Therefore, many marketers believe that a different set of marketing strategies and tactics is required to successfully deal with the dynamic nature of high-technology markets.[4] Moreover, the margin for error is much smaller with high-technology companies, thus the execution of the marketing plan must be perfect.[5] Some of the issues that make the marketing of high technology distinct from other types of products include the following:[6]

- **Market uncertainty.** Lack of confidence about customer needs relative to specific applications of the technology. This is particularly true with disruptive technologies where customer needs are generally latent.
- **Technological uncertainty.** Lack of confidence about product life cycles and obsolescence.
- **Competitive market.** Uncertainty about the impact of competitors and the likelihood of emerging competitors.
- **Integrating R&D with marketing.** Being able to identify and satisfy customer needs in the earliest stages of product development; understanding market gaps and how to fill them.
- **Managing strategic alliances.** Making sure that strategic partners also benefit from the company's marketing efforts.
- **Promotion to alleviate customer uncertainty.** Dealing with the initial customer resistance to new technology.

High-technology companies cannot succeed in an environment that separates R&D from marketing. Effective marketing strategies provide for informal networks that bridge this gap between the marketing and engineering functions.[7]

THE CHARACTERISTICS OF TECHNOLOGY-INTENSIVE MARKETS

Although specific differences can be found in different industries across the spectrum of technology, from industrial technology to information systems and biotechnology, high-technology environments share some common characteristics, in particular, market uncertainty, technology uncertainty, and competitive volatility. Each of these characteristics will be discussed in more depth in the following sections.

MARKET UNCERTAINTY

Recall that market uncertainty results from the difficulty in correctly assessing customer needs and matching those needs to a particular technology application. The principal source of market uncertainty is customers' resistance to trying a new technology they do not understand without a significant amount of education and preparation. Furthermore, to exacerbate the situation, today, customer needs are changing at a more rapid pace, often in unpredictable ways. Oftentimes, customers will not adopt a new technology until they are fairly certain that it will be the standard in the industry because the switching costs in terms of learning a new technology are high. The classic example of this is the color television, which captured only 20 percent of the market after 10 years because it was expensive and didn't offer enough value over black and white television.[8] This example points to the difference in marketing to early adopters, or visionaries, versus mainstream adopters, or pragmatists. Early adopters typically have technical backgrounds and are eager to purchase the next great thing, whereas late adopters seek a different set of benefits. Late adopters need to understand what is gained through using the applications of the technology versus not using them or using some alternative.

TECHNOLOGICAL UNCERTAINTY

Technological uncertainty speaks to the question of whether the new venture can deliver on its promises and meet the needs of customers. This includes the promise of on-time delivery, something that most technology companies with new products rarely achieve. Moreover, customers are also concerned about unintended consequences. They purchase a new technology in the hopes that it will make their business more productive, when, in fact, it often does quite the opposite because of the time involved in training employees, dealing with problems, and taking care of constant upgrades. Customers are also concerned whether the technology will quickly be rendered obsolete by newer technology, given the rapid pace of technological change. The entrepreneurial team is concerned that they will launch an application of their technology only to learn that a different application is more in demand. Deciding which features to include is not a straightforward decision, even with customer input.

COMPETITIVE UNCERTAINTY

If customers are volatile and unpredictable, competitors are equally so. In fact, many competitors for a new technology may come from outside the industry in which the technology was developed. Unfortunately, to their detriment, many companies dismiss upstarts from outside of the industry. Competitors from outside the industry frequently develop value innovations that are not based on what current competitors are doing or not doing; that is, they find new ways to create value that may not be related to the technology itself, but which build bundles of value that make the technology more desirable to customers.

What is important to understand about these characteristics is that value innovation occurs at the intersection of market, technology, and competitive uncertainty, and their existence provides the disruption in the market that the entrepreneur needs to find a unique niche.

KNOW-HOW, COMPLEXITY, AND VELOCITY EFFECTS

The nature of technology-intensive markets has important ramifications for marketing strategy and decision making. In particular, the combination of know-how or scientific and technical knowledge and tacit manufacturing and sales knowledge can create a significant competitive advantage for a company.[9] Know-how affects market advantage, but so do the complexity of the market and velocity, the speed at which technology must be developed and brought to market.

Know-how is inextricably linked with R&D expenditures. The U.S. Department of Commerce labels those industries with double the R&D expenditures to sales ratio of other industries as "high tech."[10] Although most markets are affected by know-how, the degree to which they are affected depends on the relative importance of R&D to other company assets. When know-how represents a relatively high portion of overall investment, correspondingly high R&D expenditures are typically found.[11] Know-how, unlike products, possesses the unique characteristic that it cannot be used up; it is regenerative.[12] It defies the economic principle of scarcity. In fact, the opposite seems to be true. Know-how increases and becomes more valuable with use, and the speed at which it increases accelerates as more people become more proficient at using it.[13] The cost of producing the first unit based on know-how is high, but the costs of reproduction decline precipitously, in some cases to zero. In the field of biotechnology, for example, the initial costs of developing the know-how for a pharmaceutical and bringing it to market are exorbitant, approximately $500 million, but the cost of replication, although not zero, is relatively miniscule when compared with the development costs. That is the effect of know-how.

The transfer of know-how presents unique issues as well. It is difficult, if not impossible, to place a value on know-how to the licensee or purchaser that reflects the real value of the know-how in use. Once acquired, the buyer can quite easily determine value in use, but know-how is typically not transferred until after a value has been agreed upon and the appropriate legal documents executed. Patent specifications and designs can codify know-how; it can then be transferred to the printed page or transmitted electronically. The more difficult situation occurs with tacit know-how, that is, know-how that is difficult to transfer through documentation, such as process and human expertise that are developed through informal knowledge exchange networks.

As know-how proliferation through these information networks results in rapid incremental innovation, customers have developed expectations for more and better advances at a more rapid pace and at increasingly lower prices. This phenomenon is, of course, the dilemma of technology-intensive industries. How can a company continue to provide incrementally superior products at faster speeds and lower prices? The pace of incremental innovation is stopped in its tracks when the returns on incremental innovation diminish to the point that they have no perceived value to the customer; that is, the technology has reached the upper limit of its ability to be improved or it is displaced by the announcement of a disruptive technology that makes the technology obsolete and imposes high switching costs on the buyer. Consequently, firms introducing paradigm-shifting technology must pay close attention to their migration strategies to alleviate uncertainty and resistance on the part of the buyer.

KEY DECISIONS FOR TECHNOLOGY-INTENSIVE MARKETS

The ability to transform an invention into a commercial innovation generally occurs in two ways: by market research and by the technology itself. The market-driven approach relies on internal and external knowledge to find a solution to a customer need in the market.[14] This approach can cause problems for technical people who have to try to hit a moving target with a single solution. In contrast, the technology-driven approach puts technology in the driver's seat without firm knowledge that a market even exists. This forces the scientist or engineer to develop a solution and then look for a problem. Both approaches are lacking. A more appropriate and effective approach is to use a parallel one that combines knowledge about the technology with knowledge about customer needs. This section considers the technology adoption model to describe the unique marketing issues of high-technology ventures, the issues of position and design, and how to determine a marketing approach.

DEALING WITH TORNADOES

When a company's product involves a radical technology, a different technology adoption cycle comes into play. Radical technologies shatter the equilibrium, requiring significant learning curves and exacting high switching costs from customers. Figure 12-1 provides a depiction of the technology adoption-diffusion cycle, which came out of research by the U.S. Department of Agriculture (DOA) in the 1930s. The DOA was trying to understand why farmers were reluctant to adopt new strains of seed potatoes.[15]

Prior to launching a new technology, the company gets feedback from a unique group known as innovators. Innovators are technical types who are constantly seeking new technologies, particularly before they ever reach the market. The importance of the innovators is that they provide the proof of concept for later adopters; that is, they demonstrate that the technology works. When a company is ready to launch a radical technology, it then seeks feedback from early adopters, those people who are not necessarily technically oriented but who have no fear of purchasing the latest technology. For a new company, the early market presents a time of great excitement. Preannouncements have prepared early adopters for the arrival of the technology, and

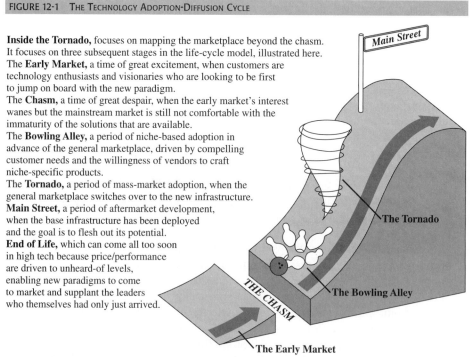

FIGURE 12-1   THE TECHNOLOGY ADOPTION-DIFFUSION CYCLE

Inside the Tornado, focuses on mapping the marketplace beyond the chasm. It focuses on three subsequent stages in the life-cycle model, illustrated here.

The **Early Market,** a time of great excitement, when customers are technology enthusiasts and visionaries who are looking to be first to jump on board with the new paradigm.

The **Chasm,** a time of great despair, when the early market's interest wanes but the mainstream market is still not comfortable with the immaturity of the solutions that are available.

The **Bowling Alley,** a period of niche-based adoption in advance of the general marketplace, driven by compelling customer needs and the willingness of vendors to craft niche-specific products.

The **Tornado,** a period of mass-market adoption, when the general marketplace switches over to the new infrastructure.

Main Street, a period of aftermarket development, when the base infrastructure has been deployed and the goal is to flesh out its potential.

End of Life, which can come all too soon in high tech because price/performance are driven to unheard-of levels, enabling new paradigms to come to market and supplant the leaders who themselves had only just arrived.

Source: "The Technology Adoption Life Cycle," from *Inside the Tornado* by Geoffrey A. Moore. Copyright © 1995 by Geoffrey A. Moore Consulting, Inc. Used by permission of Geoffery A. Moore.

their enthusiasm to try it is palpable. That enthusiasm, however, may give the entrepreneur a false sense of confidence if they do not understand that early adopter enthusiasm may not be shared by the mainstream market, and that is the crux of Moore's proposition. Between the early market and mainstream adoption lies the "chasm," a black hole of sorts where enthusiasm on the part of the early adopters has waned, but the mainstream market is not yet comfortable adopting the new technology. The vast majority of new technologies languish in the chasm because they haven't satisfied a real need on the part of customers. Some examples are artificial intelligence, global satellite positioning, and videoconferencing.

Crossing the chasm is a challenging but essential task for a technology to be adopted by the mainstream market and become the standard in its field. To do this, the new venture must begin to seek out niche markets and encourage early adopters, who are generally OEMs, to modify the technology to meet the compelling needs of customers in those niche markets. This strategy will get the company beyond the early adopters and allow it to secure the early majority customers, which comprise about one-third of the whole adoption life cycle. With the capture of each niche, the company drives out same-size competition as it marches forward. This drive to cross the chasm requires a fine balance between moving too soon with a technology that still has problems and waiting too long only to lose the competitive advantage of being the pioneer. To be successful, the drive also requires the cooperation of vendors and system integrators to craft niche-specific applications of the technology.

Once the technology has gained acceptance from a few niche markets, it finds itself in the "bowling alley," where the goal is to rack up as many niches as possible in order to generate critical mass sufficient to drive the technology into the "tornado." The tornado is a period of mass-market adoption when the mainstream market switches en masse to the new standard. When that happens, everything begins to take place very quickly. A flood of demand that is impossible to meet requires that the marketing people get out of the way and the operations people take over. All that matters in the tornado is that the company be able to manufacture and ship product as quickly as possible.

If the company survives the tornado, it will arrive at the final stage, known as "Main Street," where it immediately has to change focus and become end-user focused, something it was not during the tornado. Moore believes that the defining characteristic of Main Street is that growth no longer comes from selling to new customers, but from niche-specific extensions, in other words, from selling more products to existing customers.

To improve the chance of creating a tornado and becoming the standard, it is important to attack the competition ruthlessly to build a secure foundation. The distribution channel must be expanded rapidly to every type of outlet possible, even at the expense of the customer in the short term as the price of new technology usually declines rapidly after introduction. Customers will not mind because the technology is in such demand that all they really care about is getting their hands on it. Once the tornado has subsided, there is time to begin building the long-term customer relationships that will be necessary to sustain the company. While in the tornado, it is also important to keep moving to the next lower price point. As the leader, if the company fails to do this, it will lose customers to clones. Hewlett-Packard is one example of a company that has successfully employed this strategy, moving to the next price point to keep out competitors. Consequently, one critical component of an effective tornado strategy is to have manufacturing and distribution partners in place before the tornado occurs. As the new technology becomes the standard, these partners will become standard bearers as well.

Not every company that has experienced the tornado has benefited from it. Nearly 20 years ago, Sony hit a tornado with its Betamax technology for VCRs. Unfortunately, it attempted to control the tornado by refusing to license its technology to system integrators and application providers, so it was unable to keep up with demand. This attitude forced vendors and others to go around Sony to VHS technology, which was readily available, and VHS ended up becoming the standard. Another example of this was Word Star, which in the early days of word processing software held 50 percent of the market. In the midst of its tornado, it decided to come out with an entirely new product instead of more wisely upgrading its successful product. The impact of high switching costs to customers meant that they could just as easily switch to the competitor, WordPerfect, as to the new Word Star product.

DEALING WITH POSITIONING AND DESIGN DECISIONS

Research points to four fundamental position and design decisions that entrepreneurs must make when they operate in technology-intensive markets: the vertical positioning decision, the technology design decision, the transfer design, and the migration design.[16] These decisions are generally made without regard to what competitors are doing, because the company's intent is to innovate on value rather than benchmark on competitors' advantages and try to improve on them or fill in the gaps.

VERTICAL POSITIONING

The challenge for any high-tech entrepreneur is to convert valuable and unique know-how, which may be in the form of product/process patents, copyrights, trademarks, or trade secrets, into multiple revenue streams. Figure 12-2 shows a variety of options for doing this. From the seller's perspective—the firm that is attempting to commercialize its technology—the least risky and least costly decision is to simply sell or license the know-how to a firm that can develop it, build applications in various markets, and market it to customers. For example, a genomics company could choose to license a patented gene to another company for manufacture and distribution and continue to devote its resources to developing more know-how in its industry. Moving down the pyramid, the selling firm incurs increasing liability and costs as it must build a production-quality prototype, test it, meet regulatory requirements, design and build applications for particular markets, and create a company with a facility and equipment to manufacture and distribute the product. Conversely, moving up the pyramid, the buyer's costs go up. A buyer that licenses a technology in the know-how stage must be able to take the intangible concept and prove it by engineering a prototype and testing it.

Depending on the terms of the license agreement, the buyer could sublicense the prototype to another firm to build applications or it could decide to do all the work in-house. If the work occurs in-house, the company would need to complete all the tasks required to work its way down the pyramid. Alternatively, the company could occupy several vertical positions simultaneously by licensing core technology to application

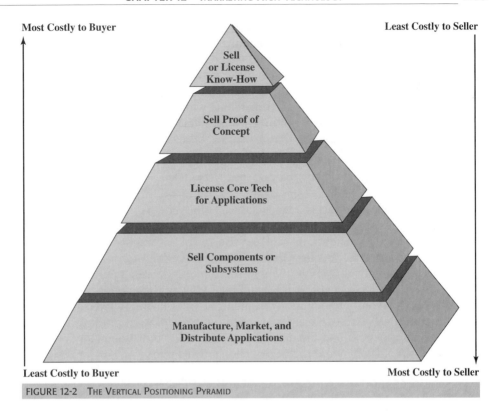

Most Costly to Buyer

Least Costly to Seller

Sell or License Know-How

Sell Proof of Concept

License Core Tech for Applications

Sell Components or Subsystems

Manufacture, Market, and Distribute Applications

Least Costly to Buyer

Most Costly to Seller

FIGURE 12-2   THE VERTICAL POSITIONING PYRAMID

developers in some market niches, developing applications and selling them itself in others, or selling or licensing components of the technology.

TECHNOLOGY DESIGN

For the vast majority of new products, designing from the voice of the customer makes sense because the company will not design features and benefits into the product that customers will not appreciate or pay for. However, in technology-intensive markets, the decision is more complex—should a design be targeted to a specific customer need or should the company design a radically new platform technology from which many applications can be derived? In industries where the unit-one costs are exceedingly high, it is usually preferable to design a platform technology so that diverse applications from the core technology with incrementally different designs can be developed, speeding the recovery of development costs. It would be far too expensive to try to reach various markets with customized products. With this strategy in mind, how would a company go about designing a core technology that would allow for a variety of incremental applications? The goal should be to recover as much of the R&D cost as possible in the first customer segment, because the first customer—the early adopter—understands the benefits of the technology, will probably demand the most in the way of features and components, and will pay more for them. Although early adopters are not necessarily representative of mainstream adopters, later versions to other customer segments could reduce the number of features and components and allow the technology to be offered at a lower price.

TRANSFER DESIGN

Although there are many alternative ways to transfer know-how and reap the rewards of that transfer, the goal should be to maximize the number of revenue streams the company can generate from the transfer design. Given the uncertainty in technology-intensive markets, it is much more difficult to achieve a single satisfactory price, which suggests that short-term license agreements with customers often make more sense. These agreements can be structured to fit a variety of circumstances, for example, licenses for individual one-time use, licenses to make and distribute into a particular market, or usage-based pricing on a specific application. The combinations are endless.

MIGRATION DESIGN

In technology-intensive industries, generations of products typically overlap one another. The new product is introduced while the older version is still selling well, usually to early adopters. By the time the mainstream market becomes aware of the new technology and its benefits over the old one, the older version is generally beginning to experience a decline in sales. Entrepreneurs have the option to withdraw an older product at the introduction of the new one and not provide migration support, that is, help to customers in dealing with switching to the new technology, or sell the two versions simultaneously for a period of time while offering migration support. Clearly, the latter approach is more customer-oriented. Providing migration assistance often entices customers who would normally wait for lower prices and more perfect versions of the technology to adopt the new version much earlier.

DETERMINING A MARKETING APPROACH

Determining how to enter a new market is a function of a variety of factors. An existing company must be aware of the its current strategies, beliefs, and associations and how they can or cannot be transferred to the new market.[17] In this situation, it is important to create a fit between the old and the new. For new ventures with new products, the situation is quite different. Not only do these new ventures have to find a fit with the needs of the new market, but also they have to demonstrate to customers that the new venture can provide that fit. One way that many new technology ventures have successfully done this is to cobrand with another firm, which can enhance the points of differentiation in the market. For example, Jordan NeuroScience (JNS), a start-up venture providing technology for remote monitoring of brainwaves of trauma patients in hospital emergency rooms, joined forces with EEG industry leader Nicolet Biomedical, a division of Viasys, to cobrand a new product uniquely suited to deliver that benefit. In general, cobranded products are more readily accepted than either brand would be alone.[18]

For new technology ventures, structuring a marketing approach is facilitated by the development of a product family architecture to maximize customer satisfaction. "Product architecture is defined as the way in which the functional elements of a product are arranged into physical units and the way in which these units interact."[19] The implications of product architecture extend to performance, manufacturability, and product variety. The product family architecture describes the underlying architecture of the technology platform and the various products and applications that are derived from it. A product family is composed of a group of products that share a similar technology platform and compatible applications.[20] Product architecture is often considered in terms of its modularity, that is, the combinations of modules and components that not only provide for more agility in manufacturing processes, but variety in the product family. Product family architecture is very important in industrial markets where the number of customers is limited. In these markets, customers tend to have more knowledge about products and their underlying product architecture. This knowledge makes it easier for entrepreneurs and marketers to identify customer requirements and for customers to express those requirements. The limited number of customers in the market makes it easier to gather market intelligence and make more informed decisions about product architecture and marketing strategy. Moreover, with industrial customers, purchasing decisions are more commonly based on product performance and functionality rather than esthetics, ergonomics, or price.

An incremental innovation can replace an existing product and provide better performance and lower cost while still offering the same functionality. However, a radical technology will exact high switching costs from customers by asking them to change their behavior and to learn a new way of doing a particular function with which they are familiar. It is important to note that the determination of how radical a technology is is not dependent on the technology, but rather on the degree of change in customer behavior when they use the technology. For example, the technology for antilock braking systems is substantially different from conventional braking systems. Antilock braking employs a microprocessor to rapidly pump the brakes, which is quite different from the mechanical braking process. However, customers do not have to change their behavior when using the antilock brakes in order for them to work. Consequently, antilock brakes are an example of an incremental innovation that is a substitute for existing systems.

The PC is an example of a radical innovation that required a significant change in behavior on the part of customers. Consider the work of accountants prior to mainstream adoption of PCs. Financial information was entered by hand into ledgers, and calculators were used to crank the numbers. It took years before many accountants trusted computers enough to make the considerable effort to learn how to use them and transfer all their record keeping to the PCs. PCs were such a radical concept that a market for them had to be created. Because they affected mission-critical activities of businesses, the adoption rate was relatively slow.

A simple two-by-two matrix provides a way to consider a potential marketing strategy for a new technology, in particular, a radical innovation that becomes the basis for a product family (See Figure 12-3). Building on Friar and Balanchandra's model, this framework looks at new and existing applications against their corresponding customer groups.[21]

When marketing a new technology, customer groups generally fall into two categories: existing and new. The existing customers are the installed base for a particular

Customer Groups

Technology		Existing	New
Incremental		Substitution	Diffusion
Radical		Early Adopter	Niche Creation

FIGURE 12-3 INNOVATION MARKETING MATRIX

technology and are a significant competitive force. They have accepted the technology and consider it their standard. Incremental innovations on the technology will usually not involve major switching costs for them, so they will be quick to adopt the innovation if it solves a need. When the same company introduces a radical innovation, early adopters will likely come from the existing pool of customers, those who are familiar with the company's products and are ready and willing to own state-of-the-art technology. New customers are then added to the mix when the incremental innovations begin to solve specific needs that earlier versions of the radical innovation did not. New customers typically follow the diffusion or cascade model of technology adoption as depicted later in Figure 12-5. With radical innovations such as the VCR, new customers enter the picture when the company begins to develop niche applications for the technology that attract new customers to the base. Once critical mass has been achieved by building out these niche markets, the radical innovation can achieve mainstream adoption.

Some evidence indicates that radical innovations are successful only in new markets or through new applications.[22] In fact, the overwhelming majority of customers for radical innovations come from existing customer groups where there was no initial interest in using a radical innovation to replace an existing application. The research of Friar and Balanchandra determined that the best strategy to achieve adoption of the radical innovation was to target existing customers of the earlier technology and to ask them what new applications should be developed rather than what should be improved.[23]

UNDERSTANDING CUSTOMER NEEDS

Most techniques that entrepreneurs and marketers use to understand customer needs are based on existing products with which customers are familiar. With a radically new innovation, there are no existing customer needs being satisfied. However, even with an incremental innovation, it is still quite difficult to collect information from customers about their specific needs because they frequently do not know how to express those needs in a way that aids engineers and marketing people in determining performance criteria. Developing an understanding of customer needs can be achieved by answering several basic questions, which are shown in Figure 12-4.

To begin to discover the answers to these questions and more, it is important to understand the factors that affect customer-purchasing decisions. Five factors appear to have an impact on the purchasing decision.[24]

1. **Cost/benefit analysis.** Customers tend to consider the benefit of purchasing the new technology relative to its costs. In other words, customers want to know that after they pay the often-higher price for the new technology, it will meet their needs and then will they be able to learn to use it quickly and correctly.
2. **Compatibility with existing technology.** Customers will tend to purchase technologies that have similar aspects to products they are currently using and that do not force them to change their current way of doing things.

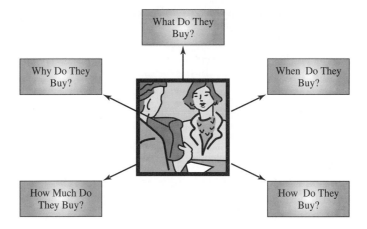

How can the company best meet their needs?

FIGURE 12-4   DETERMINING THE NEEDS OF HIGH-TECH CUSTOMERS

3. **Difficulty of use.** Customers gauge a purchase on how complex the technology is and how long it will take to learn it.
4. **Readily identifiable benefits.** Customers must be able to see what the benefits are to purchasing the technology without having to understand highly technical terms. Benefits should be intangible like convenience or ease of use and viewed from the customer's perspective. Technology companies frequently tout the features of their products. For example, HDTV has higher resolution than traditional television, but what does this mean to the customer who does not understand what resolution is? It may mean a clearer, sharper picture, but is there enough perceived difference to warrant the much higher price?
5. **Ability of benefits to be observed.** Are the benefits easily viewed by the customer using the product as well as by people watching the customer use the product? When benefits are easily observed, the desire to purchase is greater.

Considering all of these factors, it is no wonder that it takes time for technologies to achieve mass-market acceptance. Table 12-1 provides the adoption rates for several twentieth-century radical innovations.[25]

RESEARCHING CUSTOMER NEEDS

One factor that separates an effective high-tech company from an ineffective one in terms of its marketing efforts is the quality of the market intelligence it collects on its customers. For incremental innovations, the task is relatively easy and traditional market research techniques are often appropriate. However, for radical innovations, those that have no precedent, no customer awareness, and no installed base, the story is much different. Two research techniques that help to resolve this problem are empathic design and early adopter.

TABLE 12-1 Technology Adoption Rates

Internet	Compact Discs	Color TV	Answering Machines	TV	Radio
3 yrs	10 yrs	10 yrs	10 yrs	15 yrs	30 yrs
90 M users	64% mkt	3% mkt	15% mkt	60 M users	60 M users

Source: Robert Hof, "The Click Here Economy," *Business Week* (June 22, 1998): 122–128, *www.businessweek.com*.

EMPATHIC DESIGN

Oftentimes, users are unable to articulate specific performance criteria or design features and functionality that they may require. Chances are, they have developed their own "work-arounds" to fill the gap in an application. The empathic design process gives the marketer a deeper understanding of the customer's environment, what the customer's needs are, and how to translate those needs into future products.[26] For example, Intel sends its team of design ethnographers to a customer's site to spend enough time in the customer's environment to really understand their needs.[27] At the site, they are able to identify what triggers a customer to use a particular product and what problems the customer faces when using the product.

Design ethnographers can also determine various usage situations and how customers have modified a product to suit their specific needs. For example, manufacturers of pagers noticed that users were giving special codes to friends to screen out unwanted calls. This knowledge led manufacturers to produce a filtering system on pagers that improved on this work-around by customers.

Empathic design is a process that includes observation, data capture, reflection and analysis, brainstorming of solutions, and the development of prototypes.[28] It is a supplement to other market research techniques, not a substitute.

EARLY ADOPTERS

Some customers have the foresight to see their needs well into the future and are willing to pay a premium to have the technology required to meet those needs sooner than the average customer. Early adopters' needs also extend well beyond the typical needs of a mainstream adopter. Early adopters have the most stringent requirements and generally expect the most in the way of features and benefits. In fact, they often describe or even develop the application that eventually is marketed to mainstream customers because they have had more experience with the problem than the manufacturers. Since early adopters have recognized the need significantly ahead of mainstream customers, the benefit to them tends to be substantially higher. Companies such as Bose, the audio electronics manufacturer, and Cabletron, a designer of fiber-optic networks, are examples of companies that use the early adopter strategy with their customers to refine products and applications for the mainstream market.

How are early adopters identified? The best way stems from the company's relationships with its customers, but absent that (as in the case of a new venture), technology user groups are another excellent source. These groups tend to meet on a regular basis at local restaurants and continue the conversations and sharing of knowledge and resources on user groups on the Internet. Another place to find early adopters is research conferences and trade shows. Extrapolating to the mainstream market will involve asking those customers which features and benefits are most valuable and useful to them. Chances are, the mainstream customer will require fewer features and instead prefer a lower price.

RESEARCHING EMERGING MARKETS

One of the main principles of successful marketing is to focus on customer needs and find a way to solve them. That approach works well for incremental innovations on existing products or technologies.[29] The markets exist and the technology is well understood for these types of innovations. However, this approach is less successful when the company is attempting to introduce a radical innovation into a market that may not yet exist and customer needs are not known. Even when a target market can be identified, the needs of the customer may be latent, so demand-driven market research techniques will not produce useful information.[30] In this case, the technical breakthrough often comes first, followed by identification of target customers and the precise features, functions, and applications of the technology. Consequently, the level of uncertainty in this environment is twofold: technical and market. Early in the product life cycle, new technologies are often sold to users who experiment with them to discover new applications. For example, in the concept stage, PCs had no known application. Computer companies sold to computer hobbyists who liked to play around with new devices.[31] It was not until much later that the business niche was defined.

Technology diffusion in emerging markets follows a distinct pattern analogous to a cascade. Figure 12-5 presents an example of one such cascade in the adoption of VCR technology. Notice that the period of time from technology launch to mass-market acceptance was 25 years, from 1956 to 1981.

FIGURE 12-5   TECHNOLOGY DIFFUSION IN THE **VCR** INDUSTRY

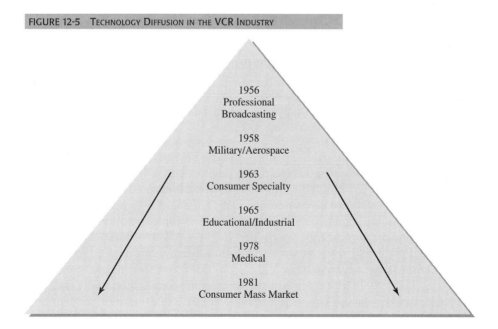

1956
Professional
Broadcasting

1958
Military/Aerospace

1963
Consumer Specialty

1965
Educational/Industrial

1978
Medical

1981
Consumer Mass Market

COLLECTING MARKET INTELLIGENCE

Understanding what is going on in the market is an ongoing process that does not stop once the new product is launched. High-technology markets are dynamic; information changes on a regular basis; new competitors emerge seemingly out of nowhere; and old competitors suddenly disappear or change form. From month to month, sometimes from week to week, the market changes; thus, gathering market intelligence is not an easy task. Fortunately, the Internet has helped marketers in their efforts to find market information. Internet resources related to market intelligence are listed at the end of the chapter, but the Internet is only the beginning. Trade journals and newspapers such as *The Wall Street Journal* can push specific industry and market information to the marketer on a regular basis to minimize having to sift through every article to find what the company needs. Press releases provide information regarding new product announcements and pricing. Journals such as *MIT Technology Review* can keep marketers current on emerging technologies being developed at universities, private institutes, and in public/private research laboratories.

The information is out there, but gathering market intelligence in a way that turns that information into useful knowledge requires a systematic approach that includes assessing what information is needed to make decisions about the customer, what sources can provide that information, and how that information can be converted to knowledge that can be used to achieve the company's goals.

FORECASTING DEMAND

There is no more difficult task for an entrepreneur than to forecast demand for a new product or service. That task is further complicated when the product is a radical innovation because historical data and trends are not available and it is difficult to extrapolate from products with different technological platforms. New products, and radical innovations in particular, do not lend themselves to traditional analytical techniques such as exponential smoothing and regression analysis because historical data on which to base an analysis does not exist. These types of products are better suited to qualitative methods. Some of these methods will be discussed in the following sections.

THE DELPHI METHOD

The most commonly used qualitative method is the Delphi Method, which brings together a panel of anonymous experts to answer critical market-research questions such as who is the customer, how does the customer buy, and when and how does the customer make purchase decisions. This method does not involve a group discussion, but begins with individual answers to a set of questions in a questionnaire format so that each expert is not influenced by the opinions of the others.[32] The first round of responses is analyzed and a second questionnaire is prepared based on the responses to the first. After the second questionnaire is completed and analyzed, a report is prepared and presented. This approach to "discussion" is useful when participants might be influenced by each other's comments or by the reputation or prestige of one or more of the experts on the panel.

It is important to be careful in the selection of the Delphi panel and to be sure to include potential customers from both the early adopter and mainstream groups. Other industry leaders would also be good additions to the panel.

SUBSTITUTE PRODUCTS

Although difficult to do with radical innovations, substitute products offer one way to estimate demand for a new product. For example, demand for compact discs was originally extrapolated from demand for cassette tapes. Looking at attributes of substitute products that are similar in nature to those of the new product can give some insight into customer response.

TRIANGULATION

The most effective approach to estimating demand for a new product is to approach it from three different angles in a process called *triangulation*. For example, to forecast demand for a new type of PDA that relies on artificial intelligence technology, the researcher can look at data on sales of similar PDAs, talk to market-channel intermediaries such as distributors and retailers, and interview potential customers. From three different sources of information, the researcher can converge on a number that makes sense and takes into consideration technical attributes and business attributes such as price, distribution, and service.

PRICING HIGH-TECHNOLOGY PRODUCTS

Although price has often been part of companies' competitive strategies, typically it has been used to gain an advantage with a commodity product. Companies rarely deliberately employ a premium pricing structure to gain a competitive advantage. In the early 1980s, however, pharmaceutical giant Glaxo introduced Zantac, an ulcer drug that was designed to compete against the leader in the market at the time, Tagamet, manufactured by SmithKline. The FDA had not identified any significant improvements in Zantac over Tagamet, so it was expected that Zantac would enter the market at a lower price to pull customers who were not brand loyal to Tagamet. In a courageous and clever move, Glaxo priced the new product at a premium and launched a marketing blitz that included developing partnerships with international competitors and approaching doctors multiple times with different sales reps touting different applications of the drug. The result of this strategy was that by 1993, Zantac had become the market leader and enjoyed huge margins from its premium pricing strategy.

Why have companies not taken a more creative approach to pricing? One reason is that many entrepreneurs think of price only as a way to cover costs and make a reasonable return. Pricing of high technology is a complicated undertaking for a variety of reasons, not the least of which is the rapid decline of price after market introduction. Some researchers have reported price declines of 20 percent or more annually.[33] To be profitable over the long term requires that a company realize huge gains in volume. The paradox is that businesses can be their most successful when prices are falling the fastest, but this requires exponential growth just to stay ahead.[34] It further requires that a firm lower its costs faster than its prices are declining. Eventually, every technology becomes a commodity, and commodity markets are somewhere that no one wants to be because the margins are slim or do not exist, volumes must remain high to compensate, and there is no room for error. In a near-commodity market, entrepreneurs must create new value apart from the original technology that will give customers a reason to pay more for the use of the technology. Many technologies end up being virtually given away while services associated with them and complementary products provide the key to continuing revenues. One factor contributing to the downward spiral of technology prices and competition based on price is the Internet, which provides a transparent market where customers can easily compare prices across many companies.

To achieve the highest price point means getting to market first or at least before that price point begins its downward slide.[35] It also means including some of the following features that are found in products that command higher prices:

- Demand for the product is strong relative to supply.
- Demand for the product is inelastic (people will buy at any price).
- The product offers additional features that are valued.
- A new technology is being introduced.
- The product is being positioned as a luxury product.

Perhaps the best way to ensure that products will not quickly become commodities despite low pricing is to develop long-term customer relationships based on a continuing dialogue and to find new ways to sell more products and services to existing customers. Furthermore, the most effective way to counter the price transparency of the Internet is to continually innovate so that customers have choices based on more than price and to create more complex pricing structures, a topic that will be taken up in a later section.

DEFINING THE COMPONENTS OF PRICE

Many factors make up the components of price, including (1) the cost of producing the product, (2) the overall price strategy, (3) promotions and discounts, (4) the degree of standardization or customization, (5) the profit required, and (6) the margins in the industry. When an entrepreneur focuses solely on covering costs without considering market demand, competition, or the company's marketing strategy, the entrepreneur loses an opportunity to price proactively for competitive advantage. Market-based pricing considers the needs and perceptions of the customer so that the value of dealing with the company and its complement of products are reflected in the price. The overall pricing strategy of the company can be proactive or reactive. A proactive strategy is what Zantac took when it entered the market at a higher price than the market leader. Reactive pricing is what happens when a firm is averse to risk and does whatever its competitors do. A risk-averse attitude can also be reflected in the standardization of prices, in other words, offering the same price to all customers. A more proactive approach allows the company to be more flexible in its pricing strategy so that it can price according to its various customer segments to account for buying habits, bundled or unbundled product offerings, and the moves of competitors. Price can be used to set up entry barriers to competitors and to provide a complex pricing structure that is difficult for competitors to untangle and compare.

CONVERGING ON A PRICE POINT

Today's chaotic market environment means that products move through their life cycles much faster, therefore management decision making must occur more rapidly and more frequently. As fast as old markets disappear, new ones emerge and competitors become more aggressive in their tactics. Consequently, it is no wonder that companies find that they must stay flexible to adapt to these changes.

Given the nature of pricing for high technology, it is not surprising that triangulation may be the solution. Converging on a price point from three perspectives makes it more likely that the price chosen will reflect the real market price, at least for a time. Figure 12-6 depicts three perspectives that are commonly used to arrive at a suitable price point: cost, competition, and customers and value chain partners.

Figuring the direct costs of producing the product is difficult in the very early stages of a new venture because prototype costs typically run about 10 times the cost of the final production-run product. Still, it is important to price the product so that costs can be covered and a profit earned, or the business will not be sustainable. The only reason to price very near cost is when cost is the company's competitive advantage and when it is sustainable over the long term against competitors that cannot achieve the same economies.

Customers and value chain partners can provide a wealth of pricing information in the same way that they supplied the entrepreneur with demand information. They both represent the market—customers in a more direct way and value chain partners as intermediaries in the process. Customers generally have no trouble expressing their feelings about price or their intolerance for a particular price point. In calculating the price the customer pays, it is vital to consider the total cost of ownership of the product, which might include delivery, installation, service, and repair. Considering all these aspects of the product and its price provides yet another way to differentiate the company from competitors. To arrive at a suitable price, the markups along the value chain must also be considered. It is one thing to cover production costs, but the cost of the value added along the channel is ultimately part of the final price as well. If that final price is beyond the tolerance of the customer, the firm must reconsider all the points along the path from the producer to the customer/end-user to reevaluate margins, costs, and markups. Many technology companies have had to resort to more direct channels of distribution to avoid the markups of intermediaries that put the final price out of range of the customer.

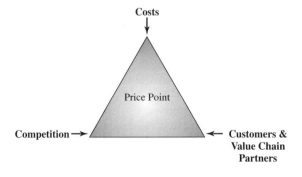

FIGURE 12-6   TRIANGULATING TO A PRICE POINT

The competition is certainly another important source of pricing information. However, benchmarking on competitors is a reactive approach to pricing and should only be a guide to determining if the price being considered is even in the ballpark of what the market will accept. If the company's technology is superior and creates new value, pricing outside the bounds of competitor pricing may be warranted, especially if it serves to put the technology in a new class all its own. Radical innovations may appear to have no direct competitors, but there are always alternatives to a new technology, and those alternatives are the competition in the form of substitute products.

CONSTRUCTING A PRICING STRATEGY

The first thing to know about pricing strategy is that one pricing strategy does not fit all. A pricing strategy will be based on the company's goals and whether the company is a start-up or established; domestic or global; or no tech, low tech, or high tech. Another point to consider is whether the pricing structure is simple or complex. A simple pricing structure will usually result in a lower price because it is easily compared across competitors' products. Conversely, a complex structure has many layers of prices and discounts, and it will be more difficult for customers to make direct comparisons. Many companies choose to begin to increase the complexity of their pricing structures by instituting two-part tariff strategies. For example, suppose the company is introducing a new software product that it is hosting via the application service provider model. It might charge a monthly flat fee for access to the ASP site and the software and a per-use charge for each time the customer accesses the site and uses the software. Customer goals will also influence the pricing strategy. For example, if customers want to use the technology to reduce costs, they will probably be focused on prices, and, therefore, the company's margins will be relatively small. On the other hand, if the customer's goal is to improve their IT effectiveness, they will focus more on the bundle of benefits the company is offering to achieve that goal. Therefore, the price will be higher and the company will experience bigger margins. Some of the goals that companies use when constructing a pricing structure include the following:

- **Increase sales.** This often means lowering prices to attract new customers that were not willing to purchase at the previous price point.
- **Maximize cash flow.** This might require raising prices and reducing costs.
- **Maximize profit.** This will probably entail raising prices and reducing costs.
- **Set up entry barriers.** This is a proactive approach to keep competitors out.
- **Define an image or control demand.** This will entail pricing high (or low) to position the product in a particular category, for example, luxury good or discount item. Pricing high is also a way to control the level of demand in the early stages of the company or when resources to produce are limited.

A number of signals indicate that the pricing strategy has problems. If prices are always based on costs or always follow competitor's pricing, the company is missing an opportunity to be proactive and use price as a competitive advantage. If prices always increase by a set amount each year or prices to all customers are one-dimensional and discounts are standardized, the pricing structure is simple and will be easily compared by customers across competitors to find the best price. The bottom line is that price should be considered a competitive weapon in the entrepreneur's arsenal of competitive advantages.

DEVELOPING A MARKETING PLAN

The plan that guides the launch of a new product is as critical to the success of that launch as the product itself. The marketing plan identifies the goals, strategies, and tactics that will be used to create product awareness and reach the customers for whom the benefits are designed. The development of the plan should be an ongoing effort that begins during feasibility analysis. Recall that one of the most important tests of feasibility analysis is the market/customer test. Primary research with the customer helps to refine the product, identify the features and benefits that create value for the customer, and determine demand. Once that information is gathered, it can be applied to developing an overall strategy for market launch and subsequent growth.

Several steps taken prior to writing a marketing plan can make the difference between an effective plan and one that does not reach its target.

1. Create a list of options that reflects all the possible strategies and tactics that might be appropriate to a particular customer market.
2. Think like a customer; in other words, imagine the company and its products from the customer's point of view. How does the customer perceive the company?
3. Know the competition. Learn what makes them successful and where they may have gaps. What is their marketing strategy? How successful is it?
4. Analyze the options and rank them according to how effectively they will help the company reach its objectives.

DEVELOPING A ONE-PARAGRAPH PLAN

Experienced marketers often suggest that it is important to put the most important components of the marketing plan into one paragraph. This forces the entrepreneur to focus on goals, strategies, and tactics to see if they are compatible. The following are the major components of this one-paragraph plan:

- **The purpose.** What will the plan accomplish?
- **The benefits of the product and any services.** How will the benefits satisfy a customer need or solve a problem?
- **The target market.** Who is the first customer for the new technology?
- **The market niche.** Where does the company fit in the market and how does it differentiate itself from the rest of the market?
- **The marketing tactics.** Which marketing tools will be employed—advertising, promotion, etc.?
- **The company's identity.** How does the customer perceive the company?

The following is an example of a one-paragraph marketing plan from a company in the business of fabricating printed circuit boards (PCBs).

> The purpose of *PCB Fab's* marketing activities is to establish *PCB Fab's* brand name in the Chinese PCB industry, help potential customers understand *PCB Fab's* services and benefits to customers, and create a market pull for the company's products and services from its target customers. *PCB Fab's* target market segment consists of foreign-owned or top Chinese PCB

fabricators that manufacture high-tech, high-end PCB devices. Its initial customers are American and European PCB manufacturers operating in China that are already *PCB Fab's* customers in the United States and Europe. Unlike other PCB fabrication material suppliers in the Chinese market that only offer customers a few limited products, *PCB Fab* provides its customers with the most comprehensive product lines so that customers only need to deal with one supplier and one invoice. In addition, *PCB Fab's* JIT total supply chain management program customizes its products and services to meet customers' specific requirements and eliminate the need for raw materials inventory. In *PCB Fab's* target market segment, the company can potentially create a highly customized, high-margin service that is valued by the target customers. *PCB Fab* will strive to create a brand image of a company that provides its customers with superior services and products with the highest quality and reliability. It also wants to be known as a company with a global reach and the capability of delivering PCB material when customers need it, where customers want it, and the way customers need it. *PCB Fab* will first create the awareness of its products and services in the International Expo of Printed Circuit Industry in Shanghai on March 20. It will then advertise its products and services in Chinese trade magazines. Meanwhile, *PCB Fab* will search and identify local distributors to distribute its proprietary product lines to leading PCB manufacturers in China. Furthermore, the company will leverage its existing strategic partnerships with American and European PCB fabricators to reach their businesses in China*

It is not within the scope of this book to discuss the marketing plan in great detail. Refer to the end-of-chapter resources for more information on the subject. Also see Figure 12-7 for an overview of the components of a marketing plan.

PROMOTING HIGH-TECHNOLOGY PRODUCTS

For whatever changes have occurred in markets and in the practice of marketing, one strategy remains constant—the practice of optimizing the marketing mix. The marketing mix is composed of product specifications, patents, brands, communication strategies, advertising, promotion, public relations, strategic alliances, services, and pricing.

For decades, innovating firms have faced an enormous problem of appropriability, that is, they had difficulty reaping the fruits of the years of work and heavy investment in R&D.[36] This problem arose out of the fact that innovations are difficult to produce but easy to imitate. Some research has suggested that competitors acquire detailed information on 70 percent of new products within 1 year of their launch, and that imitating a new innovation costs, on average, one-third of the original cost of development.[37] Today, a company's ability to effectively promote its innovations can serve to moderate the appropriability problem.[38]

---

*This one-paragraph marketing plan was adapted from a business plan drafted by Amanda Wolverton, MBA 2001, University of Southern California. The name of the actual company has been changed.

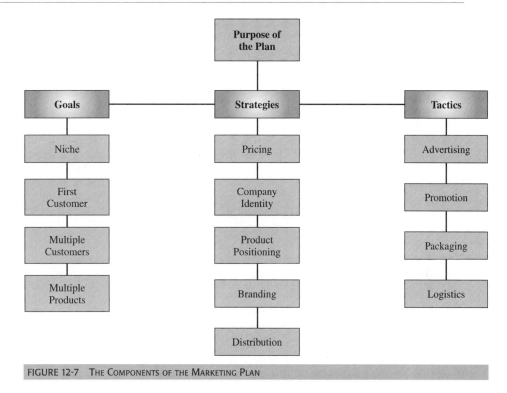

FIGURE 12-7 THE COMPONENTS OF THE MARKETING PLAN

The pharmaceutical industry serves as a good example of appropriability and the relationship between innovation and promotion. Firms that produce patented drugs experience high intensity of effort in both R&D and promotion of the drugs at market launch.[39] Because drugs are patented, they also tend to have a high degree of appropriability over the actual economic life of the patent, which is effectively shorter than the 20 years from date of application because of lengthy FDA process requirements. It is difficult to imitate a drug patent because the compound claim is very exacting and includes all formulations or uses of the chemical entity.[40] However, at the end of the patent period, the company experiences intense competition from generic drug manufacturers. Consequently, firms tend to promote heavily during the patent period to establish a secure brand to counteract the competition from generics they will experience at the end of the patent period. They may also choose to lower the price just prior to the end of the patent to discourage generic equivalents. Alternatively, the firm could use a very proactive approach such as licensing or marketing a generic version aimed at hospitals, which tend to be more price sensitive, at the same time they raise the price to pharmacies, as doctors tend to be more brand conscious.

TELLING A COMPELLING STORY

Persuasive communication is arguably the most important aspect of a promotional strategy. The ability to effectively convey the company's compelling story is what makes the difference between a successful launch and one that fizzles in a relatively short period of time. The most important piece of information that must be conveyed is the benefit to the customer. Without that, the customer has no reason to make a purchase. The company must then demonstrate that it understands the customer's pain and is offering a solution that the customer will want. Three simple questions get at the heart of the notion of a compelling story:

1. Why you?
2. Why now?
3. How will you change the world?

Many companies begin their promotional effort too early, before they are ready to deal with customers. This tactic can be fatal. For example, Dr. C. Everett Koop's site Drkoop.com had a recognized brand name, but this former surgeon general of the United States could not decide on a clear message. As a result, his public relations firm quit, and, ultimately, his company's stock fell by over 90 percent.[41]

USING PREANNOUNCEMENTS

Timing is especially critical when dealing with high-technology products. Preannouncements have become a regular tactic, particularly in the software industry, to persuade customers to delay purchasing a product until the new technology is ready.[42] It is an intentional method of providing information to competitors, customers, and shareholders to alleviate uncertainty. Preannouncements are also a good way to give a heads up to suppliers, potential partners, and company stakeholders that a new product launch will be taking place in the near future. They are a way to maintain a market position until the product actually reaches the market by spreading a sort of word-of-mouth type of advertising to channel members and customers so that they can plan their future needs.

For all of the benefits of preannouncements, they do have their drawbacks. Announcing far in advance of a launch date is a little like telling the enemy where the troops will be landing. Competitors have time to react, and generally do so in a big way when and if the product actually launches. This is one reason why pioneering firms rarely use preannouncements; they want to protect their pioneering advantage.[43] They also want to avoid cannibalizing their existing products before the new product is ready for market. Announcing far in advance also raises the probability that the product will not meet its announced date of launch due to all the normal glitches that take place in product development and prototyping. If the product is not launched on the announced date, the firm's reputation suffers and customers may cancel orders. That is what happened when Storage Technology's new product, Iceberg, was almost 2 years late on the launch of the product. Customers were so irate that they cancelled about $189 million in orders, and the company's stock dropped from $78 a share to $18.50 a share.[44] Preannouncements are known as "vaporware" when they involve software that is announced but does not exist or is years behind in a promised delivery date.[45] One Web site, Gamespot.com, publishes a Top Ten list of companies that announce vaporware.

DEVELOPING A BRAND PRESENCE

A strong brand is a significant competitive advantage in markets where customers have many choices. Branding is about creating "a deep psychological affinity to a product or service."[46] In other words, the customer wants to own the product because the brand has meaning. Compare the brand recognition versus psychological hold of Yahoo! and Intel. Although Yahoo! has brand recognition among Internet search engines, it does not generally elicit an emotional response. People do not feel bad about using another search engine. However, Intel captures both brand recognition and generates an emotional response. "Intel Inside" on the front of a PC engenders a feeling of reliability, quality, and strength. Customers think twice about purchasing a product with a non-Intel microprocessor.

A first-mover strategy requires the development of a strong brand presence, but any technology firm should make branding a significant part of its overall marketing strategy because a successful brand will ultimately bring down marketing costs. For example, in the period from 1996 to 1998 alone, AOL brought its customer acquisition costs down from $375 to $90 per customer as a result of brand recognition.[47] A successful brand commands a higher price and enjoys significantly more loyalty from customers. This means that when new products are introduced under the recognized brand, customer acceptance and adoption are almost assured because the customer's array of choices has been simplified. The most effective route to branding is to brand the company and a platform of innovations rather than a particular product or technology. Because of the rapid obsolescence of technology products, it is more important to stabilize the brand in something that will not become obsolete or that won't be for a very long time. This is why a company such as Sony always uses the trade name *Sony* in front its products, for example, the Sony Walkman and the Sony Playstation.

Cobranding or joint venturing a product is a common way to benefit from the synergy of two branded companies. For example, Microsoft and Intel joined forces to create Win-Tel. It is important when cobranding to choose partners carefully, as the brands will be inextricably tied together, perhaps for the lives of the companies.

Developing the right products in the right way is certainly an important first step in creating a successful company, but effectively marketing the company and its products to customers is critical to building sustainability.

❖ SUMMARY

Customer-centered marketing is the focus of new ventures today as they struggle to meet rapidly changing customer needs. High-technology markets display a unique blend of market uncertainty, technology uncertainty, and competitive uncertainty. In addition, know-how, complexity, and velocity all affect the market advantage of a high-tech firm. The ability to transform an invention into a commercial innovation occurs in generally two ways: by market research and by the technology itself. The market-driven approach relies on internal and external knowledge to find a solution to a customer need in the market. This approach can cause problems for technical staff that have to try to hit a moving target with a single solution. In contrast, the technology-driven approach puts technology in the driver's seat without firm knowledge that a market even exists for it. This forces the technologist to develop a solution and then look for a problem. Both approaches come up lacking. A more appropriate and effective approach is to use a parallel one that combines knowledge about the technology with knowledge about customer needs. Determining how to enter a new market is a function of a variety of factors. An existing company must be aware of its current strategies, beliefs, and associations and how they can or cannot be transferred to the new market. In this situation, it is important to create a fit between the old and the new. For new ventures with new products, the situation is quite different. Not only do these new ventures have to find a fit with the needs of the new market, but they also have to demonstrate to customers that the new venture can provide that fit. One way that many new technology ventures do this is to cobrand with another firm, which can enhance the points of differentiation in the market. Forecasting demand with new technology is a difficult task at best. The most effective approach to estimating demand for a new product is to approach it from three different sources in a process called *triangulation*. The same approach can be used to find the correct pricing for a new technology. Pricing is an important part of the bundle of competitive advantages a company has and should be dealt with proactively. All of the issues related to marketing a new technology are brought together in the marketing plan, which is designed to create awareness for the company and its products and consists of goals, strategies, and tactics. The bottom line for any company desiring to develop an effective marketing strategy is to tell a compelling story and solve a real customer need.

❖ DISCUSSION QUESTIONS

1. How do the characteristics of high-technology markets affect the marketing strategy of a new venture?
2. What is the most effective strategy for collecting market intelligence?
3. When pricing high-technology products, what factors should be taken into consideration?
4. What is the purpose of a marketing plan? What is the value of compressing the plan into one paragraph?
5. What role does branding play in the promotional strategy of a new high-tech venture?

❖ RESOURCES

Mohr, Jakki. *Marketing of High-Technology Products and Innovations.* Upper Saddle River, NJ: Prentice Hall, 2001.

Moore, Geoffrey A. *Inside the Tornado.* New York: HarperCollins, 1999.

Moore, Geoffrey A. *Crossing the Chasm: Marketing and Selling High-Tech Products to Mainstream Customers.* New York: HarperBusiness, 1999.

Ries, Al, and Laura Ries. *The 11 Immutable Laws of Internet Branding.* New York: Harperbusiness, 2000.

Winkler, Agnieszka. *Warp-Speed Branding: The Impact of Technology on Marketing.* New York: John Wiley & Sons, 1999.

❖ INTERNET RESOURCES

Hoover's Online
www.hoovers.com
Find industry and company descriptions and statistics

MarketingProfs.com
www.marketingprofs.com
A great source of articles, advice, and tools for marketing

SEC's Edgar
www.sec.gov/cgi-bin/srch-edgar
The Security and Exchange Commission's site with annual reports, 10Q and 10K filings, and regulations for selling securities

Society of Competitive Intelligence Professionals
www.scip.org
An online community for knowledge professionals with news and information to understand the competitive environment

WILL GPS EVER CROSS THE CHASM?

Twenty years ago, Charlie Trimble, a Silicon Valley entrepreneur, founded his business, Trimble Navigation Ltd., by acquiring the remnants of a Hewlett-Packard project for about $80,000. Those remnants consisted of research notes and a large circuit board (said to be the size of a coffee table). What the circuit board could do was detect a signal from the first satellite in a constellation that was to become the Navstar Global Positioning System (GPS), a worldwide radio-navigation system formed from a constellation of 24 military satellites that orbit 18,000 kilometers above the earth and their ground stations. GPS uses these "man-made stars" as reference points to calculate positions on the earth to a matter of meters.[48] GPS is a relatively simple concept with provocative implications. Basically, the GPS receiver triangulates from the satellites; that is, it measures distance using the travel time of radio signals, correcting for delays the signal might experience as it travels through the atmosphere. A GPS receiver requires three satellites to determine latitude and longitude and it gets a fix from a fourth satellite to determine altitude. The ramifications of being able to track things anywhere on earth are enormous, but, surprisingly, the system has never crossed the chasm to mainstream adoption as predicted in 1991 after the successful use of GPS in the Gulf War initiative. GPS is a classic example of the technology adoption cycle for radical innovations.

GPS was originally developed for the military for about $12 billion to enhance the precision with which the military could hit targets. It was never intended for commercial use, although the commercial businesses that have developed over time have had free access to the satellites currently in orbit with the confidence that the government will maintain them over time. A 1996 Presidential Decision Directive guaranteed that GPS would be available for citizens but under the control of the Pentagon. However, free access to government intellectual property has also caused some problems. The industry has developed technology applications far ahead of customer demand at price points too high for anyone but the hard-core early adopter. With the exception of Trimble's development of GPS for ocean navigation (its entry strategy) and desert warfare, sales have been occurring only in very small niche markets, mostly in the form of novelty gifts. For example, with handheld GPS devices, golfers can measure the length of their drive and hikers can find a trail. The reality is that few companies have found a business model that makes sense and makes money.

There are also problems with the GPS technology itself. The Department of Defense satellite constellation is often inaccurate for many of the commercial applications that require a high level of precision. Civilian applications are typically only reliable to within 70 to 100 meters, and reports of hikers walking off precipices in Scotland in the fog or dying in snowstorms because they could not find a cave point to the danger of relying on GPS in life-threatening situations. However, recently Magellan, the company that offered the first hand-held GPS device, announced that its newest upgrade would offer accuracy to within 3 meters using the Wide Area Augmentation System (WAAS), which improves positioning accuracy. Another recent problem reported by a Department of Transportation study is the susceptibility of GPS systems to jamming and interference from atmospheric effects, signal blockage from buildings, and interference from other communications equipment. As it becomes more popular, GPS will also become the target of attack by hackers and terrorists.

On a positive note, complementary technologies such as digital mapping and wireless communication are on the rise, providing the ability to combine other technologies with GPS, for example, tracking the location of a lost child and paging that child. It is projected that national adoption of GPS to track 911 callers might be the first mass adoption of the technology. The cost of GPS chips is rapidly dropping, making it more economical to install them in existing devices such as cell phones and dashboards. Bringing the price down may be enough to push the GPS industry across the chasm.

At the same time, GPS presents some additional concerns that must be addressed. Remoteness disappears when GPS is used, and that may pose a problem of invasion of privacy or a disruption of a person's life. For example, one of the early adopters of GPS tracking was United Parcel Service (UPS). UPS thought GPS would be an effective way to track trucks and monitor their whereabouts from a central location. The Teamsters union objected to continual use of GPS because it did not help workers perform their jobs better. In fact, it actually hurt productivity for the workers to know that they were being continually monitored.

The second wave of commercial applications for GPS came in 2000 with the end of selective availability and improved position accuracy; however, GPS is still not accurate enough for applications such as precision agriculture and machine control. On the horizon is a third wave of GPS products that will use Wide Area Differential DPS systems (WADGPS), making it possible for applications to access differential GPS like that used in the military, which can provide accuracy better than 1 meter.

Charlie Trimble is betting that when the price of GPS becomes more acceptable to customers and the technology is embedded in a variety of devices, people will become more location-conscious. The real questions are: Do people need that much location information? What is the pain that the technology is curing? ■

Sources: Claire Tristram, "Has GPS Lost Its Way?" *MIT Enterprise Technology Review* (July–August 1999), *www.techreview.com*; "Magellan GPS Accuracy Better than Three Meters with New Product Upgrades," *Wireless Internet* (July 2001), *www.findarticles.com;* Kathleen Hickey, "Tech War," *Traffic World* (October 1, 2001), *www.trafficworld.com.*

❖ NOTES

1. Jagdish N. Sheth, Banwari Mital, and Bruce Newman, *Customer Behavior: Consumer Behavior and Beyond* (New York: Dryden, 1999).
2. Jagdish N. Sheth, Rajendra S. Sisodia, and Arun Sharma, "The Antecedents and Consequences of Customer-Centric Marketing," *Anatomy of Marketing Science Journal* 28, no. 1 (Winter 2000): 55–66.
3. Rowland Moriarty and Thomas Kosnik, "High-Tech Marketing: Concepts, Continuity, and Change," *Sloan Management Review* 30 (Summer 1989): 7–17.
4. V. Kasturi Rangan and Kevin Bartus, "New Product Commercialization: Common Mistakes," in V. K. Rangan, Benson Shapiro, and Rowland Moriarty, eds., *Business Marketing Strategy* (Chicago, IL: Irwin, 1995), 63–75.
5. Jakki Mohr, *Marketing of High Technology Products and Innovations* (Upper Saddle River, NJ: Prentice Hall, 2001), 7–12.
6. Jakki Mohr, "The Marketing of High-Technology Products and Services: Implications for Curriculum Content and Design," *Journal of Marketing Education* 22, no. 3 (2000): 246–259.
7. John Workman, "Marketing's Limited Role in New Product Development in One Computer Systems Firm," *Journal of Marketing Research* 30 (November 1993): 5–21.
8. Geoffrey Moore, *Crossing the Chasm* (New York: HarperBusiness, 1999), 1–11.
9. George John, Allen M. Weiss, and Shantanu Dutta, "Marketing in Technology-Intensive Markets: Toward a Conceptual Framework," *Journal of Marketing* 63 (1999): 78–91.

10. William L. Shanklin and John K. Ryans, Jr., *Marketing High Technology* (Lexington, MA: D.C. Heath, 1984).

11. John et al., "Marketing in Technology-Intensive Markets," 79.

12. Rashi Glazer, "Marketing in an Information-Intensive Environment: Strategic Implications of Knowledge as an Asset," *Journal of Marketing* 55 (October 1991): 1–19.

13. Paul M. Romer, "Endogenous Technological Change," *Journal of Political Economy* 98, no. 5 (1990): 71–90.

14. R. A. Burgleman and L. Sayles, Inside Corporate Innovation (New York: The Free Press, 1986).

15. Moore, *Crossing the Chasm*, 11.

16. John et al., "Marketing in Technology-Intensive Markets," 82.

17. David A. Aaker and Kevin Lane Keller, "Consumer Evaluations of Brand Extensions," *Journal of Marketing* 54 (January 1990): 27–41.

18. C. Whan Park, Jun Sung Youl, and Allan D. Shocker, "Composite Branding Alliances: An Investigation of Extension and Feedback Effects," *Journal of Marketing Research* 33 (November 1996): 453–467.

19. Jianxin Jiao and Mitchell M. Tseng, "Fundamentals of Product Family Architecture," *Integrated Manufacturing Systems* 11, no. 7 (November 7, 2000): 469–483.

20. M. H. Meyer and J. M. Utterback, "The Product Family and the Dynamics of Core Capability," *Sloan Management Review* 34 (1993): 29–47.

21. John H. Friar and R. Balanchandra, "Spotting the Customer for Emerging Technologies," *Research-Technology Management* 42, no. 4 (July–August 1999): 37–43.

22. Joseph L. Bower and Clayton M. Christensen, "Disruptive Technologies: Catching the Wave," *Harvard Business Review* 73: 1 (January 1995): 43–53.

23. Friar and Balanchandra, "Spotting the Customer for Emerging Technologies," 37–43.

24. Everett Rogers, *Diffusion of Innovations* (New York: The Free Press, 1983).

25. Robert Hof, "The Click Here Economy," *Business Week* (June 22, 1998): 122–128. *www.businessweek.com*.

26. Dorothy Leonard-Barton and Jeffrey F. Rayport, "Spark Innovation Through Empathic Design," *Harvard Business Review* 75 (November–December 1997): 102–113.

27. Dean Takahashi, "Doing Fieldwork in the High-Tech Jungle," *Wall Street Journal*, 27 October 1998, BI, B22.

28. Leonard-Barton and Rayport, "Spark Innovation Through Empathic Design," 102–113.

29. Philip Anderson and Michael L. Tushman, "Technological Discontinuities and Dominant Designs: A Cyclical Model of Technological Change," *Administrative Science Quarterly* 35 (December 1990): 604–633.

30. Bower, J. L. and Christensen, C. M. "Disruptive Technologies: Catching the Wave," *Harvard Business Review*, Vol. 73 (January-February 1995) 43–53.

31. Friar and Balanchandra, "Spotting the Customer for Emerging Technologies," 37–43.

32. Lee, J. Krajewski, and Larry P. Ritzman, *Operations Management, Strategy and Analysis*, 5th ed. (Reading, MA: Addison–Wesley Longman, 1998), 501.

33. Bernard Wysocki, "Even High-Tech Faces Problems with Pricing," *Wall Street Journal*, 13 April 1998, A1.

34. Neil Gross and Peter Coy with Otis Port, "The Technology Paradox," *Business Week* (March 6, 1995): 76–84, *www.businessweek.com*.

35. Darren McDermott, "Cost-Consciousness Beats Pricing Power," *Wall Street Journal*, May 3, 1999, A1.

36. Kenneth J. Arrow, "Economic Welfare and Allocation of Resources for Invention," in R. Nelson, ed., *The Rate and Direction of Inventive Activity*, (Princeton, NJ: Princeton University Press, 1962), 609–624.

37. Edwin Mansfield, "How Rapidly Does New Industrial Technology Leak Out?" *Journal of Industrial Economics* 34, no. 2 (December 1985): 217–224.

38. David A. Aaker, *Managing Brand Equity* (New York: The Free Press, 1991), 1–33.

39. H. D. Vinod and P. M. Rao, "R&D and Promotion in Pharmaceuticals: A Conceptual Framework and Empirical Exploration," *Journal of Marketing Theory and Practice* 8, no. 4 (Fall 2000): 10–20.

40. Ibid.

41. Lou Hampton, "The Seven Fatal Flaws of Start-up Communications," *Public Relations Strategist* 7, no. 1 (Winter 2001): 32–35.

42. J. Eliashberg and T. Robertson, "New Product Preannouncing Behavior: A Market Signaling Study," *Journal of Marketing Research* 25 (1988): 282–292.

43. Roger Calantone and Kim Schatzel, "Strategic Foretelling: Communication-Based Antecedents of a Firm's Propensity to Preannounce," *Journal of Marketing* 64 (January 2000): 17–30.

44. Matthew Schifrin, "No Product, No Sales," Forbes (June 7, 1993): 50–52, *www.forbes.com*.

45. Stephen Kreider Yoder, "Computer Makers Defend Vaporware," *Wall Street Journal*, 16 February 1995, B1, B6.

46. Luc Hatlestad, "How to Land a High-Tech Brand," *Red Herring* (January 2000), *www.redherring.com*.

47. Marc Gunther, "The Internet Is Mr. Case's Neighborhood," *Fortune* (March 30, 1998): 69–80, *www.fortune.com*.

48. Trimble Navigation, LTD., *www.trimble.com/gps/what.html*.

13

GROWING THE HIGH-TECH VENTURE

OVERVIEW

This chapter will examine

❖ the nature of growth

❖ conventional growth strategies

❖ growth through R&D

❖ growth through cooperation

❖ strategies for setting technology standards

INTRODUCTION

Growth is something that every successful start-up attempts to achieve because it signals that the market wants what the company is offering. Consequently, entrepreneurs are in a constant search for the most effective growth strategy that will take the company through this exciting but challenging time. For at least the past 20 years, the focus of most companies looking to grow has been on competitive strategy, in other words, using the competition as a benchmark for developing a strategy. Certainly, building competitive advantages that set a company apart from the competition is necessary, but the fallacy of that approach is that focusing on doing what the competition does, only better, usually results in a strategy that is based on imitation rather than innovation, and is, therefore, inherently limited by the behaviors of the competition.[1] In both the microwave oven and VCR industries, for example, competitive benchmarking was the norm, and that strategy resulted in products that were nearly identical in every respect from the customer's point of view. Moreover, they contained too many unneeded features and, consequently, were offered at too high a price. A company that did not rely on competitive benchmarking but rather on the voice of the customer could have stepped out of the box and offered products that were easy to use.[2] The unintended consequences of choosing a competitive strategy such as this are imitative products, a reactive approach to innovation, and a failure to identify emerging markets and changing customer needs.

The solution to competitive benchmarking lies in what W. Chan Kim refers to as *value innovation.*[3] Value innovation is not related to competition; instead, it actually makes the competition irrelevant by providing a fundamentally new and superior value proposition. An example of Kim's value innovation strategy can be found in Callaway Golf's introduction of the "Big Bertha" golf club in 1991. Callaway ignored the competition's clubs and considered the needs of nonprofessionals who played regularly at country clubs. These nonprofessionals were often intimidated by the effort required to hit a very small ball with an equally small club head. Recognizing an untapped market, Callaway devised a much larger golf head that allowed amateurs to enjoy the game. In the process it captured a substantial share of existing users of standard clubs.

Kim's work further concluded that high profits and continued growth are not the result of an attractive industry, a commitment to state-of-the-art technology, being a small entrepreneurial company, or having a great team.[4] They are the result of a company making a conscious decision to pursue innovation outside the traditional context in which it is competing. Where other companies may respond to the constraints of the industry and market in which they play, value-innovation companies look for opportunities within those constraints.[5] Consider Figure 13-1, which depicts the results of a recent study of more than 100 new business start-ups. Imitator companies comprised 86 percent of the sample but generated only 39 percent of total profits. The 14 percent of all business launches that were value innovators generated 38 percent of total revenues and a surprising 61 percent of profits.[6]

A competition-based strategy has little to recommend it in an economy where supply often exceeds demand and customers are regularly barraged with new innovations. Staying ahead of the competition has become a zero-sum game that has driven many companies out of the market. In contrast, a value-innovation strategy creates new

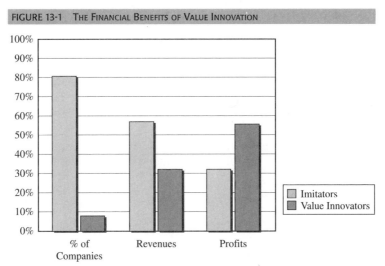

FIGURE 13-1 THE FINANCIAL BENEFITS OF VALUE INNOVATION

Source: W. Chan Kim, "Strategy, Value Innovation, and the Knowledge Economy," *Sloan Management Review* 40, no. 3 (Spring 1999): 41–55.

markets, new profits, and new growth, and it does so by using tacit knowledge created inside the company. What this means is that a firm can be successful despite industry and market conditions and can actually overcome these conditions through systematic and sustainable innovation.[7] One approach that value innovators take is to redefine a problem rather than to immediately seek its solution. Often, the most valuable solution will come from looking at the problem from a different perspective. Recall the earlier example of Callaway Golf. Its competitors thought that what customers wanted most was to hit the ball farther, so its innovations all involved accomplishing that end. Callaway redefined the problem by studying why more people chose tennis over golf at country clubs; Callaway was not concerned with the issue of performance, but rather how to get more people to play golf.

Achieving such a value innovation requires a team-based approach with team members who have diverse backgrounds and perspectives. This ensures that markets and customers can be approached from a variety of perspectives.[8]

THE NATURE OF GROWTH

To what size does a company have to grow to ensure that it will survive over the long term? In today's environment we are seeing a resurgence of mergers and acquisitions that is producing no shortage of big companies, which seems to be a return to the years prior to the decade of the entrepreneur of the 1980s. The bottom line is: Size counts, but it matters what the type of business is, what industry it is in, and what its market niche is. For some companies, being smaller in a market of big companies allows the company to seek out and serve niches that the bigger companies will not touch. The more important achievement than size then is to become the best. Patagonia Inc. is the best at what it does, making great outdoor clothing, and, after growing too fast and too large in the mid 1990s, it has now found its "natural" size, the size that allows it to perform at an optimal level.[9]

The rate at which a new venture can grow is a function of the market and the company's management. Market factors that appear to affect growth rates include size, volatility, complexity, and buying power. For example, a small, stable niche market will typically not provide an environment for rapid growth to a large size. In contrast, a global market is large enough to permit greater growth potential. A market with several large, established competitors may not be a deterrent to growth if the new venture is entering the market in a niche with innovative technology where its patent rights give it a temporary monopoly.

Some of the management factors that affect a company's ability to grow include management's reliance on successful decisions made thus far without regard for the fact that effective growth requires different skills and different decisions. The entrepreneur/CEO's inability to give up some control to others will also hurt the company's ability to grow.

THE PITFALLS OF GROWTH

Although growth is a natural by-product of a successful start-up, it does not always go smoothly. In his research with 60 entrepreneur/CEOs, Stephen Harper learned that although poor management is the common denominator in all the problems with growth, it is important to go deeper than merely lay blame on the CEO.[10] Understanding what can go wrong with growth will help entrepreneurs avoid some of the most common mistakes. The following sections describe some of the frequent pitfalls identified by these CEOs.

UNDERCAPITALIZATION

It takes money to grow, and any entrepreneur who contemplates growing a company to the next level needs a stockpile of resources to feed the greedy engine of growth. In particular, volatile markets and uncertain economic conditions demand that a growing company have contingency resources at its disposal. Problems with undercapitalization happen when new ventures start out undercapitalized and are in a constant struggle to stay afloat or when they underestimate the amount of capital that will be needed to grow successfully. For these reasons, it is important to create a financial plan for the business.

LACK OF SUFFICIENT AND QUALIFIED HUMAN CAPITAL

When a growing firm does not have the right people in the right place at the right time (before growth begins), it puts itself in jeopardy. Moreover, when the entrepreneur/CEO is unable to delegate decision-making authority to others, the company cannot make effective decisions quickly enough. However, as important as the number of personnel is, it is more important that they be the right personnel with the right skills. The company must not make the mistake of moving into territory where it does not have personnel with the skills needed to play in that market. As the saying goes, it is difficult to change a tire on a car going 100 miles an hour. Like the financial resources, the right people need to be in place prior to rapid growth.

THE INERTIA OF SUCCESS

One of the fatal mistakes that some entrepreneur/CEOs make is to believe that if the company was successfully launched, they must have done something right, so they continue down the same path. Unfortunately, the skills that were so valuable at start-up can become a hindrance or even a liability in the growth stage, particularly if the entrepreneur/CEO cannot give up control of every aspect of the business. CEOs often fall prey to what are known as the five managerial sins: arrogance, ignorance, complacency, denial, and ineptitude.[11] Arrogance has often been at the root of a company's problems during growth. The company is generating more cash flow and increased sales, so the CEO believes that it is time to enjoy some of their success with a new car, a remodeled office, and first-class airline tickets. Believing that growth will go on indefinitely, the CEO begins designing the state-of-the-art corporate headquarters and has now unwittingly put the company in jeopardy. Many companies have failed because their CEOs began spending too much money on non-revenue-generating items while not keeping the company liquid enough to endure an inevitable slowdown in growth.

FAILURE TO STAY IN TOUCH

CEOs who fail to stay in touch with what is going on in their firm's environment risk not seeing an oncoming challenge or threat. These are the CEOs who resist change because they are not aware enough of their surroundings to understand that change is necessary. By failing to stay on top of key financial, economic, company, and other indicators, they may miss trends that spell opportunity or threat. Some of the key indicators that growth is in trouble include:

- Not meeting sales forecasts
- High employee turnover
- Increasing overhead without a corresponding increase in sales
- Financial ratios falling below acceptable levels
- Missing milestones
- Not meeting delivery schedules
- Negative cash flow
- Declines in quality

WHAT IT TAKES TO GROW

Making *Fortune's* or *Inc.'s* list of fastest growing companies and sustaining that growth for at least 3 years is not easy in a volatile economy with more competition than ever before. Lee Smith reported in *Fortune* that there are five tricks to managing growth.[12] They are discussed in the following sections.

PAY ATTENTION TO DETAILS

Although keeping a watch on cash flow and profit is important, entrepreneurs often forget to manage less exciting numbers such as accounts receivable and inventory. TSI, a privately owned telecom based in Westlake Village, California, that provides corporate communication services, was so busy celebrating its revenues that it neglected to collect its receivables for more than 120 days. When it finally went to the bank to get a loan against receivables to provide some cash flow, the bank was not impressed with its old receivables. Eventually, the company had to write off about $500,000 in bad receivables. It was an expensive lesson, but now the company demands that customers pay within 45 days. Some CEOs receive daily or weekly cash flow reports to keep a handle on the company's cash position.

HIRE CAUTIOUSLY

Fast growing companies often make the mistake of hiring quickly and regretting it later. When a company is doubling or tripling in size every year, it is not difficult to hire the wrong people if hiring processes are not effective. Rapid growth requires specialization, so the jack-of-all-trades type of person that may have been appropriate at start-up now does not have the focused skills the company requires to grow. Moreover, getting rid of an employee that does not work out is more difficult than might be imagined considering the many laws that protect employees from wrongful dismissal. Therefore, the company must spend more time in the hiring process, holding multiple interviews with different people in the organization in a variety of settings to gain a better understanding of this person who will become an important part of the company.

DO NOT ASSUME THAT TREES GROW TO THE SKY

Many entrepreneurs make the mistake of assuming that rapid growth will continue indefinitely. Unfortunately, this never happens. Every highly successful company experiences periods of rapid growth followed by periods of slower growth.

Those who bet on e-commerce taking over the world believed that growth would never stop; money would always be available; everyone would buy everything over the Internet; market caps would continue to rise. Then came April 2000, and the bubble burst. For another example of rapid growth that was cut short, see the case study "From Riches to Rags" in Chapter 10.

LEARN TO SAY NO TO CUSTOMERS

It is difficult for entrepreneurs to imagine the day when they might turn away a potential customer, but learning to say no at the appropriate time may be critical to the company's survival. There is a difference between healthy growth and growth that can hurt a company. Growth that negatively affects a company comes in two forms: (1) growth that occurs before the company is ready, and, (2) hypergrowth, growth that is so rapid that it saps every resource the company has and makes it impossible for the company to see what is coming in time to stop. Growth should be a means to an end, not the end itself. In May 2001, a very successful Seattle software company, Chase Bobko, closed its doors, not from a lack of customers, but from an inability to handle growth effectively.[13] In 1998, Chase Bobko was the leader in producing programs to help clients such as Microsoft manage huge volumes of information on the Internet. During its rapid growth, Chase Bobko, in 1 week alone, brought on Boeing and Motorola as clients, but these new clients were very different from previous ones. They demanded more time and effort from Chase Bobko, and the company was unable to find and hire enough of the right people fast enough. Because the company was focusing so much of its effort on these new clients, its overall customer service declined. The dot-com bust put the final nail in the coffin. What this example clearly points to is the need for a growing company to put systems and controls in place before it begins rapid expansion and to say no if taking on a particular customer will hurt the business.

BRING IN PROFESSIONAL MANAGEMENT AT THE RIGHT TIME

The visionary, resource-building skills that the entrepreneur brought to the venture at start-up must give way to professional management skills when the company starts to grow rapidly. It is a rare entrepreneur that can see the company through its entire life cycle and do so effectively. The most difficult challenge for an entrepreneur is knowing when to turn over the reins to someone with experience in running a larger company. Planning for this succession must become part of the overall growth strategy. In some high-tech start-ups, usually those that require venture capital at the start-up stage, a management team is brought in after R&D because the original entrepreneurial team was made up of scientists and engineers with no business experience. Because these companies are designed from the beginning to grow rapidly, a significant amount of capital is invested upfront to ensure that the systems are in place to manage that growth.

❖ **The *Inc.* 500 Class of 2001**

The fastest growing U.S. companies often are not found on the stock exchanges; they are private companies, many with no thought of taking their companies public. *Inc.* magazine produces an annual report on the 500 fastest growing private companies in the United States. The following list provides the major statistics for these companies for the class of 2001.

The 2001 *Inc.* 500

Average 5-year growth rate	1,933%
Average 2000 sales	$24,976,000
Founded by two or more partners	62%
Average number of employees	160
Number of companies started from home	56%
Median number of employees	64
Percentage of companies earning a profit	76%
Average age of the companies	8 years
Percentage of companies planning to do an initial public offering	29%
Percentage of CEOs who own 100% of the company	24%
Percentage of CEOs who own less than 50% of the company	35%

Source: Susan Greco, "The *Inc* 500 Almanac," *Inc*, November 15, 2001, *www.inc.com*.

Half of the *Inc.* 500 started their businesses on less than $20,000 and more than 88 percent used their own financial resources as seed capital. In later rounds of funding, about 11 percent used strategic partners and 3 percent tapped venture capital. Venture-capital-backed firms on the list grew at more than double the 1,933 percent 5-year growth rate of the rest of the firms on the list, growing 4,619 percent over 5 years. The 2001 class reflects the effects of the dot-com debacle, with only 25 percent of the companies going after Internet sales; and of those 25 percent, only 13 percent of their revenues came from the Internet. In terms of growth strategies going forward, 57 percent of the *Inc.* 500 are planning to acquire other companies and 38 percent plan to sell their companies.

CONVENTIONAL GROWTH STRATEGIES

Conventional growth strategies—market penetration, market development, product development, and diversification—are based on three fundamental principles of growth. To grow, a company must increase users, increase usage, or increase uses.[14] In other words, the company must find new customers, increase the number of products purchased by each customer, or increase the number of ways a product can be used. The first three strategies entail growing within the current market, whereas diversification involves seeking markets outside current markets within or outside the industry.

MARKET PENETRATION

Market penetration is a strategy for growing within a company's current market, that is, exploiting the current market to the fullest extent by capturing all the potential customers and increasing the volume of sales to those customers. This strategy is typically employed first because it allows a company to operate from familiar territory and build a stronger base. Market penetration is more easily achieved if a company has defined niche markets that it can capture because its growth is more focused and its resources are used more efficiently.

MARKET DEVELOPMENT

With a market development strategy, a company is taking its products and services to new geographical areas. This can be accomplished through satellite facilities in a new region, additional sales force that focuses on the new region, or, more rapidly, through franchising and licensing.

Franchising is a popular method for growing quickly without the company having to do all the work; it is often a less expensive approach than setting up a nationwide distribution system. With a franchise, the franchisee purchases the right to implement a business plan and pays a royalty on sales in exchange for receiving a product or service with a proven market; the use of trade names; a patented design, process, or formula; an accounting and financial control system; a marketing plan and support; and the benefits of volume purchasing.[15] Franchises are typically found in retail operations. They have not been a popular strategy for high-technology companies, which typically use other distribution channels to grow.

Licensing is a means of growing a company without having to invest in plant, equipment, and employees. A license agreement is a grant to the licensee to use the company's intellectual property in the manner specified in the agreement, usually to develop applications or to make and distribute the technology. By licensing technology to application developers, system integrators, and manufacturers, a new venture gets into new markets more quickly than it would have on its own limited resources. Licensing is discussed in more detail in Chapter 6.

PRODUCT DEVELOPMENT

Another way to grow within the current market is to develop new products or new versions of existing products. Selling more products to existing customers is easier and more cost effective than seeking new customers because it takes fewer marketing dollars and it leverages the company's brand, which is already established with existing customers. Investing in R&D to come up with disruptive or radical innovations is a product development strategy that can lead to substantial growth. Using R&D to generate growth is discussed later in the chapter.

DIVERSIFICATION

Expanding the business outside the company's core capabilities through investing in or acquiring new products, services, and companies entails a diversification strategy. This strategy is often employed when the entrepreneur has exhausted other strategies.

A synergistic strategy involves looking for technologies and products that are technologically complementary to the company's current products. With conglomerate diversification, the company is seeking businesses that are not in any way related to the current business. Why would a company want to do this? The strategy may be to gain control of a related function of doing business; for example, a manufacturer might purchase the plant in which it does its manufacturing and then lease the excess capacity to another company. This strategy produces additional lease income and an asset on the balance sheet.

INDUSTRY GROWTH STRATEGIES

Growth strategies inside the industry typically involve acquisition of value chain partners or the consolidation of a fragmented industry. Moving backward or forward within the value chain is called vertical integration. With backward integration, the company acquires a supplier, whereas in forward integration, the company plans to control the distribution or downstream portion of the channel. The latter strategy gives a company more control over how products are marketed and distributed.

The consolidation strategy is used to "roll-up" a fragmented industry by acquiring as many smaller, independent businesses as possible and putting them under one umbrella organization. It is important to start by acquiring the strongest company in a particular geographic region, typically in the $7 to $20 million range in value. Acquired companies should have long track records, excellent management, and favorable reputations. It is also important to keep the original owner and key management on board to help find additional acquisitions and to ensure a smooth transition.

GROWTH THROUGH R&D

Innovation has long been a precipitator of growth in any type of company, but recently companies with world-class R&D organizations—Gillette, Lucent Technologies, and Xerox—have had serious difficulties in sustaining their previous rates of growth due to gaps in their innovation management. Some of these gaps are:[16]

- Limiting the scope and strategy of innovation and focusing resources and investment on current dominant designs or best practices in products and services, business, and markets
- Relying solely on current organizational capability and architecture for innovation management
- Creating the classic "innovator's dilemma" of restricting innovation to customers' perceived needs, thus inhibiting the ability to develop new dominant designs

As Clayton Christensen has asserted, "It's no wonder that innovation is so difficult for established firms. They employ highly capable people and then set them to work within processes and business models that doom them to failure."[17]

The work of Miller and Morris in providing a fourth-generation innovation management model has identified some basic principles that are required to sustain innovative growth.[18] These principles will be discussed in the following sections.

BROADLY DEFINE THE SCOPE OF INNOVATION

More important than incremental improvements in product performance, increasing market share, and reducing costs is creating and delivering new customer value and increasing the scope of innovation management to include the business system. This does not mean doing a static analysis of the industry and market at a single point in time, but rather adopting a sense-and-respond mentality that looks beyond the obvious market conditions to changes on the horizon. This approach entails viewing suppliers, competitors, and customers not as single sources of capabilities, but as groups or "galaxies" of ever-increasing capabilities. This new sense-and-respond capability lets the company do a more effective job of recognizing customer needs, both current and latent.

For example, the integration of atoms and bits has produced new industries and new customer markets. Cars, which are built from atoms, are now integrated with information services such as the GM OnStarsystem, which is formed of bits. GM's in-vehicle communication system created new value through the addition of information services and also fostered a new industry with higher margins than those in the very mature automobile industry.

TARGET DOMINANT DESIGN LIFE CYCLES

Given that dominant technology designs drive the evolution of industries and markets, it is possible to achieve growth, even in a mature industry, using fourth-generation innovation strategies. Dominant designs are architectures with three layers: (1) product/process platforms, (2) business models, and (3) industry/market models. Dominant designs typically arise out of a chaotic market where many players compete to become the industry standard that supplies an emerging need in the market. They have a product and know-how core that is leveraged to produce new products and applications in a variety of markets. See Figure 13-2 for a depiction of the development of dominant designs, or platforms, in the computer industry. In addition, the design architecture dictates the rules for component and raw materials suppliers who come together to form the supply chain for the new design. Even companies that have survived for years on incremental innovation find that to continue to grow, they must disrupt that incremental innovation with radical innovation that produces a new platform of products.

BUILD VALUE THROUGH ARCHITECTURE AND CAPABILITY

New technology products (capabilities) are made up of knowledge, tools, technology, and processes or practices. Knowledge or know-how explains how the new technology is used; tools represent the products and services based on the dominant design. For customers, technology falls to the background in favor of applications, whereas for OEMs and integrators, the technology itself becomes the source of new product ideas. To realize sustainable innovation and growth, value must be created from each of these capabilities.

CREATE A DISTRIBUTION AND SUPPLY ARCHITECTURE

Two types of channels exist in the distribution and supply architecture: sales and knowledge channels. The traditional sales channel includes OEMs, distributors, value-added resellers (VARs), agents, and system integrators. These channel members

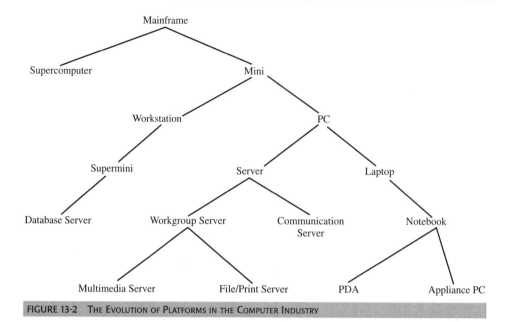

FIGURE 13-2   THE EVOLUTION OF PLATFORMS IN THE COMPUTER INDUSTRY

manage transactions, orders, accounts, and customers from the point of sale through the delivery of the product and service. The knowledge channel, by contrast, is used to build long-term relationships with customers, and value is created through personalization. Today, the knowledge channel provides more opportunities to create value than the traditional sales channel. Knowledge assets experience increasing returns and, unlike the technology itself, cannot be used up.

HELP CUSTOMERS CREATE TACIT KNOWLEDGE

Customers and other stakeholders will not appreciate a new dominant design unless they can experience it enough to provide input into its development, offer feedback on the prototype, and help to create new tacit knowledge from the experience of using the prototype. In other words, explicit knowledge is made tacit at the point at which it is internalized through experience.[19] That tacit knowledge is the crux of the value created by involving customers and other stakeholders in the entire business process. Once that tacit knowledge is observed and confirmed through field tests, it can be used to reveal latent needs.

PLAN STRATEGICALLY FOR INNOVATION

The creation of a dominant design is not a one-time experience in the evolution of a business, but rather one that must be planned as a regular piece of the innovation process. Although sustaining growth through incremental innovation is certainly part of any company's innovation portfolio, a plan for developing radical innovations that might lead to dominant designs is critical to sustainability in the long term. The strategic plan should incorporate activities that go outside the organization, such as partnering, licensing, acquisitions, and corporate venturing. This type of planning requires leadership that draws in all the functional areas of the business to share knowledge, resources, and know-how.

Growth through R&D efforts will involve both incremental and disruptive innovation. Although the majority of the effort will likely be on incremental innovations because they are less expensive and easier to introduce, a company must punctuate the evolutionary progress with technologies that leapfrog current technologies and establish new platforms on which to base further incremental innovations. DSP (digital signal processing) chips offer a classic example of this pattern. Over the past decade, the performance of DSP chips has steadily increased at the same time as the cost of those chips has decreased.[20] The new Texas Instruments TMS320C6X chip that contains more than 10 times the processing power of any currently existing commercial DSP device is a disruptive technology because it makes possible the development of new classes of DSP solutions for high-bandwidth applications such as 3D imaging and wireless base stations. When determining when to launch this disruptive technology, Texas Instruments studied future application needs and surrounded the technology with business and technical champions to increase its chance of success.

THE RISKS OF RADICAL INNOVATION

Advancing a technology can present some unusual challenges and risks. Physical risks are easily understood, for example, the risks that the Wright Brothers took as they went about perfecting the design of the first airplane. However, psychological risks are also a part of growth through R&D. Robert Goddard was a visionary who suffered much ridicule for his belief in rockets. When he launched the first liquid-fueled rocket over 75 years ago, he had no support; yet, what he accomplished formed the foundation for all that the United States has accomplished in space.[21] The risk associated with doing something new, innovative, and not understood is high. When the Hubble telescope was placed into orbit, it was discovered that an error of less than the width of a human hair in grinding the primary mirror resulted in blurry photographs. Critics of the project were quick to pronounce it a failure, but once the problem was corrected, Hubble was able to send back more than 270,000 images depicting what many call the beginning of the Universe.[22] Failure has often been the source of success. Harold Shapiro, president of Princeton University, once said, "History has shown us that failures are often just threads of a larger tapestry; until the tapestry is on the wall, the nature of the final pattern is difficult to discern. . . . A willingness to accept the risk of failure is one of the costs of leadership and, therefore, the price of all success."[23]

Those companies looking to discover the next breakthrough technology or to become the next standard need to fully prepare themselves for the risks and be willing to accept failure as part of the process.

GROWTH THROUGH CO-OPERATION AND ACQUISITION

Partnering with or acquiring other companies is an increasingly popular growth strategy in an era of rapid technological and economic change. However, a strategy that works well at start-up may not be equally effective when the company reaches maturity.

Roberts and Liu have proposed that a technology has four phases in its life cycle, and each requires a different approach to partnering with other companies: the fluid phase, the transitional phase, the mature phase, and the discontinuities phase.[24] See Figure 13-3 for an overview of the four phases and their corresponding co-operation and acquisition strategies.

The fluid phase is a time of great uncertainty and confusion as pioneering technologies enter the market in rapid succession. In general, barriers to entry are low and demand is high for the new technology. This is the time when companies seek to establish their technology as the standard through licensing and forming marketing alliances with key companies in the value chain. When Sun Microsystems introduced SPARC (scalable processor architecture) in 1989, it licensed the technology to 21 hardware manufacturers and software developers to extend its reach as quickly as possible.[25] It is also during this stage that large, established companies acquire small start-ups with unique technology that would be difficult for them to develop in-house because of their commitment to their current technology platform.

The transitional phase begins with the establishment of the dominant design that precipitates enormous demand for the technology (recall Moore's tornado in Chapter 12). The dominant design focuses the efforts of the industry toward developing applications and improvements on the standard. At this stage, large, established companies seeking to own a piece of the dominant design often acquire young companies that have adopted the dominant design and are developing extensions or improvements. New ventures that were not acquired early in their development may continue their growth and become the next generation of mature companies in the industry.

In the mature phase, the dominant design is ubiquitous, innovation in the product slows, and process innovation begins to come to the forefront. Process innovations take time and are expensive to develop. Companies often join forces to develop process innovations, as Fujitsu and Toshiba did to codevelop 1-gigabit DRAM computer chips.[26] Other companies, such as Cisco Systems, choose to acquire companies to gain access to proprietary technology. The other change that occurs during the mature stage

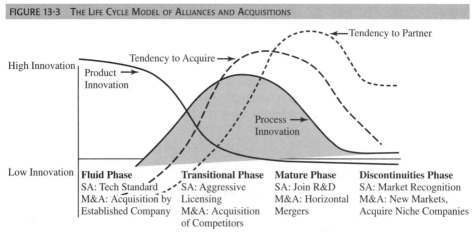

FIGURE 13-3   THE LIFE CYCLE MODEL OF ALLIANCES AND ACQUISITIONS

Source: Adapted from the work of Edward B. Roberts and Wenyun Kathy Liu, "Ally or Acquire: How Technology Leaders Decide," *MIT Sloan Management Review* 43, no. 1 (Fall 2001): 26–34.

is the commoditization of the technology, that is, competition on price becomes fierce, driving down margins, and customers tend to compare products based solely on price. In this situation, companies must reduce costs as much as possible and increase volume to make a profit. Marketing alliances are popular in this phase to pursue competitors, expand markets, and go after latent customers. Horizontal mergers such as that between Digital Equipment Corp. and Compaq in 1998 give companies a stronger base from which to compete. Some companies choose to divest themselves of noncore capabilities and focus on what they do best, as Texas Instruments did when it sold off its DRAM manufacturing facilities to Micron Technologies so that it could focus on digital-signal processing.

The entrance of a new disruptive technology that makes an established technology obsolete characterizes the discontinuities phase. Essentially, the cycle begins again with a new market being developed and new entrants appearing because of low entry barriers. Large, established companies tend to stop creating alliances and go into acquisition mode to build their capabilities, become more competitive, and simultaneously divest themselves of old technologies for which there is no longer a market. Whether cooperation or acquisition is the best strategy is a function of the stage in the life cycle of the technology.

STRATEGIC OUTSOURCING FOR KNOWLEDGE CAPABILITIES

At every stage of the technology life cycle, strategic outsourcing and partnering can be an excellent source of opportunity and profits for a growing high-tech venture. It is also a way to lower costs, risks, and fixed investments at the same time that the company increases flexibility, innovation, and value creation.[27] There are two basic categories of strategic outsourcing.

1. **Outsourcing for knowledge services or core capabilities.** Dell Computer is one of the best examples of a rapidly growing firm that concentrates on its core capabilities—customer knowledge and support—while outsourcing software and component design and manufacturing to specialized companies that provide those capabilities. By not focusing on the upstream value chain activities, Dell can devote its resources and time to building its expertise in long-term, loyal customer relationships. With more than 70 percent of its customers being large institutions, it assigns staff to each major customer to stay in touch with the customer's changing needs.

2. **Outsourcing for knowledge specialists.** Companies such as Chevron and Royal Dutch Shell regularly hire outside expertise to help them understand the sociopolitical conditions in the many countries in which they have drilling operations and refineries. They also hire real estate professionals to manage their land holdings. Other companies hire local professionals in tax, law, and insurance when they expand outside the borders of the United States.

Deciding which activities should become the company's core capabilities, that is, those activities for which it is known, is a process of exploring all the activities of the business and identifying a few "cross-functional, intellectually based service activities or knowledge and skill sets critical to customers" that the company can build to a world-class level that will define the business.[28] Although it is important to look at what competitors are doing, it is vital that the company not solely benchmark against competitors, that is, match what they are doing, because the company's core capabilities should create new value and be highly innovative, in other words, do things that competitors are not doing.

THE NATURE OF STRATEGIC ALLIANCES

A strategic alliance consists of two or more companies that join forces to undertake a joint project, share core competencies, or provide resources that one of the companies does not have. The first example of modern-day implementation of co-operation through multi-disciplinary teams came toward the end of World War II when the United States committed to the idea that splitting an atom could produce a massive explosion. With this idea, the Manhattan Project was born, and a multidisciplinary team succeeded in developing the atomic bomb. The creativity and opportunity recognition skills of the staff of the Manhattan Project and others led to a proliferation of new product ideas and technologies in the 1970s and 1980s. Unfortunately, however, very few of these ideas or products were actually commercialized.[29] At the end of the Cold War, U.S. companies faced increasing competition from Europe, with its large stable of technologies, and from Japan and other Pacific Rim countries that were taking advantage of fast-cycle product development competencies to achieve amazing rates of technological progress.[30] U.S companies were also sadly out of date in their organizational structures and processes, and decision making was influenced by the pressure to produce short-term profits. Consequently, U.S. companies were not doing what they needed to do to remain competitive, including moving new products into the market more quickly.[31] By the early 1990s, however, some companies had figured out that to be successful in geographically diverse markets, it was necessary to join forces with other companies to develop and commercialize technologies. Thus, the term "strategic alliance" became popular. Through a co-operation agreement or strategic alliance, the owner of a technology could accomplish several objectives:[32]

- Determine the feasibility of commercializing a particular technology
- Assess the utility of the technology in terms of applications and modifications of ways to use the technology in the real world
- Accurately target specific customers for the various applications of the technology
- Bring together the people who could make commercialization possible—industry partners, financial partners, etc.

The bottom line is that companies form strategic alliances to gain access to resources, skills, and knowledge that would be too costly to develop on their own and also to establish the standards for an industry. General Motors and Toyota joined forces to promote battery-powered electric, fuel-cell-powered electric, and hybrid vehicles and set the standards in the automotive industry for a new generation of automobiles. The ability to set standards for an industry is a critical achievement, one that is absolutely necessary for mainstream adoption of a new technology. When a variety of companies can produce applications from a common set of design principles, customers more readily overcome their resistance to new technology and purchase it. This encourages more companies to develop products from the core technology, creating more value. The issue of setting standards is considered in more detail later in the chapter.

Choosing a strategic partner is a critical decision that must be made as carefully as choosing an investor or a key management employee. It is important to understand why a potential company is willing to partner and what its motives are. Is the entire company behind the alliance or only the person assigned to the partnership? If that person leaves, what does that mean to the alliance? A company that is able to help its partner commercialize a technology should already work in an area that will use applications of the technology; it should also be one of the leading users of that technology and be able to assess the value of the technology to the customer. The strategic partner should see collaboration as a way to gain early access to a technology it needs. For example, a small Scandinavian manufacturer of a new water purification system assembled a panel of leaders in industries dealing with wastewater management and desalination to consider the manufacturer's technology and its potential applications. The panel found several applications, and more than half the panel committed to immediate exploration of a commercial relationship.[33] That commitment resulted in the small start-up that was able to secure government funding for additional development and marketing.

Strategic alliances occur at different points in time. Precompetitive alliances occur prior to the commercialization of the technology and are usually created for the development of a product, whereas competitive alliances are partnerships that provide competing companies with a common ground and common goals. For example, the Semiconductor Manufacturing Technology Consortium (SEMATECH) was a coalition of U.S. semiconductor manufacturers that formed in 1987 to overcome the threat of Japanese competition in their markets. SEMATECH resulted in firms pooling their resources to design and build chips faster and with more features. The industry, which had been in decline, regained its position 5 years later.[34]

VERTICAL ALLIANCES

Vertical alliances occur up and down the value chain with suppliers, distributors, or customers. The partners in a vertical alliance seek to acquire a technology or a specific core competency or resource. A technology venture may form a partnership with a supplier to secure better prices and faster access to components and raw materials. Alliances with distributors allow the company better access to customers, whereas alliances with customers provide important feedback during product development as well as for all the other activities of the business. Customers act as beta testers to check the technology in a real-world environment before it is formally launched to a wider market. At the precompetitive stage, the technology is jointly developed for the benefit of both companies. These types of alliances often weaken when the commercialization stage is reached. At the competitive stage, two competitors of equal size may join forces to develop a technology that allows them to compete effectively against a third competitor.

HORIZONTAL ALLIANCES

Horizontal alliances are formed with companies in the same position in the value chain, that is, competing firms or firms that produce products that complement the new venture firm's products. In horizontal alliances, the partners want to capture a particular market and collaborate to offer a total solution. For example, Hewlett-Packard and Kodak joined forces to capture the digital photography market by using Kodak's thermal dye transfer process to produce prints on HP printers.[35] During the precompetitive stage, the partners work to develop a common product for a common market. During the competitive stage, the alliances take the form of distribution and cross-licensing agreements, often to establish the standards in an industry by combining the strengths of two or more competitors.

THE NEGATIVES

If value chain partners were highly effective, efficient, and reliable, companies would outsource everything but their core capabilities. The reality is that strategic alliances entail risks that include delays, unexpected transaction costs, security breaches, and quality issues. For all the benefits of strategic alliances, some research has reported that their failure rate is as high as 80 percent,[36] whereas other reports put it closer to two-thirds of all alliances.[37] Part of the reason for the failure of an alliance is that small technology businesses frequently enter into a partnership agreement from a position of weakness, that is, they need resources to accomplish their goals, and the other firm, which does not really need anything from the smaller business, is placed in a position of power. Moreover, resource dependency when there are only a limited number of potential partners can result in poor performance on the part of the small firm that was unable to find the appropriate partner. Another common reason for failure is that the company that is seeking the specialized capability still tries to dictate how the activity will take place, which undermines the innovative efforts of the strategic partner that was brought on board for its core capability.

GETTING IT RIGHT

To improve the chances that a strategic alliance will be successful, a few systems and controls must be in place.

- Prepare for the alliance by conducting due diligence on the potential partner to make sure that the two firms will be compatible in their company goals and culture. The partners should develop goals, incentives, timelines, and metrics for measuring progress and performance.
- Put procurement and contract management specialists in place to track the experiences of the strategic alliance and monitor its progress.
- Develop knowledge systems to collect, evaluate, and monitor what outside suppliers are doing.
- Develop feedback mechanisms that make it possible to use the knowledge gained from the alliance to improve other areas of the business and to create a better interface between suppliers, the company, and downstream partners.

RISK FACTORS AND REMEDIES IN CO-OPERATION

Although the benefits of co-operation are many, the risks are high and should be weighed against the benefits when making any decision to partner with another company. The ultimate success of the launch of a new technology under a co-operation agreement depends on all the parties involved. No one company can ensure success for all. Consequently, one of the most vexing aspects of strategic alliances is joint decision making and giving up some control to another company, particularly where there is a size disparity between the firms. Research has confirmed that partnerships are more successful and equitable when the firms are of similar size.[38] When a start-up firm partners with a large, established firm to access resources, manufacturing, and dis-

❖ **A Study of Co-operation in the Photonics Industry**

Photonics, or opto-electronics, is an important industry because it has strategic applications in a variety of other industries such as lasers, telecommunications, and entertainment. Today, the industry is characterized by a great number of small to mid-sized enterprises concentrated in regional clusters and interacting through strategic alliances and other types of relationships with firms around the world. A multinational study conducted by Hendry, Brown, and Defillippi, found that, up to the late 1980s, the telecommunications and military markets drove growth in the U.S. and UK photonics industries.[39] After the collapse of the Soviet Union in 1989, the industry was the victim of a decline in spending on laser weapons and military equipment; telecommunications were deregulated, and fragmentation of the photonics industry occurred. Ironically, these events encouraged the collaboration now seen in the industry because larger firms are put in the position of becoming systems integrators and customers to the smaller firms.[40]

Typically, clusters of optics businesses occur around a university or a large firm, which serves as the catalyst for small business development. Most of the clusters form from spin-offs from existing companies or out of universities, and they set up shop close to the parent. For example, the Pilkington Company in North Wales has been the source of nine new start-ups, some of which supply the parent company, as well as other local firms, with services for testing equipment and marketing.[41]

tribution capability, the success of the partnership is dependent on the agreed-upon governance structure. In some cases, partners give each other control over specific aspects of the commercialization process; for example, the start-up firm makes decisions regarding design and development and the partner firm has control over manufacturing and distribution. In other cases, decisions are made jointly, which works when the companies have similar cultures and goals. Unfortunately, the fact is that most partnerships do not achieve their stated goals when they do not have compatible corporate cultures and goals.

The potential for trade secret violation is another risk of partnering.[42] Trade secrets are normally protected through contracts and nondisclosure agreements, but when two companies are working closely together, it is very difficult to completely protect trade secrets such as know-how and supplier and customer lists. That is why it so critical to choose strategic alliances carefully and to make certain that all parties are receiving equitable benefits from the arrangement and sharing equally in the risk. The transfer of trade secret information should be made in stages, with the final and most important information held back until all contracts between the parties are signed and the strategic alliance is a done deal.

Closely aligned with the risk of trade secret disclosure is the risk associated with the transference of knowledge. During the course of a strategic alliance, knowledge in the form of technical specifications, product designs, and so forth are transferred to the partner that needs them. In addition to this explicit knowledge, tacit knowledge, or know-how, is also transferred, sometimes unconsciously or unintentionally. The problem with the transference of tacit knowledge, which includes skills, procedures, thought processes, and other ways of doing things, is that once it is transferred, the firm that transferred it is no longer needed. This poses a substantial risk to the transferring firm.[43] Herein lies the dilemma of knowledge transfer: The transfer of tacit knowledge is essential to a close collaborative partnership, but that very closeness poses an increased risk to the partnering firm. Research has found that a firm that has a high level of technological innovation is less likely to use transparent types of collaborative arrangements because of the very risk of the transference of tacit knowledge that is critical to its success.[44]

Yet another risk of strategic alliances is the potential to violate U.S. antitrust laws.[45] This risk is particularly high when the partnership has the potential to affect pricing or supply within the industry. In 1999, to combat partnerships of this type, the FTC issued a set of Guidelines for Collaborations Among Competitors, which can be found at *www.ftc.gov/bc/guidelin.htm*.

STRATEGIES FOR SETTING TECHNOLOGY STANDARDS

The first mover in an industry has the potential to set the standards for all subsequent technology that later entrants might develop, but this is not an automatic advantage. To dictate standards, a company must have a well-executed strategy to achieve rapid adoption of the technology and to protect it when competitors come on the scene. When Microsoft joined forces with Intel, the goal was to capture the hardware and operating-system side of the computer industry in order to set the standard. There are a number of ways that companies with new technologies can attempt to become the standard-bearers: licensing, alliances, and diversification.[46] Table 13-1 presents an overview of the decision criteria for choosing a particular strategy.

TABLE 13-1   Decision Criteria for a Technology Standards Strategy

First Mover and Complementary Products Provider	*Licensor*	*Strategic Alliance*	*Diversification*
• Intellectual property • High barriers to entry • Required skills • Required resources • No immediate competitors	• Low entry barriers • Many potential competitors • Firm lacks all resources and skills to commercialize	• Firm cannot develop the technology alone • Barriers to entry are high • Many potential competitors capable of imitation	• Intellectual property • Sufficient resources and skills

LICENSING

Allowing others to develop applications and distribute the technology in different markets makes it possible to get the technology adopted more rapidly. This strategy helps the company quickly build an installed base of users and bring on board competitors who may otherwise have attempted to develop their own versions of the technology. Of course, licensing is not without its problems. Sometimes licensing to competitors and others can result in the inventing company losing its monopoly position in the market if a licensee develops a dominant application from the technology. It may also cause prices to drop more precipitously than if the first mover had controlled the market for a period of time.

STRATEGIC ALLIANCES

Like licensing, strategic alliances or partnerships help diffuse the technology more rapidly than a single company could accomplish on its own. Four different companies with competing technologies initially pursued digital audio technology in the form of compact discs. Philips was on a path to become the first mover but was concerned that incompatibility with emerging technologies from the other three competitors might keep it from setting the industry standard. To strengthen its position, Philips formed an alliance with Sony to develop the compact disc system, and that partnership resulted in more than 30 firms agreeing to license the new technology.[47] This is one example of how a strategic alliance can build momentum and the critical mass necessary to achieve mainstream adoption.

DIVERSIFICATION

In the early stages of a new technology, the first mover often does not have an installed base of sufficient size to encourage the development of complementary products by other companies. It is a catch-22 situation where the company needs more customers to adopt the technology, but to get more customers to adopt, it needs complementary products, which it cannot get partners to develop without more customers. Under this scenario, the firm usually opts to develop some initial complementary products itself to get the ball rolling. Unfortunately, this is a gamble because these applications or complementary products typically take the firm outside its core competency. Failure to achieve adoption of the technology after using a diversification strategy will take a tremendous toll on the business.

For a new technology venture, growth can be an exhilarating roller coaster ride or a precipitous fall into oblivion. What determines which outcome the venture experiences is the company's growth strategy and the plan to achieve it. It must be appropriate for the life cycle stage of the technology and the capabilities of the company.

❖ SUMMARY

Growth is a natural by-product of a successful start-up, and it signals that the market wants what the company is offering. A competition-based growth strategy has little to recommend it in an economy where supply often exceeds demand and customers are regularly barraged with new innovations. In contrast, a value-innovation strategy creates new markets, new profits, and new growth, and it does so by using tacit knowledge created inside the company, which means that a company can be successful despite industry and market conditions. When growth does not go smoothly, it is usually because of undercapitalization, lack of sufficient and qualified human capital, the inertia of success, and failure to stay in touch with the business. Successful growth requires that the entrepreneur pay attention to details, hire cautiously, not assume that growth will continue indefinitely, be able to turn down customers when necessary, and bring in professional management at the right time. Beyond conventional growth strategies, the new venture should consider growth through R&D. The creation of a dominant design is not a one-time experience in the evolution of a business, but rather one that must be planned as a regular part of the innovation process. Although sustaining growth through incremental innovation is certainly part of any company's innovation portfolio, a plan for developing radical innovations that might lead to dominant designs is critical to sustainability in the long term. Partnering with or acquiring other companies is an increasingly popular growth strategy in an era of rapid technological and economic change. A technology has four phases in its life cycle, and each requires a different approach to partnering with other companies: the fluid phase, the transitional phase, the mature phase, and the discontinuities phase. At every stage of the tech life cycle, strategic outsourcing and partnering can be an excellent source of opportunity and profits for a growing high-tech venture. It is also a way to lower costs, risks, and fixed investments at the same time that the company increases flexibility, innovation, and value creation.

❖ DISCUSSION QUESTIONS

1. What is the primary challenge of rapid growth? Why? How can that challenge be overcome?
2. Which strategies are appropriate at which points in the technology growth cycle, and why?
3. Why are strategic alliances a necessary component of a high-tech growth strategy?
4. How can outsourcing create growth opportunities for a new venture?
5. What are some strategies that help a company build a technology standard in an industry?

❖ RESOURCES

Catlin, Katherine, and Jana Matthews. *Leading at the Speed of Growth: Journey from Entrepreneur to CEO.* Chicago, IL: Hungry Minds, Inc., 2001.

Hill, Charles W. L. *International Business: Competing in the Global Marketplace: Postscript 2001.* New York: Irwin Professional Publishing, 2000.

McKnight, Lee W., Paul M. Vaaler, and Raul L. Katz. *Creative Destruction: Business Survival Strategies in the Global Internet Economy.* Cambridge, MA: MIT Press, 2001.

Whiteley, R., and D. Hessan. *Customer-Centered Growth.* Reading, MA: Addison-Wesley, 1996.

Wolf, J. S. *Export Profits.* Dover, NH: Upstart Publishing Company, Inc., 1992.

Woznick, Alexandra, and Edward G. Hinkelman. *A Basic Guide to Exporting,* 3d ed. Novato, CA: World Trade Press, 2000.

❖ INTERNET RESOURCES

Global Business Online
www.exporttoday.com
Tips for businesses that want to trade
internationally

International Business Forum
www.ibf.com
Site geared toward entrepreneurs who want
to get into the international marketplace.
Contains lists of resources in various countries, opportunities, and associations

The International Trade Desk
members.aol.com/tradedesk/
A screening site for key trade information

The Internationalist
www.internationalist.com
An excellent source of information on a wide
range of international issues including business, investment, and travel

International Trade Administration
www.ita.doc.gov
A division of the U.S. Department of
Commerce. Assists companies that wish to
export

RAPID GROWTH WITH BLACKBERRY?

Is there any reason to believe that a relatively boring company located in the industrial city of Waterloo in southwestern Ontario, Canada, could attract the attention of companies such as Motorola and start a buzz at one of the most important wireless trade shows in the world? Technology success story Research In Motion (RIM) set the wireless world spinning in 1999 when it launched the BlackBerry, a two-way pager the size of a pack of cigarettes with a screen for displaying text and built-in Tic-Tac-sized keys for punching in e-mail messages. It was touted as the first truly wireless communications appliance. RIM never looked back as industry giants such as IBM, Intel Corp, Merrill Lynch, and Oracle gave the devices to their employees. Despite its swift rise to prominence, RIM was not spared the steep slide of the stock market. Remarkably, while its stock declined, BlackBerry sales never slowed. In fact, in April 2001, RIM had a stellar fourth quarter with a profit of $8.3 million, an increase of 159 percent over the previous year. In 9 months, it more than doubled its workforce, to over 1,400 employees. Plans are now in place to build a second manufacturing facility to increase its capacity by sixfold.

RIM's headquarters reflects the seriousness with which it does business. A modest building houses uninspiring cubicles designed to fulfill the company's mission: to push data packets to the customer's hip. The location of the headquarters is more important than it appears on the surface. RIM's headquarters is located near the William G. Davis Computer Research Centre at the University of Waterloo, one of the most respected sources of high-technology research in the world. About 20 percent of RIM's employees come from the Davis Research Centre, and Mike Lazardis, president and co-CEO of RIM, believes

that this relationship is one of the principal reasons that RIM has been successful.

RIM was founded in 1989, several years before corporate America embraced the notion of e-mail. While professors and scientists were wired to the ARPANET, RIM's employees were already sending wireless e-mail messages to each other via a Hewlett-Packard 95LX Palmtop PC. Through the passion that its employees displayed with the concept of always-on wireless e-mail, RIM knew that it had to find a way to make this device practical and useful.

The company faced many design challenges. In addition to meeting the challenge of building a miniature, low-power, low-cost radio transceiver and reversing the flow of data on the Internet so that data would come to the user, they faced the inherent constraints of the wireless world: memory, power, and bandwidth. To attempt to overcome these challenges, RIM began the design odyssey by defining what the BlackBerry was not so that they could decide was it actually was.

In 1992, RIM was beginning to grow, and Lazaridis knew that, being an engineer, he needed help on the business side, so he brought in Jim Balsillie as co-CEO. One of the first things that Lazaridis did was to make sure the company stayed focused on its core capabilities while it was enjoying the beginnings of success. He knew that if the company was distracted by diverse projects that strained its limited resources, it would be stretched too thin during its growth and could ultimately fail.

One mistake the company made was when it sought a strategic partnership with Oracle to get wireless access to databases. Balsillie was stubborn on a couple of issues in the agreement; Oracle backed away from the deal and did not come back for 5 years. RIM learned that it is important not to go for the big win on every deal, but to make slow, steady progress.

RIM 's success put it on the industry radar screen, and it quickly learned that when you are no longer working under the radar, competitors will use any means to disrupt progress. For example, Glenayre Technologies, a competitor, filled a lawsuit against RIM for patent infringement. RIM received a favorable verdict in July 2001, but in May 2001, RIM filed an infringement suit against Glenayre alleging false advertising, unfair competition, dilution, and patent and trademark infringement. This was one of many lawsuits the company began to face.

In November 2001, RIM was hit with a complaint by a group of U.S. inventors claiming patent infringement on eight patents controlled by NTP Inc., a holding company. The complaint relates to the use of radio frequencies (RF), or wireless communications in mail systems. The eight patents were filed prior to the filing of a key process patent by RIM in May 1998. Analysts believe that RIM's process patent, which was granted in April 2001, will come under attack because as a process, it can control the market for sending and receiving e-mail from a wireless device using a single address, meaning that many of the companies competing in the wireless space would end up paying license fees to RIM. How will this affect RIM's growth strategy? Can it afford to divert its resources to fight legal battles at the same time it needs them to grow?

Meanwhile, RIM continues to partner with major companies to push its technology into more markets. Balsillie believes that RIM will compete favorably against large competitors such as Motorola and Palm because they have been in the wireless space from the beginning and have built a complex service with over 246,000 subscribers in 12,000 companies. ■

Sources: Bill Breen, "Rapid Motion," *Fast Company* (August 2001): *www.fastcompany.com*; "RIM Comments on Patent Complaint," *PR NewsWire (*August 26, 1999): *www.prnewswire.com/;* Ian Karleff, "RIM's BlackBerry Patent Challenged by U.S. Group," *Reuters*, November 21, 2001; Elizabeth Hurt, "Research in Motion Sues Competitor," *Business 2.0* (May 17, 2001): *www.business2.0.com.*

❖ NOTES

1. W. C. Kim and R. Mauborgne, "When Competitive Advantage Is Neither," *Wall Street Journal*, 21 April 1997a, 22.
2. W. Chan Kim, "Strategy, Value Innovation, and the Knowledge Economy," *Sloan Management Review* 40, no. 3 (Spring 1999): 41–55.
3. Ibid., 41–55.
4. Ibid.
5. W. Chan Kim and R. Mauborgne, "How to Leapfrog the Competition," *Wall Street Journal*, European ed., 6 March 1997e, 10.
6. Ibid.
7. C. W. L. Hill, "Differentiation Versus Low Cost or Differentiation and Low Cost," *Academy of Management Review* 13 (July 1988): 401–412.
8. T. M. Amabile, "How to Kill Creativity," *Harvard Business Review* 76 (September–October 1998): 76–87.
9. Emily Barker, "Size Counts," *Inc.* 23, no. 10 (July 2001): 42–49.
10. Stephen C. Harper, *Managing Growth in Your Emerging Business* (New York: McGraw-Hill, 1995).
11. Ibid., 39.
12. Lee Smith, "Five Secrets of Growth," *FSB: Fortune Small Business* 11, no. 6 (July–August 2001): 54.
13. Ibid.
14. Harper, *Managing Growth in Your Emerging Business*, 74.
15. Kathleen Allen, *Growing and Managing an Entrepreneurial Business* (Boston: Houghton Mifflin, 1999), 236–237.
16. William L. Miller, "Innovation for Business Growth," *Research–Technology Management* 44, no. 5 (2001): 26–41.
17. C. Christensen and M. Overdorf, "Meeting the Challenge of Disruptive Change,"

Harvard Business Review 78, no. 2 (March–April 2000): 66–76.

18. William L. Miller and Langdon Morris, *Fourth Generation R&D: Managing Knowledge, Technology, and Innovation* (New York: John Wiley & Sons, 1999).

19. Ibid. 302–303.

20. Michael Hames, "Balance Your Innovation Strategy," Electronic Business (May 1998): 1.

21. NASA FACTS: Robert H. Goddard: American Rocket Pioneer, *www.gsfc.nasa. gov/gsfc/service/gallery/fact_sheets/general/ goddard/goddard.htm.*

22. Vance D. Coffman, "The Risk of Playing It Safe: The Importance of Research and Development," *Vital Speeches of the Day* 67, no. 14 (May 1, 2001): 428–431.

23. Ibid.

24. Edward B. Roberts and Wenyun Kathy Liu, "Ally or Acquire: How Technology Leaders Decide," *MIT Sloan Management Review* 43, no. 1 (Fall 2001): 26–34.

25. Ibid., 27.

26. Ibid., 28.

27. James Brian Quinn, "Strategic Outsourcing: Leveraging Knowledge Capabilities," *Sloan Management Review* 40, no. 4 (Summer 1999): 9–21.

28. Ibid., 9–21.

29. J. W. Kunetka, *City of Fire: Los Alamos and the Birth of the Atomic Age*, 1943–1945 (Upper Saddle River, NJ: Prentice Hall, 1978).

30. G. Stalk, Jr., and A. M. Webber, "Japan's Dark Side of Time," *Harvard Business Review* 71, no. 4 (July–August 1993): 93–102.

31. Ibid.

32. Richard A. Siegel and Sten-Olof Hansen, "Accelerating the Commercialization of Technology," *Industrial Management and Data Systems* 95, no. 1 (1995): 18.

33. Ibid., 14.

34. Larry D. Browning, Janice M. Beyer, and Judy C. Shetler, "Building Cooperation in a Competitive Industry: SEMATECH and the Semiconductor Industry," (Special Research Forum: Intra- and Interorganizational

Cooperation), *Academy of Management Journal* 38 (February 1995): 113–139.

35. Mohr, 2001, p. 75.

36. Ranjay Gulati, Tarun Khanna, and Nitin Nohria, "Unilateral Commitments and the Importance of Process in Alliances," *Sloan Management Review* 35, no. 3 (Spring 1994): 61–69.

37. Benjamin Gomes-Casseres, "Joint Ventures in the Face of Global Competition," *Sloan Management Review* 30, no. 3 (Spring 1989): 17–26.

38. Louis P. Bucklin and Sanjit Sengupta, "Organizing Successful Co-Marketing Alliances," *Journal of Marketing* 57 (April 1993): 32–46.

39. Chris Hendry, James Brown, and Robert Defillippi, "Regional Clustering of High-Technology-based Firms: Opto-Electronics in Three Countries," *Regional Studies* 34, no. 2 (April 2000): 129–144.

40. G. Lorenzoni and C. Baden-Fuller, "Creating a Strategic Center to Manage a Web of Partners," *California Management Review* 37, no. 3 (1995): 146–163.

41. Hendry et al., "Regional Clustering of High-Technology-based Firms," 129–144.

42. Dale Littler, Fiona Leverick, and Margaret Bruce, "Factors Affecting the Process of Collaborative Product Development," *Journal of Product Innovation Management* 12 (1995): 16–32.

43. Shantanu Dutta and Allen M. Weiss, "The Relationship Between a Firm's Level of Technological Innovativeness and Its Pattern of Partnership Agreements," *Management Science* 43 (March 1997): 343–356.

44. Ibid.

45. Jakki Mohr, Gregory T. Gundlach, and Robert Spekman, "Legal Ramifications of Strategic Alliances," *Marketing Management* 3, no. 2 (1994): 38–46.

46. Charles Hill, "Establishing a Standard: Competitive Strategy and Technological Standards in Winner-Take-All Industries," *Academy of Management Executive* 11 (May 1997:) 7–25.

47. Mohr, 2001, p. 80.

14

ENTREPRENEURIAL VENTURING INSIDE A CORPORATION

OVERVIEW

This chapter will examine

❖ the nature of corporate venturing

❖ the role of change in facilitating corporate venturing

❖ the paths to corporate venturing

❖ success as a corporate entrepreneur

INTRODUCTION

It is logical to assume that large firms have an advantage when it comes to innovation, particularly radical innovation, because they often have the deep resources that allow them to take more risk, hire the right people, and accomplish things that young entrepreneurial ventures cannot easily do. However, the reality is that large companies do not have an excellent track record in innovation. They are not known for stimulating radical ideas at the grassroots level, mostly because of short-term thinking and bureaucratic organizational structures. The work of Clayton Christensen first introduced the idea that large companies are superior at developing incremental innovations off existing technology platforms but resistant to the development of disruptive technology that makes previous standards obsolete.[1] One of the primary reasons for this paradox is that large firms are driven by current markets and rigid financial structures that influence the way they look at new product investments. Still, the increasing rate at which large firms are developing new venture strategies and incorporating the entrepreneurial mindset into the organization stems from the need to identify "new combinations of productive resources" and extend the capabilities of the firm.[2] Successful corporate entrepreneurship helps the company acquire new capabilities,[3] develop new revenue streams,[4] enter new businesses, and improve profitability.[5]

In 1999 alone, more than 400 U.S. corporations invested in entrepreneurial start-ups, and more than 200 had formal venture programs. However, during the first 3 months of 2001, corporate venturing investment declined 81 percent, in part due to the volatility of the stock market and recessionary indicators.[6] Despite weak economic times, companies such as Boeing are moving ahead with their new venture groups and developing more effective strategies for managing intellectual property.

A corporate venture is distinct from other corporate projects in several important ways. A corporate venture is a project that is new to the company and carries a much higher risk of failure than other projects. A great deal of uncertainty is associated with the project, so it is often managed separately at some point in time. Corporate ventures are generally undertaken to move the company in new directions, reinvent the company, increase sales, or to help the company become more competitive.

To achieve successful corporate entrepreneurship requires the ongoing support of senior management, which is not always easy to gain.[7] One reason for this is that executives often do not have an ownership interest in the companies they manage, so they tend only to support projects that will increase their job security and personal wealth.[8] Moreover, corporate entrepreneurship champions endure significant risk, as less than 20 percent of new product introductions succeed, and those that do survive are usually unprofitable in the early years.[9] Even more discouraging, approximately 70 percent of all new international ventures fail.[10] Therefore, for all the benefits of corporate venturing, the risks to the financial health of the parent company and its shareholders are significant. Consequently, it is no wonder that senior management hesitates to embark on such a path.

Early research dating back to the 1970s points to the importance of corporate entrepreneurship (CE), and interest in that subject has continued to grow as large companies increasingly seek ways to become more entrepreneurial, and, therefore, more competitive. Research on corporate entrepreneurship has found that:

- CE is an effective way to create new revenue streams.[11]
- Entrepreneurial activities stimulate product/process innovation.[12]
- Corporate venturing is a source of organizational growth.[13]
- Entrepreneurial activities spur the company to take risks and pioneer new product/process development, thereby making it more competitive.[14]
- Entrepreneurial activities help the company overcome resource limitations.[15]

Many large companies look at corporate venturing as a way to become more entrepreneurial and to attract entrepreneurs into their businesses. Cisco, the network infrastructure company, has been acquiring small start-ups for a long time. Cisco looks for companies offering a promising technology that is due for launch in 6 to 12 months. In the first 6 months of 2000, Cisco acquired one new start-up every 2 weeks.[16]

Large, established companies such as Chrysler have used CE to turn their companies around. By empowering employees to make decisions and putting customer needs first, Chrysler was able to launch the era of the minivan, revolutionizing the auto industry and leading to a series of design innovations that brought Chrysler back from a near-death experience. The entrepreneurial spirit, coupled with a flexible organizational structure, facilitates a market orientation that is proactive about seeking competitive intelligence, recombining resources in new ways, and implementing strategic responses.[17]

THE NATURE OF CORPORATE VENTURING

Corporate ventures can access one critical resource that most new start-ups cannot—the core competencies and tacit knowledge that have developed in the organization over time. This competitive advantage gives the corporate venture a significant edge over the independent start-up. However, the drawbacks of starting a venture inside a large corporation will frequently temper that advantage. One of those drawbacks is core competency. The term *core competency* has three dimensions. One dimension is resources—the knowledge, capabilities, and assets that the firm has developed.[18] The second dimension is the ability of the firm to make use of those resources, also called the capabilities of the firm. The third dimension is the company culture, which involves the decision making that links the resources with the capabilities. The problem is that frequently in large organizations knowledge and skills become habits that are institutionalized over time, creating what are known as *core rigidities*. The qualitative research of Dougherty on Techco Chemical Ltd. provides some insight into the issue of core competencies and core rigidities when it comes to innovation.[19] Techco is a chemical products company whose core competencies include a "deep knowledge" of a particular chemical technology and the ability to deal creatively with user needs. The firm was built on an initial radical innovation in a chemical process. Over several decades, the founder instilled his vision into the employees, which included being technology focused and developing inventive solutions to customer needs. Over time, however, and with little competition, their core competencies began to become sources of incompetence. If a technology was "neat," unique, and could be produced at a low cost, the company would make it, regardless of whether it was creating value or needed by customers. Its success at technology development led the company to focus most of its efforts on the product side of the business rather than on marketing. Techco was considered a technology push company; if they built it, customers would come. Unfortunately, the technology life cycle caught up with the company; their core business began to experience declining sales, which forced the company to begin looking for new uses for its technology.

Techco had developed a power source with a special packaging that would prevent chemicals in a power source from leaking inside machinery. The engineers decided that this packaging could be sold as a separate product and began to look for a market. They settled on an industry that used a lot of batteries—the toy industry—figuring that they would provide a power source that had a longer shelf life, was more reliable, and was less likely to leak than conventional alkaline batteries. The product had an odd shape and was priced higher than batteries, but it was "neat" and unique, so they pursued it. It took the company 6 months, during which it applied for several patents, to learn that they did not understand who the customer was. Toy makers were not interested in including the new power source in their toys because it would raise the price of their product, and consumers consider price when they purchase toys. Consumers, they found, were just as happy using cheaper alkaline batteries. After 3 years of failed effort, Techno decided to end that product line. Their core competency—product design—had become their core incompetency because they did not realize that customers in this new industry might not appreciate uniqueness over a commodity product such as a battery.

The resources of both corporate ventures and independent start-ups are affected by three environmental conditions: time, success hurdles, and boundaries.[20] The gestation period for a corporate venture tends to be nearly twice as long as that for an independent start-up, taking much longer to reach profitability.[21] One of the reasons for this difference is that corporate ventures are generally insulated from external environments by a parent company that can afford to suffer a negative cash flow for a longer period of time because the new venture is just one item in their portfolio of products and ventures. In contrast, the independent start-up has more limited resources; the entrepreneur must not only fund the business, but also take care of their personal life as well.

Another issue related to time is that in the corporate venture the development schedule is typically set by people external to the project so that the schedule meshes with corporate objectives. Thus, the project moves more slowly through the development process and accesses resources at a slower pace because it is subject to the systems and controls of the parent company.

Yet another difference between corporate ventures and entrepreneurial start-ups is that corporate ventures are subject to success hurdles, externally imposed objectives in terms of financial performance and strategic fit. A new corporate venture may have to achieve an overall return on investment in excess of 30 percent and 10 percent annual profit before taxes. One large oil company will not look at a new venture possibility unless it can achieve $1 billion in sales within 2 years. Moreover, the new venture opportunity must fit strategically with the parent corporation, which explains why so many large companies are not successful at radical innovation. By definition, the new venture does not have a strategic fit with the current platform of technologies. Entrepreneurial ventures have the freedom to set whatever success hurdles they deem appropriate or desirable.

Finally, corporate ventures tend to inherit the rigid hierarchies of their parents. Although these existing structures may offer some incubation protection for the new venture, they also shelter it from opportunity and resources that do not fit within the parent's strategic plan. On the other hand, the new venture can trade on the reputation and legitimacy of the parent company to seek outside financing more easily than the independent entrepreneur can.

THE ROLE OF CHANGE IN FACILITATING CORPORATE VENTURING

Organizations tend to learn from previous experience; therefore, change comes about only as it is related to the organizational history.[22] An organization's performance, then, can affect its ability to change. Two factors appear to true about organizational change: (1) it involves risk, and (2) risk-taking is related to goals. Typically, a firm will not change its behavior, even in the face of feedback that suggests that changing would be prudent, if there is a goal associated with that behavior. The reason for this is that decision makers often commit and stay committed to activities doomed to failure because they resist change unless they can readily see an attractive alternative.[23] Firms are more likely to change if they have developed routines and procedures for making changes.[24]

CORE COMPETENCY VERSUS CHANGE

Most companies succeed in building a core competency or primary capability for which they are known. However, this same competency can be their downfall if they succumb to the inertia of success. Believing that they must be doing something right, they fear changing their pattern of success, and in doing so leave themselves vulnerable to a competing company that finds a gap in what they are doing or creates new value in a completely different way. Relying on a core set of skills or a core technology often prevents a firm from making the important leap to a new technological platform that will enable it to diversify its product offerings. History speaks to the benefit of taking on the risk associated with change. Hewlett-Packard had no expertise in computers when it decided to become a leader in that industry; Disney had no experience with theme parks when it designed and developed Disneyland. Companies such as these took an enormous risk and moved outside their core competency to radically innovate.

To survive in today's rapidly changing environment, large firms must explore technologies that will make their core competencies obsolete or face being made obsolete by someone else. Classical economist Joseph Schumpeter referred to this notion as "creative destruction." The willingness of a firm to cannibalize its own technologies may actually be the secret to its ultimate success.[25] Companies typically apply incremental improvements to existing technology, but at some point the return on investment in incremental improvements begins to diminish. If the firm does not introduce a new platform of technologies before those diminishing returns reach zero, it risks losing its place in the market. Consequently, it is vital that large firms pursue radical innovation on a regular basis. However, developing and marketing radical or disruptive technologies inside a large corporation is no simple task, as the pressure to produce incremental technologies is very powerful. Incremental innovations improve product performance, are immediately perceived as more valuable by customers, are easier to take to the mainstream market, and provide high profit margins.[26] Incremental innovations by competitors rarely cause the downfall of a strong firm, but established firms are threatened by companies competing with radical innovations, even though those innovations typically have lower initial performance, are not yet valued by mainstream customers, and provide low profit margins.

Why are established firms threatened by disruptive technologies? The very nature of these companies and their responsibility to stakeholders makes them vulnerable. Large firms are resource dependent, so they typically only invest in projects that provide a quick and reasonably secure return on their investment. These projects generally have high profit margins, are technologically feasible, have large markets, and satisfy current customer needs. Radical innovations initially serve niche markets and do not provide rapid growth with high returns. Radical innovations are inherently risky. It is difficult, if not impossible, to identify in advance all the potential applications for the technology, so the company is at risk that a competitor will identify a market opportunity with its technology and in some cases even patent the new use.

❖ How Xerox Learned to Innovate Radically

For years, Xerox Corporation, the document company, had no trouble developing both incremental and radical technologies, but it had significant difficulty commercializing its radical technologies. In 1995, the company created Xerox New Enterprises (XNE) to facilitate investment in new businesses outside Xerox's core competencies. Xerox saw this as a way to become more flexible, create parallel business models, and enhance the value of its stock. XNE would implement a set of best practices for commercializing their software and other business solutions. These best practices were defined against four challenges to radical innovation that Xerox had identified in its markets: (1) resource dependency (the need to achieve return-on-investment hurdles), (2) smaller markets than corporate parameters allowed for, (3) the inability to successfully identify all potential applications and opportunities, and (4) the inability of technology supply to meet market demand when the technology achieved mainstream adoption,

Rather than find ways around these challenges, Xerox chose to meet them head on. It figured that by creating independent organizations for radical innovation and putting early adopter customers onto development teams, it would ensure that the projects chosen and the technologies developed would meet real emerging customer needs. These new ventures would be small and flexible, and their environment would encourage quick failures and the celebration of small wins.

Over a period of 6 years, Xerox started more than a dozen companies, including Liveworks, Inc., Document Sciences, and E-Signage. These companies were structured as independent subsidiaries whose financial function was managed by the parent company. Employees of the subsidiaries had their own stock option pool and benefits package. Early on, Xerox knew that it had to find a way to maintain a constant flow of new ideas through XNE. It created the Corporate Innovation Council (CIC) in 1996 to develop some strategies for identifying and screening new opportunities. In particular, Xerox was interested in pursuing the emerging document market. The CIC developed a four-step process that included (1) scanning for opportunities, (2) developing of a business concept and testing it, (3) upon funding, pulling together a team for product development and the creation of a business plan, and (4) incubating the new business. At the end of the four steps, the new venture was either offered to one of Xerox's business groups, established as a new business group, spun out of Xerox as an independent company, or licensed to third parties. Although this model is not 100 percent successful for every new venture, it has become an excellent model for encouraging radical innovation inside a large corporate environment. Xerox believes that its ultimate success will come from putting in place formal processes and structures that facilitate new ideas and an entrepreneurial culture.

Sources: Rafik Loutfy and Lotfi Belkhir, "Managing Innovation at Xerox," *Research–Technology Management* 44, no. 4 (July–August 2001):15–24; William L. Miller, "Innovation for Business Growth," *Research–Technology Management* 44, no. 5 (September–October 2001): 26–41; Frederick D. Buggie, "The Four Phases of Innovation," *The Journal of Business Strategy* 22, no. 5 (September–October 2001): 36.

THE PIONEERING FIRM

Because the project life cycle of radical innovation is vastly different from that of incremental innovation, it requires different strategies at the project and organizational levels. Radical innovation projects are generally characterized by a long discovery and development period, exploration and experimentation, highly unpredictable and uncertain outcomes, sporadic results, and turnover of key participants. In this type of environment, conventional management and organizational approaches are not appropriate.

Pioneering with a radical innovation is a difficult strategy that large, established firms have not executed well. The work of Christensen, mentioned earlier, demonstrates that there are powerful forces that work against large companies when they attempt to pioneer with a disruptive technology.[27]

- **Dependency on customers and investors for resources.** The reality is that customers and investors (shareholders) control how money is spent in a large organization. Investors want a quick return and customers want products to satisfy current needs, so large companies that are performing well will quickly kill ideas that customers do not want immediately.
- **Small markets are not compatible with large company growth needs.** A $40-million company needs to find an $8-million revenue market to grow at 20 percent, but a $4-billion company needs to find $800 million in new sales.[28] New markets do not come that large, and the formal structure and overhead of the large company makes it impossible to focus on small markets.
- **A nonexistent market cannot be analyzed.** Most large companies act on the basis of thorough market research and industry analysis, but with a disruptive technology, the markets do not yet exist, so the company is forced to move forward on faith alone. There is no way to accurately predict emerging markets. However, being a pioneer in a market that cannot be analyzed is a huge competitive advantage if done well because the company will face no competitors for a long time.

Every firm should consider the advantages and disadvantages to the pioneering strategy. Pioneering requires substantial resources and marketing effort to make the technology the standard in the industry.

ADVANTAGES OF PIONEERING

The first company into a market with a proprietary technology has the advantage of setting the rules that others will have to follow. The first mover has the opportunity to establish its brand before competitors are able to enter the market. During the temporary quiet time that the company experiences by pioneering, it gains significant learning curve advantages and begins to create the economies of scale that are difficult for later entering firms to replicate.[29] In addition, because of the reduction in production costs that typically comes with time, the pioneer's profitability level will naturally be higher than an entering competitor. However, to achieve the benefits of a pioneering market entry, a company must have vision, good systems in place, and market and distribution strategies that will help it sustain that lead throughout a rapid growth period.

DISADVANTAGES OF PIONEERING

Being first to market is not always the best position to be in. For example, Apple was the first mover in the PDA market with its Newton MessagePad. The Message-Pad was designed to recognize a person's handwriting; however, it was technically flawed. Because it was required to recognize millions of keystrokes, it is understandable that performance was not up to customer expectations, which is typical of a disruptive technology. The second mover, Palm, was able to capitalize on the weaknesses of MessagePad and produce a technically more accurate PDA at a lower price that was targeted to a specific customer, the business user. First movers are hampered by high development costs and the need to get to market quickly to preserve their first-mover advantage. Later entrants can take their time, learn from their predecessor's mistakes, and overcome the pioneers through superior strategies and even by changing the rules as Palm did when it developed its own handwriting script, Graffiti.[30]

MANAGING PIONEERING WITH RADICAL INNOVATION

The Industrial Research Institute, in collaboration with the Rensselaer Radical Innovation Research Project, attempted to "identify and understand the management practices used by IRI member firms to cope with the high uncertainty associated with developing and commercializing radical innovations."[31] The IRI's research identified four means of stimulating the development of radical innovation in firms:

1. **Identifying the "holy grails" in the industry.** Every industry has technical challenges that must be overcome before the next technological breakthrough can occur. For example, a firm that developed a new way to improve fuel efficiency in the auto industry would reap the benefits of a breakthrough innovation that would revolutionize the industry.
2. **Issuing company-wide requests for proposals.** These requests usually come about when the company is facing an imminent threat to its core capability.
3. **Establishing formal venture boards.** The purpose of these boards is to review proposals and help determine the direction the company will take technologically.
4. **Small group idea generation.** Many companies have found that small teams scanning the environment can come up with ideas that would otherwise not have been discovered.

Christensen's work adds to these four stimuli by addressing how successful companies deal with the forces working against radical innovation in large firms.[32]

- They put disruptive innovation projects with the right customers so that the project has a higher likelihood of getting funded.
- They put disruptive technology projects inside small organizations so that small wins are appreciated.
- They plan for fast failures and quick experiments.
- They find new markets for the disruptive technology so that it will not have to compete as a sustaining technology in the mainstream market.

THE ROLE OF VENTURE CHAMPIONS

Every new venture inside a large corporation requires a champion to tear down the speed bumps that threaten the project and to act as a liaison with key corporate decision makers. Venture champions are the corporate entrepreneurs who are willing to take a high degree of risk to make the venture happen.[33,34] They have the technical skills and the negotiating talent to get the firm past its natural tendency to stick to its core competency and rely on incremental innovation.[35] Venture champions are the keepers of the entrepreneurial spirit inside large companies, and they fight for the freedom of the scientist or engineer to deviate from the core technologies. Venture champions are more likely to emerge in highly innovative companies such as 3M, where employees are able to allocate 15 percent of their time to pursuing innovation. Other companies give their champions and those creating the innovations a financial stake in those innovations to prevent the brain drain that often occurs when scientists and engineers are not able to reap the rewards of their inventions.

Most projects require multiple champions who promote various aspects of the project: technical, overall project, senior management, and business unit champions. Research has identified four types of venture champion roles: champions of ideas, opportunistic behavior, resources, and incorporation.[36] The champion of ideas is the person who must convince stakeholders, both internal and external to the company, that the idea has merit. Those that champion opportunistic behavior serve as leading blockers when conventional routines are disrupted, and they set acceptable boundaries for activities that disrupt the equilibrium. Resource champions see that the new venture has the needed resources, and incorporation champions prepare to integrate the new venture into the parent corporation.

In radical innovation projects, one of the venture champion's primary roles is to give the project legitimacy. Incremental innovations have inherent legitimacy because they are based on the core technology of the company. However, radical innovations do not have legitimacy. Leifer et al. found several ways that venture champions created legitimacy for a radical innovation project. For example, with Texas Instruments' Digital Light Processing project, a formal, secure communication system was set up between the project and the rest of the company to make sure that key people were in touch with what was going on.[37] That system enhanced the project's legitimacy. Venture champions must also continually emphasize the benefits of the project to the company, as the risks will be very apparent. They counter the naysayers with hard data supporting the progress that is being made. That evidence of progress makes it easier to gain additional funding when it is needed. Completion of a prototype and positive feedback from lead users will further convince senior management of the wisdom of continuing the project. Finding a "brand name" partner for the project is another effective way to stamp it with legitimacy, as is assembling a powerful board of advisers, both internal and external. Finally, the venture champion can attract company "superstars" to the team, those whose reputation in the company will help smooth the way for the project.

THE PATHS TO CORPORATE VENTURING

The easiest road to entrepreneurship inside a large organization may be through incremental innovation on existing products. Unfortunately, that will not increase the competitiveness of the firm and rarely leads to commercially viable products. Moreover, these types of innovations are easily copied, erasing any advantage gained by undertaking them.[38] The second route to entrepreneurship entails integrating technologies that may never have been associated with one another and producing new knowledge from that integration. Recombining existing resources to create new uses is one of the fundamental activities of entrepreneurship. This technological integration produces tacit know-how that is unique to the firm and offers a distinct competitive advantage in the market.[39] The third route to entrepreneurship involves discovering new ways to exploit technology and company know-how through commercialization, producing new sources of revenue.

Taking advantage of all three routes is actually the most effective way to achieve a spirit of entrepreneurship inside the corporation. New knowledge must be embedded in the culture of the organization so that new competencies are developed and all possible uses for the knowledge are considered and implemented. To achieve the successful integration of new knowledge inside large organizations, corporate entrepreneurs typically rely on their social capital, that is, their network of like-minded (in terms of the entrepreneurial spirit) individuals, both inside and external to the company, who will help build the necessary critical mass of support. Corporate entrepreneurs use their informal networks to pursue the required resources to implement their ventures. Corporate entrepreneurs, like independent entrepreneurs, undertake a variety of atypical activities to overcome the constraints of the typical corporate environment. These entrepreneurial activities include bartering, bootstrapping, stealing personnel time, appropriating materials, concealing activities, and trading on favors.[40]

Corporate entrepreneurs have the critical opportunity recognition and sensemaking skills required to add meaning to the knowledge created and inspire its implementation. Valuable insights also come from people outside the entrepreneurial activities of the company. Because they are not as close to the activities of the corporate entrepreneurs, they can often see relationships and possibilities that the originators cannot. It is then the job of the corporate entrepreneur to aggregate the various insights and knowledge, interpret them, and put them in a form that will be readily understood and accepted by key decision makers in the organization.

There are three fundamental paths to corporate venturing: skunk works, strategic integration, and entrepreneurial immersion (see Figure 14-1). Two of the approaches lead to the creation of autonomous new ventures. Each of the three paths incorporates varying degrees of difficulty and requires different levels of commitment (see Figure 14-2).

SKUNK WORKS

It is difficult to foster radical innovation inside a large, established corporate culture that has thrived on incremental innovation. As a result, many companies have gone to the Lockheed skunk works model. *Skunk works* is a term that dates back to the 1940s when a group of engineers at Lockheed Martin developed the first jet fighter. The skunk works removed the new venture from the straitjacket of the parent company and isolated it so that it could develop and grow in a more entrepreneurial environment.[41] Similarly, IBM located its PC development team in Florida so that it could function without being inhibited by any particular IBM unit from the parent company. In general, the only large firms that have been successful with disruptive technologies have done so by setting up an autonomous organization that focuses on customers who are early adopters.[42]

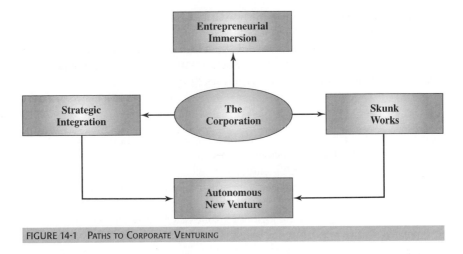

FIGURE 14-1   PATHS TO CORPORATE VENTURING

Today, the biggest stumbling block in most corporate entrepreneurship efforts is that employees do not share in the wealth they create for the parent company. Until 1996, Xerox ran one of the most successful venture programs in the United States with 56 percent IRR (internal rate of return) over the previous 10 years.[43] However, they abandoned it because staff kept leaving to start their own companies or work where they could more easily reap the rewards of their inventions. At Xerox, an inventor was paid a salary and received bonuses, but did not share in the venture's success. Other roadblocks to a skunk works type of venturing are lack of commitment on the part of decision makers, too much devotion to the core technology of the business, and an unstable organizational structure that is easy to disband when the company no longer wants to support it.

Lockheed skunk works founder Clarence L. "Kelly" Johnson created a set of guidelines for the skunk works:[44] (1) each engineer must be able to multitask, being at once a designer, parts tracker, or mechanic; (2) managers must be able to access all

FIGURE 14-2   PATHS TO CORPORATE VENTURING: LEVELS OF COMMITMENT

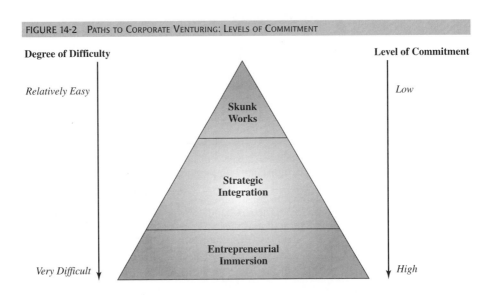

plans and understand how each part contributes to the whole; and (3) the project must operate without the typical red tape.

Critics of the skunk works model claim that organizations must encourage innovation and entrepreneurial thinking inside the larger company if they are to build a sustainable innovation strategy, a difficult task at best.[45]

STRATEGIC INTEGRATION

Firms with multiple businesses or divisions face a unique situation; they must maximize the profitability of all of their businesses over the long term. In the early 1990s, the focus was on operational integration, which included reengineering to enhance speed, quality, and efficiency. It also meant getting rid of business activities that were not profitable and no longer met company goals. By the late 1990s, the strategic integration of resources and competencies became the focus of the majority of businesses.[46] Today, the goal of most companies is to recognize future opportunities long before they make themselves apparent and match those opportunities to strategies that the company has never before utilized. Burgelman and Doz have identified five integrative strategies, outlined in Table 14-1.[47]

Successful strategic integration is the result of overcoming two significant challenges: (1) effectively managing the conflict between maintaining and protecting the company's core competencies and growing and diversifying the business strategy, and (2) effectively managing the transfer and sharing of resources among the various business units. Companies that focus on protecting their core tend to choose a scope-driven strategy and grow by extending their scope. For example, the Walt Disney Co. under the leadership of Michael Eisner tends to find opportunity by extending its scope, in

TABLE 14-1 Strategic Integration

Strategy	Definition	Example
Scope	Collaboration with existing business units to pursue a new business opportunity	Intel's chipset and motherboard businesses collaborate to develop new products
Reach	The original corporate strategy is altered by changing a unit or creating a new one	ThermoElectron spins off new business units to develop new products
Overambitious	No trade-off between scope and reach	American Express's effort to become a financial supermarket
Minimal integration	Limits on scope and reach	Traditional approaches based on capital investment and portfolio-planning decisions
Complex	Maximum strategic-opportunity set with as much scope and reach as possible within the constraints of the market. Discovery and creation of new business opportunities that combine resources from many company units.	Cisco Systems identifies, acquires, and integrates newly emerging industry segments that are important to their corporate strategy

other words, finding opportunity within the arena in which it has already been successful.[48] Contrast that strategy with the radical innovation of Walt Disney when he took the company into the theme park business. For companies such as this, a reach strategy is risky and difficult to execute. For corporate entrepreneurs with opportunities that fall outside the strategic scope, it is very difficult to get management to commit sufficient company resources to exploit the opportunity.

In contrast, large organizations with an entrepreneurial culture will be comfortable with a reach-driven strategy that recognizes opportunity in technology gaps that can result in technological disruption. Because these companies have a flatter, team-based structure, middle management is closer to the point of discovery. Corporate entrepreneurs have been the source of disruptive technology opportunities at 3M, Johnson & Johnson, and Hewlett-Packard. However, these same companies often have difficulty with scope-driven strategic integration because their business units are so accustomed to operating somewhat autonomously that their managers often forget that they are part of a much larger organization. One excellent example of this was Johnson & Johnson's plan to create a Hospital Services Group (HSG) during the 1980s.[49] The goal of HSG was to present a unified interface to customers for ordering, billing, and logistics; doing that meant requiring its independent product divisions to work together.[50] The project was so radical that it took several years and significant intervention from top management to achieve.

Effectively managing the transfer and sharing of company resources is yet another challenge in the effort to achieve strategic integration. Those resources consist of tangible assets such as money, equipment, raw materials, and labor, and intangible assets such as patents, brands, know-how, and skills. For companies with limited resources, whenever a tangible asset is transferred to one business unit, it creates a vacuum in another, whereas all groups can use intangible assets simultaneously without fear of their running out.

The complex integration strategy must satisfy dynamic interdependencies among existing business units and new venture units. Companies such as Nokia and Intel have used new-venture groups to facilitate complex integration strategies. Another approach is to use senior executives as integrators. At Hewlett-Packard, a senior executive is in charge of a major functional unit or activity while also being accountable for new-business development involving complex strategic integration across several business units.[51] At 3M, technologies belong to everyone; everyone can access them, and business units can own the products they create from those technologies.

With all types of strategic integration, the issue of rewarding or providing incentives for performance is a touchy issue. In a complex or entrepreneurial organization where rewards have been predicated on business unit performance, getting people to work on strategic integration is difficult because they cannot perceive the rewards for doing so. Management faces the daunting challenge of devising incentives that reward people across business units and entice business units to work together toward a common goal.

ENTREPRENEURIAL IMMERSION

It is easier to create an entrepreneurial culture at start-up than to attempt to reengineer an entire company that has lived with the bureaucratic mindset for years. However, even a company that began with an entrepreneurial spirit can lose the spirit as it grows and adds layers of management and commitment to resources. One company that has maintained its entrepreneurial spirit throughout its growth is Clovis, California-based Pelco Inc. Pelco, the leading manufacturer of video surveillance systems, has its products installed everywhere, from Buckingham Palace to the Pentagon to the local street corner. At Pelco, the entrepreneurial mindset and customer focus are apparent in every area of the business. Although this company has over 1,000 employees, it is nearly impossible to walk onto the factory or assembly floor and talk to a worker without hearing the word *customer* within a few seconds. When a customer such as the Mirage Hotel in Las Vegas has an idea for an innovation in one of Pelco's products, Pelco brings them to the manufacturing floor and fast prototypes the innovation. If the innovation works the way the customer wants, it is immediately put into production. Everyone at Pelco, including the janitor, is expected to find new and innovative ways to improve the business, its products, and its services. Another example of entrepreneurial immersion is New Pig Corporation, the subject of the Case Study at the end of the chapter.

SUCCESS AS A CORPORATE ENTREPRENEUR

Corporate entrepreneurship will never be the same experience as pure entrepreneurship with a start-up venture. By definition, the corporate entrepreneur is working with a different set of variables and a different kind of risk. Successful negotiation of the roadblocks and speed bumps that can stall or derail a radical innovation requires a plan built on an understanding of the nature of those roadblocks. One of the major roadblocks for corporate entrepreneurs is people. It is easy to find the people in the organization who have the power to say no. What the corporate entrepreneur needs to do is find others with an entrepreneurial mindset who will say yes. These allies can come from within or outside the organization; even customers and suppliers can become strong allies for a corporate venture project.

Oftentimes, the idea for a new project is first disclosed to a trusted colleague, then it is time to put something on paper. One of the critical talents a corporate entrepreneur must have is the ability to put an idea into a short memo in a very compelling way. Doing so helps the corporate entrepreneur focus the idea, give it some structure, and consider how it might be implemented. Here are some of the questions that this initial memo should answer:

- Why will this idea work?
- Why is the entrepreneur the one to do it?
- How does it fit with the company's strategy?
- What is the risk? Is the risk worth it?
- Does the company have the resources and talent to make the idea happen?

The corporate entrepreneur should plan to ask for resources to achieve a specific goal on the way to the larger objective. In other words, the corporate entrepreneur will get farther faster by asking for commitments in stages and only asking for what is needed to get to the next stage. At each stage, some of the risk has been reduced. It is important to commit to less than is possible to achieve. If the project has the potential to reach $6 million in sales at the end of 2 years, commit to achieving $4 million but reach the $6 million. To go farther faster requires that the project not be made public until some milestones have been attained. Announcing what is planned just sets the project up for attack by people who are not part of it and gives competitors notice that this new technology is in the works. This tactic is known as working "under the radar" until enough of the pieces are in place to ensure a better chance that decision makers will listen.

Even when a new venture project fails, it may boost the team's careers in the parent company. Anshu Prasad and Jim Carew, Nortel employees, developed a software package called Guru that was designed to help programmers debug their programs. The Business Ventures Group at Nortel decided that the market was too small and killed the project during its development. That decision did not hurt Prasad and Carew, because people at the highest levels in the company now knew them, they had developed new skills while working on the project, and they had taken a risk that gave them credibility with the right people in the company.[52]

A WINNING CLIMATE FOR CORPORATE VENTURING

All the efforts of a venture champion will be wasted if the climate of the company does not foster entrepreneurship. 3M is regularly touted as a master of innovation and entrepreneurship, generating new products and services faster than old ones become obsolete. Approximately 30 percent of their 60,000 products are new within a 5-year period.[53] See the Case Study at the end of the chapter to learn how New Pig Corporation encourages innovation and entrepreneurship in ways that rival the much larger 3M Corporation.

What are the characteristics of a winning climate for corporate venturing and the entrepreneurial spirit? The following are some of the factors that must be in place to nurture a winning climate.

- **An entrepreneurial vision.** For corporate venturing to succeed, a vision for infusing the entrepreneurial spirit of innovation throughout the organization must be in place. If there is no support for entrepreneurship at the top, it will be difficult for the company to achieve and sustain it.
- **The customer is on the team.** When customers help to drive innovation, the company is often better able to see the benefits of innovation and corporate venturing.
- **Experimentation and failure are accepted.** The freedom to try new things, take risks, and learn from quick failures is critical to an entrepreneurial learning environment. The new venture team must be able to define challenges in creative ways and not be constrained by the resources of the parent company.
- **Time for innovation.** At 3M, employees are expected to devote about 15 percent of their time exploring new ideas and inventing without having to get permission from supervisors or management. Making innovation part of everyone's job increases the chances that radical innovation will occur.
- **Resources available for innovation.** Discretionary resources should be available for innovation projects, and the ability to tap those resources needs to be at the lowest levels possible.
- **Cross-disciplinary teams.** Teams composed of a number of different functions and empowered with decision-making abilities are more likely to come up with

radical innovations than those that must report to upper management on every idea and decision. People need to be moved around and out of their comfort zones so that their creative thinking skills can be encouraged.

- **Champions or sponsors.** Every company needs to have people empowered to influence and support a project from start to finish. They become the liaisons to upper management and smooth the way for the project team.
- **Employee-flight incentives.** The company must give employees a stake in the new venture—the ability to share in the risks and the rewards.
- **Preserve core values but challenge everything else.** Only the fundamental values of the firm remain immutable; everything else is subject to change and must change for the company to survive and grow.

A PLAN FOR LIVING WITH CHAOS

In their research on established firms engaging in radical innovation, Leifer et al. determined that a learning plan was more compatible with the nature of corporate venturing with radical innovations than a static plan based on current knowledge at a specific point in time.[54] The premise is that with radical innovation, the firm does not have all the knowledge it needs to develop an effective plan because there are no precedents— the company is navigating through unknown territory. The learning plan would enable the company to build a plan as it went through the project. The learning plan would:

- Catalogue the effects and results of all the project uncertainties
- Detail the assumptions related to each uncertainty
- Prioritize the tasks based on the assumptions and define the path going forward
- Log the project's history as a guide to future projects

Rather than tightly controlling the development of the project as is typically done with incremental innovations, the learning plan would provide a means for learning from what happens during the project, making adjustments, and creating new knowledge that can be used in future projects.

Too many times companies focus their strategy on where they want to go. Once that objective is identified, they go on to think about how they are going to get there. Unfortunately, traditional approaches to strategy such as this fall apart in unpredictable, uncertain environments. It becomes impossible to predict which strategies, which competencies, and which industries will remain viable for any length of time. Brown and Eisenhardt found that successful companies manage change at three levels: sometimes they lead the change; other times they anticipate it; and sometimes they react to change.[55] For example, Intel, the leader in semiconductor technology, uses all three levels of change. When Sun Microsystems, Oracle, and IBM pioneered the network computer as an inexpensive alternative to the PC for Internet computing, Intel, which saw its business being attacked, responded by creating an Internet division and partnering with Microsoft to develop a hybrid targeted at the network computer market. Intel also anticipates change. Early in the 1990s, it saw the importance of graphics and multimedia to its business, so Intel quickly developed strategic alliances with telecommunications, cable, and movie companies. It also invested more than $500 billion in more than 50 entrepreneurial ventures in the graphics and multimedia space. Intel is well known for leading change and is the pacesetter in its industry.[56]

Recognizing that the ability to change is a critical capability of successful firms, Brown and Eisenhardt developed 10 "laws" for successfully competing in dynamic environments, which are summarized in Table 14-2.[57]

ACQUIRING RESOURCES

Resource acquisition is a constant activity that consumes a great deal of the champion's time. Resources will have to be accessed not only internally but also externally at various stages in the project's life. Although large companies generally have a wealth of resources, these resources are usually committed to incremental innovations, which are the mainstay of the company. Consequently, in the earliest stages of a new project, known as the fuzzy front end, the funding comes through informal sources in the form of discretionary funds from the CEO, a business unit, or R&D. However, discretionary funds are volatile and can disappear overnight if the company suddenly faces a downturn. Radical innovation development is a lengthy process that can test the patience of any corporate investor who is under pressure to demonstrate a return on investment. It is also a dynamic process where funding comes from many sources at many different points in time.

Although a shortage of funding can put a lot of stress on the team, an overabundance of funding can be just as devastating and even cause the project to be delayed. A radical innovation often receives large government grants in the early stages; this has two negative effects: (1) it sets high expectations for the project before early exploration has had a chance to take place, and (2) it gives the team a financial comfort level that does not put it under pressure to get the work done quickly. In other words, it escalates the commitment and reduces the chance that the project will be stopped if it appears infeasible and should be stopped. Moreover, the administrative requirement associated with government funding puts an additional burden on the team and distracts it from the product development process.

Because the bootstrap method of funding is ineffective and time consuming, many companies approach the funding dilemma from a venture capital perspective. For example, Nortel Networks, a global telecommunications company, created a venture board that examines strategies such as acquisitions, divestitures, spin-offs, and strategic partnerships.[58] At Nortel, funding a new venture involves a three-pronged approach. First, a three-member qualification team evaluates ideas and recommends those that should receive seed funding for initial research to see if the opportunity is worthy of a venture. If the idea is aligned with Nortel's current efforts, the decision is relatively easy, but if it involves a truly radical innovation, it goes on to the second stage—new business commercialization. Here, the criterion is that the target market has to be at least $100 million, providing for a potential annual growth rate of 15 percent. The new venture also has to prove that it is sustainable and lends itself to differentiated products. Projects that do not fit in with the current business units at this point are spun out as independent businesses, with Nortel Networks holding an equity stake. In this way, a radical innovation project does not get killed because it does not fit with current technological efforts.

The need for resources by the new venture team goes well beyond capital. Often it is necessary to bring in partners to fill competency gaps in such areas as market and business model development, technology development and acquisition, and manufacturing expertise. The tacit knowledge that these partners bring to the team would take

TABLE 14-2   Laws for Competing in Dynamic Environments

The Rule	What It Means
1. Advantage is temporary	Nothing is forever. Competitive advantage is a moving target that must be reassessed on a regular basis.
2. Strategy is diverse, emergent, and complicated	There are no simple strategies. Effective strategies emerge and evolve through exploration and experimentation.
3. Reinvention is the goal	The effective firm worries less about efficiency and focuses its efforts more on creating new value in every area of the business, but particularly in new product innovation.
4. Minimize structure	Structure should be kept to a minimum—a few strict rules and metrics. Use just enough structure to keep the business moving forward, but not enough to constrain it.
5. Learn from the past	The history of the company is often a clue to its future success. An existing business concept can be given new life if reinvented using new venture models, new markets, and new technologies.
6. Reach into the future	Because the future is uncertain, successful firms reach out to it by taking risks and experimenting with new products and nascent markets.
7. Time pace change	The pace of change is as important as the speed. The company should establish a rhythm and tempo around new products that get a momentum going. The tempo matches the change of demand in the market while the rhythm matches that of other firms in the market.
8. Grow the strategy	To build a new strategy, the company has to first rejuvenate or eliminate the old strategies. Instead of starting with the future, they start with the present.
9. Drive strategy from the business level	Strategy cannot be driven from the top down in rapidly growing businesses. Strategy and change must come from the business or operating level.
10. Continually realign businesses with markets and opportunities	In dynamic markets, the firm must continually look for patterns of change and emerging markets.

Source: Based on Shona L. Brown and Kathleen M. Eisenhardt, *Competing on the Edge: Strategy as Structured Chaos* (Boston: Harvard Business School Press, 1998), 241–247.

years to develop inside the new venture team. By taking on partners, the team can move forward more quickly.

INTERACTING WITH THE PARENT COMPANY

Interacting with the parent organization is another reality of corporate venturing inside a large organization. Frequently, companies that undertake corporate venturing believe that the radical innovation project should be kept away from the rest of the organization in a kind of skunk works environment. The problem with that approach is that corporate venturing teams rarely have all the skills and resources they need to operate autonomously; yet they are detached from the very skills and resources they need that are available in the parent company. The firms that Leifer et al. studied all benefited from interaction with the parent company.[59] The parent company maintains an enormous database of tacit knowledge through its informal networks that can be tapped and used to move the project along more quickly. These networks of embedded knowledge help to reduce the uncertainties associated with the radical innovation process.

If there was ever a time that was right for corporate entrepreneurship, it is now. There are no stable industries and no stable companies. The companies that survive and thrive in the next decade will be those that make radical innovation a priority and that organize for flexibility and change.

❖ SUMMARY

Although it is often thought that large firms have the advantage when it comes to innovation because of their deep resources, the reality is that they do not have a good track record in innovation, particularly radical innovation. One reason for this is that large firms are driven by current markets and rigid financial structures that influence the way they look at new product investments. A corporate venture is distinct from other corporate projects in several important ways. It is a project that is new to the company and carries with it much higher risk of failure than other projects. There is more uncertainty associated with the project, so it is often managed separately at some point in time. Corporate ventures are generally undertaken to move the company in new directions, reinvent the company, increase sales, or to help the company become more competitive. Corporate ventures can access one critical resource that most new start-ups do not enjoy: the core competencies and tacit knowledge that have developed in the organization over time. These competitive advantages give the corporate venture a significant edge over the independent start-up. One problem that frequently occurs in large organizations is that knowledge and skills become habits that are institutionalized over time, creating what are known as *core rigidities,* so the company resists going beyond what it knows. Yet another difference between corporate ventures and entrepreneurial start-ups is that corporate ventures are subject to success hurdles, externally imposed objectives in terms of financial performance and strategic fit. Large firms are resource dependent, so they typically invest only in projects that provide a quick and reasonably secure return on their investment. These projects generally have high profit margins, are technologically feasible, have large markets, and satisfy current customer needs. Every new venture inside a large corporation requires a champion who is a corporate entrepreneur who is willing to take a high degree of risk to make the venture happen. Most projects require multiple champions that promote various aspects of the project: technical, overall project, senior management, and business unit champions. There are basically three routes to corporate entrepreneurship: skunk works, strategic integration, and entrepreneurial immersion. A winning climate for corporate venturing and the entrepreneurial spirit will include an entrepreneurial vision, putting the customer on the team, promoting experimentation and failure, making time for innovation, having resources available for innovation, promoting champions or sponsors, establishing employee-flight incentives, and preserving core values.

❖ DISCUSSION QUESTIONS

1. How are corporate ventures distinguished from other projects inside large organizations and from entrepreneurial start-ups?
2. What are some of the reasons that corporate venturing has had a relatively poor track record?
3. What is the role of the venture champion in taking a new idea to the project stage and beyond?
4. Consider the three paths to corporate venturing discussed in the chapter (skunk works, strategic integration, entrepreneurial immersion). What are the ramifications of each to the company in terms of the level of commitment and difficulty?
5. What are the critical factors in becoming a successful corporate entrepreneur?

❖ RESOURCES

Block, Zenas, and Ian C. MacMillan. *Corporate Venturing: Creating New Businesses Within the Firm.* Boston: Harvard Business School Press, 1995.

Brown, Shona L., and Kathleen M. Eisenhardt. *Competing on the Edge: Strategy As Structured Chaos.* Boston: Harvard Business School Press, 1998.

Oden, Howard W. *Managing Corporate Culture, Innovation, and Intrapreneurship.* Westport, CT: Greenwood Publishing Group, 1997.

❖ INTERNET RESOURCES

Intrapreneurship
entrepreneurs.about.com/cs/intrapreneurship/
Articles on intrapreneurship and how to infuse entrepreneurship into a corporation

A Process for Intrapreneurship
www.bradfuller.com/Publications/innovate.html
Article on how intrapreneurship works

Corporate Venturing
www.corporateventuring.com/
A source of information on what's going on in the world of corporate venturing

NEW PIG CORPORATION: A STUDY IN CORPORATE INNOVATION

It may not be the most glamorous of businesses, but New Pig Corporation is using technology and a sense of humor to solve real problems in the world of manufacturing. One issue that factories face is how to clean greasy spills and leaks on floors. For years, the industry solution was cat litter, but it was messy and tended to get tracked into the machinery. Don Beaver and Ben Stapelfeld were in the industrial cleaning business at that time and decided that they were going to find a way to solve the problem. They began experimenting with all types of absorbent materials, putting them into everything from athletic socks to pantyhose to see what worked, then throwing the sock away when it became saturated. They finally settled on using corncobs as an absorbent material. Now that they had a product, it was time to build a company. In 1985, with $500,000 from banks and private investors, they started the business. When it was time to put together a board of directors and advisers, they chose people who could help them in everything from pricing to suppliers to packaging. One of the board members even leased a part of his plant to New Pig for a year until it could build its own.

Realizing that they had to find a way to stand out in the traditional industrial distribution channels, Beaver and Stapelfeld dubbed the company New Pig Corporation and the new invention the Original PIG Absorbent Sock. They then began spending about 40 percent of their revenues on promotion, using the pig theme to create the packaged absorbents market. Throughout its catalogue are Pig Tech Tips, Boar Facts, and products such as the Ham-O PIG Mat, which soaks up spills around a machine. Its company headquarters are at One Pork Avenue, and its phone number is 800–HOT-HOGS. More importantly, however, they defined their business broadly, saying that New Pig is in the problem-solving business, encouraging their customers to tell New Pig their industrial cleaning problems so that the company could invent ways to solve them.

In industrial channels, purchasing through catalogs (online or off) is common, so New Pig developed the Pigalog through which it sells almost all of its 2,500 products. Its customer base spreads to over 155,000 customers in 40 countries, a number that is growing at about 10 percent annually.

The strategy was a success. By 1998, the Tipton, Pennsylvania, company had over 300 employees and sales of $77 million. The New Pig brand was now recognized and established. Even competitors that tried to copy the concept using snakes and gators could not make a dent in the company's brand. New Pig spread the brand in every conceivable location.

In 1990, New Pig was at a crossroads; it needed to work on building better customer relationships that would help it move into new markets, beyond packaged absorbents to overall workplace safety. Stapelfeld decided to make the CFO his new CEO and paid him more than he was paying himself in his position as Chairman. That turned out to be a wise decision, because Nino Vella put needed systems and controls in place and helped the company maximize profits in a very narrow market. More importantly, Vella got the company thinking about where it should go next. Under his leadership, the $13 million in sales the company had in 1990 grew to $77 million in 1998.

In 1997, four employees from accounting, customer service, marketing, and new product development, went to Vella with the idea for a consumer products catalog, saying that it was time for New Pig to enter that $10 billion market. Recognizing that New Pig might lose these bright young employees if they could not take on a new product development challenge, Vella gave them the opportunity to do so. Then he encouraged everyone at New Pig to contribute to its database of new product innovations. Several hundred new product ideas are generated by employees every year.

Over the years, New Pig has become legendary for its fanatical service to customers. For example, one evening Betty Narehood, a New Pig employee, responded to a frantic call from a customer whose hazardous materials business was on fire. She put New Pig in emergency response mode and put together a special order of products to absorb liquids and contain spills. With no commercial trucking available at that hour of the night, a New Pig employee volunteered to drive one of the company's trucks the four-hour distance to the customer. Throughout the entire ordeal, Narehood made all the decisions but kept the President and Vice President aware of what she was doing. The reason that Narehood was able to make rapid decisions on behalf of the customer is that New Pig has created a corporate culture where the vision is shared by everyone and everyone is empowered to satisfy the customer.

On another front, New Pig is going after new markets so that it can sell more products to its existing customers. Instead of just letting the catalog speak for the company, New Pig is going out and meeting face-to-face with customers to learn their needs and build stronger relationships. One customer came up with a product that diverts liquid rather than absorbing it. New Pig developed it, and the product generated more than $1 million in sales the first year.

New Pig has successfully avoided the big corporate mentality and inertia of success, but it has been so busy doing what it does well that it has not spent much time looking to the future and how it might position itself given its declining manufacturing market. New Pig is now grappling with this new change. ■

Sources: New Pig Corporation, *www.newpig.com*; Joanna Brandi, "Customer Care Bulletin No. 5," *www.cus tomerretention.com/library*; Doug Laplante, "Build a Berm," *Visions Magazine*, April 1996, *www.pdma.org/ visions/apr96/newpig.html*.

❖ NOTES

1. Clayton M. Christensen. *The Innovator's Dilemma* (Boston: Harvard Business School Press, 1997).

2. Patricia G. Greene, Candida G. Brush, Myra M. Hart, "The Corporate Venture Champion: A Resource-Based Approach to Role and Process," *Entrepreneurship Theory and Practice* 23, no. 3 (Spring 1999): 103–122.

3. J. Stopford and C. Baden-Fuller, "Creating Corporate Entrepreneurship," *Strategic Management Journal* 15 (1994): 521–536.

4. Z. Block and I. C. MacMillan, *Corporate Venturing* (Boston: Harvard Business School Press, 1995).

5. J. G. Covin and D. Slevin, "A Conceptual Model of Entrepreneurship as Firm Behavior," *Entrepreneurship Theory and Practice* 16 (1991): 1, 7–25.

6. "Study Probes Corporate Venturing," *www.uoregon.edu/newscenter/corpventure. html*, November 16, 2001.

7. T. Nakahara, "Innovation in a Borderless World Economy," *Research–Technology Management* 40 (1997): 3, 7–9.

8. P. Wright et al., "Impact of Corporate Insider, Blockholder, and Institutional Equity Ownership on Firm Risk Taking," *Academy of Management Journal* 39, no. 2 (1996): 441–464.

9. Zenas Block and Ian MacMillan, "Stimuli and Stumbling Blocks in a New Venture," in Sue Birley and David F. Muzyka, eds., *Mastering Entrepreneurship* (London: Financial Times-Prentice Hall, 350–356.

10. J. M. Geringer and L. Herbert, "Measuring Performance of International Joint Ventures," *Journal of International Business Studies* 22 (1991): 249–263.

11. R. Peterson and D. Berger, "Entrepreneurship in Organizations," *Administrative Science Quarterly* 16 (1971): 97–106.

12. R. A. Burgelman, "A Model of the Interaction of Strategic Behavior, Corporate Context, and the Concept of Strategy," *Academy of Management Review* 8, no. 1 (1983): 61–70; "A Process Model of Internal Corporate Venturing in the Diversified Major Firm," *Administrative Science Quarterly* 28, no. 2 (1983): 223–244; "Intraorganizational Ecology of Strategy-making and Organizational Adaptation: Theory and Field Research," *Organization Science* 2 (1991): 239–262.

13. D. Miller, "The Correlates of Entrepreneurship in Three Types of Firms," *Management Science* 29, no. 7 (1983): 770–791; S. Zahra and J. G. Covin, "Contextual Influences on the Corporate Entrepreneurship-Performance Relationship: A Longitudinal Analysis," *Journal of Business Venturing* 10, no. 1 (1995): 43–58.

14. D. Kuratko, R. Montagno, and J. Hornsby, "Developing an Intrapreneurial Assessment Instrument for Effective Corporate Entrepreneurial Environment." *Strategic Management Journal* 11 (Summer 1990): 49–58.

15. G. Hamel and C. K. Prahalad, *Competing for the Future* (Boston:Harvard Business School Press, 1994).

16. Klaus Macharzina, "Entrepreneurship on a Global Rise," *Management International Review* 40, no. 3 (2000): 199–202.

17. Hilton Barrett and Art Weinstein, "The Effect of Market Orientation and Organizational Flexibility on Corporate Entrepreneurship," *Entrepreneurship Theory and Practice* 23, no. 1 (Fall 1998): 57–70.

18. J. Barney, "Firm Resources and Sustained Competitive Advantage," *Journal of Management* 17, no. 1 (1991): 99–120.

19. Deborah Dougherty, "Managing Your Core Incompetencies for Corporate Venturing," *Entrepreneurship Theory and Practice* 19 (Spring 1995): 113–135.

20. Greene et al., "The Corporate Venture Champion," 103–122.

21. J. A. Starr and I. C. MacMillan, "Resource Cooptation via Social Contracting: Resource Acquisition Strategies for New Ventures," *Strategic Management Journal* 11 (1990): 79–92.

22. Barbara Levitt and James G. March, "A Model of Adaptive Organizational Search," *Journal of Economic Behavior and Organization* 2 (1988): 307–333.

23. Frances J. Milliken and Theresa K. Lant, "The Effects of an Organization's Recent Performance History on Strategic Persistence and Change: The Role of Managerial Interpretations," in Paul Shrivastava, Anne Huff, and Jane Dutton, eds., *Advances in Strategic Management* (Greenwich, CT: JAI Press, 1991), 7:129–156.

24. Dawn Kelly and Terry L. Amburgey, "Organizational Inertia and Momentum: A Dynamic Model of Strategic Change," *Academy of Management Journal* 34 (1991): 591–612.

25. Joseph Schumpeter. *The Theory of Economic Development* (Cambridge, MA: Harvard University Press, 1934).

26. Rafik Loutfy and Lotfi Belkhir, "Managing Innovation at Xerox," *Research–Technology Management* 44, no. 4 (2001): 15–24.

27. Clayton Christensen, *The Innovator's Dilemma* (New York: HarperBusiness, 2000), xix-xxii.

28. Ibid., xx.

29. Roger A. Kerin, P. Rajan Varadarajan, and Robert A. Peterson, "First–Mover Advantage: A Synthesis, Conceptual Framework, and Research Propositions," *Journal of Marketing* 56 (October 1992): 33–52.

30. Venkates Shankar, Gregory S. Carpenter, and Lakshman Krishnamurthi, "Late Mover Advantage: How Innovative Late Entrants Outsell Pioneers," *Journal of Marketing Research* 35 (February 1998): 57–70.

31. Mark P. Rice, Colarelli O'Connor, Lois S. Peters, "Managing Discontinuous Innovation," *Research–Technology Management* 41, no. 3 (May–June 1998): 52–58.

32. Clayton Christensen, *The Innovator's Dilemma* (Boston: Harvard Business School Press, 1997).

33. Modesto Maidique, "Entrepreneurs, Champions, and Technological Innovations," *Sloan Management Review* 21 (Spring 1980): 59–70.

34. Jane Howell, "Champions of Technological Innovation," *Administrative Science Quarterly* 35 (June 1990): 317–341.

35. Rajesh K. Chandy and Gerard J. Tellis, "Organizing for Radical Product Innovation: The Overlooked Role of Willingness to Cannibalize," *Journal of Marketing Research* 35 (November 1998): 474–487.

36. S. Venkataraman, I. C. MacMilan, and R. G. McGrath, "Progress in Research on Corporate Venturing," in D. L. Sexton and J. D. Kasarda, eds., *The State of the Art of Entrepreneurship* (Boston: PWS-Kent, 1992), 487–519.

37. Richard Leifer et al. *Radical Innovation* (Boston: Harvard Business School Press, 2000), 68.

38. J. Barney, "Firm Resources and Sustained Competitive Advantage." *Journal of Management* 17 (1991): 99–120; K. B. Clark and T. Fujimoto, *Product Development Performance* (Boston: Harvard Business School Press, 1991).

39. H. Itami, *Mobilizing Invisible Assets* (Boston: Harvard University Press, 1987); S. A. Zahra, A. P. Nielsen, and W. C. Bogner, "Corporate Entrepreneurship, Knowledge, and Competence Development," *Entrepreneurship Theory and Practice* 23, no. 3 (1999): 169.

40. Starr and MacMillan, "Resource Cooptation Via Social Contracting," 75–92.

41. Behnam Tabrizi and Rick Walleigh, "Defining Next-Generation Products: An Inside Look," *Harvard Business Review* 75:6 (November–December 1997): 116–124.

42. Christensen, *The Innovator's Dilemma* (1997): 110.

43. Ibid.

44. Clarence L. "Kelly" Johnson, *Lockheed Aviation Legend: 1910–1990, A Biography,* *www.wvi.com/~lelandh/kelly1.htm.*

45. Gary Hamel, "Killer Strategies That Make Shareholders Rich," *Fortune* (June 23, 1997): 70–84.

46. Robert A. Burgelman and Yves l. Doz, "The Power of Strategic Integration," *MIT Sloan Management Review* 42, no. 3 (2001): 28–38.

47. Ibid., 5.

48. J. Kolotouros, J. Maggioncalda, and R. A. Burgelman, "Disney in a Digital World," Stanford Business School Case No. SM-29, Stanford Business School (Palo Alto, CA: 1996); J. Kolotouros and R. Burgelman, "Disney in a Digital World (B)," Stanford Business School Case No. SM-29B, Stanford Business School (Palo Alto, CA, 1998).

49. Ibid., 13; F. Aguilar, "Johnson & Johnson (B): Hospital Services," Harvard Business School Case No. 9–384–054 (Boston: Harvard Business School Publishing Corp., 1983).

50. Burgelman and Doz, "The Power of Strategic Integration," 14.

51. R. A. Burgelman and P. Meza, "The New HP Way," Stanford Business School case no. SM-7, Stanford Business School (Palo Alto, CA, 2000).

52. Lieber, Ron, "Start-ups—The 'Inside' Stories," *Fast Company* (March 2000), Issue 32, p. 284.

53. Shona L. Brown and Kathleen M. Eisenhardt, *Competing on the Edge: Strategy as Structured Chaos* (Boston: Harvard Business School Press, 1998), 15–17.

54. Leifer et al. *Radical Innovation*, 55–56.

55. Brown and Eisenhardt, *Competing on the Edge: Strategy as Structured Chaos*, 163–167.

56. Ibid., 163–167.

57. Ibid., 241–247.

58. Ibid., 118.

59. Leifer, 2000.

DEVELOPING A BUSINESS PLAN FOR SUSTAINED INNOVATION

OVERVIEW

This chapter will examine

❖ the audience for the business plan

❖ the components of the business plan

❖ the timeline for start-up

INTRODUCTION

Whether an entrepreneurial start-up or a new venture inside a large corporation, any new venture requires a plan if it intends to be successful and sustainable over the long term. Especially in today's chaotic and unpredictable environment, there are many variables to consider in launching a venture, and it would be difficult to determine all the interactions and ramifications of those variables without mapping out a strategy in advance. Although preparing a business plan is no guarantee of success, it can go a long way toward increasing the odds in favor of it. Perhaps more importantly, it is an excellent way for an entrepreneur to ensure that she really understands the business.

Business plans have a different purpose than feasibility analyses. Recall that feasibility analysis is designed to test a concept in the market and determine the conditions under which the business should go forward. In contrast, the business plan is about designing a company to execute the business concept. In that role, the business plan serves as a reality check for entrepreneurs to make sure that they are committed to the concept. The process of doing a business plan uncovers flaws and potential challenges that might not otherwise have been seen and might save the entrepreneur from continuing with a business that will always be a struggle. It can also be the source of opportunity. In 1992, Dari Shalon, a Stanford Ph.D. student, coinvented a DNA chip that had huge commercial potential. The DNA chip is a combination of "chemistry, imaging equipment, and genetics that allows scientists to peer into a cell and measure the activity of its genes, tens of thousands at a time."[1] Ahead of his competitors, Shalon wrote a business plan for a company he called Synteni that would perform inexpensive experiments for customers rather than asking them to purchase a costly system. The business was such a success that it was eventually acquired by Incyte Pharmaceuticals.

The business plan provides a living guide to the business, a blueprint for start-up and growth, and a comprehensive picture of the business in a changing environment. Once completed, the business plan is not a static document. The estimates and assumptions for what is expected to happen change with new information and more experience with the business. It is rare to find an entrepreneur whose projections were right on the mark prior to start-up, but those business plan projections put the company close enough to the real numbers to make starting the venture feasible. The business plan is also a statement of intent for third parties; that is, investors, key management, advisors, strategic partners, and others, who want to know more about the business before they get involved. The particular needs of these third parties will be considered in a later section.

THE AUDIENCE FOR THE BUSINESS PLAN

A variety of interested parties will want to read the business plan to understand how the business works and what the entrepreneur plans for its future. The most important audience is the entrepreneur because the business plan will reflect the current status and direction of the business. Other interested parties include investors, strategic partners, potential management, and bankers, among others.

INVESTORS

Investors are principally interested in how much their investment will appreciate and when they can pull their money out of the venture, reaping the rewards of their investment. Consequently, they will look most closely at those factors that will most affect their return on investment. First and foremost, investors examine the qualifications and track record of the management team in an effort to learn if their investment is in capable hands. If the team does not pass muster, there is no point considering the rest of the plan. For high-tech ventures, they will expect to see expert scientists or engineers who will lead the technical side of the business. It is also advantageous if the new venture has a management team that includes people with business experience in the industry. This is less necessary in the biotech field, where venture capital investors may wish to bring in professional management that they have chosen. Investors will then look at the technology and the market to make sure that it is large enough to give them the return on investment they require. They will also investigate the deal structure in terms of how much equity their investment will buy and what liquidity event is planned that will allow them to cash out of their investment.

STRATEGIC PARTNERS AND FUTURE MANAGEMENT

Partnering with other companies that have core competencies that the new venture needs is a common strategy. Strategic partners will look at the business plan to determine how much business they might get in the future. They also want to know that the new venture can pay for the work the partner does on behalf of the venture.

At some point, the company will need to attract professional management to handle certain aspects of the business or fill in gaps in expertise. The business plan will give these candidates a better idea of the role they might play in the company and what the potential is for moving up in the company.

BANKERS/LENDERS

Bankers are most interested in the company's ability to repay any loan that the bank may choose to extend. Consequently, bankers look at gross profit margins to find out how much room the company has for error between the cost to produce and the selling price. If margins are slim and the company has to lower its prices to compete, it may not be able to pay off its loans in a timely fashion. Bankers also look at cash flow to see if the company can pay all its expenses and still have money left over and at the management team to determine if personal guarantees will be required.

COMPONENTS OF THE BUSINESS PLAN

Although a lot of information needs to be included in the business plan, it is not a game of whoever has the biggest plan wins. In fact, quite the opposite is often true. Investors believe that if the entrepreneur has done his homework and really understands the business, it can be presented in 25 pages or less (preferably less) with supporting documents in an appendix. The writer's goal should be to make it easy for the reader to find information rapidly. That means that the business plan should not read like a novel; it should have headers, lots of white space, charts, and graphs so the reader can navigate it quickly. Investors typically read lots of plans, so they are not interested in spending a long time on a plan to understand the concept. Table 15-1 outlines the key questions that the business plan should answer.

There is no one way to organize a business plan, but there are some components that are common to all plans. They provide the information required to completely understand the business and the intentions of the founders. See Table 15-2 for an outline of the business plan.

THE BUSINESS CONCEPT

The business concept describes the product/service, the primary customer, the benefits being delivered to that customer, and the distribution channel through which the benefits are delivered. The business concept also includes a discussion of the business model, that is, how the company intends to make money, and the status of development of the prototype technology. In this section, the company will spell out its

TABLE 15-1   The Basics of the Business Plan

The Question	Elaboration
What is the need that is being met? Is it compelling?	The answers to these questions come from the market research. Is there a market for the opportunity? How big is that market? Who is the most likely customer? What is the demand?
Is there a team that can serve the need?	Does the new venture team have the passion, experience, and expertise to execute this business concept?
Why now?	Why is this business concept the right one to do now? Why is no one else doing it? Is the current environment right for this concept?
Will the venture return enough on the effort and investment to make it worthwhile to do?	Some concepts are feasible but the market is not large enough to allow the company to grow and return an adequate profit. What is the opportunity cost of this venture?
Is there an effective execution plan for the business?	Does the business plan outline an effective strategy for building a company and launching the first product?

vision and major goals. One of the big mistakes that many entrepreneurs make is to identify broad, sweeping goals such as "dominate the market through customer service," without ever specifying how they will accomplish this enormous task. One of the ways to give the plan focus is to provide a vision and a mission statement. The vision statement paints a picture of what the company will look like 5 or 10 years into the future. It is derived from the company's core values—its fundamental, unchanging beliefs—and its purpose—the company's reason for existence. For example, pharmaceutical giant Merck sees itself as the leader in preserving and improving human life. Incorporated as part of the company's Web site, *www.merck.com*, the core values that support this vision are:

- Preserving and improving human life
- Commitment to the highest standards of ethics and integrity
- Dedication to the highest level of scientific excellence and commitment to research to improve human and animal health and quality of life
- Expectation of profits, but only from work that satisfies customer needs and benefits humanity
- Recognition that the ability to excel depends on the integrity, knowledge, imagination, skill, diversity, and teamwork of employees

The mission, in contrast, is a statement of a clear and compelling, but broad, goal that focuses the effort of the company and tells the world why it is in business. For example:

> The mission of **Merck** is to provide society with superior products and services—innovations and solutions that improve the quality of life and satisfy customer needs—to provide employees with meaningful work and advancement opportunities and investors with a superior rate of return.

www.merck.com

TABLE 15-2 The Business Plan Outline

Main Heading	Possible Subheadings
Proof of Concept/Executive Summary	No more than two pages with key findings from all sections of the business plan
Business Concept	Concept (product/service, customer, benefit, distribution), vision, mission, core values, growth potential
Management Team	Qualifications, needs or gap analysis
Industry/Market Analysis	Industry size, status, potential, trends and patterns of change, profit potential, sales patterns, and gross margins.
	Primary target market demographics, secondary markets, results of primary research, customer profile, needs analysis, distribution channels, entry strategy, competitive analysis, competitive advantage, pricing strategy
Process or Operations Plan	Technical description of product, current status of development, tasks to be completed, time and cost to complete, government approvals required, physical distribution plan, process and work flow, materials and manufacturing requirements, inventory requirements, labor requirements
Management and Organization Plan	Philosophy of management and company culture, legal structure, organizational chart, compensation, and main policies
Marketing Plan	Purpose, target market, unique niche, business identity, plan to reach first customer, media plan, promotional plan
Financial Plan	Summary of key points and capital requirements, breakeven analysis, assumptions, complete financial statements, plan for funding
Growth Plan	Strategy for growth, resources, infrastructure changes
Contingency Plan	Strategies for dealing with change
Harvest or Exit Strategy	What is the liquidity event that will allow the investors to cash out of the deal? How will the founding team harvest its wealth?
Supporting Documents	Resumes, maps, etc.

Another example of a vision and mission statement comes from a new venture, Application Technologies Inc., which is featured in the sidebar "Great Idea; Poor Business Plan":

Vision: Application Technologies will become a leading developer of proprietary, innovative, and value-added packaging delivery systems for consumable products.

Mission: Application Technologies' primary goal is to deliver innovative and value-added unit dose-packaging technologies that create better efficacy and ease of use in topical consumable products. By supplying superior packaging to the consumer, Application Technologies will provide an optimum return on investment to our investors, our strategic partners, and our employees.

www.businessplans.org/Applicat/Applic01.html

THE INDUSTRY/MARKET ANALYSIS

This section of the business plan presents an overview of the industry in which the company will do business: the life cycle stage of the industry; major competitors and competitive rivalry; issues of volatility, uncertainty, and complexity; status of the technology; and typical gross margins. It will also describe the primary and secondary markets for the new technology, who the customer is, what is known about the customer, how big the market is, and how great the demand is. The industry and the economy are the contexts in which the new venture will do business, so it is important that the business plan demonstrate that the entrepreneur understands that context and what the ramifications are for the business. Putting an infeasible business into a new context can often make it feasible. Likewise, taking a successful business and moving it to a new environment can hurt the business. For example, several years ago, one packaging company was facing bankruptcy when the Tylenol-package-tampering incident occurred, causing several deaths. As it happened, the packaging company had the means to install tamper-proof seals in the Tylenol packaging. That single event turned the company around. Every entrepreneur needs to consider what can be done to affect the context in which a new venture will emerge.

In addition to the section on the management team, the market analysis provides the most compelling information for potential investors. Investors do not want to just hear about the size of the market, they want details, particularly about competitors and their strategies and how they compare to the new venture's competitive strategy. For example, do competitors have a core competency that could easily be transferred to the niche the new venture has created? Investors also want to see solid evidence that customers will not only purchase the product, but that they will purchase it from the new company. This is an important distinction. One young entrepreneur developed a very credible business plan in the telecommunications industry. The purpose of the business and its technology was to more effectively use satellite capacity. His potential customers were major broadcasters and cable companies. The entrepreneur was able to prove a substantial demand for his service, but the broadcasters were clearly reluctant to buy from him because he was young, inexperienced, and did not have a credible team. In other words, they did not believe that his team could execute on the concept no matter how good it was.

Where bona fide customers have not been secured, the team needs to present the results from beta customers who have used the product and provided feedback. Sales and distribution partnerships with established companies also boost the credibility of a young start-up and provide evidence for a market demand.

THE FOUNDING TEAM

The founding team component of the business plan provides important evidence that the management team possesses the required knowledge, skills, and experience to execute the business plan. It addresses gaps in these areas and how the team plans to compensate for them. It also discusses the board of directors and board of advisors, as well as any strategic partnerships the company may be engaged in. The quality of the people on the board is a testament to the entrepreneur's business network, access to funding, and various capabilities. William Sahlman has suggested that there are some important questions that potential investors often ask themselves when they view the resumes of the founding team:[2]

- Where do the founders come from?
- Where did they receive their education?
- What is their work experience? For whom have they worked? Is it relevant to the current venture?
- What have they accomplished in both their professional and personal lives?
- What is the team's reputation in their community?
- What skills, knowledge, and abilities do they have?
- How committed is the team to this venture?
- What is the team's motivation for starting the business?

Again, investors and others must be satisfied that the team can make the business happen.

THE OPERATIONS PLAN

In the operations plan, a detailed description of the operations of the business and workflow are presented, including a discussion of the distribution channels that will be used to move the product to the customer. Details about raw material acquisition, manufacturing, assembly, and labor are also addressed. Mapping out the business processes is a way to justify the labor, supply, and equipment needs of the new venture.

MANAGEMENT AND ORGANIZATION PLAN

This section addresses the management philosophy, the company culture, the legal structure, the management organization, and key policies related to employees and compensation. Investors prefer to see a qualified management team in place, particularly a CEO and sales and marketing management. Investors also like to see management teams receiving equity as incentives. They do not mind seeing the use of advisers or people who are moonlighting from full-time jobs to temporarily fill in gaps in the new venture.[3]

TECHNOLOGY PLAN

This section discusses how the company will use technology to create a competitive advantage, both as a product and as an enabler of business goals. The initial technology and its first application are only the beginning. The company needs to map out its innovation strategy several years into the future while at the same time remaining flexible enough to take advantage of new opportunities involving disruptive technology or responding to the technology moves of competitors.

MARKETING PLAN

The marketing plan is based on the company's market research and describes the strategy for creating customer awareness and desire to purchase the product. It includes a discussion of the market niche, the business identity, marketing and promotional tools that will be used to reach the customer, a media plan, and a marketing budget. See the resources at the end of the chapter for more information on marketing plans for high-tech ventures.

FINANCIAL PLAN

This section presents a complete financial picture of the company in the form of pro forma financial statements and an analysis of start-up capital requirements. The premises the founders used in deriving the financial statements are an important component of this section of the business plan because they let the reader understand the rationale behind the numbers. The financial plan demonstrates that the claims about the technology, the market, and the operational strategy will create a business that can be sustained and grow over the long term. Investors are also concerned about gross margins and cash flow. They want to know when the company will break even, that is, cover all its direct costs and begin to make a profit. If the company can make a profit within 18 months, investors will look more seriously at the deal. One rule of thumb is that the company should achieve profitability in about half the time as the investment capital covers. Thus, if the team is seeking capital to cover a year's worth of activity, the company should achieve a profit in half that time, or 6 months. Any projections should take into consideration the state of the economy at the time of the project and over the term of the projections. In general, sales cycles tend to run longer than entrepreneurs project.

CONTINGENCY PLAN

This component of the business plan lets the reader know that the founding team realizes that the best-laid plans may go astray. It presents potential scenarios, usually those with the highest probability of occurring, and describes a plan for minimizing their effects on the new venture. What will happen if one of the founding team leaves the venture? What will the company do if a new competitor emerges that threatens the venture's market? Typically only major events are considered and those with a higher probability of occurring.

GROWTH PLAN

This section is critical because it describes the entrepreneur's plan for taking the company beyond start-up with the primary customer to multiple customers and multiple products. A growth timeline will include trigger points or milestones that will signal the starting point for the next level of growth. For example, a marketing campaign to create awareness and acquire new customers in a particular market segment will probably trigger the need for additional sales people, which is an added expense. It will also trigger increased revenues. These triggers serve as justification for the numbers presented in the financial plan.

DEAL STRUCTURE AND EXIT OR HARVEST STRATEGY

This section is written to address the needs of a potential investor and justifies how much capital is required and at which stages in the life of the venture. It is important that the founding team not include in the business plan how much equity it is willing to relinquish in exchange for investment capital. The terms of an investment deal are always subject to negotiation, and telling a potential investor up front what the team is willing to do diminishes its capacity to negotiate the best deal for the company. This section should also discuss a future liquidity event that would occur within the 5-to-7-year time frame that most investors are looking at for an exit. IPOs are not always in favor, and in the early 2000s, acquisitions seem to be the more popular liquidity event. In that case, the deal structure should include the mention of some potential acquirers and why they are compatible with the new venture. In any event, the exit strategy should show investors how they will recoup their investment and make a return on that investment.

THE EXECUTIVE SUMMARY

The executive summary is perhaps the most important document relative to the business plan because it is the first document an interested party typically sees. The executive summary is designed to give a potential investor or other interested party enough information to stimulate their interest, but not enough to disclose anything proprietary. The goal is to get the person interested enough to begin a dialogue and request a copy of the full business plan. The summary should contain all the important points from the various sections of the business plan. See Table 15-3 for some of the key questions that should be answered in the executive summary.

Many entrepreneurs fail to capture the attention of potential investors because they do not open their executive summary with the compelling story of their business. What is the pain that their product is solving? What customer need is being addressed by their product or service? Provocative statistics and anecdotes are often excellent ways to capture attention quickly. For example, Sudden Presence LLC is a software developer that funds its development of video games through its consulting practice. It caught attention in its executive summary by stating that 99 percent of all software developers do not make a profit and proceeded to describe its concept, which will change that model.[4] Another mistake that is often made is not clearly stating in the first paragraph the business concept—product/service, customer, value proposition,

TABLE 15-3   Executive Summary: Key Questions to Answer

1. What is the business concept? (Business, customer, benefit, distribution)
2. Does the industry support the feasibility of the concept? How? Is it structurally attractive? Are there trends that are favorable to the growth of the new venture?
3. Is the market large enough to permit rapid growth to a reasonable size? (i.e., $50 million in 5 years)
4. Is there customer acceptance for the business and its products/services? What is the demand?
5. What is the entry strategy? How are initial market penetration and the first customer achieved?
6. Who are the key competitors? How will the business differentiate itself?
7. What is the pricing strategy? How is it justified?
8. Does the company have the capabilities in the founding team to successfully implement the plan? If not, how will it fill them?
9. How will the business be organized to facilitate implementation in terms of legal structure, organizational structure, and process?
10. What is the marketing plan in one paragraph?
11. Does the financial plan support a viable business? Summary of key points and capital requirements (needs assessment)
12. How will the business be funded?
13. Does the market support a potential for growth? What are the key growth plans?

and distribution—so that the reader immediately gets a complete picture of the business. Sudden Presence's concept statement is as follows[5]:

> Sudden Presence ("Sudden Presence," "Company," and "SP") is a software developer and technology consultant that designs and directly distributes interactive software for consulting clients and character rich interactive entertainment software for video game publishers. Sudden Presence provides peace of mind and confidence to its customers by funding its own development and providing results that are innovative, on time, marketable, and cross-licensable.

Other areas that should be emphasized in the executive summary include the business model, the profitability potential, and the capability for growth. Investors want to see a solid business model that will make a profit within a reasonable period of time.[6]

A BUSINESS PLAN FOR A GROWING BUSINESS

A start-up business plan focuses on the business concept, but the business plan for an existing business that is attempting to grow has a different focus. It must show how the business will use the capital it secures to grow the business to a particular milestone. Much more is expected of a young company with a track record. Investors will want to see a qualified management team in place that knows how to run a business during rapid growth. They will look for a board with outside directors who bring successful track records to the mix. Investors want to see at least $20 million in revenues with sales occurring in an expanding market and operating margins of at least 10 percent.[7] An existing company has a trend line of sales, a pattern it has developed since start-up. Any major deviation from that pattern when projecting into the future must be substantiated by a serious change in some aspect of the business that will allow it to increase its historical rate of growth. This change could be new management, a proprietary process, or a disruptive technology. The company must also defend its competitive advantages in the market and show how they can be sustained.

THE PLAN OF ATTACK

Understanding what goes into the business plan is only half the process. Having a plan of attack or strategy for writing the business plan is the other half. Here are several steps that will make the writing of a business plan more manageable.

ESTABLISH OBJECTIVES

A business plan should be prepared with a particular audience in mind, despite the fact that many of the components are in common no matter who the audience is. This is why companies often have more than one version of their plan, each plan addressing the specific needs of a particular audience. Furthermore, what is the company attempting to communicate with the plan? Is the company seeking funding? Strategic partners? Key management?

PREPARE AN OUTLINE

With the objectives firmly in mind, an outline can be prepared that will identify all the key points that will be brought out in the plan. Working from an outline such as the one depicted in Table 15-2 makes it easier to get through the process and not leave anything out.

WRITE THE PLAN

One of the easiest ways to begin writing the business plan (and beginning is always the difficult part) is to gather all the research that has been collected in one place. Then set up a template on the computer that contains headers for all the sections of the business plan as identified in the outline. Moving through the stack of research, enter the findings in the appropriate category in the business plan. Then go back through the plan to fill in the gaps, draw conclusions, and generally smooth out the transitions between ideas. It is important not to wait until the very end to prepare the financial statements because many of the decisions made in the plan will be predicated on results obtained in the financial projections. Before preparing the financials, detail the assumptions that support the numbers that appear in the statements. The executive summary is generally prepared last so that it contains all of the key findings from the major sections of the business plan.

HAVE THE PLAN REVIEWED

It is always a wise idea to have someone knowledgeable in business plans review the plan. The entrepreneur is too close to the concept and will often read things into the plan that are not there. Modify the plan based on the reviewer's comments. If the plan is for a technology concept that is fairly complex, it might be a good idea to have someone who does not understand the technology read the plan to see if it has been explained clearly enough for the average reader. Be sure to keep the plan updated as new information comes in or as the company begins to gain experience and the financial projections become more realistic.

THE BUSINESS PLAN PRESENTATION

Entrepreneurs are often asked to present their business plans in a formal or informal presentation before potential investors. This will typically happen after the potential investors have read the executive summary and perhaps the complete business plan. With a presentation, the investor's goal is to learn more about the founding team, their passion for the project, and their ability to withstand the intense questioning that usually follows a presentation. In general, the presentation should be designed to answer the fundamental questions about the business (see Table 15-1) in less than half an hour. Like the executive summary, it is important to catch the audience's attention in the first 60 seconds with a provocative statistic or anecdote that describes the pain or compelling story behind the business concept.

The best presenter among the founding team should make the presentation. However, if the team as a whole is generally effective as speakers, then perhaps the technical side of the team could present the technical issues and the business side of the team present the business issues. In either case, it is important not to spend the bulk of the time on the technology itself and short change the business model and market research, which are of great importance to the investors. Entrepreneurs are frequently "in love" with their technologies and fail to recognize that investors are more interested in the team and the market than the technology itself. Visual aids in the form of presentation slides and demos are vital to getting the concept across to the audience, but they should not overwhelm the presentation so that the focus is on the visual aids rather than on what the presenter is saying. They should be a supplement to the presentation, not the presentation itself. Of vital importance is testing any demonstrations of technology in advance of the presentation to make sure they work as intended, especially if the technology is in prototype form.

The presentation is the first hurdle; the more important hurdle is the question-and-answer period. Some things to remember about the Q&A are that investors usually know the answers to the questions they are asking, and they will often ask questions that require impossibly precise answers or are so broad that it is not easy to know what the investor is looking for in an answer. A question that poses real problems for most presenters is the one that is very complex with many underlying assumptions. For example, "If I were to consider your venture in terms of its operational strategy before and after this investment, how might that strategy change, and how would that change affect your financial projections?" There is no way to answer such a question without considerable thought and clarification. One approach is to ask the questioner to repeat the question; that gives the team time to digest it and then repeat back the various parts in an effort to clarify the intention of the questioner. What the questioner really wants to know with this type of question is if the team can make snap decisions about strategy and if they can be pushed to change their strategy just because a potential investor suggests that they should. The team should not commit to any course of action or changes in the financial projections at the presentation. Telling the investor that this is an important question that requires time to consider will signal to the investor that the team does not make precipitous decisions without considering all the ramifications.

If the investor group criticizes the team or the concept, it does not mean that they are not interested. They may merely be testing the team's ability to withstand criticism and defend their decisions. It is important in this situation not to become defensive but to restate the basis for any strategy, decision, or finding firmly and confidently.

❖ Great Idea; Poor Business Plan

Johann Verheem had a difficult decision to make. He was about to take a big risk and leave a very successful position at Guthy-Renker, the infomercial leader, where he was director of product development, to start a business for which he had developed a plan while at San Diego State University earning an MBA. Verheem had already taken one big risk when he left his family and friends in South Africa and came to the United States to find a new life. At the time he was deciding whether to leave his job and start a business, his wife was expecting their first child and his company was doing everything possible to entice him to stay.

An acquaintance approached Verheem with the idea for Appli-K pouch, a pillow-shaped sealed container made from Mylar or any of a number of other materials used for dispensing medications. The two agreed that it would be a great project to undertake in Verheem's business plan class. To use the pouch, the consumer would simply peel two sealed flaps back over the pouch to open it, and then squeeze. The flaps protected the fingers so a person could apply a medication without ever touching the wound or blemish. Because the class required that students work in teams, Verheem chose Natasha King, who specialized in market research, and the two took on the project together. By the fall of 1998, they had developed a strategy for bringing the product to market. The business plan called for strategic partnerships with manufacturers who would make the product, then Verheem and King would license it to large consumer products manufacturers such as Procter & Gamble. In this way, they would not incur the heavy costs of building a manufacturing facility and hiring labor, yet they would have real assets and continuing revenue streams. The team believed that the pain they were solving was the unnecessary mess on a person's hand and contamination to the medication or cream prior to its application to a wound. After hundreds of hours of work, the business plan received a B– from their professor, who ironically would later serve on their board of directors. He claimed that they had not done a good job of articulating their vision for the business. Little did they know that the B– would actually predict the eventual outcome of the business.

In the meantime, their professor entered the team in multiple business plan competitions, and in the fall of 1999, Verheem and King won the NASDAQ-Amex/SDSU Business Plan Competition and its $10,000 prize. By that time, Verheem was receiving plenty of encouragement to start the business from friends and even the professor who had given him a B– on his business plan. Finally, he made the decision to go for it and gave a large chunk of the equity in the new company to Kurt Koptis, the inventor, in exchange for rights to other inventions, including the Appli-Can, a spray container with a brush molded into the cap. His business plan projected that the pouch product alone would turn the company into a $20 million business. He could easily see a $100 million company in his future.

In January 1999, Verheem started Application Technologies with $230,000 in seed capital, which covered start-up costs and the cost of building the production prototypes. In April of that same year, Verheem raised another $225,000 to bring management on board full time. The company began filing for four additional patents for packaging products and acquired several strategic partners for design and manufacturing. By January 2001, Verheem was admitting that he had succeeded in introducing pouch packaging as a revolutionary technology, but he had not succeeded in building the company as he had projected in the business plan. The business plan had projected $1.2 million in revenues and four employees in 2000. The actual numbers came in at $750,000 and three employees. Realizing that the company was not what he had wanted, he then entered into an acquisition agreement to sell the company for $4 million, which would provide a decent return for the stockholders.

Verheem learned several valuable lessons from the experience. First and foremost, it is important to start a business in an industry for which the entrepreneur has passion. Verheem's passion was marketing, but he found himself in the packaging business. He wanted to start a company, but his business model had him licensing his product. The second important lesson was that "when you work for

(continued)

somebody else, you don't necessarily know what it takes to get that paycheck to you."[8] Now he definitely understands in a very profound way what it feels like to be accountable.

Source: Michael Warshaw, "The Start-Up Diaries: Plan B-Minus," *Inc Magazine,* January 1, 2000, *www.inc.com;* "Confidence Man," *Inc Magazine,* January 1, 2001, *www.inc.com;* "Application Technologies Inc." MOOT CORP Competition, *www.businessplans.org/Applicat/Applic01.html.*

TIME IS OF THE ESSENCE

Entrepreneurs are typically optimistic about the amount of time it takes to start a business and reach its various milestones (see Figure 15-1). They are particularly optimistic about the amount of time the start-up will spend in what is termed *the valley of death,* that is, the period during which a lot of money is being spent, but no revenues are coming into the business.[9] R&D, beta testing, and final product development all generally occur within this period. Biotech start-ups typically have the longest valley of death. Many potentially great biotech discoveries never make it to market because the team cannot secure enough capital to sustain the business until revenues begin.

Product development always takes much longer than predicted. Because a technology works in the laboratory does not mean that it is ready for the market. It will have to be tested under the toughest of conditions many times before the team can feel confident that it is ready for sale to its customer market.

Securing customers, suppliers, distributors, employees, and strategic partners takes more time than most entrepreneurs plan for. Companies that are producing products

FIGURE 15-1 BUSINESS DEVELOPMENT TIMELINE

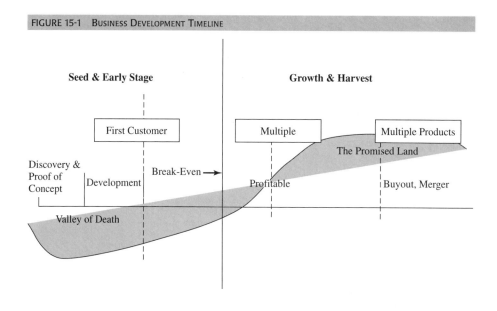

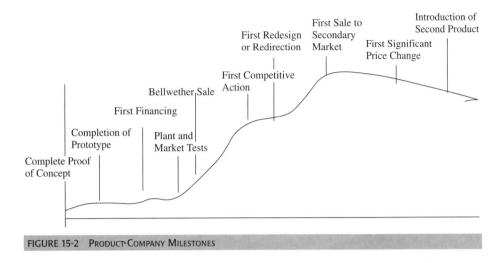

FIGURE 15-2   PRODUCT-COMPANY MILESTONES

under the regulatory control of the FDA need to check out the timelines for approvals, which can take from a few months to several years, as in the case of pharmaceutical development. Safety regulations and certifications come into play in nearly every industry, which is why it is so important to understand the nature of the industry in which the company will operate.

Securing start-up capital is a test of endurance for the team. Even identifying the appropriate sources of funding at particular stages is a difficult and time-intensive task taking several months if not a year or more. Once the investor is identified, a period of due diligence and negotiation adds additional time to the projections. See Figure 15-2 for a typical timeline with milestones.

To survive the ravages and frustrations of time delays, it is important that the team be realistic about their projections and anticipate what could possibly cause delays in their progress. Because starting a technology venture is a test of endurance, it is important to also plan for providing balance in the lives of the founding team and any employees. All work and no play create a frantic environment and a level of pressure that few people can tolerate. Start-up is a journey, not a destination; it is a marathon, not a sprint. Therefore, the team must go into the process prepared to last for the long term.

The business plan is a worthy undertaking, but make no mistake about it; it takes a lot of time and effort to do it well. Nevertheless, the rewards are great. High-tech entrepreneurs with business plans generally are far better informed about the industry in which they will do business, the company they will run, the competitors they will meet in the marketplace, and the customers who determine the success of the business than those who move forward without a plan. Entering a volatile market equipped with vital information and a strategy for going forward increases the odds of success.

❖ SUMMARY

It is important for a high-tech venture to develop a business plan, whether that venture is a start-up, a rapidly growing company, or a new venture inside a large corporation. Business plans have a different purpose than feasibility analyses. Recall that feasibility analysis is designed to test a concept in the market and determine the conditions under which the business should go forward. In contrast, the business plan is about designing a company to execute the business concept. In that role, the business plan serves as a reality check for the entrepreneur to make sure that they are committed to the concept, a living guide to the business or blueprint for start-up and growth, and a statement of intent for interested parties. Those interested parties may include investors, lenders, suppliers, key management, or strategic partners. The business plan answers the questions: (1) What is the need that is being met? (2) Is there a team that can serve the need? (3) Why should this business be done now? (4) Will the venture return enough on the effort and investment to make it worthwhile to do? and (5) Is there an effective execution plan for the business? The business plan consists of a description of the concept, the industry/market analysis, the founding team, the operations plan, the management and organization plan, the technology plan, the marketing plan, the financial plan, the contingency plan, the growth plan, and the deal structure or exit plan. The executive summary is perhaps the most important piece of information because most investors will not read the business plan unless they find the executive summary compelling. The business planning process involves establishing objectives, preparing an outline, writing the plan, and having the plan reviewed. Entrepreneurs are often asked to present their business plans in a formal or informal presentation before potential investors. This will typically happen after the potential investors have read the executive summary and perhaps the complete business plan. With a presentation, the investor's goal is to learn more about the founding team, their passion for the project, and their ability to withstand the intense questioning that usually follows a presentation.

❖ DISCUSSION QUESTIONS

1. In what ways is a business plan different from a feasibility analysis?
2. How would an investor's view of the business plan be different from a banker's view? A strategic partner's view?
3. What is the strategic role of the executive summary?
4. How is a business plan for a growing company different from one for a start-up?

❖ RESOURCES

Covello, Joseph, and Brian J. Hazelgren. *Your First Business Plan,* 3d ed. Naperville, IL: Sourcebooks Trade, 1998.

Hoff, R. *I Can See You Naked*. Kansas City, MO: Andrews McMeel Publishing, 1992.

Horan, James T, Jr., Jim Horan, and Rebecca S. Shaw. *The One-Page Business Plan.* El Sobrante, CA: The One-Page Business Plan Company, 1998.

Mohr, Jakki. *Marketing of High-Technology Products and Innovations.* Upper Saddle River, NJ: Prentice Hall, 2001.

Pinson, Linda, and Jerry Jinnett. *Anatomy of a Business Plan*, 4th ed. Chicago, IL: Dearborn Publishing, 1999.

❖ INTERNET RESOURCES

BizPlanit

www.bizplanit.com/vplan.htm
Site that helps entrepreneurs create, evaluate, and improve business plans

Build a Strong Business Plan, Section by Section

www.inc.com/guide/item/0,7462, CHL1_GDE66,00.html
Inc.'s guide to writing business plans

Business Plan Templates

www.vfinance.com/
Business plan templates that can be downloaded and viewed in Microsoft Word

SBA: The Business Plan Roadmap to Success

www.sba.gov/starting/indexbusplans.html
An SBA site dedicated to helping entrepreneurs write business plans

AN ILLUMINATING BUSINESS PLAN

How does a company such as Color Kinetics move from a 1997 start date to listing Disney, Sony, Loews, Marriott, Royal Caribbean Cruise Lines, and Boston Symphony Hall as a few of its customers in October 2001? It takes a plan. George Mueller and his cofounder, Ihor Lys, met at Carnegie Mellon University, where Lys was earning a doctorate in electrical engineering and Mueller was majoring in computer and electrical engineering and minoring in fine art. After graduation, the R&D work that would ultimately lead to a patent began as a sporadic effort on the weekends as they met in Mueller's Boston apartment. In 1992, they entered the world of lighting by building a novelty sign that consisted of a single vertical row of LEDs that displayed "slices of an image, one column at a time."[10] The first sign was dedicated to Mueller's mother and said "love," the second read "beer." As Mueller was taking business classes, they decided to write a business plan to develop this concept and the company that would execute it, Stone Age Technologies. At the time, the only goals they had were to earn some money and get some free signs. However, Stone Age Technologies was quickly put into hibernation when Mueller decided to found an economics research firm, Internet Securities, Inc., with his brother, Gary. That firm was a success, and in 1999 the brothers sold 80 percent of the company for $43 million.

Meanwhile, by 1997, still dreaming about LEDs, Mueller went back to the concept of digital lighting, and he and Lys began working seriously on the concept from Muellers' fourth-floor walkup in Boston. It was there that they founded their company, calling it Color Kinetics. They had discovered a way to hook an LED device to a computer chip board to create an array of light-ing effects. Rather than the traditional dimmers, sleeves, and gels that lighting designers typically used, their system used red, green, and blue LEDs to create more than 16 million colors and hues. Furthermore, instead of a complex and costly maze of circuitry, switches, and levers, their system ran off PC or DMX intelligence. The flexibility of their system allowed them to create a variety of different color environments.

Color Kinetic's first employee was David Johnson, who took on the role of president of finance in October 1997. Johnson brought experience in managing high-end software companies to the team. Later that year, Mueller and his team lugged 30 Color Kinetics prototypes—everything they had—to Las Vegas for the Dimensions International show. In the middle of million-dollar, high-tech booths, Color Kinetics set up a tent, laid down some old carpet, and plugged in a laser printer to print out promotional material for attendees. Despite the bootstrapped presentation, it was obvious that Color Kinetics had created a radically new innovation in lighting, and people wanted to place orders even though the team had yet to determine its pricing model. At the show, Color Kinetics managed to win the Architectural Lighting product of the Year award, the first of many awards to follow. The orders began pouring in, far more than they had ever predicted. One of their first major customers was Focus Lighting in New York, which integrated the Color Kinetics system into its sign for the Loews 42nd Street E Walk Theatre. That project cost almost $2 million, more than three times the price of a neon sign, but the Color Kinetics lighting will last 11.7 years of continuous use.

Unlike many high-tech ventures, in its fourth year of business, Color Kinetics already had product and revenues, as well as two patents on its core technology, Chromacore, which generates colored light using a microprocessor and additive color mixing. Based on LEDs, it offers a life of 100,000 hours, uses very little power, produces no heat or UV emissions, and has the ability to create dynamic color without moving parts. This means that the lighting effects can be used in a variety of environments.

THE INDUSTRY

The global market for incandescent bulbs, fluorescent tubes, and halogen lamps is about $11.5 billion. In contrast, the market for visible-light LEDs is a tiny $680 million, with an expected growth to $1.8 billion within 5 years. LEDs were first developed in the 1960s. They consist of tiny chips of semiconductor material encased in clear epoxy. When electricity runs through them, they give off a white light. The positively charged regions of the material are called "holes," and negatively charged electrons, which produce a photon of light, fill them. The greater the energy gap, the higher the photon energy, and the level of energy determine the light that is displayed. On the color spectrum, blue and violet photons contain the most energy. Engineers can change the amount of energy by using different materials.

LEDs have become popular for many uses because they are efficient, using only 15 watts of electricity versus the normal 150 watts, and they last longer. For example, many of the red traffic lights in the United States are LEDs, and they are expected to do their job of halting traffic for about 10 years. Still, for mainstream consumer adoption, they will be too expensive for the foreseeable future. Agilent Technologies is predicting that it will produce a 1,500 lumen LED (equivalent to a 100-watt incandescent bulb) that will carry a price of $150 in a few years, which is still very high for the average consumer. A group of researchers is seeking government funding to advance the state of LED technology to the point that it can compete with traditional lighting technology and provide a significant savings in energy.

For mass-market adoption, there is another challenge. Incandescent light has a yellow cast, which gives it a warm feel that is compatible with skin tones. In contrast, white phosphor LEDs emit a blue tone, which gives human skin a deathly pallor. It is expected that over time, LED users will be able to dial up the color tone they want.

THE PLAN

When they founded Color Kinetics in 1997, Mueller and Lys did not envision "conquering the world." Instead, they were focused on giving customers what they wanted, nothing more, nothing less. By 2001, the company had received a third round of funding of $13 million and was poised to enter the international market with 29 distributors. In April 2001, Color Kinetics opened its first office in Japan as a joint venture with ALS, Inc., the planning division of a leading professional light company in Japan that had been distributing the company's products in Japan. Locating an office in Japan would give Color Kinetics the ability to focus on the unique needs of Japanese customers and build its visibility as the digital technology leader in the lighting industry.

In September 2001, the company brought on William J. Sims as President and Chief Operating Officer to position the company for rapid growth in the illumination market, which analysts now predict will reach $30 billion by 2010. Sims brought upper-level management experience from such notable companies as Zenith, JVC, and e-SIM, where in every case he improved profitability significantly and expanded the company's worldwide markets. What made it possible to attract this level of talent was Color Kinetics' business model, the technological potential, and the culture of innovation that Mueller and Lys had built.

Today, the company has nearly 100 employees in 40,000 square feet on Milk Street in downtown Boston and revenues of over $21 million. Its patent portfolio is growing as it seeks to protect the use of multiple colored LEDs to generate fully controllable white light. In October 2001, the company was awarded its fifth patent (#6,292,901), which covers its Smartjuice intelligent power technology that involves methods and systems for multiplexing power and data over conventional wiring to permit control of intelligent digital light fixtures.

Having captured significant success in the professional lighting space, Color Kinetics is now expanding into the pool and spa arena as a first step into the consumer products space. Having successfully executed a business plan for starting the company, they must now develop a plan for growing into a new arena. What are some of the challenges they face? How will business planning help them overcome those challenges? ▪

Sources: Neil Savage, "LEDs Light the Future," *MIT Technology Review*, (September–October 2000): *www.techreview.com*; Ken Shulman, "The Color of Money," *Metropolis Magazine* (May 2001): *www. metropolismag.com/html/content_0501/ent/index.html*; "Color Kinetics Continues Global Expansion with the Formation of Color Kinetics Japan," *PR Newswire*, March 7, 2001; "Color Kinetics Appoints New President and Chief Operating Officer to Lead Company's Continued Expansion and Technology Innovation," *PR Newswire*, September 25, 2001; "Color Kinetics Expands Intellectual Property Portfolio with Fifth U.S. Patent for Intelligent Illumination Technologies," *PR Newswire*, October 11, 2001.

❖ NOTES

1. "The 1999 TR100," *MIT Technology Review* (November–December 1999), *www.techreview.com*.
2. Ibid.
3. Emily Barker, "The Bulletproof Business Plan," *Inc.* (October 1, 2001), *www.inc.com*.
4. Ara Grigorian, Armen Grigorian, Gary Kirschner, *Sudden Presence LLC*, written as a course project at the University of Southern California, Fall 2001.
5. Ibid.
6. Ibid.
7. Business Briefs:, "Business Plans for Private Equity Seekers," *Financial Executive* 17, no. 8 (November 2001): 11.
8. Michael Warshaw, "The Start-Up Diaries: Plan B-Minus, *Inc.*, January 1, 2000, *www.inc.com*.
9. Daniel Muzyka and Sue Birley, "Time Pressures Can Cloud the Mind," in Sue Birley and Daniel F. Muzyka, eds., *Mastering Entrepreneurship* (London: Financial Times-Prentice Hall, 2000), 159–163.
10. Neil Savage, "LEDs Light the Future," *MIT Technology Review* (September–October 2000) *www.techreview.com*.

A

Acquisition
  See Growing the high-tech venture
Addante, Frank, 78, 81
Adoption-Diffusion (A-D) model, 175–176, 260
Aligned companies, 212
Amazon.com, 114, 118, 223
Amazon.com v. Barnesandnoble.com, 122
*American Express v. American Express
    Limousine Service*, 116
*American Home Products Corp. v. Johnson
    Chemical Co., Inc.*, 153
America Online (AOL), 4
Angel investors, 196–197
Antidilution provision, 218
Apple's Newton Message Pad, 4, 236, 318
Application, 29–30
Application Technologies, Inc., 339–340
Autodesk, 109–110
Avery Dennison Corporation, 150

B

Backward integration, 294
Balanced portfolio, 176
Balsillie, Jim, 308–309
Bankers, as audience for a business plan, 337
Barriers to entry, 57
Beaver, Don, 331–332
Benefit measurement, 91
Bezos, Jeff, 223
BioForce Laboratory, Inc., 12
Biometrics, 7
Biotechnology, funding for, 199–201
BountyQuest, 152
Bracketing, 149–150
Brain-machine interfaces, 6
Brand, 145
Brand presence, 278–279
Build, 18
Building, 32
Build-to-sell model, 19
Built to flip, 19, 85
Built to Last, 4, 19

Burn rate, 180
Business concept, 337–340
  See also Technology business concept
Business method patents, 122–123
Business model, 146
Business model, building and valuing, 168
  constructing effective models, 172–173
  drivers of value, 173
    added growth, 174, 175
    balanced portfolio, 176
    license agreement, 176–178
    new application, 174–176
    valuation process example, 178–180
    when value is discounted, 178
  financial models for assessing value, 180
    intellectual capital management, 181
    pro forma discounted cash flow model,
      182–183
    real options model, 183
    royalty method, 183
    valuations based on cost, 181
    venture capital methods, 183–184
  Pixstream Inc.: The Value of Intangible Assets
    (case study), 186–187
  radical innovation models, 169
    incremental environment, 171
    multiple revenue streams, 171–172
    strategic positioning in the value chain,
      170–171
Business models for innovation, 18
  build-to-sell model, 19
  inventor platform, 19
Business plan, 137
  basics of (table), 338
  for a growing business, 344–345
  outline (table), 339
  prelaunch, 97
  presentation, 345–346
  for sustained innovation, 335
    audience for, 336–337
    components of, 337–348
    An Illuminating Business Plan (case study),
      352–354
    time is of the essence, 348–349

Business valuation, 218–219
Buyer's power, 57

C

Cadence Design Systems, Inc., 94, 99–100
Callaway Golf, 287, 288
Callidus Software, 228
Campari (lending gauge), 210–211
Canitano, Nick, 227
Capital
    cost of raising, 203–204
    difficulty in securing, 190
    start-up, 349
Carbon Nantechnologies Inc. (CNI), 12
Cardiometrics, 19
Caretaker strategy (manufacturing), 243
Carew, Jim, 324
Change, corporate venturing and, 314–319
Chan, K. W., 287
Charmed Technology, 13–14
Chase Bobko, 291
Chen, Humphrey, 206–207
Chesebrough, Robert, 8
Chevron, 299
Christensen, Clayton, 9, 294, 311, 317
Chrysler, 312
Cisco, 312
Citation trees, 161
Cobranding, 279
Coca-Cola, 145, 155
Collaboration on inventions, 158–160
Collins, Jim, 4, 19
Color Kinetics, 352–354
Combinatorial research, 95–96
Commercialization
    graphical depiction of, 87–88
    prior to patent protection, 156–157
    See also Innovation and commercialization
Commoditization of technology, 299
Comparable transaction method, 184
Competition analysis, 58–61
Competition-based strategy, 287
Competitive advantage, 5–6
    patents as
        building a coalition, 150–151
        creating a patent wall, 149–150
        maintaining patents, 151
        running, 150
Competitive market, 257

Competitive uncertainty, 258
Competitor rivalry, 58
Complexity, 258–259
Computer-aided systems, 96
Computer Motion, 165–166
Concept investigation, 93
Concept testing, 62
Conglomerate diversification, 294
Connection, 29
ConneXus Corp., 206–207
ContentGuard, 6
Contingency plan, 342
Control rights, 219–220
Convergent thinking, 31
Co-operation
    See Growing the high-tech venture
Cooper, Robert, 86–88
Copyrights
    See Intellectual property
Core competencies, 313
    vs. change, 315
Core rigidities, 313
Corporate entrepreneurship, 312, 320
    source of disruptive technology
        opportunities, 323
    stumbling blocks, 321
    See also Entrepreneurial venturing inside a
        corporation
Corporate funding, 201
Corporate venture
    defined, 312
    environmental conditions' influence on, 314
    winning climate for, 325–326
Corporations, 247–248
Cost-based valuations, 181
Creative destruction, 5, 315
Creative thinking, challenges to, 30
Creativity
    in innovation, 7–8
    See also Technology opportunities
Credit cards, as funding for a start-up, 193
Cross-licensing, 146
Customer profiles, 66
Customers, 190
    creating tacit knowledge for, 296
    learning to say no to, 291
    sophisticated, 14–15
    understanding needs of, 266–269
Customer uncertainty, 257
Cycle time, reducing, 95–96

D

Data mining, 6
da Vinci, Leonardo, 29–30
da Vinci (robotic surgery system), 165–166
Deal structure, 342–343
Debt, 210–211
Dell Computer Corp., 174, 299
Delphi Method, 270–271
Demand, forecasting, 66–67, 270–271
de Mestral, George, 8
Design, development, platform testing, 93–94
Designing right the first time, 94
Design patents, 121–122
Details, paying attention to, 290
Deterministic problems, 31
Diamond v. Chakrabarty, 120
Differentiation strategy (entry), 238–239
Digital Equipment Corporation, 168
Digital Light Processing, 319
Digital Millenium Copyright Act
        (DCMA), 115
Digital rights management, 6
Direct public offering: Regulation A, 222–223
Disclosure Document Program, 123
Discontinuities phase in technology life
        cycle, 299
Discounted cash flow (DCF), 92
    business model, 182–183
Discovery, 29, 88–89
Disincentives of intellectual property, 111–112
Disruptive (radical) model of innovation, 9–12
Disruptive technology, 299, 315
    large companies' challenges with, 317
Distribution architecture, 295–296
Distribution channel analysis, 67–70
Distributors, 189–190
Divergent thinking, 30–31
Diversification, 293–294, 305
Diversity, 256
Doctrine of equivalents, 148
Domain names, 118
Dominant design life cycles, 295, 296
Dot-com implosion, 2–3
Drivers of value
    See Value
DR-LINK software, 161
Drucker, Peter, 88–89
Dubinsky, Donna, 23–25
Due diligence, 133, 216

E

Early adopters, 175, 268–269
Early majority, 176
Early stage capital, 191
        See also Funding the technology start-up
Eaton Corporation, 195
Economic Commercial Value (ECV), 92
Economic Espionage Act of 1996, 155
Economic life of a technology, 40
Economic models, 91–92
Economies of scale, 4–5
Eisner, Michael, 322–323
Eli Lilly Co., 152
Emerging markets, 269
Empathic design, 268
EndoSonics, 19
Engineering approach to creative problem
        solving, 32
Entrepreneurial immersion, 323–324
Entrepreneurial opportunity recognition
        process, 34
Entrepreneurial venturing inside a corporation,
        311–312
    nature of, 313–314
    New Pig Corporation: A Study in Corporate
        Innovation (case study), 331–332
    paths to, 319
        entrepreneurial immersion, 323–324
        skunk works, 320–322
        strategic integration, 322–323
    role of change in facilitating, 314
        core competency vs. change, 315
        how Xerox learned to innovate
            radically, 316
        pioneering firm, 317–318
        venture champions, 318–319
    success as a corporate entrepreneur, 324
        living with chaos, 326–329
        winning climate, 325–326
Entry strategy, 238–239
Equity, 211
Equity arrangements, 193–194
Executive summary, 343–344
Exit strategy, 342–343

F

Fair use, 115
Fayyad, Usama, 6

FDA phase I testing for biotechnology, 200
Feasibility
    questions prior to, 53–54
    See also Technical feasibility analysis
Feasibility analysis, 51
    conducting, 54–55
Feasible business model, constructing, 71–73
Festo Corp. v. Shoketsu Kinzoku Kogyo
            Kabushiki Co., 148
Fiber-optic industry, 169–170
Financial models for assessing value
    See Business model, building and valuing
Financial plan, 342
Financing strategy for growth, 211–213, 214
    See also Funding growth
First-mover advantage, 3–4, 15, 150
First-mover strategy, 279
Five Cs (lending gauge), 210–211
Flexible manufacturing, 243–244
Flexible transistors, 6
Fluid phase in technology life cycle, 298
Focus groups, 65–66
Forecasting demand, 66–67, 270–271
Foreign patents, 125–126
Forward integration, 294
Founding team, 70–71, 340–341
Framing, 154
Franchising, 293
Friendly money, 192–193
Fullerenes, 12
Fully Integrated Pharmaceutical Company
            (FIPCO) (business model), 200–201
Funding growth, 209
    debt, 210–211
    equity, 211
    financing strategy for, 211–213
    initial public offering, 223
        failure of, 227
        measures of success, 224
        process of, 224–227
    presenting the company to investors, 228
        tools of the trade, 229
    private offering, 221
        direct public offering: Regulation A,
            222–223
        small corporate offering registration, 222
    From Riches to Rags and Back?: When Going
            Public May Not Be the Right Path
            (case study), 231–232
    venture capital funding, 213
        aftermath, 220–221

business valuation, 218–219
control rights, 219–220
due diligence, 216
risk and return assessment, 216–218
screening criteria, 214–220
timing of funding, 220
Funding the technology start-up, 189
    cost of raising capital, 203–204
    early stage capital, 195
        angel investors and networks, 195–197
        biotechnology funding, 199–201
        corporate funding, 201
        venture capital at start-up, 197–199
    government sources
        Small Business Administration
            (SBA), 203
        Small Business Innovation Research
            (SBIR) grants, 202
        Small Business Investment Company, 203
        Small Business Technology Transfer
            Research (STTR) program, 202–203
    Prepare for the Money Hunt (case study),
            206–207
    risks and stages of financing, 190–192
    seed capital
        credit cards and other debt, 193
        equity arrangements, 193–194
        friendly money, 192–193
        R&D partnerships, 195
        strategic partnerships and other intermedi-
            aries, 194–195
Fuzzy Front End (FFE), 38

G

Gallo, Robert, 160
Gates, Bill, 19
Genentech, 2, 169
Gene patents, 121
General Agreement of Tariffs and
            Trade (GATT)
    trademarks and, 117
General Motors, 300
Gentech Corporation, 62–63
Gerstner, Louis, Jr., 12
Gillette, 149
Glaxo, 271
Globalization, 14
Goddard, Robert, 297
Gordon, Robert, 11
Gould, Gordon, 128–129

Governance structure, 303
Government funding sources
  See Funding the technology start-up
Gower, Bob, 12
Grantback clause, 138–139
Grant clause, 138
Greene, Todd, 52
Grove, Andy, 2, 10
Growing the high-tech venture, 286–287
  conventional growth strategies, 292
    diversification, 293–294
    of industry, 294
    market development, 293
    market penetration, 293
    product development, 293
  co-operation in the photonics
      industry, 303
  growth through co-operation and acquisition,
      297–298
    outsourcing for knowledge capabilities,
      299–300
    risk factors and remedies in co-operation,
      302–304
    strategic alliances, 300–302
  growth through R&D, 294
    build value through architecture and capa-
      bility, 295
    create a distribution and supply architec-
      ture, 295–296
    define scope of innovation, 295
    help customers create tacit knowledge, 296
    plan strategically for innovation, 296–297
    risks of radical innovation, 297
    target dominant design life cycles,
      295, 296
  nature of growth
    pitfalls, 288–290
    what it takes to grow, 290–292
  Rapid Growth with BlackBerry? (case study),
      308–309
  strategies for setting technology
      standards, 304
    diversification, 305
    licensing, 305
    strategic alliances, 305
Growth
  value of added, 174, 175
  See also Funding growth; Growing the high-
      tech venture
Growth funding, 191
Growth plan, 342

H

Harper, Stephen, 289
Harvest strategy, 342–343
Hauser, John R., 100
Hawkins, Jeff, 23–25
HeadBlade, 52–53
Hewlett-Packard, 4, 86, 112–113, 301–302,
    315, 323
High technology product development
      strategies, 84
  identifying winners, 86–87
  IDEO: Where Innovation Is the Culture (case
      study), 105–106
  metrics for success, 97
    increasing R&D effectiveness, 99–100
    managing risk of R&D, 98–99
    measuring R&D effectiveness, 100
  new product development, 87
    in-house product testing, 96
    phase 1: opportunity recognition or discov-
      ery, 88–89
    phase 1: technology screening and platform
      identification, 89–92
    phase 2: concept investigation, 93
    phase 2: design, development, platform test-
      ing, 93–94
    phase 2: predevelopment financial
      analysis, 93
    phase 3: design and development of the
      product family, 94–96
    phase 4: limited market trial, 96
    phase 4: market launch to full
      operation, 97
    phase 4: prelaunch business plan, 97
  new product failure, 85–86
  outsourcing technology innovation,
      100–103
High-tech ventures
  See Growing the high-tech venture
Hiring, 290
Hitachi, 161
Hockey stick approach, 184
Horizontal alliances, 301–302
Horizontal mergers, 299
Human capital, 146
  lack of sufficient and qualified, 289
Human Genome Project, 3, 12–13
Human Genome Sciences, 121
Hyatt, Gilbert, 148
Hybrid license, 156

I

IBM, 134, 147, 320, 326
Idea, 27
IDEO (design company), 105–106
Incentives
    to commercialize, 111
    to disclose, 111
    to invent, 110–111
Incremental environment, radical innovation
    in, 171
Incremental innovation, 265
Incumbent's curse, 10–11
Indeterminate problems, 31
Industry analysis, 340
    framework for, 56
        barriers to entry, 57
        buyers' power, 57
        competitor rivalry, 58
        substitute products, 57
        suppliers' power, 57
        technology, 58
    industry growth cycle, 55–56
    plan for, 61–62
Industry growth cycle, 55–56
Industry growth strategies, 294
Inflection points, 10
Information asymmetry, 190–191
Information-based products, 4
In-house product testing, 96
Initial public offering, 223
    failure of, 227
    measures of success, 224
    process of, 224–227
Innovation
    defined, 8–9
    large companies' track record, 311
    plan for, 296–297
    scope of, 295
    See also Business plan, for sustained
        innovation
Innovation and commercialization, 1
    foundations of technological
        company success, 15–16
        creativity and invention, 7–8
        customers, sophisticated, 14–15
        disruptive (radical) model of innovation,
            9–11
        globalization, 14
        Human Genome Project, 12–13
        incumbent's curse, 10–11

innovation defined, 8–9
    key disruptive technologies, 11–12
    nano economy, 12
    nanotechnology, 13
    product development timelines,
        shrinking, 15
    rapid changes, 15
    research, 8
    stimulating innovation, 14–15
    sustaining model of innovation, 9–10
    wireless technology, 13–14
Innovation in the Palm of His Hand (case
    study), 23–25
process of
    build, 18
    build-to-sell model, 19
    developing and testing the business con-
        cept, 18
    developing the business, 18–19
    intellectual property assets, 17
    inventing and innovating, 16–17
    inventor platform, 19
    launching the business, 19–20
    license, 18
    opportunity recognition, 17
    patents, 17
    product development, 17–18
    prototyping, 17–18
    sell, 18
    technological feasibility, 17–18
technological change and economic princi-
    ples, 2
    better, faster, cheaper, 5
    financial revolution, 3
    first mover to scale, 3–4
    key technologies to watch, 6–7
    monopolies, 5
    scarcity, 4–5
Innovation and Entrepreneurship, 88–89
Innovation management, gaps in, 294–297
Innovators, 175
Innovator strategy (manufacturing), 243
In re Alappat, 122
Integrating R&D with marketing, 257
Integration
    backward, 294
    forward, 294
    strategic, 322–323
    vertical, 294
Intel, 2, 10, 147, 279, 326
Intellectual capital management, 181

Intellectual property, 109
  copyrights, 114
    Digital Millenium Copyright Act
        (DCMA), 115
    fair use, 115
    Gordon Gould: The Father of Laser
        Technology (case study), 128–129
  patents, 118
    business method patents, 122–123
    categories of, 120
    design patents, 121–122
    Disclosure Document Program, 123
    filing for, 123–126
    foreign patents, 125–126
    nonobviousness, 121
    nonprovisional patent, 124–125
    no prior art, 120–121
    patentable inventions, 119–123
    plant patents, 122
    provisional patent, 123–124
    utility of invention, 120
    utility patents, 121
  protection of, 17
  theory behind
    disincentives of, 111–112
    incentives to commercialize, 111
    incentives to disclose, 111
    incentives to invent, 110
  trademarks, 117
    domain names, 118
    Internet and, 117–118
  trade secrets, 112
    nondisclosure agreements, 113–114
  See also Licensing intellectual property
Intellectual Property Asset Management soft-
    ware, 161
Intellectual property strategy, 144–145
  developing, 146
    improving the company's financial
        position, 151
    invalid patents, 152
    patent audits, 151–152
    patent infringement, 148–149
    patents as competitive advantage, 149–151
    success of, 147
    when the patent runs out, 152
  issues in, 155
    applying protection to a technology or
        product/process, 156
    avoiding litigation, 158
    choosing not to patent, 157–158
    collaborating on inventions, 158–160
    commercialization prior to patent protec-
        tion, 156–157
    intellectual property management, 160–163
    patent application, guidelines for, 162
    risks to intellectual assets, 145–146
    Robotic Surgery to the Rescue (case study),
        165–166
    trademark strategies, 152–153
      framing, linking, and metatags, 154
      trade secrets, 154–155
Interests (LLC), 248
Intermediaries, 227
Internet
  as a disruptive technology, 11–12
  surveys, 66
  trademarks and, 117–118
Interviews, 65–66
Intuitive Surgical, 165–166
Invalid patents, 152
Invention, 29
  court definition of, 157
  in innovation, 7–8
Invention Development Organizations, 122
Inventor platform, 19
Investment risk, 98
Investors, 190
  as audience for a business plan, 336
IP.com, 152

J

Jefferson, Thomas, 118
Joannopoulos, John, 7
Johnson, Clarence L. "Kelly", 321–322
Johnson, David, 352
Johnson & Johnson, 323
Joint venturing, 279
JordanNeuroScience (JNS), 264

K

Kagan, Cherie, 6
Kelley, David M., 105–106
*Kenner Parker Toys Inc. v. Rose Art Industries
    Inc.*, 153
King, Natasha, 347
Know-how, 258–259
Knowledge
  tacit, 304
  transference of, 303–304
Knowledge channels, 295–296

Knowledge products, 4
Kodak, 301–302
Koptis, Kurt, 347

L

Laggards, 176
Land, Edwin, 19
Lanham Act (1946), 116, 118
Late majority, 176
Late stage capital, 191
Lazardis, Mike, 308–309
Legal forms of organization
  See Moving from R&D to operations
Lemelson, Jerome, 149
Lenders, 210–211
  as audience for a business plan, 337
  See also Funding growth
Lending gauges, 210–211
License, 18, 43
License agreement, 137–139, 176–178, 293
License exchanges, 137
Licensing, 293, 305
Licensing intellectual property, 131
  license agreement, 137–139
  licensee's view of the process
    negotiating favorable terms, 137
    preparing a business plan, 137
    searching for the right technology,
      136–137
  licensing strategy, 139–140
  licensor's view of the process
    conduct market research, 132–133
    decide what will be licensed, 132
    define benefits to licensee, 132
    determine value of license
      agreement, 134
    due diligence, 133
    understand the process, 135–136
  P&G: Finding the Value of the Licensing
    Network (case study), 142–143
Licensing model, 200, 201
Licensing strategy, 139–140
Lightman, Alex, 13–14
Limited Liability Company (LLC), 248
Limited market trial, 96–97
Linking, 154
Listerine, 156
Lockheed Martin, 320–322
Lowe, Frederick, 78
Lys, Ihor, 352–354

M

Mail surveys, 66
Management plan, 341
Manhattan Project, 300
Manufacturing structures, 243
Market analysis, 340
  information needs, 64
  testing the customer, 64
    customer profile, 66
    focus groups and interviews, 65–66
    forecasting demand, 66–67
    surveys, 66
Market-based pricing, 272
Market comparison method, 184
Market development, 293
Market entry strategy, 238–239
Marketer strategy (manufacturing), 243
Marketing approach, determining, 264–266
Marketing high technology, 256
  customer needs
    emerging markets, 269
    researching, 267–269
    understanding, 266–267
  marketing plan, 275–276
  market intelligence
    Delphi Method, 270–271
    forecasting demand, 270–271
    substitute products, 271
    triangulation, 271
  pricing high-technology products, 271
    components of price, 272
    price point, 273–274
    pricing strategy, 274
  promoting high-technology products, 276
    brand presence, 278–279
    preannouncements, 278
    telling a compelling story, 277–278
  technology-intensive markets, characteristics of
    competitive uncertainty, 258
    know-how, complexity, and velocity effects,
      258–259
    market uncertainty, 257–258
    technological uncertainty, 258
  technology-intensive markets, key decisions
    for, 259
    determining a market approach,
      264–266
    positioning and design decisions,
      262–264
    tornadoes, 260–262

Will GPS Ever Cross the Chasm? (case study), 282–283
Marketing plan, 275–276, 341
Market intelligence, 270–271
Market penetration, 293
Market research, for licensing purposes, 132–133
Market uncertainty, 257–258
Mattel, Inc., 149
Mature phase in technology life cycle, 298–299
Maybach, Wilhelm, 7
MCI, 102
Mellinger, Doug, 231–232
Members (LLC), 248
Merck, 338
Metatags, 154
Micro Chemical, Inc. v. Great Plains Chemical Co., 157
Microfluidics, 7
Microphotonics, 7
Microsoft, 326
Microsoft Windows, 4–5
Migration design, 264
Mission development, 237–238
Mission statement, 338–340
Monopolies, 5
    temporary (in patents), 147
Monsanto, 71–72
Moving from R&D to operations, 235
    legal forms of organization, 244
        changing, 249
        corporations, 247–248
        Limited Liability Company (LLC), 248
        making a decision, 248–249
        partnerships, 246–247
        protection for owners, 247–248
        R&D prelaunch forms, 246–247
        sole proprietorships, 246
        stock, 249–251
    organizational models, 240–241
        operational strategy, 243
        process flow, 243–244, 245
        Silicon Valley, 239, 242–243
    Quantum Dots Corporation (case study), 253–254
    transitioning from project to operations
        entry strategy, 238–239
        successful, 236–238
Mueller, Gary, 352
Mueller, George, 352–354
Multiple revenue streams, 171–172

N

Nakamatsu, Yoshiro, 28, 30, 46–47
Nano economy, 12
Nanotechnology, 13
Napster, 115
Narehood, Betty, 332
Natural language processing, 7
Navigating, 32
Navstar Global Positioning System (GPS), 282–283
Near-production quality, 63
Netscape Communications, 2, 153
Network, 146
Network effects, 4
Network externalities, 4
Networks (funding), 196–197
New product development
    See High technology product development strategies
New product failure, 85–86
Niche strategy (entry), 239
Nicolelis, Miguel, 6
Nicolet, 264
Nonaligned companies, 212
Nondisclosure agreements, 113–114
Nonobviousness, 121
Nonprovisional patent, 124–125
No prior art, 120–121
Nortel Networks, 325, 327
North American Industry Classification System (NAICS), 61

O

Office of the Independent Inventor, 119
Olson, Ken, 168
Operations
    See Moving from R&D to operations
Operations plan, 341
Opportunity, 27
Opportunity recognition, 17, 88–89
    See also Technology opportunities
Opportunity, sources of
    See Technology opportunities
Options approach, 92
Options pricing theory, 92
Optiva Corp., 227
Oracle, 326
Organizational models
    See Moving from R&D to operations
Organization plan, 341

Outsourcing
    for knowledge services or core capabilities, 299
    for knowledge specialists, 299
    of technology innovation, 100–103

P

PaineWebber, Inc. v. WWWPainewebber.com, 153
PalmPilot, 23–25
Partnerships, 102–103, 246–247
Patent audits, 151–152
Patent Cooperation Treaty of 1970, 126
Patent infringement, 148–149
Patent pending, 123–124
Patents, 17, 36
    See also Intellectual property; Intellectual
        property strategy
Patent wall, 149–150
Payment clause, 138
Pelco Inc., 324
Performance clause, 138
Pfaff v. Wells Electronics, 157
Pharmaceutical development, risk associated
        with, 99
Philips, 305
Phone surveys, 66
Pioneering firm
    advantages, 317
    disadvantages, 318
    radical innovation and, 318
Plant patents, 122
Platform identification
    See Technology screening and platform
        identification
Platform projects, 89
*Playboy Enterprises Inc. v. Calvin Designer
        Label*, 154
Polaroid, 146
Prasad, Anshu, 324
Preannouncements, 278
Predevelopment financial analysis, 93
Prelaunch business plan, 97
Price point, 273–274
Pricing and prices
    of high-technology products, 271
        components of price, 272
        price point, 273–274
        pricing strategy, 274
Private offering, 221
    direct public offering: Regulation A, 222–223
    small corporate offering registration, 222

Proactive pricing strategy, 272
Problems
    four types of, 31
    restating, 31
Problem solving, engineering approach to, 32
Process flow, 243–244
Procter & Gamble (P&G), 142–143
Product development, 17–18, 293, 348
Product development success, 97
    increasing R&D effectiveness, 99–100
    managing risk of R&D
        investment risk, 98
        project management risk, 98–99
        risk with pharmaceutical develop-
            ment, 99
    measuring R&D effectiveness, 100
Professional management, 291
Project management risk, 98–99
Promotion, 257
    of high-technology products, 276–279
Prototyping, 17–18, 62–63
Provisional patent, 123–124
Purchasing decisions, factors impacting,
        266–267

Q

Q-Sort method, 91
Qualitex Co. V. Jacobson Products Co., 116

R

Radical Innovation, 171
Radical innovation, 269, 311, 315, 319
    chaos and, 326
    developing, 31
    pioneering firm and, 317–318
    risks of, 297
Radical innovation business models
    See Business model, building and valuing
Radical technologies, 260–262, 265–266
Random problems, 31
Ravindra, Rekha, 78
R&D
    integrating with marketing, 257
    partnerships, 195
    See also Moving from R&D to operations;
        Research and development
Reactive pricing strategy, 272
Real options model, 183
Reorganizer strategy (manufacturing), 243
Research, in innovation, 8

Research and development
  increasing effectiveness, 99–100
  managing the risk of, 98–99
  measuring effectiveness, 100
  reducing time needed for, 95–96
  shift in, 84
  See also Growing the high-tech venture; High
      technology product development
      strategies; R&D
Research In Motion (RIM), 308–309
Resource acquisition, 327–328
Resource partners, 190
Resources, 189
Retain-as-much-equity-as-possible approach, 190
Return assessment, 216–218
Risk
  in co-operation, 302–304
  in corporate venturing
  investment, 98
  pharmaceutical development, 99
  project management, 98–99
  of radical innovation, 297
  in venture capital funding, 216–218
Risk-averse attitude, 272
Risks, 190
  associated with development, 41–42
  See also Funding the technology start-up
Robot design, 7
Royal Dutch Shell, 299
Royalty method, 183

S

S3 (company), 147
Sales channels, 295–296
Scarcity, 4–5
Schumpeter, Joseph, 5, 315
Scope of innovation, 295
S-corporation, 248
*Seal-Flex, Inc. v. Athletic Track and Court
    Construction*, 157
Searle, George, 206–207
Secrecy and negotiation, 135–136
Secrecy clause, 138
Seed capital, 191
  See also Funding the technology start-up
Sell, 18
Semiconductor Manufacturing Technology
    Consortium (SEMATECH), 301
Sense-and-respond mentality, 295
Shalon, Dari, 335–336

Shane, Scott, 172
Shannon, Claude Elwood, 28, 46–47
Shapiro, Harold, 297
Silicon Valley, 239, 242–243
Simplistic problems, 31
Sims, William J., 353
Singh, Ranjit, 6
Skunk works, 320–322
Small Business Administration (SBA), 203
Small Business Innovation Research (SBIR)
    grants, 202
Small Business Investment Company (SBIC)
    program, 203
Small Business Technology Transfer Research
    (STTR) program, 202–203
Small corporate offering registration, 222
Smalley, Richard, 12
Smith, Adam, 4
SmithKline, 271
Social capital, 158–159
Sole proprietorships, 246
Sonny Bono Copyright Extension Act of 1998,
    114–115
Sony, 262, 305
Speed, 5–6
Stapelfeld, Ben, 331–332
Start-up companies
  See Funding the technology start-up
*State Street Bank & Trust Co. v. Signature
    Financial Group*, 122
Step-up ratio, 178
Stock, 249–251
Strategic alliances, 257, 305
  nature of, 300–302
Strategic integration, 322–323
Strategic partners, as audience for a business
    plan, 337
Strategic partnerships, 194–195
  choosing a partner, 301
Strategic positioning in the value chain, 170–171
Structural Dynamics Research Corp.
    (SDRC), 96
Substitute products, 57, 271
Success
  as a corporate entrepreneur, 324
    plan for living with chaos, 326–329
    winning climate for corporate venturing,
      325–326
  determinants of, 86–87
  inertia of, 289
Success hurdles, 314

Sufield analysis, 33
Sun Microsystems, 298, 326
Suppliers, 189
Suppliers' power, 57
Supply architecture, 295–296
Surveying, 32
Surveys, 66
Sustaining model of innovation, 9–10
Synergistic strategy, 294

T

Tacit knowledge, 296, 304
Taussig, Reed, 227
Teams, 237
Tech Coast Angels, 196
Techco Chemical Ltd., 313–314
Technical feasibility analysis
  product risks and benefits, 63
  questions to answer, 64
  stage one: concept testing, 62
  stage three: near-production quality, 63
  stage two: primitive prototype, 62–63
Technological change
  See Innovation and commercialization
Technological innovation
  See Innovation and commercialization
Technological uncertainty, 257, 258
Technology, influence on industry, 58
Technology business concept, 50
  competition analysis, 58–61
  developing, 51
    benefits, 53
    defining the business, 52–53
    feasibility, 53–54
  distribution channel analysis, 67–70
  feasibility analysis, 54–55
    outline, 73–74
  feasible business model, constructing, 71–73
  founding team analysis, 70–71
  industry analysis, 55–56, 61–62
    barriers to entry, 57
    buyers' power, 57
    competitor rivalry, 58
    substitute products, 57
    suppliers' power, 57
    technology, 58
  market analysis
    information needs, 64
    questions to answer, 67
    testing the customer, 64–67

technical feasibility analysis
  product risks and benefits, 63
  questions to answer, 64
  stage one: concept testing, 62
  stage three: near-production quality, 63
  stage two: primitive prototype, 62–63
  Zondigo: Chaos in the Wireless World (case study), 77–82
Technology design, 263
Technology feasibility, 17–18
Technology-intensive markets
  See Marketing high technology
Technology life cycle, phases of, 298–299
Technology opportunities, 27
  Art of Invention (The): Yoshiro Nakamatsu and Claude Elwood Shannon (case study), 46–47
  creativity as spark, 28
    challenges to, 30
    creative process, 29–30
    engineering approach to problem solving, 32
    problem-solving skills, 30–32
    TRIZ approach to innovation, 32–33
  opportunity recognition, 34–35
  opportunity, sources of
    customers, 36
    existing technology, 37
    government, 37
    industry, 35–36
    other sources, 37
    patent literature, 36
    universities, 36
  screening, 37–38
    classifying technologies after screening, 42–44
    stand-alone opportunities, 39–42
Technology plan, 341
Technology screening and platform identification
  benefit measurement, 91
  business development, 90
  customers, 89–90
  economic models, 91–92
  existing architecture and company capabilities, 90
  impact of the project, 90–91
Technology standards, 304–305
Technology start-ups
  See Funding the technology start-up
Three Dimensional Printing Process (3DP), 172
3M (company), 323, 325

Time to market
  computer-aided systems and, 96
  reducing, 94–95
Tornadoes, 260–262
TotalNews.com, 154
Toyota, 300
Trademarks, 116
  developing a strategy for, 152–155
  Internet and, 117–118
  See also Intellectual property; Intellectual
      property strategy
Trade secrets
  in the lab, 160
  protecting and defending, 154–155
  violation of, 303
  See also Intellectual property
Transfer design, 264
Transference of knowledge, 303–304
Transfer pricing, 134
Transitional phase in technology life cycle, 298
Triangulation, 271
Trimble, Charlie, 282–283
Trimble Navigation Ltd., 282–283
TRIZ approach to innovation, 32–33
Tylenol-package-tampering incident, 340

U

Undercapitalization, 289
Untangling code, 7
U.S. Patent and Trademark Office, 5, 17, 36,
      116–117
Utility, of inventions, 120
Utility patents, 121

V

Valley of death, 348
Valuation process example, 178–180
Value, 173
  added growth, 174, 175
  balanced portfolio, 176
  building through architecture and
      capability, 295
  discounted, 178
  financial models for assessing, 180–184
  license agreement, 176–178
  new application, 174–176
Value chain, strategic positioning in, 170–171
Value innovation, 287
Value-innovation strategy, 287–288
Vella, Nino, 331–332

Velocity effects, 258–259
Venture capital
  methods of valuation, 183–184
  at start-up, 197–199
Venture capital funding, 3, 213
  screening criteria, 214–215
    aftermath, 220–221
    business valuation, 218–219
    control rights, 219–220
    due diligence, 216
    risk and return assessment, 216–218
    timing of funding, 220
Venture champions, 318–319
Verheem, Johann, 346–348
Vertical alliances, 301
Vertical integration, 294
Vertical positioning, 262–263
Vito, Rob, 50–51
Volta, Alessandro, 7
VORAD Safety Systems, 195

W

Wall of invention, 93–94
Wallpapering, 150
Wal-Mart Stores, Inc., 114
Walt Disney Co., 315, 322–323
*WarnerLambert Pharmaceutical Company, Inc.
      v. John J. Reynolds, Inc.*, 156
Washington Post Co. et al. v. TotalNews, 154
Waymaking, 32
Weaver, Warren, 46–47
Wireless technology, 13–14
Woodstream Corporation of Pennsylvania, 119
Woodward, Dan, 232
World Intellectual Property Organization
      (WIPO), 154

X

Xerox, 147, 149, 321
  radical innovation and, 316

Y

Yahoo!, 279
Yansouni, Cyril, 4
Yet2.com, 137

Z

Zcore, 77–82
Zeus Robotic Surgical Systems, 165–166
Zondigo, 77–82